— The BIG BOOK of —
PALEO
RECIPES

The BIG BOOK of
PALEO
RECIPES

More Than 500 Recipes for Healthy, Grain-Free, and Dairy-Free Foods

Linda Larsen

Avon, Massachusetts

Published by
Adams Media, a division of F+W Media, Inc.
57 Littlefield Street, Avon, MA 02322. U.S.A.
www.adamsmedia.com

Contains material adapted and abridged from *The Everything® Weeknight Paleo Cookbook,* edited by Michelle Fagone, copyright © 2014 by F+W Media, Inc., ISBN 10: 1-4405-7229-1, ISBN 13: 978-1-4405-7229-6.

ISBN 10: 1-4405-8629-2
ISBN 13: 978-1-4405-8629-3
eISBN 10: 1-4405-8630-6
eISBN 13: 978-1-4405-8630-9

Printed in the United States of America.

10 9 8 7 6 5 4 3 2 1

Library of Congress Cataloging-in-Publication Data

Larsen, Linda.
  The big book of paleo recipes / Linda Larsen.
    pages cm
  Includes index.
   ISBN 978-1-4405-8629-3 (pb) -- ISBN 1-4405-8629-2 (pb) -- ISBN 978-1-4405-8630-9 (ebook) -- ISBN 1-4405-8630-6 (ebook)
  1. Cooking (Natural foods) 2. High-protein diet--Recipes. 3. Prehistoric peoples--Nutrition. I. Title.
  RM237.55.L37 2015
  641.5'637--dc23

                    2014038771

Cover design by Erin Alexander.
Cover images © subbotina/luiscarceller/123RF.

This book is available at quantity discounts for bulk purchases.
For information, please call 1-800-289-0963.

CONTENTS

2   Sauces and Spreads 61

3   Salads and Dressings 91

4 Stocks, Soups, and Stews 137

5 Grain-Free Baked Goods and Pasta 191

6 Vegetarian 207

9

10 Fish and Seafood.............349

11 Side Dishes......393

12 Gluten- and Dairy-Free Meals 425

INTRODUCTION

ARE YOU LOOKING FOR FLAVORFUL, NUTRITIOUS MEALS THAT WILL FUEL YOUR BODY? The Paleolithic diet is for you.

The Paleolithic diet or "Paleo lifestyle" has become increasingly popular in recent years. Also known as the "Caveman Diet," the name refers to a period of time when people only ate grass-fed game, wild-caught fish, nuts, seeds, vegetables, berries, and occasionally other fruits. These people lived before the time of modern agriculture and the domestication of animals. They hunted for their meat and gathered their berries and nuts. There were no grains planted in fields, no milk past weaning, and, subsequently, the population wasn't plagued by many of the diseases that are seen today. Back then, there were no fast-food restaurants or packaged microwavable meals.

Ridding your body of toxins found in inflammatory foods such as grains and processed ingredients will contribute to increased energy levels. Your natural circadian rhythm, or body clock, will start working better, allowing you to pop out of bed after a great night's sleep. Your prescription medication and over-the-counter drugs may become a thing of the past. Aches and pains from arthritis or swelling joints may subside because you are consuming foods that do not irritate your body.
If this sounds too easy to be true, it's not. If you're thinking that you need to move to the forest and take up hunting, fishing, and gardening to be on today's Paleolithic diet, that could not be further from the truth. The Paleo lifestyle simply requires a shift in your thinking. First, you will need to learn what foods are considered Paleo "yes" or Paleo "no."

PALEO-FRIENDLY FOODS

Although the list of Paleo-acceptable foods is long, there are some choices that are more beneficial than others. Foods rich in omega-3 fatty acids promote optimal health and well-being. Some great omega-3 choices include:

Protein Sources of Omega-3

- Wild-caught salmon
- Cold-water fish such as mackerel, herring, and sturgeon
- Free-range poultry
- Grass-fed beef

Fat Sources of Omega-3

- Walnuts (particularly black walnuts)
- Brazil nuts
- Flaxseed

Carbohydrate Sources of Omega-3

- Broccoli
- Collard greens
- Raspberries
- Strawberries

On the Paleolithic plan, you will want to find fruits and vegetables with lower glycemic levels. These foods will not have a big impact on the blood sugar and insulin levels in your body. By keeping these levels lower and in balance you will promote wellness and reduce any unnecessary inflammation.

Foods with lower glycemic levels include:

Low-Glycemic Level Fruits

- Apple
- Apricot
- Cherries
- Grapefruit
- Kiwi
- Orange

- Lemon
- Pear
- Plum
- Strawberries
- Raspberries

Low-Glycemic Level Vegetables

- Asparagus
- Beet greens
- Broccoli
- Cabbage
- Carrots
- Cauliflower
- Celery
- Mushrooms
- Onions
- Red peppers
- Swiss chard
- Collard greens

FOODS TO AVOID ON THE PALEO DIET

Paleolithic hunter-gatherers ate foods that were pre-agricultural. They did not farm the land or herd animals for sustenance. Grains such as wheat, oats, barley, quinoa, and rice were not a part of their diet. Neither were potatoes or legumes of any sort, including soybeans and peanuts. When these foods are in their natural, raw state they are toxic for the human body because of the presence of toxins called lectins. Lectins have been linked to many ailments, but predominantly they cause "leaky gut" syndromes in human intestinal tracts. There are several symptoms of leaky gut syndrome. These symptoms include abdominal discomfort and pain, heartburn, bloating, gluten and food intolerance, and muscle cramps. In addition to lectin, diets high in processed foods, low in fiber and nutrients, and with high levels of additives contribute to this disorder. On the Paleolithic diet you would avoid all foods linked to this and many other diseases.

Some Paleo adherents avoid vegetables in the nightshade family which include tomatoes, eggplant, peppers, and paprika. Those foods were considered poisonous in the Paleolithic era, even though they are safe and nutritious. Nightshade vegetables do contain alkaloids, a natural pesticide, along with saponins and lectins that can contribute to leaky gut. If you have problems with inflammation, you may want to avoid these foods.

The use of salt in the Paleo diet is controversial. Some who interpret the diet strictly do not add salt to their foods. Others think that salt has been used for centuries and can be used in foods eaten on this diet. It is true that most Americans eat too much salt, but most of that is found in processed foods. Since processed foods are not allowed on the Paleo diet, adding small amounts of salt to recipes is not problematic. If you do choose to use salt, look for salt that is minimally processed with no additives.

Dairy Products

The plight of animals in the dairy and factory farm industry is alarming. As farmers inject livestock with hormones to boost productivity and feed them antibiotics to mitigate disease that can thrive in crowded conditions, consumers are slowly ingesting these compounds themselves. And antibiotic-resistant bacteria are becoming more common, making foodborne illnesses more serious and difficult to treat because of factory farming practices. Always look for grass-fed and organic beef and bison products and free-range chicken and poultry products to avoid hormones and antibiotics.

Many people on the Paleo diet do not consume any dairy products. Some people on the Paleo diet do eat dairy products such as heavy cream, butter, and cheese. Others do not eat dairy because they are lactose-intolerant or just feel better on a dairy-free diet. Some of the latest nutritional research shows that those who eat high-fat dairy products have a lower risk of developing diabetes. Dairy can add nutrition and interest to many foods, if used in moderation.

If you do choose to eat dairy, make sure you only buy organic cream, butter, yogurt, sour cream, and cheese made from grass-fed, free range cows. Avoid products made with added coloring such as Yellow No. 5 and annatto. Raw dairy can be risky, since unpasteurized milk and cream and raw milk cheese can contain pathogenic bacteria that can make you very sick.

You can add dairy or leave it out in all of these recipes. Substitutions are offered for a dairy ingredient if you choose to avoid those products. Use coconut cream in place of heavy cream, olive, avocado, or coconut oil in place of butter; almond or coconut yogurt instead of dairy yogurt; and vegan cheese for regular cheese.

At any rate, consider adding calcium-fortified foods and supplements to your diet as well as eating the following vegetables that contain calcium.

Calcium-Rich Foods

- Bok choy
- Dandelion greens
- Collard greens
- Sweet potato
- Swiss chard

Remember that there are different variations of the Paleo diet. Those on the strict version of the diet do not eat dairy, alcohol, nightshade vegetables, coffee, or any grains or legumes. Others include wine, dairy, and tomatoes and eggplant. Many experts recommend the 85/15 rule so you don't become bored and fall off the wagon: 85% of the foods you should eat are strict Paleo; the other 15% of your diet can be less strict, such as cheese, tomatoes, coffee, dairy, and wild rice. Here's the bottom line: Choose the foods that you are comfortable eating and that make your body work, look, and feel its best.

Now, all you need to start on your journey toward Paleo success is a simple shopping list, an open mind, and a whole bunch of recipes. And you've come to the right place! Read on for hundreds of Paleo-friendly recipes your whole family is sure to enjoy, no matter what time of the day! As you prepare and enjoy these dishes, you'll find yourself energized and fueled—and amazed by just how easily you too can enjoy the Paleolithic lifestyle.

CHAPTER 1

APPETIZERS AND SNACKS

CURRIED KALE CHIPS

Kale and curry powder together in one recipe make a nutrition powerhouse. Kale contains powerful antioxidants, including at least forty different flavonoids, which fight cancer and also help reduce inflammation in your body. The leafy green is also a fabulous source of fiber. And curry powder is made with turmeric, which contains cucurmin, a compound that helps reduce the risk of cancer. But the best thing about this combination is that it tastes wonderful!

Serves 6

2 bunches kale

2 tablespoons extra-virgin olive oil

1 tablespoon coconut oil, melted

2 tablespoons curry powder

1 teaspoon ground ginger

½ teaspoon ground cardamom

¼ teaspoon cayenne pepper

1 teaspoon salt, if desired

1. Preheat oven to 350°F. Wash the kale well and dry thoroughly. Cut out any large ribs and discard. Cut the kale leaves into 3" pieces.

2. In small bowl combine the olive oil and coconut oil and mix well. Stir in the curry powder, ginger, cardamom, and cayenne pepper and mix until combined.

3. Pour this mixture over the kale leaves and massage with your hands until the leaves are coated. Arrange leaves in a single layer on two baking sheets. Bake for 15–18 minutes, rotating pans after 10 minutes. The kale will not be crisp.

4. Remove from oven and sprinkle with salt, if using. Let stand until leaves are crisp. Store at room temperature in airtight container.

SWEET AND SPICY NUT MIX

Nuts are a wonderful snack when you're eating a primal diet. They are full of fiber, healthy fats, and vitamins and minerals. And they are very satisfying. There is no way you'll eat this nut mix and be hungry again an hour later. Use your favorite nuts in this easy recipe and adjust the spice mixture to your taste.

Yields 6 cups

2 egg whites

1 teaspoon lemon juice

Pinch salt

2 tablespoons honey or agave nectar

1½ teaspoons cinnamon

1 teaspoon chili powder

½ teaspoon cayenne pepper

½ cup finely chopped coconut

2 cups walnuts

2 cups pecans

2 cups hazelnuts

¼ cup butter, melted or ¼ cup extra-virgin olive oil

3 tablespoons coconut oil, melted

1. Preheat oven to 325°F. In large bowl, beat egg whites with lemon juice and salt until stiff peaks form. Beat in honey, cinnamon, chili powder, and cayenne pepper until combined. Stir in coconut.

2. Fold in walnuts, pecans, and hazelnuts until nuts are coated.

3. Place melted butter or olive oil and coconut oil in 15" x 10" jellyroll pan. Spread the nuts over the fat mixture. Bake for 40 minutes, stirring every 10 minutes, until nuts are light golden brown and crisp and the fat is absorbed. Let cool, then store in an airtight container at room temperature.

SEVEN-LAYER GERMAN DIP

Seven-layer dips are popular for a reason—they're beautiful and delicious! Most are flavored with Mexican or Greek ingredients. This dip from Germany is a bit different and very hearty. Make it ahead of time and store it in the fridge. Serve with celery sticks, red pepper slices, and baby carrots for dipping.

Serves 10

1 (8-ounce) package cream cheese, softened, or 1 cup Yogurt Cheese (see Chapter 2)

½ cup sour cream or coconut cream or Almond Yogurt (see recipe in this chapter)

2 tablespoons Dijon mustard

½ teaspoon caraway seeds

1½ cups naturally fermented sauerkraut, drained

1 cup zucchini, sliced and peeled

½ pound spicy pork sausage, cooked and drained

1 red bell pepper, chopped

1 cup diced Swiss cheese, if desired

⅓ cup sliced green onions

1. In large bowl, beat cream cheese or Yogurt Cheese until smooth. Beat in sour cream or coconut cream and mustard until well blended. Stir in caraway seeds. Spread in a circle on a serving platter.

2. Top with, in order, sauerkraut, zucchini, sausage, red bell pepper, Swiss cheese, and green onions. Cover and refrigerate for 1–2 hours to blend flavors.

SAUERKRAUT BALLS

Despite the strange name, this appetizer recipe is really delicious; it's crisp and creamy and flavorful. Be sure to use naturally fermented sauerkraut, as it has the most probiotics. These little tidbits should be served soon after they are made, but you can keep them warm in a 200°F oven for about an hour.

Serves 8

2 tablespoons butter or olive oil

1 onion, finely chopped

3 tablespoons almond flour

⅓ cup beef broth

3 tablespoons grainy mustard

½ cup shredded Gruyère cheese, if desired

1½ cups naturally fermented sauerkraut, well drained

2 eggs, beaten

1 cup ground almonds

Salt and pepper to taste

2 cups coconut or palm oil

1. Melt butter or oil in medium saucepan over medium heat. Add onion; cook until tender, about 5–6 minutes. Add almond flour; cook and stir for 2 minutes longer.

2. Stir in beef broth and cook until thick. Remove from heat and add mustard and Gruyère. Let cool for 10 minutes, then stir in sauerkraut. Cover and chill for at least one hour.

3. When ready to fry, place eggs in a shallow bowl and ground almonds in another. Season both mixtures with salt and pepper.

4. Roll the sauerkraut mixture into 1" balls. Dip into egg, then into almonds and place on wire rack.

5. Heat oil in large saucepan to 375°F. Drop the sauerkraut balls, one at a time, into the oil and fry for 2–3 minutes until golden brown. Remove from oil and place on paper towels to drain. Serve warm.

CURRIED NUTS AND FRUIT

Curry powder is a blend of spices unique to India. Most Indian families develop their own blend. You can buy good quality curry powder at any grocery store, or make your own. It is usually made from cinnamon, turmeric, cumin, mustard and fennel seeds, pepper, nutmeg, cardamom, ginger, and cayenne pepper, among other spices. It's delicious when combined with crunchy nuts and tart dried fruit in this easy recipe.

Yields 4 cups

1 cup broken walnuts

1 cup small whole pecans

2 tablespoons coconut oil

1 tablespoon butter or extra-virgin olive oil

1 tablespoon curry powder

1 cup sunflower seeds

1 cup dried unsweetened cranberries

½ cup chopped dried unsulfured apricots

1. Combine walnuts and pecans in medium bowl; set aside.

2. In large saucepan, combine coconut oil and butter or olive oil; melt over medium heat. Add curry powder; cook and stir for about 1 minute until fragrant.

3. Add walnuts and pecans; cook, stirring frequently, until nuts are toasted and slightly crisp. Remove walnuts and pecans from heat and transfer nuts to bowl. Add sunflower seeds to pan and toast for 1–2 minutes. Add to bowl.

4. Stir in cranberries and apricots and toss to coat. Spread on paper towel and let cool. Store tightly covered in airtight container.

MINI CURRIED QUICHES

Tiny quiches are the perfect appetizer for entertaining. These do not have a crust, but the filling is sturdy enough to hold together quite nicely. You can vary the amount of curry powder to your taste. More than a teaspoon will make the quiches quite spicy.

Yields 24 quiches

2 tablespoons butter or coconut oil

1 small onion, finely chopped

2 cloves garlic, minced

1 teaspoon curry powder

½ cup chopped cooked shrimp

4 eggs

⅓ cup heavy cream or coconut cream

½ teaspoon salt

⅛ teaspoon pepper

½ cup shredded fontina cheese, if desired

Additional ¼ cup shrimp, if not using cheese

1. Preheat oven to 375°F. Grease 24 mini muffin cups with unsalted butter and set aside.

2. In medium saucepan, melt butter or coconut oil over medium heat. Add onion and garlic; cook and stir until tender, about 5 minutes. Add curry powder and cook for 1 minute; remove from heat. Stir in shrimp and set aside.

3. In medium bowl, beat eggs with cream or coconut cream, salt, and pepper.

4. Divide onion mixture and cheese, if using, among prepared muffin cups, then top each with egg mixture, filling to the top. If not using cheese, add ¼ cup more shrimp.

5. Bake for 15–20 minutes or until the quiches are puffed and light golden brown. Serve warm or at room temperature. Refrigerate leftovers.

PRIMAL MEATBALLS

Meatballs make a wonderful appetizer. You can mix them with salsa or tomato sauce, or add them to any type of dip. Serve with little toothpicks. This recipe uses ground nuts instead of bread crumbs to add texture to the ground meat. You can use any type of nut you'd like—hazelnuts and walnuts are especially meaty-tasting. These meatballs freeze very well. Let the meatballs cool on the baking sheet for 20 minutes, then transfer to the refrigerator to cool completely. Pack into freezer containers and freeze up to 3 months. Do not freeze the meatballs uncooked. To thaw, let stand in the fridge overnight, then gently reheat in a sauce and serve.

Yields 36 meatballs

2 tablespoons butter or coconut oil

1 onion, finely chopped

3 cloves garlic, minced

1 egg, beaten

½ cup ground hazelnuts

1 teaspoon salt

⅛ teaspoon pepper

1 teaspoon dried marjoram leaves

1 pound lean ground beef

½ pound lean ground pork

1. Preheat oven to 400°F. Line a rimmed baking sheet with parchment paper and set aside.

2. In medium skillet, melt butter or coconut oil over medium heat. Add onion and garlic; cook and stir until tender, about 5 minutes. Remove to large bowl and let cool 10 minutes.

3. Stir egg, hazelnuts, salt, pepper, and marjoram into the onion mixture. Then add beef and pork and work gently but thoroughly with your hands.

4. Form mixture into 1½" meatballs and place on prepared pan. Bake for 18–23 minutes or until a meat thermometer registers 165°F and meatballs are done. Serve immediately, or cool, refrigerate, and reheat to serve later.

CHICKEN PISTACHIO PÂTÉ

Pâté is an elegant appetizer that has gone out of style. Let's bring it back! Pâtés are rich and flavorful and can be beautiful when made with the right ingredients. This is a country-style pâté, which means that the ingredients are cut a little coarser than a traditional smooth pâté. No food processor is used or needed for this recipe.

Serves 8–10

3 slices bacon

2 tablespoons butter or olive oil

1 onion, finely chopped

2 cloves garlic, minced

¼ pound chicken livers, cleaned and chopped

1 pound ground chicken, dark and light meat

3 tablespoons brandy, if desired

2 tablespoons heavy cream or coconut cream

2 eggs, beaten

1 teaspoon dried marjoram

1 teaspoon dried sage leaves

1 teaspoon salt

¼ teaspoon white pepper

1 cup pistachios, coarsely chopped

1. In small skillet, cook bacon until crisp. Remove bacon from pan, drain on paper towels, crumble, and set aside.

2. Add butter or olive oil to drippings remaining in skillet and place over medium-low heat. Add onion and garlic; cook and stir until softened, about 4–5 minutes; do not let brown. Remove to large bowl and cool for 10 minutes.

3. Add the chicken livers, ground chicken, brandy, cream, eggs, marjoram, sage, salt, and pepper to the onion mixture and mix gently but thoroughly. Stir in the pistachios and reserved bacon.

4. Line an 8" x 4" loaf pan with parchment paper and add the chicken mixture. Smooth the top and rap the pan sharply on the counter to remove any air pockets.

5. Bake the pâté for 60–70 minutes until a meat thermometer registers 165°F. Let cool on a wire rack for 30 minutes, then cover and refrigerate for at least 8 hours.

6. When ready to serve, drain off any liquid and unmold the pâté onto a serving platter. Slice to serve.

FLINTSTONE GUACAMOLE

Guacamole is a wonderful appetizer or sandwich spread that is easy to make and very healthy. But finding ripe avocados in the grocery store can be a challenge. Buy avocados that are firm and heavy for their size, then store them together in a paper bag on the counter. They'll be ready to use in a few days. But be warned—avocados tend to ripen all at once! Enjoy them in this wonderful recipe.

Yields 1½ cups

2 tablespoons lemon juice

½ teaspoon salt

3 ripe avocados, peeled and cubed

3 tablespoons sour cream, coconut cream, or Wilma's Mayonnaise (see Chapter 2)

1 cup grape tomatoes, chopped, if desired

1 green onion, finely chopped

1 clove garlic, minced

1 jalapeño pepper, minced

1. In medium bowl, combine lemon juice and salt; stir until salt dissolves.

2. Add the avocados and mash with a potato masher until almost smooth. Leave some avocado pieces for added texture.

3. Stir in sour cream, coconut cream, or mayonnaise, tomatoes, green onion, garlic, and jalapeño pepper. Taste and correct seasonings, if desired. Serve immediately.

Hot Pepper Precautions

Wear gloves or sandwich bags over your hands when you clean and dice hot peppers. It's important to avoid having the peppers come into contact with your skin and, especially, your eyes. As an added precaution, wash your hands (and under your fingernails) thoroughly with hot, soapy water after you remove the gloves or sandwich bags.

CAVEMAN DEVILED EGGS

Deviled eggs are a wonderful appetizer or snack recipe. They are easy to make, despite the undeserved "difficult" reputation of hard-cooked eggs. Just keep an eye on the pot and the time and use eggs that aren't brand-spanking new, and you won't have a problem. You can add everything from tiny shrimp to blue cheese to this classic recipe. But bacon, of course, makes everything taste better.

Serves 12

12 large eggs

4 slices bacon

⅓ cup Wilma's Mayonnaise (see Chapter 2) or Almond Yogurt (see recipe in this chapter)

2 tablespoons Dijon mustard

1 tablespoon grainy mustard

½ teaspoon salt

⅛ teaspoon white pepper

1. Place the eggs in a large deep saucepan and cover with cold water. Bring to a boil over high heat. Let the eggs boil for exactly one minute, then cover pan and remove from heat. Let stand for 11 minutes.

2. Meanwhile, fry the bacon until crisp; drain on paper towels, crumble, and set aside. Reserve 1 tablespoon bacon drippings.

3. When the 11 minutes is up, drain eggs and run cold water into the saucepan. Add a few ice cubes to the pan and let stand for 7 minutes.

4. Then gently tap the eggs, still under the water, on the sides of the pan to crack the shells. Let stand for 3 more minutes, then peel the eggs.

5. Cut the eggs in half and carefully remove the yolks. Place the yolks in a food processor.

6. Add reserved bacon drippings, mayonnaise or Almond Yogurt, Dijon mustard, grainy mustard, salt, and pepper to the egg yolks and process until smooth. Remove processing blade and stir in the reserved bacon.

7. Spoon or pipe the egg yolk mixture back into the egg white halves. Serve immediately, or cover and store in the refrigerator up to 3 days.

SAUSAGE-STUFFED MUSHROOMS

Grocery stores sell several different sizes of mushrooms. Buy the largest white mushrooms you can find for this recipe. Snap off the stems, then trim the stem ends and chop to use in the filling. Before filling the mushrooms, you may want to scrape away the dark brown gills, since they tend to be bitter.

Serves 6

12 large white mushrooms

¾ pound spicy pork sausage

1 small onion, chopped

3 cloves garlic, minced

1 stalk celery, finely chopped

⅓ cup finely chopped walnuts

1 teaspoon dried marjoram leaves

½ teaspoon dried tarragon leaves

1 tablespoon lemon juice

1 egg, beaten

½ teaspoon salt

⅛ teaspoon pepper

1. Preheat oven to 350°F. Rinse mushrooms to remove dirt and dry. Remove stems from mushrooms, trim stem ends, and chop stems; set aside.

2. In medium skillet, cook sausage with onion, garlic, and chopped mushroom stems until meat is brown, stirring to break up meat. Drain, then add celery and cook for another 2 minutes.

3. Remove from heat and stir in walnuts, marjoram, tarragon, lemon juice, egg, salt, and pepper. Use this mixture to stuff the mushrooms.

4. Place mushrooms in a baking dish and bake for 20–30 minutes or until stuffing is browned and crisp on top.

CHEESY BACON FIGS

This is a wonderful appetizer recipe worthy of company. Fresh figs can be hard to find, but when you do find them, buy all you can. They are tender and sweet with a wonderful texture, totally unlike the dried fruit. Stuff with your favorite cheese, wrap with bacon, and bake. If you're not eating cheese, stuff the figs with a whole almond or pecan. You can make this recipe with dried figs too.

Serves 6

12 fresh figs or 12 dried figs

12 small pieces Asiago or Fontina cheese

6 slices bacon, cut in half

2 tablespoons apricot preserves

1. Preheat oven to 400°F. Cut a slit in the side of each fig and insert the cheese. Set aside.

2. Partially cook the bacon until some of the fat is rendered out but the strips are still pliable. Remove from heat and let cool for 10 minutes.

3. Wrap a slice of bacon around each fig, covering the cheese. Secure with a toothpick.

4. In a small bowl, combine 2 tablespoons bacon fat with apricot preserves and mix well. Brush this mixture over the bacon-wrapped figs.

5. Bake for 15–20 minutes or until bacon is crisp and cheese is melted. Let cool for 5–10 minutes, then remove toothpicks and serve.

NUTTY CHICKEN NUGGETS

Chicken nuggets are a wonderful snack, but most recipes use bread crumbs or crushed cereal to make the crisp crust. Using nuts is a better idea—the nuts add more flavor and protein. You can use any type of nut you'd like in this easy recipe. Serve these with mustard or a barbecue sauce for dipping. You can also wrap these little bites in lettuce leaves with some mayo or mustard for a delicious sandwich.

Serves 4–6

1 pound boneless, skinless chicken breasts

2 tablespoons lime juice

1 tablespoon olive oil

1 clove garlic, minced

½ cup hazelnut flour

½ teaspoon salt

⅛ teaspoon pepper

1 egg, beaten

1⅓ cups finely chopped toasted hazelnuts

1. Preheat oven to 375°F. Cut chicken breasts into 1" pieces and place in shallow dish. Top with lime juice, olive oil, and garlic; mix well and set aside.

2. In a shallow dish, combine hazelnut flour, salt, and pepper. In a second shallow dish, place egg. In a third dish, place chopped hazelnuts.

3. Drain chicken, then dip each chicken piece into the hazelnut flour mixture, then into the egg, then into the hazelnuts to coat. Place on a rimmed baking sheet.

4. Bake for 15–20 minutes or until chicken registers 165°F and juices run clear. Serve with any sauce for dipping.

SALMON NORI ROLLS

Nori, or dried sheets of seaweed, is an excellent wrapper for sandwiches and snacks. It is high in iodine, a nutrient that can be missing in the Paleo diet. These little rolls are delicious, easy to make, and gorgeous to look at. Rice, which is usually used in nori rolls to hold everything together, is omitted, but you won't miss it.

Serves 6

2 (4-ounce) salmon fillets

1 tablespoon olive oil

1 teaspoon dried thyme leaves

½ teaspoon salt

⅛ teaspoon white pepper

2 avocados, peeled and thinly sliced

2 tablespoons lemon juice

1 teaspoon sesame oil

2 tablespoons prepared horseradish

3 tablespoons Wilma's Mayonnaise (see Chapter 2)

4 sheets pressed seaweed (nori)

2 cups shredded cauliflower

1. Preheat oven to 350°F. Place salmon in baking dish and drizzle with olive oil. Sprinkle with thyme, salt, and pepper. Bake the salmon for 13–18 minutes or until the salmon just flakes when tested with fork. Remove from oven, remove the salmon from the dish, and let cool.

2. When salmon is cool, flake into large pieces.

3. Sprinkle avocado slices with the lemon juice and sesame oil. In small bowl, combine horseradish and mayonnaise.

4. Place nori sheets, shiny side down, on work surface. Leaving a 1" border at the top and bottom of each sheet, spread sheets with some of the horseradish mixture. Place rows of the salmon, avocado, and cauliflower next to each other on the sheets, filling about ½ of the sheet.

5. Roll up tightly (you can use a bamboo mat that is made specifically for this purpose to roll the seaweed) and seal the edge with some water.

6. Cut the roll into several pieces using a sharp knife. Repeat with remaining ingredients. Serve immediately, or cover with damp towel and store in the fridge for 2–3 hours before serving.

BACON-WRAPPED OYSTERS

Oysters are very high in protein and contain healthy omega-3 fatty acids, as well as a good supply of calcium and zinc. These shellfish can be eaten raw, but are also delicious cooked. You can ask your seafood supplier to shuck the oysters for you, or do it yourself if you have an oyster knife and know how to accomplish this task. When wrapped in bacon along with a piece of sweet date and baked, they make a wonderful appetizer.

Serves 4

6 slices bacon, cut in half crosswise

12 live oysters, shucked and drained, or 12 smoked oysters

6 large Medjool dates, pitted and cut in half lengthwise

1. Preheat oven to 400°F. Place bacon on work surface.

2. Place each oyster on the bacon strips and place a date half next to the oyster.

3. Roll up, enclosing the oyster and date in the bacon. Secure with a toothpick.

4. Place the oysters on a rimmed baking sheet and bake for 10–15 minutes or until the bacon is golden brown and crisp. Serve warm.

CAPRESE BITES

Caprese salad is an Italian invention, comprising fresh tomatoes, fresh basil, and mozzarella cheese. You can certainly use cheese if you're eating it, but this version using scallops looks just the same and is just as delicious. These pretty appetizers are ideal served to company when you're grilling in the summer. The tomatoes and basil must be in season for this recipe. You'll need 4" wooden skewers.

Serves 4

2 tablespoons butter or coconut oil

1 clove garlic, minced

6 sea scallops, each cut in half crosswise

12 grape tomatoes

12 basil leaves

1 tablespoon balsamic vinegar

2 tablespoons olive oil

¼ teaspoon salt

Pinch white pepper

1. Melt butter or coconut oil in medium saucepan over medium heat. Add garlic and cook for 30 seconds. Add the scallops, cut-side down, and cook for 1 minute. Turn over and cook for 1–2 minutes longer or until the scallops are opaque. Remove from heat and let cool for 10 minutes.

2. Skewer the ingredients in this order: grape tomato, scallop, and basil leaf.

3. Combine vinegar, olive oil, salt, and pepper in small bowl and drizzle over the skewers. Serve immediately.

BACON BLUE CHEESE DIP

Bacon and blue cheese is a natural combination. You can use any type of blue cheese in this recipe: Gorgonzola, blue cheese from Iowa, or whatever you find in your grocery store. Serve with lots of fresh veggies for dipping or Paleo Crackers (see Chapter 5).

Yields 1 cup

4 slices bacon

1 onion, chopped

½ cup Wilma's Mayonnaise (see Chapter 2)

2 tablespoons heavy cream or coconut cream

⅓ cup crumbled blue cheese

1 tablespoon chopped fresh chives

1. Cook bacon until crisp in small skillet. Drain bacon on paper towels, crumble, and set aside.

2. Drain all but 1 tablespoon bacon drippings from pan. Cook onion in drippings until tender, about 5–6 minutes.

3. In small bowl, combine mayonnaise and heavy cream and beat well. Stir in bacon, onion, blue cheese, and chives. Serve immediately, or cover and refrigerate up to 2 hours.

SWEET POTATO SKINS

Potato skins are a classic bar appetizer that is rich and delicious. Did you know that you can make them with sweet potatoes? Save the flesh of the sweet potatoes to make Sweet Potato–Topped Meat Loaf (see Chapter 8). You can top these tender and crisp wedges with bacon, sausage, mayonnaise, shrimp, lettuce, chopped vegetables, or anything that catches your fancy. For this recipe, if you're not eating cheese, mash the avocado and spread that on the finished potato skins to hold the other toppings.

Serves 6–8

4 medium sweet potatoes, scrubbed

2 tablespoons coconut oil

1 teaspoon salt

¼ teaspoon white pepper

3 tablespoons butter, melted or olive oil

1 cup shredded Cheddar or Gruyère cheese, if desired

1 cup sour cream, Wilma's Mayonnaise (see Chapter 2), or Yogurt Cheese (Chapter 2)

4 slices bacon, crisply cooked and crumbled

1 cup shredded lettuce or kale

1 cup seeded chopped tomatoes, if desired

2 avocados, peeled and chopped

1. Preheat oven to 425°F. Rub the sweet potatoes with coconut oil, sprinkle with salt and pepper, pierce with a fork, and place on a baking sheet. Bake until tender, about 45–55 minutes. Let cool for 30 minutes on a wire rack.

2. Cut the sweet potatoes in half lengthwise and scoop out most of the flesh, leaving about ¼" of flesh next to the skin. Reserve flesh for another use.

3. Cut the halves in half lengthwise, then in half crosswise. You'll have 32 pieces of sweet potato skin. Place, skin-side down, on baking sheet in a single layer. Drizzle with melted butter or olive oil and sprinkle with salt and white pepper.

4. Bake the potato skins 8–11 minutes longer, or until crisp.

5. Top with cheese, if using, and let stand until cheese melts. (If not using cheese, mash avocado and spread over potato skins as the first topping instead of the last.) Top with sour cream, bacon, lettuce, tomatoes if using, and avocado, and serve immediately.

SPANAKOPITA-STUFFED MUSHROOMS

Spanakopita is a Greek recipe that combines yogurt, cheese, garlic, and spinach layered between crisp layers of phyllo dough. But phyllo is made from wheat and isn't acceptable on the Paleo plan. So use that filling to stuff mushrooms! This delectable appetizer can be made ahead of time; bake the mushrooms right before serving.

Serves 6–8

18 large mushrooms

2 tablespoons butter or olive oil

1 medium onion, chopped

2 cloves garlic, minced

½ cup Yogurt Cheese (see Chapter 2)

1 cup shredded mozzarella cheese

1 cup frozen chopped spinach, thawed and well drained

⅓ cup crumbled feta cheese

½ teaspoon salt

⅛ teaspoon pepper

1. Preheat oven to 375°F. Briefly rinse the mushrooms under cool running water and dry. Trim and discard ends from mushroom stems. Remove stems from caps and chop stems.

2. In medium skillet, melt butter over medium heat. Add onion, garlic, and chopped mushroom stems; cook and stir until tender, about 5 minutes. Remove from heat and place in bowl; let cool 10 minutes.

3. Add Yogurt Cheese, mozzarella cheese, spinach, feta, salt, and pepper to onion mixture. Stuff the mushroom caps with this mixture.

4. Bake immediately for 15–20 minutes or until mushrooms are hot. You can also cover and refrigerate up to 12 hours at this stage; add another 5 minutes to baking time.

FRICO

This is a simple, delicious recipe if cheese is part of your diet. Just get a hard grating cheese such as Parmesan or Romano, place it in little piles on a Silpat-lined baking sheet, and bake until light brown. The little rounds harden as they cool. They're perfect to serve along with soup or chili, or serve them with Flintstone Guacamole (see recipe in this chapter) or any other dip from this chapter.

Serves 8

1 cup grated fresh Parmesan or Romano cheese

1 tablespoon almond flour

½ teaspoon dried thyme or basil leaves

Pinch black pepper

1. Preheat oven to 400°F. Line two baking sheets with Silpat or other silicone liners.

2. In medium bowl, combine cheese, almond flour, thyme, and pepper and toss to mix. Place on baking sheets by rounded tablespoon measure, about 5" apart. Flatten to form 3" rounds.

3. Bake for 4–7 minutes or until light golden brown. Cool on baking sheet for 2 minutes, then remove to a wire rack to cool completely. Store in airtight container at room temperature.

ROASTED KALE

This simple recipe makes a crisp, chewy kale that is irresistible. You can slice up some collard greens or Swiss chard as a substitute for kale, or mix them all together for a tasty medley.

Serves 2

6 cups kale

1 tablespoon avocado oil

1 teaspoon garlic powder

1. Preheat oven to 375°F.

2. Wash, dry, and trim kale by pulling the leaves off the tough stems or running a sharp knife down the length of the stems.

3. Place leaves in a medium-sized bowl; toss with oil and garlic powder.

4. Roast for 5 minutes on a roasting pan; turn leaves over and roast another 7–10 minutes, until kale turns brown and becomes paper-thin and brittle.

5. Remove from oven and serve immediately.

BAKED STUFFED CLAMS

Try to use fresh clams rather than canned in this dish. Once you do, you'll never go back to canned! Cherrystone clams are hard-shell quahogs and are generally 2½" in diameter.

Serves 4

4 fresh cherrystone clams, well-scrubbed and opened, meat removed and reserved

1 tablespoon lemon juice

¼ cup almond flour

1 egg

1 tablespoon Wilma's Mayonnaise (see Chapter 2)

½ teaspoon dried dill

2 tablespoons organic butter or Ghee (see Chapter 2), melted

Salt and pepper, to taste

1. Preheat the oven to 350°F. Place the clam shells on a baking sheet.

2. Add the clam meat and the rest of the ingredients to a food processor or blender and pulse until mixed but not puréed.

3. Spoon the stuffing into the clam shells and bake for about 20 minutes. Serve immediately.

Follow Your Nose—and Your Ears!

When buying any kind of seafood, ask to smell it first. A fresh, salty aroma is fine; anything else is suspect—don't buy it! When selecting clams, make sure that they are tightly closed and make a sharp click when you tap them together. Clams should be tightly closed before cooking, and when cooked they should open.

SCALLOP CEVICHE

This recipe calls for overnight preparation, so plan accordingly. The scallops can be cooked before serving if you'd like. Bake at 400°F for 10–15 minutes until firm.

Serves 8

2 pounds small bay scallops

1 cup lime juice

1 large onion, chopped

20 black olives, chopped

½ cup water

3 medium tomatoes, peeled and diced

½ cup extra-virgin olive oil

1 teaspoon oregano

⅛ teaspoon white or black pepper

1. Marinate scallops in lime juice for 3–4 hours.

2. Drain and rinse scallops in cold water.

3. Place scallops in a medium-sized bowl and add remaining ingredients. Mix and store overnight in refrigerator.

4. Serve chilled.

Eating Raw Food

Many people advocate eating only raw food. However, you should be aware that the cooking process kills bacteria and small organisms that can cause illness. Eating uncooked food is a risk, no matter how tasty the dish.

SCALLOPS WRAPPED IN BACON

This common party appetizer has been revamped for Paleo with nitrate/nitrite-free bacon.

Serves 10

2 tablespoons almond oil

20 large scallops

2 tablespoons minced garlic

20 slices uncured, nitrate/nitrite-free bacon

1. Preheat oven to 375°F. Heat oil in a large skillet over medium-high heat. Sauté scallops in oil with garlic 3–4 minutes, or until scallops are lightly browned. Set aside to cool.

2. Cook bacon about 1 minute on each side until some of the fat is rendered out but the bacon is still pliable, and use to wrap scallops. Make sure bacon is not overcooked or it will not wrap around scallops.

3. Secure each appetizer with a toothpick. Place on baking pan. Bake for 15–18 minutes or until bacon is crisp and scallops are cooked.

TURKEY-STUFFED MUSHROOM CAPS

These appetizers are a bit more exciting than traditional recipes using bread crumbs. They are stuffed with protein and fats to ensure more macronutrients in each bite.

Serves 10

20 white mushrooms

2 tablespoons walnut oil

½ pound ground turkey

¼ cup minced onion

4 cloves garlic, minced

½ cup finely chopped walnuts

½ teaspoon sea salt

½ teaspoon black pepper

1. Preheat oven to 350°F.

2. Remove stems from mushrooms and hollow out mushroom caps. Dice mushroom stems and place in medium-sized bowl.

3. Heat walnut oil in a medium-sized skillet and cook ground turkey, onion, and garlic for 5–8 minutes, or until turkey is no longer pink.

4. Add mushroom stems, walnuts, salt, and pepper to the ground turkey and cook until mushroom stems are soft, about 8 minutes.

5. Stuff turkey mixture into mushroom caps and place on baking sheet.

6. Bake for 20 minutes or until golden brown on top.

EXOTIC FRUIT GUACAMOLE

Papaya and mango add an exotic twist to a traditional dish. The mix of sour and sweet will make your taste buds pop. If you aren't eating tomatoes, just increase the amounts of the other fruits.

Serves 4

1 medium papaya, peeled and cubed

1 medium mango, peeled and cubed

1 medium ripe avocado, pitted, peeled, and diced

1 tablespoon lime juice

2 cups seeded, diced tomato, if desired

¼ cup diced onion

2 tablespoons minced fresh cilantro

1 teaspoon seeded, finely chopped jalapeño pepper

1 garlic clove, minced

In a medium-sized bowl, combine all ingredients. Mix well and serve.

BAKED CHICKEN WINGS

Cayenne pepper is known for its metabolism-boosting properties. Blended with paprika and garlic, cayenne is sure to kick up the heat in these chicken wings.

Serves 4

12 chicken wings

3 tablespoons coconut aminos

½ tablespoon garlic powder

1 teaspoon paprika

1 teaspoon cayenne pepper

2 teaspoons raw honey

½ teaspoon salt

¼ teaspoon pepper

1 tablespoon avocado oil

1. Wash the chicken wings and pat dry with paper towels.

2. Combine remaining ingredients except oil in a bowl. Add wings and coat with mixture. Cover and refrigerate for 1–2 hours or overnight.

3. Preheat oven to 425°F. Line a baking dish with aluminum foil. Drizzle foil with oil. Place wings in one layer in baking dish.

4. Bake for 40 minutes or until golden brown. Turn the wings over after 20 minutes for even cooking.

BUFFALO CHICKEN WINGS

These spicy wings make the perfect tailgate treat.

Serves 12

4 tablespoons almond oil

4 tablespoons hot sauce

1 tablespoon lime juice

Ground pepper, to taste

4 pounds chicken wings with wing tips
   removed, cut in half

1. Add oil, hot sauce, and lime juice to a 4- or 6-quart slow cooker. Cook on high, about 15–20 minutes.

2. Add small amount of pepper to wings and place them on a broiler pan or baking sheet. Broil in the oven until lightly browned, about 5–6 minutes on each side.

3. Add chicken wings to slow cooker, and stir to coat with the sauce. Cover and cook on high for 3–4 hours.

Try Them Boneless!

For the boneless version of this classic appetizer, replace wings with 4 pounds of boneless, skinless tenders. Be prepared to eat with a fork! Serve as an appetizer as-is or over a bed of salad greens.

LOLLIPOP LAMB CHOPS

Baby lamb chops are expensive, but this appetizer is worth every penny for a special occasion.

Serves 14

4 cloves garlic

4 tablespoons minced parsley

3 tablespoons rosemary

Grated zest of ½ lemon

3 tablespoons Dijon mustard

2 tablespoons avocado oil

Salt and pepper, to taste

14 baby rib lamb chops, trimmed, with
   long bones left on

1. Blend everything but the chops in a mini food processor or blender until combined.

2. Pour mixture into a large dish and add lamb chops, turning to coat both sides.

3. Broil or grill lamb chops over medium-high heat for 3 minutes per side.

Crowd Pleaser

Baby lamb chops are the star of the show at parties and special occasions. Your guests will love these delicious finger foods. They are fun to eat like chicken wings but make less of a mess.

CRAB MEAT– OR SHRIMP-STUFFED MUSHROOMS

These can be made in advance and frozen. This is very good party fare, but be sure you make enough—they go quickly!

Yields 12 mushrooms

¼ pound cooked shrimp or crab meat (canned or fresh)

1 cup almond meal

½ cup Wilma's Mayonnaise (see Chapter 2)

Juice of ½ lemon

1 teaspoon fresh dill, or 1 teaspoon dried dill

Salt and pepper, to taste

12 white mushrooms, 1–1½" across, stems removed

1. In a large bowl, mix all the ingredients except the mushrooms.

2. At this point, you can stuff the mushrooms and refrigerate or freeze, or you can continue the recipe.

3. Preheat oven to 400°F. Place stuffed mushrooms on a baking sheet and bake for 15–20 minutes. Serve hot.

Buying Mushrooms

Buy only the whitest, crispest mushrooms. If you buy them from a grower, you'll see that they stay white and unblemished for at least three weeks. Old mushrooms are tan to brown with black/brown flecks.

SPICY BEEF–STUFFED MUSHROOMS

These disappear rapidly at a party—people love them! Just like the Crab Meat– or Shrimp-Stuffed Mushrooms (see previous recipe), you can make them in advance and either refrigerate or freeze them.

Yields 12 mushrooms

2 tablespoons avocado oil

¼ pound ground sirloin (very lean)

2 shallots, minced

1 clove garlic, minced

Salt and pepper, to taste

1 teaspoon hot sauce

1 teaspoon minced fresh ginger

1 large egg

1 teaspoon Worcestershire or other steak sauce

12 white mushrooms, 1–1½" across, stems removed

6 teaspoons almond meal

1. Preheat the oven to 400°F. Heat the oil over medium-high heat in a medium skillet and brown the sirloin, shallots, and garlic until the meat is thoroughly cooked. Stir in the salt and pepper, hot sauce, ginger, egg, and Worcestershire sauce. Remove from heat and set aside.

2. Set mushrooms on a baking sheet lined with parchment paper. Stuff mushrooms with meat mix. Sprinkle with almond meal.

3. Bake for 30 minutes until tops are brown and mushrooms are sizzling.

BACON-AND-HERB STUFFED MUSHROOMS

This is a delicious appetizer for a brunch! You could also serve these on the side with eggs.

Yields 16 mushrooms

16 white mushrooms, 1–1½" across, stems reserved and chopped

2 strips nitrate/nitrite-free bacon, cut in small pieces

½ red onion, minced

¼ cup almond meal

Pinch nutmeg

2 teaspoons minced fresh parsley

2 teaspoons minced fresh sage

1 large egg

1. Preheat the oven to 350°F. Clean mushrooms and place caps on a baking sheet lined with parchment paper.

2. In a medium-sized skillet, sauté bacon, onion, and mushroom stems over medium-high heat until the bacon is crisp. Stir in almond meal, nutmeg, parsley, and sage. Take off heat, let cool slightly, and mix in the egg.

3. Spoon mixture into mushrooms. Bake for 20 minutes or until lightly browned and very hot.

CLAMS CASINO

This recipe is great with tiny littleneck clams, which are sweet and tasty. Some are saltier than others, so between the combination of the clams and bacon, you do not need to add any salt at all.

Serves 4

16 littleneck clams, opened, juices reserved

4 tablespoons organic butter or Ghee (see Chapter 2)

1 small onion, finely minced

Juice of ½ fresh lemon

2 teaspoons chopped fresh parsley

½ teaspoon dried oregano

½ cup finely chopped roasted sweet red pepper

3 tablespoons almond meal

Freshly ground black pepper, to taste

3 slices nitrate/nitrite-free bacon, cut into 1" pieces

1. Preheat oven to 400°F. Place the open clams on a baking pan.

2. In a saucepan over medium heat, add the butter, onion, lemon juice, herbs, and red pepper. Mix well; when butter melts, sauté for about 4 minutes. Mix in almond meal and sprinkle with pepper. Moisten with reserved clam juice.

3. Divide the mixture among the clams.

4. Put a piece of bacon on top of each stuffed clam. Bake for 12 minutes, or until the bacon is crisp and the clams are bubbling.

Littleneck Clams

Littleneck clams are the smallest variety of hard-shell clams and can be found off the northeastern and northwestern coasts of the United States. They have a sweet taste and are delicious in soup, steamed and dipped in melted butter, battered and fried, or baked.

DEVILED EGGS WITH CAPERS

If deviled eggs aren't spicy, they aren't devilish enough! This recipe can be adapted if you want less heat.

Yields 12 deviled eggs

6 hard-cooked eggs, shelled and cut in half

½ avocado, mashed

1 teaspoon hot sauce

1 teaspoon celery salt

1 teaspoon onion powder

1 teaspoon garlic powder

1 chili pepper, finely minced, or to taste

2 tablespoons extra-small capers

Garnish of paprika or chopped chives

Brine-Packed Capers

Capers are actually caper berries that have been pickled. You can get them packed in salt, but they are better when packed in brine. You can get larger ones or very, very small ones—the tiny ones are tastier.

1. Scoop out egg yolks and place in food processor along with avocado, hot sauce, celery salt, onion powder, garlic powder, chili pepper, and capers.

2. Blend until smooth and spoon into the hollows in the egg whites.

3. Garnish with paprika or chives and cover loosely with foil. Refrigerate for at least 3 hours before serving.

PALEO CHIPS

Most Paleolithic diet enthusiasts say they miss tortilla chips the most. This is a close substitute and goes well with guacamole and salsa.

Serves 3

1½ cups almond flour

1 large egg

1 tablespoon minced garlic

1 tablespoon organic, no-salt-added tomato paste

1 jalapeño pepper, seeded and chopped

1 teaspoon chili powder

½ teaspoon onion powder

1. Preheat oven to 350°F.

2. Combine all ingredients in food processor and blend completely.

3. Spread evenly on a baking sheet covered with parchment paper.

4. Bake for 10 minutes.

5. Remove from the oven and cut into squares.

Complex Carbohydrates and the Paleolithic Diet

The most difficult part of the transition from a Neolithic diet to a Paleolithic diet is letting go of high-carbohydrate snack foods such as chips and pretzels. Those comfort foods are associated with gatherings, parties, and celebrations. It will take a while to detox your body from such foods, but once you make the switch, you will not look back. The great way your body feels a couple of weeks into the plan more than makes up for the withdrawal from complex carbohydrates and refined sugar.

ROASTED PARSNIP CHIPS

The parsnip is a root vegetable related to the carrot. It has a sweet taste and a lower glycemic load than a potato.

Serves 6

6 parsnips

3 tablespoons avocado oil

⅛ teaspoon nutmeg

1 teaspoon cinnamon

1. Preheat oven to 400°F. Line a baking sheet with parchment paper.

2. Peel parsnips and cut thinly at an angle to make long oval shapes.

3. In bowl, combine parsnips, oil, and spices. Mix well.

4. Spread parsnips out on baking sheet in a single layer. Cook 30 minutes. Remove from oven.

5. Turn on broiler and broil 5 minutes to make crispier chips.

SARDINES IN RED PEPPER CUP

These cups can be put together in a few minutes and are ideal snacks for transporting. Additionally, this recipe is a great source of omega-3.

Serves 1

1 (3.75-ounce) can no-salt-added, boneless, skinless sardines

1 red pepper

Juice of 1 lemon

Black pepper, to taste

1. Open and drain container of sardines.

2. Cut red pepper in half, lengthwise, remove ribs and seeds, and fill with sardines. The sardines could be added whole or chopped, whichever you prefer.

3. Sprinkle with lemon juice and pepper. Serve.

SHRIMP COCKTAIL

Shrimp is another flavorful, low-fat shellfish that is a nice addition to the Paleolithic lifestyle.

Serves 4

6 tablespoons grated horseradish root

1 tablespoon raw honey

1 (6-ounce) can organic, no-salt-added tomato paste

Juice of 1 lemon

½ teaspoon red pepper flakes

1 pound jumbo cooked shrimp, peeled

In a small bowl, blend the horseradish, honey, tomato paste, lemon juice, and red pepper flakes. Serve immediately with jumbo shrimp.

Shrimp Facts

Shrimp is a great protein source. A single (4-ounce) serving of shrimp contains 24 grams of protein with less than 1 gram of fat. It contains a high level of selenium, vitamin D, and vitamin B12. Selenium has been linked with cancer-fighting properties and is utilized in DNA repair.

ROASTED SPICY PUMPKIN SEEDS

This spicy seed recipe is sure to be a family favorite. It is quick to prepare and easy to grab for an on-the-go snack.

Serves 6

3 cups raw pumpkin seeds

½ cup almond oil

½ teaspoon garlic powder

Freshly ground black pepper, to taste

1. Preheat oven to 300°F.

2. In a medium-sized bowl, mix together all ingredients until the pumpkin seeds are evenly coated.

3. Spread in an even layer on a baking sheet.

4. Bake for 1 hour and 15 minutes, stirring every 10–15 minutes until toasted.

Pumpkin Seed Benefits

Pumpkin seeds have great health benefits. They contain L-tryptophan, a compound found to naturally fight depression, and they are high in zinc, a mineral that protects against osteoporosis.

HOT AND SPICY NUTS

Serve these at a cocktail party as an alternative to plain salted nuts. They are also delicious in trail mix.

Yields 2½ cups

2½ cups skin-on almonds or mixed nuts

1 teaspoon almond oil

½ teaspoon ground jalapeño pepper

½ teaspoon garlic powder

½ teaspoon cayenne pepper

½ teaspoon ground chipotle

½ teaspoon paprika

1. Place the nuts into a 1- to 2-quart slow cooker. Drizzle with the oil and stir. Add the spices, and then stir again to distribute the seasonings evenly.

2. Cover the slow cooker, and cook on low for 1 hour. Then uncover and cook on low for 15 minutes or until the nuts look dry. Let cool and store in airtight container at room temperature.

STUFFED GRAPE LEAVES

Although there are many versions of stuffed grape leaves served across the Mediterranean, these grape leaves are inspired by the flavors of Greece.

Serves 30

16 ounces jarred grape leaves (about 60 leaves)

2 teaspoons bacon fat

¾ pound ground beef, chicken, or pork

1 shallot, minced

¼ cup minced dill

½ cup lemon juice, divided

2 tablespoons minced parsley

1 tablespoon dried mint

1 tablespoon ground fennel

¼ teaspoon freshly ground black pepper

2 cups water

1. Prepare the grape leaves according to package instructions. Set aside.

2. Heat bacon fat in a large skillet over medium-high heat. Sauté the meat and shallot for 8–10 minutes, or until the meat is thoroughly cooked. Drain off any excess fat. Scrape into a bowl and add the dill, ¼ cup of the lemon juice, parsley, mint, fennel, and pepper. Stir to incorporate all ingredients.

3. Place a leaf, stem-side up, with the top of the leaf pointing away from you, on a clean work surface. Place 1 teaspoon of filling in the middle of the leaf. Fold the bottom toward the middle and then fold in the sides. Roll it toward the top to seal. Repeat until all leaves are used.

4. Place the rolled grape leaves in two or three layers in a 4-quart slow cooker. Pour in the water and remaining lemon juice. Cover and cook on low for 4–6 hours. Serve warm or cold.

SLOW-COOKED ALMONDS WITH A KICK

These crunchy, heart-healthy snacks are hard to resist.

Serves 24

6 cups skin-on almonds

4 tablespoons coconut oil, melted

3 cloves garlic, minced

2–3 teaspoons coarsely ground black
   pepper

1. Heat a 2-quart slow cooker on high for 15 minutes. Add the almonds.

2. Drizzle oil over almonds and stir. Sprinkle with garlic and pepper and stir.

3. Cover and cook on low for 2 hours. Stir every 30 minutes.

4. Turn heat up to high and cook uncovered for 30 minutes, stirring every 15 minutes.

5. Turn heat to low and serve warm, or remove from heat and allow to cool.

EGGPLANT RELISH

This recipe calls for Almond Yogurt, which is made from almond milk. It's a good substitute for cow's or sheep's milk yogurt. You can find it at co-ops and specialty stores, or make your own (see recipe in this chapter). Serve with grilled or raw veggies for dipping.

Serves 6

1 large eggplant, pierced all over with a
   fork

2 tablespoons extra-virgin olive oil

½ cup finely chopped tomato

¼ cup finely chopped onion

¼ cup Almond Yogurt (see recipe in this
   chapter)

3 cloves garlic, minced

½ teaspoon dried oregano

1–2 tablespoons lemon juice

Pepper, to taste

1. Place pierced eggplant in a 4-quart slow cooker, cover, and cook on low until tender, 4–5 hours. Cool to room temperature.

2. Cut eggplant in half and remove eggplant pulp (including seeds) from the peel with a spoon. Mash eggplant pulp and mix with oil, tomato, onion, Almond Yogurt, garlic, and dried oregano. Season with lemon juice and pepper and serve.

ALMOND OR COCONUT YOGURT

Almond or Coconut Yogurt is a great substitute for yogurt made from cow's, goat's, or sheep's milk. It is simply almond or coconut milk that has been cultured with a vegan yogurt starter or probiotics (lactobacillus bacteria). The bacteria eat the sugar in the milk and the protein coagulates to make a firm mixture. Yogurt can be tricky to make, but every batch you make will get better. A yogurt maker makes the process easier. Homemade yogurt will usually be thinner than purchased yogurt.

Yields 2 cups

2 cups almond or coconut milk

1 tablespoon probiotics or vegan yogurt starter

1. Place the milk in a small saucepan over low heat. Heat the milk to 170°F to kill any undesirable bacteria. Let cool to 110°F, stirring occasionally.

2. Add the probiotics or the vegan yogurt starter.

3. Place the mixture in a clean bowl that has been sterilized in the dishwasher, or use a yogurt machine.

4. If using a machine, turn it on according to the appliance directions. If you are not using a machine, cover the bowl and place the yogurt on a heating pad or in a water bath. Make sure the temperature stays at 100°F or close to it.

5. After 7–9 hours, the mixture should be thickened. Refrigerate, covered, up to 1 week. You can reserve a tablespoon of this yogurt to use as a starter for your next batch.

SPICED HAZELNUTS

This fiery favorite can liven up any appetizer menu.

Serves 24

6 cups hazelnuts

3 tablespoons almond oil

3 tablespoons crushed dried rosemary

1 tablespoon raw honey

¾ teaspoon cayenne pepper

½ teaspoon garlic powder

1. Heat a 2- or 3-quart slow cooker on high for 15 minutes; add hazelnuts. Drizzle oil over hazelnuts and toss; add remaining ingredients and toss.

2. Cover and cook on low for 2 hours, stirring every hour. Turn heat to high, uncover, and cook 30 minutes, stirring after 15 minutes.

3. Turn heat to low to keep warm for serving or remove from slow cooker.

APPETIZER MEATBALLS

Combine the cooked meatballs in a slow cooker with your favorite tomato sauce or Jalapeño Tomatillo Sauce (see Chapter 2) to enhance the flavor of these versatile meatballs.

Yields 24 meatballs

1 pound ground beef

1 large egg

2 tablespoons dried minced onion

1 teaspoon garlic powder

½ teaspoon pepper

1. Add all the ingredients to a large mixing bowl and combine with your clean hands. Shape the resulting mixture into approximately 24 small meatballs.

2. Add meatballs to a 2- or 3-quart slow cooker, cover, and cook on high until meatballs are cooked through, about 4 hours.

3. Turn heat to low and keep warm before serving.

SLOW-COOKED PALEO PARTY MIX

Grab it while it's hot, because it won't last long once the guests arrive!

Serves 24

4 tablespoons walnut oil

3 tablespoons lime juice

2 teaspoons garlic powder

2 teaspoons onion powder

1 cup raw almonds

1 cup raw pecans

1 cup raw walnut pieces

2 cups raw shelled pumpkin seeds

1 cup raw shelled sunflower seeds

1. Add oil to a 2-quart slow cooker. Then add the lime juice, garlic powder, and onion powder and stir all together.

2. Add the nuts and seeds. Stir well until all are evenly coated. Cover and cook on low for 5–6 hours, stirring occasionally.

3. Uncover slow cooker, stir, and cook another 45–60 minutes, to dry the nuts and seeds.

4. Cool and store in an airtight container.

SPINACH DIP

Serve with vegetables for dipping or Paleo-friendly crisps!

Serves 8

1 (10-ounce) package frozen spinach, thawed and undrained

1 small onion, finely chopped

1 stalk celery, thickly sliced

2 cloves garlic

2 tablespoons almond oil

½ teaspoon dried basil

½ teaspoon dried thyme

⅛ teaspoon ground nutmeg

Pepper, to taste

2 large eggs

1. In a food processor, process the spinach, onion, celery, garlic, oil, basil, thyme, and nutmeg until finely chopped.

2. Season to taste with pepper. Add eggs and process until smooth.

3. Spoon the mixture into greased, 1-quart soufflé dish, and place the dish inside a 6-quart slow cooker.

4. Cover and cook on low about 4 hours.

HOT CINNAMON-CHILI WALNUTS

These seasoned walnuts are a sweet-and-spicy hit with chili powder, cinnamon, and honey.

Serves 6

1½ cups walnuts

¼ cup raw honey

2 teaspoons cinnamon

1½ teaspoons chili powder

2 teaspoons coconut oil

1. Combine all the ingredients and place in a greased 2½-quart slow cooker.

2. Cover slow cooker and vent lid with a chopstick or the handle of a wooden spoon. Cook on high for 2 hours or on low for 4 hours.

3. Pour walnut mixture out onto a baking sheet lined with parchment paper. Allow to cool and dry and then transfer to an airtight container. Store in the pantry for up to 2 weeks.

ROASTED PISTACHIOS

Raw pistachios are available at Trader Joe's and health food stores. Roasting your own lets you avoid salt on the nuts, which makes them a snack that perfectly matches your Paleo palate.

Serves 16

1 pound raw pistachios

2 tablespoons almond oil

1. Add the nuts and oil to a 2-quart slow cooker. Stir to combine. Cover and cook on low for 1 hour.

2. Stir the mixture again. Cover and cook for 2 more hours, stirring the mixture again after 1 hour. Cool and store in an airtight container.

Putting Roasted Pistachios to Work

You can make 8 servings of a delicious coleslaw alternative by mixing together 3 very thinly sliced heads of fennel; ½ cup roasted, chopped pistachios; 3 tablespoons almond oil; 2 tablespoons freshly squeezed lemon juice; and 1 teaspoon finely grated lemon zest. Add freshly ground black pepper and additional lemon juice if desired. Serve immediately, or cover and refrigerate up to 1 day.

ASPARAGUS AND AVOCADO LETTUCE WRAPS

This recipe is a great side dish for any main course, or add protein to make a complete meal. You can spice these wraps up with a few drops of your favorite hot sauce.

Serves 4

24 asparagus spears, trimmed

1 ripe avocado, pitted and peeled

1 tablespoon freshly squeezed lime juice

1 clove garlic, minced

2 cups chopped tomatoes

2 tablespoons chopped red onion

3–4 whole romaine lettuce leaves

⅓ cup fresh cilantro leaves, chopped

Health Benefits of Asparagus

Asparagus is an often undervalued vegetable in the kitchen. This healthy stalk weighs in at 60 percent RDA of folic acid. Additionally, it is high in vitamins A, B6, and C, as well as potassium. Asparagus is a great vegetable to eat if you're trying to lose weight. It has a diuretic effect and helps to release excess water from the body.

1. In a medium-sized saucepan over high heat, bring 2" of water to a boil.

2. Place the asparagus in a steamer basket, cover, and steam until just tender. Be careful not to overcook. The asparagus should still have a bit of crunch after about 5 minutes of steaming.

3. Remove asparagus and immediately rinse in cold water. Drain thoroughly.

4. In a small bowl, mash the avocado, lime juice, and garlic into a coarse purée.

5. In another bowl, stir together the tomatoes and onion.

6. Lay the lettuce leaves flat and spread avocado mixture equally among the lettuce leaves, then add asparagus and tomato-onion mixture.

7. Top with a dash of fresh cilantro leaves.

8. Fold in both sides and the bottom of each lettuce leaf and roll up.

CHAPTER 2

SAUCES AND SPREADS

GHEE

While not technically a sauce, ghee is a wonderful fat to use while cooking. It is the clear fat from butter, without the milk solids or water. You can drizzle ghee over grilled steaks or chicken for the perfect finishing touch. Ghee isn't difficult to make; it just takes some time. Use unsalted organic butter from grass-fed cows, cook it slowly, and refrigerate the finished product, well covered, up to 1 month.

Yields ¾ cup

1 pound unsalted butter

1. Place the butter in a saucepan over medium-high heat until it starts to simmer. When the butter simmers, reduce heat to medium and watch carefully. Foam will appear on the top; carefully skim this off and discard.

2. When the butter becomes a deeper gold in color, after about 8–10 minutes, the bubbling will stop and darker gold milk solids will be in the bottom of the pan.

3. Pour the mixture through three layers of cheesecloth set into a strainer. Discard the milk solids. Pour the clear liquid into a container, cover, and refrigerate. Use in place of butter or olive oil in recipes.

YOGURT CHEESE

If you are including dairy in your Paleo diet, Yogurt Cheese is an essential. This thick and creamy mixture can be substituted for cream cheese and for mayonnaise in just about any recipe. And it's so easy to make. You should use full-fat yogurt, just because it's more in line with the Paleo philosophy. Plus, it tastes wonderful! You can make Yogurt Cheese using Almond Yogurt (Chapter 1) if you are avoiding dairy. Try flavoring your yogurt cheese with herbs, spices, mustard, or sautéed vegetables. You can reserve the whey to use in soups or smoothies.

Yields 1 cup

3 cups full-fat yogurt

1. Place 4–6 layers of cheesecloth into a colander. Place the colander in a larger bowl. Place the yogurt in the cheesecloth, cover, and put in the refrigerator for 8–12 hours. The whey will drain out of the yogurt and collect in the bowl.

2. When the yogurt cheese is done draining, remove from the cheesecloth and place in a bowl; cover and refrigerate. If you want to add something to the cheese, stir it in gently so the cheese doesn't separate or break down.

WILMA'S MAYONNAISE

Homemade mayonnaise is one of the joys of the Paleo diet. This creamy, flavorful, and unctuous dressing is perfect for making salads and for sandwich spreads. If you are part of a high-risk group, healthwise, please use pasteurized eggs, since raw eggs can carry salmonella bacteria. You can find pasteurized eggs in regular supermarkets. Be sure to abide by use-by dates for food safety reasons. Also, vary the types of oils you use in this recipe until you find the ones with the best flavor for your palate. If you are following a vegetarian Paleo diet, omit the bacon and add another tablespoon of olive oil to the recipe.

Yields 1¼ cups

1 slice bacon

2 egg yolks

⅛ teaspoon salt

1 tablespoon Dijon mustard

1 tablespoon lemon juice

½ cup light olive oil

½ cup avocado or hazelnut oil

1. Cook the bacon in a small skillet until most of the fat has rendered. Do not brown the fat. Remove bacon from the pan; drain and reserve the fat. You can discard the bacon or return it to the pan, cook it to your liking, and eat it—it's your cook's treat.

2. In blender or food processor, combine egg yolks, salt, mustard, and lemon juice and blend until smooth.

3. Gradually add the bacon fat, olive oil, and avocado or hazelnut oil and process until the mixture is smooth and thick. Cover and refrigerate up to 5 days.

4. You can also make this by hand: Whisk all the ingredients except the bacon fat and oils together, then add the fat and oils in a thin stream, whisking constantly until mixture is thick.

NUT BUTTER SPREAD

Nut butters are a delicious alternative to peanut butter or mayonnaise when making a sandwich or a salad dressing. And they're easy to make, as long as you have a sturdy food processor. For best flavor, roast the nuts before you process them. Add anything you wish to this basic recipe, including melted chocolate for your own homemade Nutella, vanilla for more flavor, or spices such as cinnamon or cardamom. Cover and refrigerate up to a week.

Yields 1 cup

2 cups roasted pecans, almonds, or hazelnuts

Pinch sea salt

1. To toast nuts, place in a single layer on a rimmed baking sheet. Roast in a 400°F oven for 15–20 minutes or until nuts are fragrant and light golden. Let the nuts cool before you process them.

2. Place the nuts in a heavy duty food processor or blender. Cover and process for 5–10 minutes or until the nut butter is desired consistency. Season with salt.

SLOW-COOKER MARINARA

Marinara is simply a tomato sauce that is simmered until the tomatoes fall apart and the flavors blend. Making it in the slow cooker is a great way to prepare this Italian recipe. Use fresh tomatoes for the best flavor, but only when they're in season. During the winter, make this using boxed tomatoes, which are better quality than canned.

Yields 8 cups

2 tablespoons olive oil

1 onion, finely chopped

2 pounds Roma or plum tomatoes, chopped

2 cups water

½ cup dry red wine, if desired

4 cloves garlic, sliced

1 teaspoon salt

¼ teaspoon black pepper

1 teaspoon dried oregano leaves

2 teaspoons dried basil leaves

1 teaspoon agave nectar

1. In small saucepan, heat olive oil over medium heat. Add onion; cook and stir until onions are tender, about 5–6 minutes. Transfer to a 4-quart slow cooker.

2. Add remaining ingredients except agave nectar to slow cooker. Cover and cook on low for 5–7 hours or until tomatoes have fallen apart. Stir to blend, or use a stick blender for a smoother sauce.

3. Taste to correct seasonings; you may want to add more herbs, since the long cooking time diminishes their flavor. Add agave nectar and use, or ladle into jars and keep in the refrigerator for up to 1 week. You can freeze this sauce up to 3 months; let stand in the refrigerator overnight to thaw.

SLOW-COOKER APPLESAUCE

Applesauce is so simple to make, especially when you use the slow cooker. You can use any apples that are sweet and tart and that become soft when cooked. And remember, when you use flavorful organic apples, you don't need to add any sweetener. Use as many apples as you'd like; just make sure that the slow cooker is filled between ½ and ¾ full for best results. You can flavor this recipe with any warm spice: cinnamon, nutmeg, ginger, and cardamom are good choices.

Yields 5 cups

3 McIntosh apples

3 Granny Smith apples

3 Golden Delicious apples

2 tablespoons lemon juice

⅓ cup water

1 teaspoon cinnamon

¼ teaspoon nutmeg

Pinch salt

2 teaspoons vanilla

1 tablespoon butter or coconut oil

1. Peel and core the apples and cut into chunks. As you work, put the pieces in the slow cooker and sprinkle with lemon juice.

2. Add water, cinnamon, nutmeg, and salt and stir. Cover and cook on high for 4–6 hours or until apples are soft.

3. Mash the apples using a potato masher or large fork. Make the mixture as smooth or as chunky as you'd like. Add the vanilla and butter or coconut oil, cool, and store in the refrigerator up to 2 weeks.

CRUNCHY TUNA SPREAD

Keep some spreads on hand for hungry teenagers and adults. This recipe stores well, tightly covered in the fridge, for up to 5 days. Use it as a dip for veggies, or spread it on romaine lettuce leaves and roll up for a quick wrap sandwich. If you can find Italian tuna packed in oil, use it. It has much more flavor than the American type packed in water.

Yields 2 cups

3 slices bacon

⅔ cup Wilma's Mayonnaise (see recipe in this chapter)

¼ cup Dijon mustard

1 teaspoon dried thyme leaves

¼ cup chopped red onion

1½ cups chopped red cabbage

1 yellow bell pepper, chopped

1 (12-ounce) can tuna in oil, drained

¼ cup toasted pine nuts

1. In medium skillet, cook bacon until crisp. Remove from pan, drain on paper towels, crumble, and set aside. Reserve 1 tablespoon bacon drippings.

2. In medium bowl, combine reserved bacon drippings, mayonnaise, mustard, and thyme leaves and mix well.

3. Stir in red onion, cabbage, bell pepper, tuna, pine nuts, and reserved bacon and mix gently. Cover and refrigerate up to 4 days.

SMOKED SALMON SPREAD

There are two types of smoked salmon: hot-smoked and cold-smoked. Hot-smoked salmon is firm and flakes easily and tastes strongly of smoke. Cold-smoked salmon is tender and usually sliced very thinly. You can use either type in this recipe, or substitute a 6-ounce can of red sockeye salmon, drained. Spread it on Paleo Crackers (see Chapter 5) for a quick snack, or use it to fill avocados or celery sticks for a light lunch.

Yields 1½ cups

1 (8-ounce) package cream cheese, softened, or 1 cup Yogurt Cheese (see recipe in this chapter)

¼ cup sour cream or coconut cream

2 tablespoons butter, softened

1 tablespoon prepared horseradish

2 tablespoons small capers, rinsed and drained

2 tablespoons lemon juice

1 tablespoon chopped fresh dill weed

⅔ cup chopped smoked salmon

1. In medium bowl, beat cream cheese until smooth. If using Yogurt Cheese, skip this step.

2. Add sour cream and butter and stir until blended. Stir in remaining ingredients and mix until combined. Use immediately, or cover and store in the refrigerator up to 3 days.

HONEY PECAN SPREAD

This delicious spread can be served on sliced apples or celery, or you can spread it on any of the bread recipes in this book. It is really good for breakfast on the run; try it on the Nuts and Seeds Granola Bars from the Children's Favorites chapter (Chapter 13). You can also use walnuts or hazelnuts in place of the pecans.

Yields 1 cup

1½ cups pecans, coarsely chopped

½ cup butter, divided

2 tablespoons honey

1 teaspoon cinnamon

⅛ teaspoon nutmeg

Pinch salt

1. Place pecans and 2 tablespoons of the butter in a medium saucepan over medium-low heat. Toast the pecans, stirring frequently, for 8–9 minutes or until the pecans are fragrant and turn a slightly darker brown color. Remove from heat and cool completely.

2. When the pecans are cool, combine remaining butter with honey, cinnamon, nutmeg, and salt in a medium bowl and beat until smooth. Stir in pecans.

3. Store covered in the refrigerator. Let stand 15 minutes before using so the mixture softens enough to spread easily.

KALE PESTO

Kale is a nutritional powerhouse and is very popular. Its cholesterol-reducing properties are stronger if it's cooked before eating. Steaming also reduces the leafy green's strong taste and helps it retain its bright color. This pesto can be served on chicken, fish, or pork, and can be stirred into mayonnaise for a dip or salad dressing. It freezes well too; freeze in small portions and thaw in the fridge overnight before using.

Yields 2½ cups

2 cups packed fresh kale

1 cup fresh basil leaves

½ cup toasted chopped hazelnuts

1 tablespoon lemon juice

1 clove garlic, minced

½ teaspoon salt

⅛ teaspoon pepper

⅓ cup olive oil

2 tablespoons hazelnut oil

¼ cup water

1. Place the kale in a steamer and turn it on. You can also bring 2 cups water to a boil in a medium saucepan. Add a steamer basket or insert. Cover. Steam the kale for 2–3 minutes or until slightly softened. Remove to colander to drain. Press in kitchen towel to remove excess water.

2. Combine kale, basil, hazelnuts, lemon juice, garlic, salt, and pepper in a food processor. Process until finely chopped.

3. With motor running, add olive oil and hazelnut oil gradually through the feed tube. Add enough water as needed for desired consistency. Correct seasoning. Store, covered, in the refrigerator up to a week or freeze for longer storage.

SPINACH PISTACHIO PESTO

If you aren't eating cheese, pesto is off the table. But this delicious and flavorful sauce is a must for adding interest to many foods, including salads, grilled meats, and Italian dishes. So substitute pistachios! This tender nut adds lots of flavor to pesto without any dairy at all. It can be frozen in small amounts; just thaw in the fridge overnight before using in recipes.

Yields 3 cups

1 (10-ounce) package frozen chopped spinach

1½ cups pistachios

1 cup fresh basil leaves

⅔ cup olive oil

1 teaspoon salt

1. In blender or food processor, combine spinach, pistachios, and basil and blend until finely chopped.

2. With motor running, slowly add olive oil through the feed tube until mixture is smooth and thick. Add salt.

3. Add enough water for desired consistency. Refrigerate, covered, up to 3 days, or freeze for longer storage.

CHIMICHURRI SAUCE

Chimichurri Sauce comes from Argentina. This flavorful herb sauce is primarily used for grilled meat, especially beef, but it can be used on seafood, pork, chicken, or vegetables. It is very easy to make. Store it covered in the refrigerator for up to 5 days. You can freeze it for longer storage; just thaw in the fridge overnight.

Yields 2 cups

1½ cups packed flat-leaf parsley

⅓ cup cilantro or oregano leaves

1 shallot, chopped

3 cloves garlic, chopped

¼ cup red wine vinegar

2 tablespoons lemon juice

⅔ cup olive oil

½ teaspoon salt

⅛ teaspoon pepper

1. Combine parsley, cilantro, shallot, and garlic in food processor and process until finely chopped. You can chop all these ingredients by hand if you'd like.

2. Transfer to a medium bowl and add vinegar, lemon juice, olive oil, salt, and pepper and stir with a whisk until combined. Refrigerate until serving time.

ROASTED VEGGIE SALSA

Most salsas are made from raw vegetables. Roasting the veggies adds another layer of flavor and makes this salsa a bit different. Serve with lots of vegetables and Paleo Chips (see recipe in Chapter 1) for dipping. Tomatillos look like little green tomatoes, but they have a tart and fresh taste. The color contrast in this salsa recipe is beautiful.

Yields 4 cups

½ pound fresh tomatillos, husk removed

½ pound Roma tomatoes

1 zucchini

2 tablespoons olive oil

1 onion, chopped

1–2 jalapeño peppers, chopped

4 cloves garlic, chopped

2 tablespoons lemon juice

½ teaspoon salt

⅛ teaspoon pepper

½ teaspoon crushed red pepper flakes

2 tablespoons chopped cilantro

1. Preheat oven to 400°F. Coarsely chop the tomatillos, tomatoes, and zucchini and place on a rimmed baking sheet. Drizzle with the olive oil and stir to coat. Top with onion.

2. Roast for 20–25 minutes or until vegetables are soft and light brown on the edges. Remove from oven and place in large bowl.

3. Stir in jalapeño peppers, garlic, lemon juice, salt, pepper, red pepper flakes, and cilantro. Cool, then store in refrigerator.

MINT PESTO

Pesto can be made with just about any herb or vegetable. Mint is a great choice for pesto, especially when serving it with lamb or chicken. The sharp sweet smell of mint is refreshing and an appetite stimulant. Mint is also rich in carotenes, those precursors to vitamin A, and vitamin C. It grows very well in the garden—almost too well! This recipe doesn't use cheese.

Yields 2 cups

2 cups packed fresh mint leaves

1 clove garlic, minced

2 tablespoons lemon juice

⅓ cup toasted pine nuts

¼ teaspoon salt

⅓ cup extra-virgin olive oil

2–3 tablespoons water

1. In blender or food processor, chop mint with garlic until finely chopped.

2. Add lemon juice, pine nuts, and salt and process again.

3. With the machine running, add oil and water until a sauce forms. You may need to add more oil or water. Store covered in the refrigerator for 3 days; freeze for longer storage.

PARTY GUACAMOLE

Guacamole is a party favorite that is also quite healthy.

Serves 6

4 ripe avocados

2 vine-ripe tomatoes, diced, if desired

½ cup diced green onions

1 tablespoon seeded, diced jalapeño peppers

2 cloves garlic, minced

Juice of 1 lime

¾ teaspoon sea salt

½ teaspoon freshly ground black pepper

1. Scoop out the flesh of the avocados and place in a small bowl. Mash the avocados with a fork.

2. Add the tomatoes, onions, jalapeños, and garlic. Mix together.

3. Add fresh lime juice and mix.

4. Stir in salt and black pepper and serve immediately.

SLOW-COOKED SALSA

This may be the easiest salsa recipe ever, and it tastes so much fresher than jarred salsa.

Serves 10

4 cups halved grape tomatoes

1 small onion, thinly sliced

2 jalapeño peppers, diced

⅛ teaspoon salt

1. Place all ingredients into a 2-quart slow cooker. Stir. Cook on low for 5 hours.

2. Stir and lightly smash the tomatoes before serving, if desired.

ROCKING SALSA

This salsa is sure to be a winner at any party. Serve with Paleo Chips (see Chapter 1) for a great appetizer before dinner.

Serves 4

½ cup chopped fresh cilantro

1½ cups chopped tomatoes

¼ cup sun-dried tomatoes

½ cup olive oil

2 teaspoons freshly squeezed lime juice

1 teaspoon minced ginger

1½ teaspoons minced garlic

1 teaspoon minced jalapeño pepper

Combine all ingredients in a food processor and pulse quickly to blend. Be careful not to over-pulse and completely liquefy this salsa. It should have a slight chunky texture.

FRESH PEPPER SALSA

Tomatoes are a great source of the antioxidant vitamin C. You can also get creative and make your salsa with other vegetables, fruits, and spices.

Yields 1 pint

1 yellow bell pepper

1 orange bell pepper

2 poblano chilies

2 Anaheim chilies

2 small jalapeño peppers

2 cloves garlic

¼ red onion

Juice of ½ lime

Freshly ground black pepper, to taste

1 tablespoon avocado oil

Chopped cilantro (optional)

1. Place all ingredients except the oil and cilantro (if using) in a food processor and pulse until desired chunkiness results. Taste and adjust for saltiness and heat.

2. In a medium-sized pot, heat oil until slightly smoking. Add blended pepper mixture. Cook on high for 8–10 minutes, stirring occasionally. Sprinkle some chopped cilantro on top before serving, if desired. Serve hot, cold, or at room temperature with veggies, as a garnish for fish or poultry, or in your favorite burrito.

MELON SALSA

This sweet melon salsa is a fun alternative to traditional vegetable-based salsas.

Serves 4

3 tomatoes, seeded and finely diced

½ honeydew melon, peeled and finely diced

1 cantaloupe, peeled and finely diced

1 cup minced red onion

½ jalapeño pepper, seeded and minced

½ cup chopped fresh cilantro

Juice of 1 large lime

1. In a large serving bowl, combine all ingredients and mix well.

2. Chill for 4 hours and serve.

Melons

Melon has a very low sugar content. One fruit serving of cantaloupe is half a melon. This is a good choice when you're watching calories or counting fruit servings per day.

SALSA VERDE

Tomatillos, relatives of the tomato, are in peak season in the summer and early autumn. Salsa verde *means "green salsa."*

Yields 3 cups

1½ pounds fresh tomatillos

2 jalapeño peppers

½ cup chopped fresh cilantro

1 onion, chopped

Juice of 1 lime

2 teaspoons salt

1. Preheat oven to 400°F. Remove husks from the tomatillos, rinse in warm water, and place on a baking sheet with the jalapeños. Place jalapeños and tomatillos in the oven to roast until slightly charred, about 10 minutes.

2. Place tomatillos, jalapeños, cilantro, onion, lime juice, and salt in a blender. Purée until salsa is well-blended.

AIOLI

Aioli is a basic French mayonnaise used throughout the Mediterranean. It's loaded with garlic and can include a variety of different herbs. You can also add tomatoes and spices.

Yields 1 cup

2 pasteurized eggs, at room temperature

1 teaspoon lemon juice

1 teaspoon white wine vinegar

½ teaspoon Dijon mustard

4 cloves garlic, or to taste

¾ cup avocado oil

Choice of ½ teaspoon oregano, tarragon, or rosemary

Salt and pepper, to taste

1. Combine the eggs, lemon juice, vinegar, mustard, and garlic in a blender.

2. Add the oil a little at a time and continue to blend. When the mixture is creamy, taste. Add herb of choice and salt and pepper. Pulse to blend. Store in the refrigerator or serve.

Storing Aioli

Aioli will keep in the refrigerator for a day or two, but it's best made and used the same day. Don't freeze aioli or it will separate and become greasy.

FRESH TOMATO DRIZZLE

This is perfect over shrimp, drizzled onto avocados, or even used as a sauce for hot or cold chicken or fish. It tastes summery!

Yields 2 cups

1 pint cherry tomatoes

4 cloves roasted garlic

2 shallots

2 jalapeño peppers, cored and seeded

¼ cup stemmed, loosely packed fresh basil

¼ cup red wine vinegar or balsamic vinegar

½ cup almond oil

½ teaspoon celery salt

2 teaspoons Worcestershire sauce

Freshly ground black pepper, to taste

½ teaspoon cayenne pepper, or to taste

Purée all ingredients in a blender. Taste and add more celery salt and pepper if desired. This dressing improves with age—try making it a day or two in advance.

Balsamic Vinegar

There are various types of Italian vinegar, but perhaps the most famous is balsamic vinegar. Balsamic vinegar is made from reduced wine and aged in special wood barrels for years. Each year's barrels are made of a different type of wood—the vinegar absorbs the flavor of the wood. Authentic balsamic vinegar ages for a minimum of ten and up to thirty years.

WASABI MAYONNAISE

Traditional wasabi paste is made with real mayonnaise. This version is Paleo-friendly and can be used with sushi or other types of proteins.

Serves 8

2 large eggs, preferably pasteurized

2 tablespoons lemon juice

1 teaspoon dry mustard

2 tablespoons wasabi powder

1½ cups avocado oil

1. Combine eggs, lemon juice, dry mustard, and wasabi powder in a food processor and pulse until blended.

2. Drizzle oil into egg mixture slowly and continue to pulse until completely blended.

Eating Raw Proteins

There has been some debate as to whether you should eat proteins raw. Certain vitamins, such as C, B6, and B9, are diminished in the cooking process but other nutrients, such as egg protein, are more digestible. But you don't consume protein for vitamin C. And raw eggs can be contaminated with salmonella bacteria and can make you sick. If you are pregnant, elderly, or have a chronic illness or a compromised immune system, do not consume raw or undercooked eggs, raw milk, or raw or undercooked meats. In the last 20 years, more virulent and antibiotic-resistant bacteria have emerged that were not around in the Paleolithic era.

CHIPOTLE MAYONNAISE

This dressing will add a nice flavor to most meat, poultry, and fish dishes.

Serves 8

2 large eggs, preferably pasteurized

2 tablespoons lemon juice

1 teaspoon dry mustard

2 tablespoons minced chipotle peppers

1½ cups avocado oil

1. Combine eggs, lemon juice, dry mustard, and chipotle peppers in food processor and pulse until blended.

2. Drizzle oil into egg mixture slowly and continue to pulse until completely blended. Store covered in the refrigerator up to 2 days.

HOMEMADE KETCHUP

Ketchups are traditionally high in sugar, and sugar-free versions usually contain a chemical sweetener. If you make your own, you'll know exactly what ingredients are in your specially made ketchup!

Serves 5

1 (15-ounce) can no-salt-added tomato sauce

2 teaspoons water

½ teaspoon onion powder

¾ cup raw honey

⅓ cup lime juice

¼ teaspoon cinnamon

⅛ teaspoon ground cloves

Pinch ground allspice

Pinch nutmeg

Pinch freshly ground black pepper

⅔ teaspoon sweet paprika

1. Combine all the ingredients in a 2½-quart slow cooker. Cover and cook on low, stirring occasionally, for 2–4 hours or until ketchup reaches desired consistency.

2. Turn off the slow cooker and allow mixture to cool, then transfer to a covered container (such as a recycled ketchup bottle). Store in the refrigerator for up to a month.

Ketchup with a Kick

If you like zesty ketchup, you can add red pepper flakes or salt-free chili powder along with, or instead of, the cinnamon and other seasonings. Another alternative is to use hot paprika rather than sweet paprika.

WALNUT PARSLEY PESTO

Walnuts add a significant blast of omega-3 fatty acids to this delicious pesto.

Serves 4

½ cup walnuts

8 cloves garlic

1 bunch parsley, roughly chopped

¼ cup walnut oil

Freshly ground black pepper, to taste

1. Chop the walnuts in a food processor or blender. Add the garlic and process to form a paste. Add the parsley; pulse into the walnut mixture.

2. While the blender is running, drizzle in the oil until the mixture is smooth. Add pepper to taste.

Pesto for All

"Pesto" is a generic term for anything made by pounding the ingredients in a mortar and pestle or processing them in a food processor or blender. Most people are familiar with traditional pesto, which is made with basil and pine nuts, but many prefer this variation with parsley and walnuts.

RED PEPPER COULIS

A coulis is a thick sauce made from puréed fruits or vegetables. You can make it with any fruit or vegetable you like. To add more flavor, experiment with the addition of herbs and spices.

Serves 8

6 red peppers

1 tablespoon walnut oil

Freshly ground black pepper, to taste

1. Preheat oven to 375°F.

2. Toss the red peppers with the oil in a medium-sized bowl. Place the peppers on a racked sheet pan and put in the oven for 15–20 minutes, until the skins begin to blister and the red peppers wilt.

3. Remove from oven and immediately place the red peppers in a glass or ceramic container with a top. Let sit covered for approximately 5 minutes, then remove the peppers and peel off the skin. Stem, seed, and dice the peppers.

4. Place the red peppers in a blender and purée until smooth. Season with black pepper.

SERRANO MINT SAUCE

This mint sauce is great with fish, poultry, and steak. Use this in place of other condiments or as a salad dressing.

Serves 6

1 cup tightly packed mint leaves

2 serrano chili peppers, chopped

4 cloves garlic, chopped

1 (1") piece fresh ginger, peeled and chopped

¼ cup lime juice

2 tablespoons olive oil

Combine all ingredients in food processor and pulse to coarsely blend.

HABANERO BASIL SAUCE

This sauce is very spicy and goes well with meats and poultry.

Serves 6

2 cups chopped basil leaves

3 habanero peppers, stemmed

2 cloves garlic

¼ cup lime juice

3 tablespoons olive oil

Combine all ingredients in food processor and pulse to coarsely blend.

MINT CHIMICHURRI SAUCE

Instead of the traditional mint jelly, use this mint chimichurri sauce to make a lamb recipe extra special.

Yields 2 cups

2 cups fresh parsley

2 cups fresh cilantro

1 cup fresh mint

¾ cup olive oil

3 tablespoons red wine vinegar

Juice of 1 lemon

3 cloves garlic, minced

1 large shallot, quartered

1 teaspoon salt

1 small jalapeño pepper, seeded and chopped

1. Wash herbs, remove stems, and chop leaves.

2. In a blender, combine oil, vinegar, lemon juice, garlic, shallot, salt, and jalapeño; blend ingredients together.

3. Add chopped parsley, cilantro, and mint to the blender in batches and blend until sauce is smooth.

JALAPEÑO TOMATILLO SAUCE

Serve this sauce over riced cauliflower or roasted root vegetables for a fiery Southwestern dish.

Serves 4

1 teaspoon avocado oil

2 cloves garlic, minced

1 medium onion, sliced

7 large tomatillos, peeled and diced

2 jalapeño peppers, minced

½ cup water

1. Heat the oil in a medium-sized skillet over medium heat. Sauté the garlic, onion, tomatillos, and jalapeño peppers for 5–10 minutes, until softened.

2. Place the mixture in a 2½-quart slow cooker. Add the water and stir. Cook on low for 8 hours.

FRUITY BALSAMIC BARBECUE SAUCE

Use this sauce in pulled pork, as a dipping sauce, over chicken or burgers, or even as a marinade.

Yield: 1–½ cups of sauce

¼ cup balsamic vinegar

2½ cups cubed mango

2 chipotle peppers in adobo sauce, puréed

1 teaspoon raw honey

1. Place all ingredients in a 2-quart slow cooker. Stir. Cook on low for 6–8 hours.

2. Mash the sauce with a potato masher. Store in an airtight container for up to 2 weeks in the refrigerator.

LEMON DILL SAUCE

Serve this delicious, tangy sauce over salmon, asparagus, or chicken.

Serves 4

2 cups chicken broth

½ cup lemon juice

½ cup chopped fresh dill

¼ teaspoon white pepper

Place all ingredients in a 2-quart slow cooker. Cook on high, uncovered, for 3 hours or until the sauce reduces by one-third.

A Peek at Peppercorns

Black peppercorns are the mature fruit of the black pepper plant, which grows in tropical areas. Green peppercorns are the immature fruit of the black pepper plant. White peppercorns are mature black peppercorns with the black husks removed. Pink peppercorns are the dried berries of the Brazilian pepper plant.

RASPBERRY COULIS

In this recipe, the slow cooking causes the fruit to cook down enough that straining is unnecessary. This is delicious as both a breakfast fruit spread and a sweet dessert topping.

Serves 8

12 ounces fresh or frozen raspberries

1 teaspoon lemon juice

2 tablespoons raw honey

Place all the ingredients in a 2-quart slow cooker. Mash gently with a potato masher. Cook on low, uncovered, for 4 hours. Stir before serving.

Taste, Taste, Taste

When using fresh berries, it is important to taste them prior to sweetening. One batch of berries might be tart while the next might be very sweet. Reduce or eliminate honey in this recipe if using very ripe, sweet berries.

FENNEL AND CAPER SAUCE

Try this sauce over boneless pork chops or boneless, skinless chicken breasts and grilled summer vegetables.

Serves 4

2 fennel bulbs with fronds, thinly sliced

2 tablespoons nonpareil capers

½ cup chicken broth

2 shallots, thinly sliced

2 cups diced fresh tomatoes

½ teaspoon freshly ground black pepper

⅓ cup fresh minced parsley

1. Place all ingredients except the parsley in a 3-quart slow cooker.

2. Cook on low for 2 hours, and then add the parsley. Cook on high for an additional 15–30 minutes.

SUMMER BERRY SAUCE

Drizzle this sauce over desserts and breakfast foods.

Serves 20

1 cup raspberries

1 cup blackberries

1 cup golden raspberries

½ cup water

½ teaspoon raw honey

Place all the ingredients in a 2-quart slow cooker. Lightly mash the berries with the back of a spoon or potato masher. Cover and cook on low for 2 hours, then uncover and cook on high for ½ hour.

ARTICHOKE SAUCE

Slow-cooking artichoke hearts gives them a velvety texture.

Serves 4

1 teaspoon almond oil

8 ounces frozen artichoke hearts, defrosted

3 cloves garlic, minced

1 medium onion, minced

2 tablespoons capote capers

1 (28-ounce) can crushed tomatoes

1. Heat the oil in a nonstick skillet over medium heat. Sauté the artichoke hearts, garlic, and onion for about 10–15 minutes, until the onion is translucent and most of the liquid has evaporated.

2. Put the mixture into a 4-quart slow cooker. Stir in the capers and crushed tomatoes.

3. Cook on high for 4 hours or on low for 8 hours.

Cleaning Slow Cookers

Do not use very abrasive tools or cleansers on a slow-cooker insert. They may scratch the surface, allowing bacteria and food to remain in the appliance. Use a soft sponge and baking soda for stubborn stains. You can also soak the slow cooker insert in warm soapy water before scrubbing clean.

MANGO CHUTNEY

This fruity, cool chutney is a nice accompaniment to spicy dishes. To peel a ripe mango, you can slide a spoon, bottom-side up, under the skin to remove it easily, without damaging the fruit.

Serves 8

3 mangoes

1 red onion

½ bunch fresh cilantro

1 teaspoon fresh lime juice

½ teaspoon freshly grated lime zest

Freshly ground black pepper, to taste

Peel and dice the mangoes and onion. Chop the cilantro. Mix together all the ingredients in a medium-sized bowl and adjust seasonings to taste.

APPLE CHUTNEY

Try this as a side for pork dishes instead of applesauce. It is also wonderful with hearty winter squash.

Serves 4

2 cups ice water

1 tablespoon fresh lemon juice

3 Granny Smith apples

1 shallot

3 sprigs fresh mint

1 tablespoon freshly grated lemon zest

¼ cup white raisins

½ teaspoon cinnamon

1. Combine the water and lemon juice in a large mixing bowl. Core and dice the apples, leaving peels on, and place them in the lemon water.

2. Thinly slice the shallot and chop the mint.

3. Thoroughly drain the apples, then mix together all the ingredients in a medium-sized bowl. Cover and store in the refrigerator up to 3 days.

PLUM SAUCE

Plum sauce is usually served with egg rolls, which are generally not Paleo-approved. But this delicious sauce is also wonderful brushed on chicken or pork ribs; doing so near the end of the grilling time will add a succulent glaze to the grilled meat.

Serves 16

8 cups pitted, halved plums (about 3 pounds)

1 small sweet onion, finely diced

1 cup water

1 teaspoon peeled, minced fresh ginger

1 clove garlic, minced

¾ cup raw honey

½ cup lemon juice

1 teaspoon ground coriander

½ teaspoon cinnamon

¼ teaspoon cayenne pepper

¼ teaspoon ground cloves

1. Add the plums, onion, water, ginger, and garlic to a 4-quart slow cooker. Cover and cook on low, stirring occasionally, for 4 hours or until plums and onion are tender.

2. Use an immersion blender to pulverize the contents of the slow cooker before straining it, or press the cooked plum mixture through a sieve.

3. Return the liquefied and strained plum mixture to the slow cooker and stir in honey, lemon juice, coriander, cinnamon, cayenne pepper, and cloves. Cover and cook on low, stirring occasionally, for 2 hours or until the sauce reaches the consistency of applesauce.

TOMATO AND CHICKEN SAUSAGE SAUCE

Sausage is a delicious alternative to meatballs in this rich tomato sauce.

Serves 6

4 Italian chicken sausages, diced

2 tablespoons tomato paste

1 (28-ounce) can crushed tomatoes

3 cloves garlic, minced

1 large onion, minced

3 tablespoons minced basil

1 tablespoon minced Italian parsley

¼ teaspoon crushed rosemary

¼ teaspoon freshly ground black pepper

1. Quickly brown the sausage on both sides in a nonstick skillet over medium-high heat, about 1 minute on each side. Drain any grease.

2. Add the sausage to a 4-quart slow cooker, along with the remaining ingredients. Stir.

3. Cook on low for 8 hours. Serve over cooked spaghetti squash or shirataki noodles.

CHIPOTLE TOMATO SAUCE

Try this Southwestern take on the classic Italian tomato sauce over spaghetti squash or as salsa on a Southwestern dish of choice.

Serves 6

3 cloves garlic, minced

1 large onion, minced

1 (28-ounce) can crushed tomatoes

1 (14.5-ounce) can diced tomatoes

3 chipotle peppers in adobo sauce, minced

1 teaspoon dried oregano

1 tablespoon fresh cilantro, minced

½ teaspoon freshly ground black pepper

Place all ingredients in a 4-quart slow cooker. Cook on low for 8–10 hours. Stir before serving.

Know Your Slow Cooker

When using a new or new-to-you slow cooker for the first time, pick a day when someone can be there to keep tabs on it. In general, older slow cookers cook at a lower temperature than newer models, but even new slow cookers can vary. It is a good idea to know the quirks of a particular slow cooker so food is not overcooked or undercooked. You can test a used slow cooker by filling it half full with water. Cover and turn on low. After 8 hours, test the water temperature with a food thermometer. It should be at least 185°F. If it is not, the slow cooker is not safe to use.

BOLOGNESE SAUCE

Also called Bolognese or ragù alla Bolognese, this recipe combines vegetables and meat to create the perfect sauce for pouring over just about any beef and/or veggie dish.

Serves 6

2 teaspoons avocado oil

½ pound lean, grass-fed ground beef

½ pound ground pork

1 large onion, minced

1 large carrot, minced

1 stalk celery, minced

3 ounces tomato paste

1 (28-ounce) can diced tomatoes

½ cup canned, unsweetened coconut milk

1 tablespoon Italian seasoning

¼ teaspoon ground black pepper

⅛ teaspoon nutmeg

1. Heat the oil in a nonstick skillet over medium heat. Brown the ground beef and pork, about 5–10 minutes. Drain off any excess fat.

2. Add the meats and the remaining ingredients to a 4-quart slow cooker. Cook on low for 8–10 hours. Stir before serving.

SUN-DRIED TOMATO SAUCE

Sun-dried tomatoes are an excellent source of lycopene, a micronutrient shown to be associated with cardiovascular health benefits and disease prevention.

Serves 4

1½ cups chopped sun-dried tomatoes

1 (28-ounce) can tomatoes, chopped

1 (14.5-ounce) can tomatoes, chopped

1 medium onion, chopped

2 cloves garlic, minced

1 cup chopped celery

⅔ cup vegetable broth

1½ teaspoons basil

1 teaspoon dried fennel seed

½ teaspoon oregano

½ teaspoon pepper

8 ounces sliced mushrooms (optional)

Place all the ingredients in a 4- or 6-quart slow cooker, cover, and cook on low for 6–8 hours.

SPINACH MARINARA SAUCE

Powerfully flavored and nutrient-rich, this sauce goes well with chicken, beef, or turkey meatballs, or over a vegetable medley side dish or main course.

Serves 8

1 (28-ounce) can peeled, crushed tomatoes, with liquid

1 (10-ounce) package frozen, chopped spinach, thawed and drained

2⅔ (6-ounce) cans tomato paste (16 ounces)

1 (4.5-ounce) can sliced mushrooms, drained

1 medium onion, chopped

5 cloves garlic, minced

2 bay leaves

⅓ cup peeled and grated carrot

¼ cup avocado oil

2½ tablespoons red pepper flakes

2 tablespoons lemon juice

2 tablespoons dried oregano

2 tablespoons dried basil

1. In a 4- or 6-quart slow cooker, combine all the ingredients, cover, and cook on high for 4 hours.

2. Stir, reduce heat to low, and cook for 1–2 more hours. Remove and discard bay leaves.

GROUND TURKEY TOMATO SAUCE

This sauce is packed full of fresh, natural flavor. It's an excellent complement to just about any Italian dish.

Serves 6

2 tablespoons avocado oil

1 pound ground turkey

1 (14.5-ounce) can stewed tomatoes

1 (6-ounce) can tomato paste

½ teaspoon dried thyme

1 teaspoon dried basil

½ teaspoon oregano

½–1 teaspoon raw honey (optional)

1 yellow onion, chopped

1 bell pepper, chopped

2 cloves garlic, crushed

1 bay leaf

¼ cup water

4 ounces chopped or sliced mushrooms, fresh or canned, drained

1. Heat the oil in a skillet over medium heat. Add the ground turkey and cook for 5–7 minutes until brown.

2. While browning turkey, place stewed tomatoes, tomato paste, thyme, basil, oregano, and honey in a 4- or 6-quart slow cooker. Stir well and turn slow cooker to low heat.

3. Transfer browned turkey to slow cooker with slotted spoon. In pan with ground-turkey drippings, sauté onion, pepper, garlic, and bay leaf for 3–5 minutes until softened.

4. Add the sautéed vegetables, water, and chopped mushrooms to the slow cooker. Cover and cook on low 4–6 hours. Thin with a little water if necessary; remove and discard bay leaf.

CRANBERRY SAUCE

Serve this sweet-tart cranberry sauce with a holiday meal. You can also use it as a spread or pour it over your favorite dessert.

Serves 10

12 ounces fresh cranberries

½ cup freshly squeezed orange juice

½ cup water

½ teaspoon orange zest

½ teaspoon raw honey

Place all ingredients into a 1½- or 2-quart slow cooker. Cook on high for 2½ hours. Stir before serving.

CRAN-APPLE SAUCE

This sauce is simple, sweet, and loaded with antioxidants like vitamin C.

Serves 6

1 cup fresh cranberries

8 apples, peeled, cored, and chopped

½ cup raw honey

1 cinnamon stick, halved

6 whole cloves

1. Combine cranberries, apples, and honey in a 4- or 6-quart slow cooker.

2. Place cinnamon stick and cloves in center of a 6" square of cheesecloth. Pull up sides and tie to form a pouch. Place in slow cooker.

3. Cover and cook on low for 4–5 hours or until cranberries and apples are very soft. Remove and discard cheesecloth bundle.

ROSEMARY MUSHROOM SAUCE

This sauce can be used as a marinade as well as a sauce to enhance the flavor and texture of many beef and chicken dishes.

Serves 4

8 ounces fresh mushrooms, sliced

1 large onion, thinly sliced

1 teaspoon avocado oil

1 tablespoon crushed rosemary

3 cups chicken broth

1. In a skillet over medium heat, sauté the mushrooms and onions in oil for about 5 minutes, until onions are soft.

2. Place onions and mushrooms in a 3-quart slow cooker. Add the rosemary and broth and stir.

3. Cook on low for 6–8 hours or on high for 3 hours.

RED PEPPER RELISH

This sauce has a little kick, spicing up the flavor of just about any entrée or side.

Serves 8

4 large red bell peppers, stemmed, seeded, and cut into thin strips

2 small Vidalia onions, thinly sliced

6 tablespoons lemon juice

¼ cup raw honey

½ teaspoon dried thyme

½ teaspoon red pepper flakes

½ teaspoon black pepper

1. Combine all the ingredients in a 3-quart slow cooker and mix well.

2. Cover and cook on low for 4 hours.

CHAPTER 3

SALADS AND DRESSINGS

HONEY DIJON SALAD DRESSING

Salad dressings are the finishing touch for any salad. They can also be used as a dip with the addition of some Yogurt Cheese or Wilma's Mayonnaise (both recipes are in Chapter 2). Make them in small quantities, since these homemade dressings don't last as long as commercial varieties. And, as always, use your favorite herbs and spices in this easy recipe.

Yields 1 cup

2 tablespoons Dijon mustard

2 tablespoons grainy mustard

3 tablespoons pure honey

2 tablespoons apple cider vinegar

¼ cup extra-virgin olive oil

2 tablespoons Wilma's Mayonnaise (see Chapter 2)

1. In medium bowl, combine both mustards with honey and vinegar and beat well with wire whisk. Gradually add the olive oil and beat until thick and smooth.

2. Beat in the mayonnaise until smooth; season to taste. Cover and refrigerate up to 1 week.

ROQUEFORT SALAD DRESSING

Roquefort is a type of blue cheese. Technically, only cheese made in a certain region in France can be called Roquefort. Whether you use true Roquefort, Gorgonzola, or another blue cheese for this recipe, it will still be delicious. Blue cheese is made from a combination of milks, usually goat's milk and sheep's milk. It is inoculated with penicillium mold, which makes the typical blue veins in the cheese.

Yields 1 cup

½ cup Wilma's Mayonnaise (see Chapter 2)

⅓ cup buttermilk or coconut cream

1 tablespoon lemon juice

⅓ cup crumbled Roquefort or blue cheese

1 teaspoon grated garlic

Pinch freshly ground pepper

1. In bowl, combine mayonnaise and buttermilk and whisk until combined. Gradually beat in lemon juice until thick.

2. Stir in cheese, garlic, and pepper; season to taste. Store, covered, in the refrigerator for up to 1 week.

TARRAGON VINAIGRETTE

Fresh tarragon is a wonderful herb that adds flavor to any dish. It's especially good with chicken and fish and in salad dressings. You can make a quantity of this recipe and store it in the fridge, covered, for up to 2 weeks. Just shake it before using it to dress spinach or lettuce salads.

Yields 1 cup

2 tablespoons Dijon mustard

2 tablespoons apple cider vinegar

1 tablespoon lemon juice

4 teaspoons chopped fresh tarragon

⅔ cup olive oil

¼ teaspoon salt

In small jar with screw-on lid, combine all ingredients. Cover jar tightly and shake well. Store in refrigerator; shake before each use.

AVOCADO SALAD DRESSING

Avocados are so good for you. They are full of vitamins and minerals, especially potassium and vitamins C and B6. They have lots of very healthy fats that help your body absorb vitamin A. Plus, they're delicious! This dressing doesn't keep as long as most because, even with lemon juice, avocado flesh will turn dark fairly quickly. So make it and use it the same day.

Yields ½ cup

1 ripe avocado, peeled and cubed

2 tablespoons lemon or lime juice

¼ teaspoon salt

Pinch white pepper

2 tablespoons olive oil

¼ cup Wilma's Mayonnaise (see Chapter 2)

Combine all ingredients in a food processor or blender. Cover and process or blend until smooth. You can thin this dressing with a bit of water or coconut milk until it reaches the consistency you want. Cover and store in the refrigerator up to 1 day.

HONEY CINNAMON SALAD DRESSING

This delicious salad dressing is good on a plain spinach salad, or try it on a fruit salad made of blueberries, apples, cherries, grapes, and sliced figs. It keeps well in the fridge and is easy to whip up when you get a craving for a fresh fruit salad.

Yields ¾ cup

⅓ cup raw honey

¼ cup apple cider vinegar

2 tablespoons hazelnut oil

3 tablespoons olive oil

½ teaspoon cinnamon

Pinch cardamom

Pinch salt

In small jar with a tight-fitting lid, combine all ingredients and shake well. Use immediately, or cover and store in the refrigerator up to 1 week.

FRENCH DRESSING

French dressing is a delicious addition to salads, and some people like it on cottage cheese for a snack. But bottled commercial French dressing is loaded with all kinds of sweeteners such as high fructose corn syrup, stabilizers such as xanthan gum, and thickeners such as food starch—not what you want on the Paleo diet. This easy recipe tastes much better than any French dressing you've had before!

Yields 1¼ cups

1 small onion, finely chopped

2 cloves garlic, minced

¼ cup apple cider vinegar

1 tablespoon lemon juice

2 tablespoons tomato paste

2 tablespoons Homemade Ketchup (see Chapter 2)

1 tablespoon Dijon mustard

2 teaspoons agave nectar

2 tablespoons raw honey

½ cup olive oil

½ teaspoon smoked paprika

¼ teaspoon salt

⅛ teaspoon white pepper

1. Combine all ingredients in a food processor or blender. Cover and blend until smooth.

2. Cover and refrigerate for 2–3 hours to let flavors blend. Store tightly covered in the fridge for up to 5 days.

ITALIAN DRESSING

Try doubling this recipe and storing in a glass jar. It will keep for several days and is much better than supermarket dressings.

Yields 1 cup

⅓ cup balsamic vinegar

½ teaspoon dry mustard

1 teaspoon lemon juice

2 cloves garlic, chopped

1 teaspoon dried oregano or 1 tablespoon fresh oregano leaves

½ teaspoon salt

½ teaspoon ground black pepper

½ cup extra-virgin olive oil

Place all ingredients except the oil in a blender. With the blender running on a medium setting, slowly pour the oil into the jar. Blend until very smooth. Serve immediately on salad or cover and store in the refrigerator for up to 7 days.

BUTTERMILK DILL SALAD DRESSING

Buttermilk is the liquid left behind when butter is made. Despite its name, it is low in fat, creamy, and rich. You can use this recipe as a dip for vegetables or as a topping for steak or chicken. It keeps well in the fridge, covered, up to a week. If you aren't eating dairy, substitute coconut cream for the buttermilk.

Yields 1 cup

½ cup Wilma's Mayonnaise (see Chapter 2)

⅓ cup buttermilk or coconut cream

2 tablespoons lemon juice

1 clove garlic, minced

1 tablespoon chopped fresh dill weed

1 teaspoon dill seed

1 tablespoon chopped fresh chives

½ teaspoon salt

⅛ teaspoon white pepper

1. In blender or food processor, combine mayonnaise, buttermilk, lemon juice, and garlic and blend or process until smooth.

2. Pour into small jar and add dill weed, dill seed, chives, salt, and pepper. Mix well and store in refrigerator.

CREAMY BACON SALAD DRESSING

This recipe uses bacon fat, not the actual bacon itself, to add fabulous flavor. Whenever you use it to dress a salad, you could add some crisply cooked, crumbled bacon. Freeze the cooked bacon for later use, refrigerate it to use within a day or two, or eat it as your cook's treat.

Yields ¾ cup

5 slices bacon

⅔ cup Wilma's Mayonnaise (see Chapter 2)

2 tablespoons heavy cream or coconut cream

2 tablespoons apple cider vinegar

1 tablespoon lemon juice

¼ teaspoon salt

⅛ teaspoon pepper

1. Cook bacon over low heat until crisp. Remove bacon, drain on paper towels, and reserve for another use. Strain the bacon fat through cheesecloth.

2. In food processor, combine bacon fat, mayonnaise, and heavy cream or coconut cream and process until smooth. Add vinegar, lemon juice, salt, and pepper and process until smooth.

3. Store, covered, in refrigerator up to 1 week. Before use, thin with lemon juice or heavy cream, as desired, if necessary.

BALSAMIC VINAIGRETTE AND MARINADE

Because balsamic vinegar is very sweet, it needs a slightly sour counterpoint—in this recipe, lemon juice. It also needs a bit of zip, such as pepper or mustard. You can use this recipe as a dressing or a marinade.

Yields 1 cup

2 cloves garlic, minced

2 shallots, minced

⅓ cup balsamic vinegar

Juice of ½ lemon

½ teaspoon salt

½ teaspoon freshly ground pepper

½ teaspoon Dijon mustard

½ cup avocado oil

Place all ingredients except the oil in a blender. With the blender running on a medium setting, slowly pour the oil into the jar. Blend until very smooth. Cover and store in the refrigerator for up to 7 days.

The Condiment of Kings

Mustard is one of the oldest condiments, having been used for over 3,000 years. The first mustards were made from crushed black or brown mustard seeds mixed with vinegar. In 1856, Jean Naigeon of Dijon, France, created Dijon mustard by mixing crushed mustard seeds with sour juice made from unripe grapes.

CURRY SALAD DRESSING

This dressing goes well on any salad and has a nice flavor from the curry powder.

Serves 1

Juice of 1 lime

1 teaspoon curry powder

½ teaspoon ground black pepper

1 teaspoon dried basil

3 tablespoons olive oil

Place all ingredients except the oil in a blender. With the blender running on a medium setting, slowly pour the oil into the jar. Blend until very smooth. Serve immediately on salad or cover and store in the refrigerator for up to 7 days.

Curry Powder Power

Curry powder is a mixture of spices commonly used in South Asian cooking. While it does not correlate directly to any particular kind of curry, it is popular in Europe and North America to add an Indian flair to dishes. It can contain any number of spices but nearly always includes turmeric, which gives it its distinctive yellow color.

ASIAN DRESSING

Asian dressing is perfect with poultry. When you crave the taste of Chinese food, add this dressing to any plain dish to spice things up a bit.

Serves 4

2 tablespoons sesame oil

2 tablespoons coconut aminos

½ teaspoon ground black pepper

1 teaspoon dried thyme

2 tablespoons olive oil

Place all ingredients except olive oil in a blender. With the blender running on a medium setting, slowly pour the oil into the jar. Blend until very smooth. Serve immediately on salad or cover and store in the refrigerator for up to 7 days.

LEMON DILL DRESSING

This traditional dressing is best on fish recipes.

Serves 2

Juice of 1 lemon

1 teaspoon fresh dill

½ teaspoon ground black pepper

2 tablespoons olive oil

In a small bowl, combine lemon juice, dill, and pepper. Whisk in olive oil until blended. Serve immediately or cover and refrigerate up to 7 days.

Oils

Many salad dressing recipes call for olive oil, but you should feel free to experiment with various Paleo-friendly oils. Each oil has a different flavor and, more important, a different fat profile. Flaxseed oil is higher in omega-3 fatty acids than others. Walnut oil has a lower omega-6 to omega-3 ratio compared with others. Udo's Oil is a good blend of oils with various omega-3s, 6s, and 9s. These oils together have a nice flavor and have the best to offer in a fat profile.

PALEO COBB SALAD

Cobb salads were invented at the Brown Derby Restaurant in Hollywood and named after the owner. They are delicious and hearty and usually contain chicken, bacon, egg, and avocado, so are perfect for the Paleo diet. You can also make this salad with cooked shrimp or cooked sliced roast beef. If you aren't eating tomatoes, substitute sliced mushrooms. Serve this salad as soon as it is made.

Serves 4

4 eggs

6 slices bacon

3 boneless, skinless chicken breasts

½ teaspoon salt

⅛ teaspoon pepper

¼ cup extra-virgin olive oil

1 clove garlic, minced

3 tablespoons lemon juice

2 tablespoons Dijon mustard

¼ teaspoon salt

⅛ teaspoon pepper

1 head romaine lettuce, chopped

1 avocado, peeled and chopped

2 cups cherry or grape tomatoes, if desired

½ cup chopped pecans

1. Place eggs in a medium saucepan, cover with cold water, and place over high heat. Bring to a rolling boil, boil for 1 minute, then cover pan, remove from heat, and let stand 11 minutes. Drain eggs and place in a bowl of ice water; let stand 5 minutes. Tap eggs on the sides of the bowl to break the shells, then set aside.

2. In large skillet, cook bacon until crisp. Remove bacon to paper towels to drain, then crumble. Remove 2 tablespoons bacon drippings to small bowl and set aside.

3. Sprinkle chicken with salt and pepper; cut into 1½" pieces. Sauté chicken in the bacon drippings remaining in the skillet until chicken is thoroughly cooked to 165°F, about 5–7 minutes. Remove chicken from skillet and set aside.

4. Beat olive oil, minced garlic, lemon juice, and mustard into reserved bacon drippings in small bowl to make the dressing. Season to taste with salt and pepper.

5. Peel eggs and slice into quarters.

6. Arrange romaine lettuce on a large platter. Arrange chicken, bacon, eggs, avocado, and tomatoes on lettuce and drizzle with the dressing. Sprinkle pecans over all and serve immediately.

SHRIMP-STUFFED AVOCADOS

Shrimp is an excellent and delicious source of protein. When it's the main ingredient in a salad, choose the largest shrimp you can afford for the nicest presentation. Shrimp are graded by the number of the little shellfish per pound—the larger the shrimp, the fewer there are per pound. Shrimp labeled "Jumbo" shrimp, for instance, are usually about 20 per pound, whereas large shrimp are about 30 per pound.

Serves 4

½ pound large raw shrimp, peeled and deveined

4 tablespoons olive oil, divided

3 tablespoons Wilma's Mayonnaise (see Chapter 2)

2 tablespoons chopped fresh dill weed

1 tablespoon lemon juice

⅛ teaspoon pepper

3 ripe avocados, cut in half, pit removed

2 stalks celery, chopped

½ cup chopped, peeled, seeded cucumber

¼ cup sliced green olives

1. Prepare the shrimp, pat dry, and set aside.

2. In large skillet, heat 1 tablespoon olive oil over medium heat. Add the shrimp in a single layer. Cook, turning once, for 4–6 minutes or until the shrimp curl, turn pink, and feel firm to the touch. Remove from the skillet and set aside on a plate. Let the shrimp cool and coarsely chop.

3. In a food processor or blender, combine 3 tablespoons olive oil, mayonnaise, dill, lemon juice, and pepper and blend until smooth.

4. Chop up 1 avocado and add to the mayonnaise mixture; blend until smooth.

5. In a large bowl, combine the shrimp, celery, cucumber, and olives and mix gently. Add the mayonnaise mixture and stir to coat. Serve in 4 avocado halves.

SALMON BERRY SALAD

Always try to find wild salmon; the flavor, texture, and nutrition are much better than those of farm-raised salmon. Wild salmon has more omega-3 fatty acids and less overall fat than farmed salmon, and it has not been raised on antibiotics. This salad is fresh and pretty. Use the nicest berries you can find in the market.

Serves 4

2 (6-ounce) salmon fillets

⅓ cup extra-virgin olive oil

2 tablespoons raspberry vinegar

2 tablespoons lemon juice

2 tablespoons Dijon mustard

2 teaspoons chopped fresh thyme leaves

¼ teaspoon salt

⅛ teaspoon pepper

6 cups mixed lettuces

2 cups blueberries

1 cup raspberries

¾ cup chopped toasted hazelnuts

1. Place salmon fillets, skin-side down, on a broiler rack. Preheat broiler to high. Broil salmon 6" from the heat source for 8–12 minutes until the salmon flakes when tested with a fork. Set aside to cool for a few minutes.

2. In small bowl, combine olive oil, raspberry vinegar, lemon juice, mustard, thyme, salt, and pepper; mix well with a whisk until blended

3. Place the lettuce in a large serving bowl. Break salmon apart with your fingers, discarding the skin, and add to lettuce along with the blueberries.

4. Drizzle dressing over all and toss gently. Top with raspberries and hazelnuts and serve immediately.

NUTTY CHICKEN SALAD

Main dish salads are so versatile. You could make this into a more savory salad by using broccoli florets, red bell pepper, and green beans instead of the apple and cranberries. Or substitute cooked salmon or shrimp for the chicken. It will keep for several days, well covered, in the fridge. When you're hungry, just dig in!

Serves 8

2 pounds bone-in, skin-on chicken breast

1 tablespoon olive oil

5 tablespoons Dijon mustard, divided

3 teaspoons chopped fresh thyme leaves, divided

1 teaspoon salt

¼ teaspoon pepper

1 cup Wilma's Mayonnaise (see Chapter 2)

¼ cup lemon juice

1 tablespoon agave nectar or honey

⅛ teaspoon red pepper flakes

1 cup chopped toasted walnuts

½ cup toasted slivered almonds

6 stalks celery, sliced

2 Granny Smith apples, chopped

1 cup dried unsweetened cranberries, if desired

1. Preheat oven to 350°F. Arrange chicken, skin-side up, in a baking dish.

2. In small bowl, combine olive oil, 2 tablespoons mustard, 1 teaspoon thyme, salt, and pepper. Loosen chicken skin from flesh and rub olive oil mixture over chicken flesh. Smooth skin back over the meat.

3. Bake chicken for 55–65 minutes or until internal temperature registers 165°F. Remove chicken from oven and let rest for 20 minutes.

4. In large bowl, combine mayonnaise, 3 tablespoons mustard, lemon juice, agave or honey, 2 teaspoons thyme, and red pepper flakes and mix well.

5. Remove chicken meat from bone; discard skin and bones. Shred chicken or cut into 1" pieces. Add to mayonnaise mixture and stir to coat. Stir in walnuts, almonds, celery, apple, and cranberries. Cover and chill for 1–2 hours before serving.

CABBAGE AND BACON SLAW

Cabbage is a cruciferous vegetable. That means it contains antioxidants and fiber to help fight the formation of cancer cells; in fact, raw cabbage shows more cancer prevention benefits than cooked cabbage. It also helps lower cholesterol. Plus, it's delicious, especially combined with more veggies and bacon in this wonderful salad.

Serves 6

½ head green cabbage, shredded

½ head red cabbage, shredded

4 stalks celery, sliced

6 slices bacon

1 red onion, chopped

3 cloves garlic, minced

1 cup olive oil mayonnaise or Wilma's Mayonnaise (see Chapter 2)

¼ cup Dijon mustard

2 tablespoons lemon juice

¼ cup chopped flat-leaf parsley

2 tablespoons fresh thyme leaves

½ teaspoon salt

⅛ teaspoon white pepper

1. Combine both kinds of cabbage and celery in large bowl; toss to combine and set aside.

2. In large skillet, cook bacon until crisp. Drain bacon on paper towels, crumble, and set aside. Remove all but 2 tablespoons drippings from skillet and discard.

3. In drippings remaining in skillet, cook red onion and garlic just until the vegetables begin to soften. Add to cabbage mixture and toss.

4. In small bowl, combine mayonnaise, mustard, lemon juice, parsley, thyme, salt, and pepper and mix well. Pour over cabbage mixture and stir to coat. Cover and refrigerate for 1–2 hours to blend flavors before serving.

FRUIT AND NUT SALAD

Fruits and nuts make a delightful salad with excellent flavor and texture. You can use any fruits that look good in the market, and any nuts you like. Put this salad together right before serving; it doesn't keep well in the fridge. Pair it with grilled steak or chicken for a wonderful dinner.

Serves 4

1 tablespoon hazelnut oil

2 tablespoons olive oil

2 tablespoons lemon juice

2 tablespoons chopped fresh basil leaves

1 tablespoon chopped mint leaves

¼ teaspoon salt

2 cups sliced strawberries

2 cups blueberries

2 cups cubed watermelon

½ cup chopped toasted hazelnuts

¼ cup toasted pine nuts

1. In large bowl, combine both oils, lemon juice, basil, mint, and salt and whisk until combined.

2. Add the fruits and toss gently until coated. Top with nuts and serve immediately.

CHOPPED CHICKEN SALAD

A chopped salad is simply a salad in which all the ingredients are, well, chopped. This creates a nice texture and a beautiful composition. You can use any of your favorite fruits in this salad, but try this combination first. Make it ahead of time and store it in the fridge. Then when anyone in the family is hungry, tell them to dish it up and eat.

Serves 6

2 tablespoons hazelnut oil

3 tablespoons olive oil

2 tablespoons lemon juice

3 tablespoons apple cider vinegar

½ teaspoon salt

⅛ teaspoon pepper

1 teaspoon agave nectar

½ teaspoon dried thyme leaves

2 tablespoons coconut milk

3 cups cooked cubed chicken

1 red bell pepper, chopped

1 yellow bell pepper, chopped

2 cups chopped endive

1 cup chopped mushrooms

½ cup chopped toasted hazelnuts

1. In small bowl, combine hazelnut oil, olive oil, lemon juice, vinegar, salt, and pepper and whisk well. Add agave nectar, thyme, and coconut milk and whisk until combined; set aside.

2. In large bowl, combine all remaining ingredients except hazelnuts. Pour dressing over and toss to coat. Garnish with hazelnuts and serve immediately.

STEAK SALAD

Crisp and tender greens and lots of flavorful veggies are topped with juicy grilled steak and a creamy salad dressing in this wonderful recipe. It's a meal in itself—all you need to add is a glass of wine. You can vary the types of vegetables you use in this recipe, and add some cubed cheese if you like.

Serves 4

¼ cup olive oil

5 tablespoons red wine vinegar

2 cloves garlic, minced

½ teaspoon salt

⅛ teaspoon pepper

1½ pounds sirloin or flank steak

¾ cup Wilma's Mayonnaise (see Chapter 2)

3 tablespoons lemon juice

2 tablespoons prepared horseradish

½ cup almond milk

2 tablespoons chopped fresh chives

6 cups romaine or butter lettuce

2 cups grape tomatoes, if desired

1 (8-ounce) package mushrooms, sliced

1 yellow bell pepper, sliced

1. In large bowl, combine olive oil, vinegar, garlic, salt, and pepper. Add steak; cover, and marinate in the refrigerator for 2–4 hours.

2. In small bowl, combine mayonnaise, lemon juice, horseradish, almond milk, and chives; cover and refrigerate.

3. When ready to eat, prepare and preheat grill.

4. In large bowl, combine lettuce, tomatoes, mushrooms, and yellow bell pepper.

5. Remove steak from marinade; discard marinade. Grill 6" from medium coals for 8–14 minutes or until desired doneness.

6. Slice steak thinly across the grain and add to lettuce mixture. Drizzle with dressing and serve immediately.

TUNA CARROT SALAD

There are several types of canned tuna. The kind you want to buy, because it is lower in mercury content, is chunk light tuna. For flavor, the best tuna is sold packed in olive oil; try brands that are imported from Italy. Drain off the olive oil and use it in the recipe for more flavor. This easy recipe can be used to make lettuce wraps or enjoyed on its own, or served over mixed lettuces.

Serves 4

3 (4-ounce) cans tuna in oil, drained, oil reserved

1½ cups grated carrots

1½ cups sliced celery

½ cup chopped red onion

¾ cup Wilma's Mayonnaise (see Chapter 2)

3 tablespoons reserved tuna oil

3 tablespoons lemon juice

3 tablespoons Dijon mustard

1 tablespoon grainy mustard

2 tablespoons chopped fresh basil

1. In medium bowl, combine tuna, carrots, celery, and red onion.

2. In small bowl, combine mayonnaise, tuna oil, lemon juice, Dijon mustard, grainy mustard, and basil and mix well. Add to tuna mixture and stir to coat. Cover and refrigerate until serving time.

BROCCOLI SALAD

Broccoli pairs beautifully with any kind of pork. This wonderful recipe is very satisfying, and it's easy to make. And it uses two kinds of pork: sausage and bacon! Something slightly sweet is important to the balance of flavors in this salad. Dried cherries are a good choice, but you could also use golden raisins or dried cranberries.

Serves 6

2 heads broccoli, broken into florets

½ pound spicy ground pork sausage

6 slices bacon

1 red onion, chopped

3 cloves garlic, minced

⅔ cup Wilma's Mayonnaise (see Chapter 2)

3 tablespoons olive oil

3 tablespoons honey

2 tablespoons lemon juice

½ teaspoon salt

⅛ teaspoon pepper

1 cup dried cherries

½ cup sliced almonds

1. Steam the broccoli over boiling water for 5–7 minutes until tender. Drain well and set aside.

2. In large skillet, cook sausage until browned and cooked through; remove from skillet and drain fat.

3. Add bacon to same skillet; cook until crisp. Drain on paper towels, crumble, and set aside.

4. Drain fat from the skillet, but do not wipe out. Add onion and garlic; cook and stir, scraping up pan drippings, for 5–6 minutes until tender. Remove from heat.

5. In large bowl, combine mayonnaise, olive oil, honey, lemon juice, salt, and pepper. Add broccoli, sausage, bacon, onions, and garlic.

6. Stir in dried cherries and sliced almonds. Cover and refrigerate for at least 3 hours before serving.

SWEET POTATO SALAD

Canned foods aren't strictly Paleo, but if you need some help in the kitchen, canned foods that are pure—just the main ingredient plus salt—can be included in your plan. Read labels carefully to make sure the canned foods you buy aren't full of hidden sugars and artificial ingredients! Canned sweet potatoes are a great choice in this easy salad because you don't have to heat up the kitchen to make it.

Serves 6

½ cup yogurt

½ cup Wilma's Mayonnaise (see Chapter 2)

2 tablespoons Dijon mustard

2 tablespoons honey

2 tablespoons lemon juice

2 tablespoons minced fresh chives

1 tablespoon chopped fresh dill

½ teaspoon salt

⅛ teaspoon white pepper

2 (15-ounce) cans sweet potatoes, drained

1 Granny Smith apple, chopped

3 stalks celery, sliced

4 green onions, sliced

1. In large bowl, combine yogurt, mayonnaise, mustard, honey, lemon juice, chives, dill, salt, and pepper and mix well.

2. Add drained sweet potatoes and mash slightly, leaving some pieces whole. Stir in apple, celery, and green onions. Refrigerate, covered, for 2–3 hours before serving.

GRILLED TUNA SALAD

Fresh tuna tastes completely different from canned tuna. And it grills beautifully. You can grill fresh tuna to rare, if that's what you like. It's good whether cooked rare, medium, or well done; it's completely up to you. As long as the sides and edges are cooked, rare tuna is safe. Enjoy it in this refreshing salad. If you aren't eating tomatoes, substitute sliced mushrooms.

Serves 4

¼ cup lemon juice

¼ cup extra-virgin olive oil

2 tablespoons Dijon mustard

2 teaspoons chopped fresh oregano leaves

½ teaspoon salt

⅛ teaspoon pepper

1½ pounds tuna steak

2 cups baby spinach

2 cups kale leaves, torn into little pieces

1 cup curly endive

2 cups grape tomatoes, if desired

2 avocados, peeled and cubed

1. In large bowl, combine lemon juice, olive oil, mustard, oregano, salt, and pepper and whisk until combined.

2. Prepare and preheat grill. Remove 2 tablespoons of the dressing to another bowl. Brush this onto both sides of the tuna.

3. Grill tuna until desired doneness, turning once. Remove to plate and cover to keep warm.

4. Add spinach, kale, endive, and grape tomatoes to dressing in large bowl and toss.

5. Cut tuna into 1½" pieces and add to salad; toss again. Top with avocado and serve immediately.

KALE AND FRUIT SALAD

Kale is skyrocketing in popularity. It's also very good for you; it's high in vitamins A, C, and K. It's also a good source of iron, manganese, and potassium. Because it's a cruciferous vegetable, it is rich in antioxidants. Its bitter flavor is actually delicious, especially when paired with sweet fruits.

Serves 4

1 head curly kale

1 cup Bing cherries, pitted

1 cup sliced strawberries

1 cup cubed cantaloupe

¼ cup Wilma's Mayonnaise (see Chapter 2)

¼ cup raspberry vinegar

3 tablespoons extra-virgin olive oil

⅛ teaspoon salt

1. Remove kale leaves from the stems; discard stems. Tear kale into small pieces.

2. Combine kale in serving bowl with cherries, strawberries, and cantaloupe.

3. In small bowl, combine mayonnaise, raspberry vinegar, olive oil, and salt and whisk until combined. Drizzle over salad, gently toss to coat, and serve immediately.

TOMATO SALAD

There are many different types and colors of tomatoes in the market today. If you go to a farmers' market, you can usually find many heirloom varieties, such as Brandywine, Marglobe, Red Zebra, and others. They are beautiful with a very rich taste and perfect in this salad if nightshade vegetables are on your diet plan. Serve with grilled chicken or steak for a wonderful summer meal.

Serves 4

¼ cup white wine vinegar

2 tablespoons lemon juice

¼ teaspoon salt

2 cloves garlic, minced

¼ cup extra-virgin olive oil

1 tablespoon honey

1 tablespoon chopped chives

2 cups grape tomatoes

2 yellow tomatoes, chopped

4 Roma tomatoes, sliced

2 beefsteak tomatoes, sliced

1. In small bowl, combine vinegar, lemon juice, salt, and garlic and mix well. Add olive oil gradually, whisking to combine. Add honey and chives and mix well; set aside.

2. Arrange all of the tomatoes on a large plate. Drizzle with the dressing and let stand for 10–15 minutes, then serve.

GREEN-ON-GREEN SALAD

Lots of light and tender greens mixed with heartier, more substantial greens makes an interesting and varied salad. Use the greens that look the best in the market to make this easy recipe. You could make it a main dish salad by adding some cooked chopped chicken or beef, or leftover cooked shrimp or salmon.

Serves 4

2 cups torn kale

1 cup torn curly endive

1 cup butter lettuce

1 cup red lettuce

1 cup baby spinach leaves

1 avocado, peeled and cubed

1 green bell pepper, chopped

3 green onions, sliced

⅔ cup Avocado Salad Dressing (see recipe in this chapter)

½ cup broken shelled pistachios

1. Combine kale, endive, butter lettuce, red lettuce, spinach, avocado, green bell pepper, and green onions in large salad bowl; toss gently.

2. Drizzle with the Avocado Salad Dressing and toss gently again. Serve immediately, topped with pistachios.

KALE AND BEEF SALAD

The hearty and bitter flavor of kale pairs well with grilled or broiled beef in this one-dish meal. The kale marinates in the dressing while you cook the beef. Then you let the beef rest for a few minutes, slice it thinly, top the salad, and dig in.

Serves 4

1½-pound ribeye steak

½ teaspoon salt, divided

⅛ teaspoon pepper

1 head kale, stems removed, torn

3 green onions, sliced

1 large tomato, seeded and chopped, if desired

¼ cup extra-virgin olive oil

2 tablespoons lemon juice

2 tablespoons honey

½ teaspoon dry mustard powder

½ cup slivered almonds, toasted

1. Prepare and preheat grill. Sprinkle steak with ¼ teaspoon salt and pepper; set aside.

2. In large salad bowl, combine kale, green onions, and tomato. In small bowl, combine olive oil, lemon juice, honey, mustard powder, and remaining ¼ teaspoon salt and mix well. Drizzle over kale and toss well. Sprinkle with almonds.

3. Grill steak to desired doneness, about 5 minutes per side, turning once, for medium rare. Let steak stand for 5 minutes, then slice thinly. Arrange on salad and serve immediately.

WILTED TWO-BACON SALAD

Regular strip bacon and Canadian bacon are both used in this recipe. Canadian bacon is made from pork loin, and it is leaner than regular bacon. Its taste and texture are closer to ham. Canadian bacon is sometimes called "back bacon." Both are delicious served with spinach and romaine lettuce wilted with a hot dressing. Lots of onion and garlic add flavor and nutrition to this easy recipe.

Serves 4

4 cups torn romaine lettuce

3 cups baby spinach leaves

6 slices bacon

½ pound Canadian bacon, chopped

1 onion, chopped

4 cloves garlic, sliced

1 tablespoon Dijon mustard

1 tablespoon honey

¼ cup red wine vinegar

3 hard-cooked eggs, sliced

1. Combine romaine lettuce and spinach in large salad bowl; set aside.

2. Cook bacon in large skillet until crisp. Drain on paper towels, crumble, and set aside.

3. Cook Canadian bacon in the bacon fat in pan for about 2–3 minutes or until heated. Add to crumbled bacon.

4. Add onion and garlic to pan; cook until tender, about 4–5 minutes.

5. Standing back because it will spatter, add mustard, honey, and vinegar to hot pan. Stir with a wire whisk until combined. Immediately pour over greens in bowl.

6. Add both types of bacon and eggs to salad bowl; toss gently to mix and serve immediately.

PORK AND BEET SALAD

Beets are delicious when roasted and combined with a spicy dressing and tender and juicy pork tenderloin. This salad is unusual and special enough for company. Serve with some Paleo-friendly bread spread with garlic butter and toasted, along with a glass of white wine. Some Dark Chocolate Brownies (see Chapter 15) for dessert would be perfect.

Serves 4

3 beets

⅓ cup water

1 (1-pound) pork tenderloin

3 tablespoons hazelnut oil, divided

½ teaspoon salt

⅛ teaspoon pepper

½ teaspoon dried thyme leaves

2 tablespoons extra-virgin olive oil

3 tablespoons red wine vinegar

2 tablespoons Dijon mustard

2 tablespoons Wilma's Mayonnaise (see Chapter 2)

4 cups baby spinach

2 cups torn red leaf lettuce

½ cup toasted chopped hazelnuts

1. Preheat oven to 375°F. Place beets in a baking dish, add water, and cover tightly. Roast for 60–70 minutes or until a knife slides easily into a beet. Cool on wire rack.

2. Peel the beets and slice into ¼" slices. Set aside.

3. Place pork tenderloin in a baking dish. Drizzle with 1 tablespoon hazelnut oil and sprinkle with salt, pepper, and thyme leaves. Roast for 30–35 minutes or until a meat thermometer registers 145°F. Cover and set aside.

4. In large salad bowl, combine remaining 2 tablespoons hazelnut oil, olive oil, red wine vinegar, mustard, and mayonnaise; mix well. Add spinach and lettuce; toss to coat. Top with beets.

5. Slice the pork tenderloin and arrange over the salad. Sprinkle with hazelnuts and serve immediately.

CHOPPED SALAD

Chopped salads were first served in steakhouses as Chef or Cobb salads. They can be made of just about anything you have in the fridge. But this salad is something special, with lots of delicious ingredients. It's really a meal in one; you don't need to serve anything else with it but some sliced fruit.

Serves 4

½ cup Wilma's Mayonnaise (see Chapter 2)

2 avocados, peeled and mashed

3 tablespoons lemon juice

¼ cup buttermilk

2 tablespoons chopped fresh dill

3 cups chopped cooked chicken breast

6 slices bacon, cooked crisp and chopped

1 red bell pepper, chopped

1 yellow bell pepper, chopped

4 green onions, chopped

4 cups chopped romaine lettuce

2 cups chopped fresh spinach

4 hard-cooked eggs, chopped

½ cup chopped walnuts

1. In large bowl, combine mayonnaise, avocados, lemon juice, buttermilk, and dill and mix well.

2. Add chicken, bacon, bell peppers, and green onions and toss to coat.

3. Place lettuce and spinach in large serving bowl. Top with chicken mixture and toss gently. Garnish with eggs and walnuts and serve immediately.

SWEET MELON SALAD

There are lots of different kinds of melons in the market, and all are on the Paleo diet list. Some people shun melons because they feel they are too sweet, but others embrace them as a great source of vitamin C, fiber, and water. This salad combines three different types of melons with a fresh mint dressing. It's luscious.

Serves 6

2 tablespoons lemon juice

2 tablespoons honey

2 tablespoons coconut milk

2 tablespoons chopped fresh mint

Pinch salt

3 cups cubed cantaloupe

3 cups cubed watermelon

2 cups cubed honeydew melon

1. In large serving bowl, combine lemon juice, honey, coconut milk, mint, and salt and mix well.

2. Add the melons and stir gently to coat. Serve immediately, or cover and chill up to 6 hours before serving.

CAULIFLOWER "RICE" SALAD

Cauliflower "rice" can also be made into a salad! The shreds are very briefly cooked to give them more of a cooked rice texture, but you can leave them raw if you'd like. This colorful and flavorful salad is great as a side dish for grilled steak or chicken, or it can be served as a vegetarian main dish salad.

Serves 4

1 head cauliflower, shredded

1 tablespoon lemon juice

1 tablespoon coconut oil

4 stalks celery, sliced

1 yellow bell pepper, chopped

2 carrots, shredded

⅓ cup finely chopped dill pickle

⅓ cup extra-virgin olive oil

3 tablespoons lemon juice

1 tablespoon honey

1 tablespoon chopped fresh dill

¼ teaspoon salt

⅛ teaspoon pepper

1. Toss shredded cauliflower with lemon juice.

2. Heat coconut oil in skillet over medium heat. Add shredded cauliflower and cook for 1–2 minutes or until crisp-tender. Scrape cauliflower into a bowl and set aside to cool for 15 minutes.

3. Stir celery, bell pepper, carrot, and dill pickle into cauliflower.

4. In small bowl, combine olive oil, lemon juice, honey, dill, salt, and pepper and mix well. Pour over salad and stir to coat. Cover and chill for 1–3 hours before serving.

MEDITERRANEAN SALAD

Mediterranean ingredients include feta cheese, olives, lemons, artichokes, red onions, and cucumbers. They all combine in this easy and fresh-tasting salad. You could add some chopped cooked chicken or some medium grilled shrimp to this salad to make it a meal in one. Serve with a glass of wine on a screened-in porch.

Serves 4

¼ cup extra-virgin olive oil

2 tablespoons lemon juice

1 tablespoon Dijon mustard

1 clove garlic, minced

½ teaspoon dried oregano

¼ teaspoon salt

⅛ teaspoon pepper

2 cups curly endive

2 cups butter lettuce

1 cup baby spinach leaves

1 (14-ounce) can plain artichokes, drained and sliced

1 red onion, chopped

1 cucumber, seeded and chopped

½ cup black olives

½ cup crumbled feta cheese, if desired

1. In large salad bowl, combine olive oil, lemon juice, mustard, garlic, oregano, salt, and pepper and mix well.

2. Add endive, lettuce, and spinach and toss to coat.

3. Top with artichokes, red onion, cucumber, and black olives and toss to coat. Top with cheese and serve.

ZESTY PECAN CHICKEN AND GRAPE SALAD

Coating your chicken with nuts adds a crispy skin that keeps the meat moist and tender.

Serves 6

¼ cup toasted chopped pecans

1 teaspoon chili powder

¼ cup avocado oil

1½ pounds boneless, skinless chicken breasts

1½ cups white grapes

6 cups salad greens

1. Preheat oven to 400°F.

2. In a blender, mix the pecans and chili powder. Pour in the oil while the blender is running. When the mixture is thoroughly combined, pour it into a shallow bowl.

3. Coat the chicken with the pecan mixture and place on racked baking dish; roast for 40–50 minutes, until the chicken is thoroughly cooked. Remove from oven, let cool for 5 minutes, and thinly slice.

4. Slice the grapes and tear the greens into bite-sized pieces. To serve, fan the chicken over the greens and sprinkle with sliced grapes.

Toasting Nuts for Fresher Flavor and Crispness

To bring out the natural flavor of the nuts, heat them on the stovetop or in the oven for a few minutes. For the stovetop, spread nuts in a dry skillet and heat over a medium flame until their natural oils come to the surface. For the oven, spread the nuts in a single layer on a baking sheet and toast for 5–10 minutes at 350°F, until the oils are visible. Cool nuts before serving.

MACKEREL WITH TOMATO AND CUCUMBER SALAD

According to the USDA National Nutrient Database for Standard Reference, mackerel contains 2.3 grams of omega-3 for every 100 grams of fish. That makes mackerel the fish with the most essential fatty acids (EFAs).

Serves 4

15 ounces mackerel fillets, drained

1 clove garlic, crushed

1½ tablespoons coconut oil

1 tablespoon chopped fresh basil

½ teaspoon ground black pepper

10 cherry tomatoes, halved

½ cucumber, peeled and diced

1 small onion, chopped

2 cups mixed lettuce greens

1. Place mackerel in a medium-sized bowl with garlic and coconut oil.

2. Add basil and pepper to mackerel mixture, turn fish to coat evenly, and transfer to a medium-sized skillet. Sauté over medium heat for 5–8 minutes on each side, or until brown.

3. Cut cooked mackerel into bite-sized pieces and place in a clean bowl.

4. Stir in tomatoes, cucumber, onion, and lettuce and serve.

AVOCADO CHICKEN SALAD

This recipe makes a great party salad. You can serve it in lettuce cups for a meal or in small cups with spoons as an appetizer.

Serves 3

3 avocados, pitted and peeled

2 boneless, skinless chicken breasts, cooked and shredded

½ red onion, chopped

1 large tomato, chopped

¼ cup chopped cilantro

Juice of 1 large lime

1. In a medium-sized bowl, mash avocados. Add chicken and mix well.

2. Add onion, tomato, cilantro, and lime juice to the avocado and chicken mixture. Mix well and serve.

CRISP AVOCADO SALAD

This recipe works well as a side dish to spicy entrées.

Serves 4

3 cups iceberg lettuce, shredded

2 cups chopped avocado

½ cup sliced red onion

1 (3-ounce) can sliced black olives, drained

1 tablespoon lime juice

2 tablespoons toasted pine nuts

Toss lettuce, avocado, onion, and olives together in a large salad bowl. Sprinkle salad with lime juice. Toss well to coat. Sprinkle with pine nuts and serve.

APPLE COLESLAW

This coleslaw recipe is a refreshing and sweet alternative to the traditional coleslaw with mayonnaise. Additionally, the sesame seeds give it a nice nutty flavor.

Serves 4

2 cups packaged coleslaw mix

1 unpeeled tart apple, chopped

½ cup chopped celery

½ cup chopped green pepper

¼ cup extra-virgin olive oil

2 tablespoons lemon juice

½ cup halved seedless grapes

½ cup toasted pecan pieces

1. In a medium bowl, combine the coleslaw mix, apple, celery, and green pepper.

2. In a separate small bowl, whisk together olive oil and lemon juice. Stir in grapes and pecans. Pour over coleslaw and toss to coat.

Seeds versus Nuts

Nuts have a higher omega-6 to omega-3 ratio. Seeds, on the other hand, have a different profile. Seeds have much lower saturated fat content and are more easily digested by individuals with intestinal issues.

AVOCADO AND SHRIMP SALAD

Creamy avocado and refreshing citrus bring out the sweetness of shrimp. This is a salad you will want to have again and again.

Serves 4

24 raw medium shrimp, shelled and deveined

2 tablespoons avocado oil

4 green onions, sliced, divided

2 garlic cloves, finely minced

2 tablespoons dry white wine or chicken broth

Salt and pepper, to taste

1 red grapefruit, cut in half

8 ounces butter lettuce, washed and torn into bite-sized pieces

1 ripe avocado, sliced

1. Peel and devein the shrimp.

2. In a skillet set over medium-high heat, add the oil. Add shrimp and half of the green onions. Cook, stirring frequently, until shrimp are half-cooked. Add garlic and white wine or broth, cook for an additional minute, then add salt and pepper.

3. Add juice of one grapefruit half to the pan; cook for 2–3 minutes. Cut the peel off the remaining grapefruit half and cut fruit into bite-sized pieces.

4. Place lettuce, avocado slices, and remaining green onions on salad plates for serving. Transfer cooked shrimp to plates.

5. Drizzle sauce from pan over top and garnish with remaining grapefruit pieces.

ORANGE SALAD

This is a healthful salad that makes a visual impact.

Serves 4

3 cups cubed butternut squash, drizzled with olive oil and roasted

2 carrots, peeled and shredded

2 cups peeled and diced papaya

2 tablespoons shredded fresh ginger

Juice of 1 lime

1 tablespoon raw honey, or to taste

1 tablespoon olive oil

Freshly ground black pepper

1. Combine the squash, carrots, and papaya in a large salad bowl. Set aside.

2. In a separate bowl, whisk together the ginger, lime juice, honey, olive oil, and pepper until well combined. Toss the dressing with the salad ingredients and serve.

GREEK SALAD

Olives are a rich source of oleic acid, a heart-healthy monounsaturated fat. While various types of olives are commonly used in Mediterranean dishes, Greek salads often feature kalamata olives.

Serves 4

4 cups chopped romaine lettuce

1 large tomato, seeded and chopped

1 small cucumber, sliced

1 green bell pepper, seeded and cut into rings

¼ cup red wine vinegar

Juice of 1 lemon

1 tablespoon Italian seasoning

Salt and pepper, to taste

¼ cup extra-virgin olive oil

2 teaspoons capers

16 kalamata olives

1. Place lettuce, tomato, cucumber, and bell pepper in a large bowl.

2. To make dressing, whisk vinegar, lemon juice, Italian seasoning, and salt and pepper in a small bowl. Mix in olive oil.

3. Coat vegetables with dressing.

4. Place salad on plates. Top salad plates with capers and olives.

CHICKEN SALAD

This salad is the perfect lunch made with extra chicken from last night's dinner.

Serves 4

1 head romaine lettuce

¼ cup red wine vinegar

2 cloves garlic, minced

2 tablespoons Dijon mustard

1 teaspoon dried rosemary

Salt and pepper, to taste

¼ cup olive oil

¼ cup diced carrot

1 medium red bell pepper, seeded and minced

¼ cup sliced radish

2 cups shredded cooked chicken breast

1. Wash romaine lettuce, remove core, and chop leaves into 1" pieces.

2. Combine vinegar, garlic, mustard, rosemary, and salt and pepper in small bowl. Whisk olive oil into vinegar mixture.

3. Place romaine lettuce, carrot, bell pepper, radish, and chicken in a large bowl. Pour dressing over salad and toss to coat.

Not Your Typical Chicken Salad

Using herbs and vegetables brightens up the typical deli-style chicken salad. Adding carrot, radish, bell pepper, and herbs not only spruces up the color on your plate, it also adds crunch and increases the amount of essential vitamins and fiber.

MEDITERRANEAN TOMATO SALAD

Use juicy tomatoes for this recipe, such as heirloom varieties or beefsteak. You can substitute orange bell pepper for the yellow if needed.

Serves 4

2 cups sliced tomatoes

1 cup peeled, chopped cucumber

⅓ cup diced yellow bell pepper

¼ cup sliced radish

¼ cup flat-leaf parsley, chopped

1 garlic clove, finely minced

1 tablespoon lemon juice

3 tablespoons extra-virgin olive oil

Salt and pepper, to taste

2 cups baby spinach leaves, torn

1. Toss tomatoes, cucumber, bell pepper, radish, and parsley together in a large salad bowl.

2. Sprinkle garlic, lemon juice, and oil over tomato mixture. Toss to coat. Add salt and pepper to taste. Split spinach between four plates and top with tomato mixture. Serve immediately.

MINTY BLUEBERRY MELON SALAD

Seedless watermelons can sometimes have small white seeds scattered within the flesh. Use a fork to remove any noticeable seeds from the cubed watermelon before making the salad.

Serves 4

1½ cups cubed cantaloupe (1" cubes)

1 cup cubed seedless watermelon (1" cubes)

¾ cup blueberries

1 cup halved green grapes

1 tablespoon minced mint leaves

1 teaspoon minced flat-leaf parsley

1. Gently toss the cantaloupe, watermelon, blueberries, and grapes together in a large salad bowl.

2. Add mint and parsley and toss to mix. Serve immediately, or chill in fridge for up to 2 hours.

RAINBOW FRUIT SALAD

You can't go wrong with this salad—it's juicy, fresh, naturally low in fat and sodium, and cholesterol-free. Enjoy it as a salad or as a dessert.

Serves 12

1 large mango, peeled and diced

2 cups fresh blueberries

1 cup sliced bananas

2 cups halved fresh strawberries

2 cups seedless grapes

1 cup unpeeled, sliced nectarines

½ cup peeled, sliced kiwi fruit

⅓ cup freshly squeezed orange juice

2 tablespoons lemon juice

1½ tablespoons raw honey

¼ teaspoon ground ginger

⅛ teaspoon ground nutmeg

1. Gently toss mango, blueberries, bananas, strawberries, grapes, nectarines, and kiwi together in a large mixing bowl.

2. In a separate bowl, whisk together orange juice, lemon juice, honey, ginger, and nutmeg.

3. Chill fruit until needed, up to 3 hours. Just before serving, pour honey-orange sauce over fruit and toss gently to coat.

SALMON SPINACH SALAD

This salad makes perfect use of leftover salmon. Salmon will only remain good in the fridge for two days, so make sure you find a use for it quickly!

Serves 1

1 (5-ounce) salmon fillet, cooked

1 cup spinach leaves

½ cup red grapes

¼ cup shredded carrots

1 tablespoon sliced almonds

1 tablespoon fresh raspberries

Combine ingredients in a bowl and enjoy.

BLOOD ORANGE SALAD WITH SHRIMP AND BABY SPINACH

For an elegant supper or luncheon salad, this is a crowd-pleaser. The deep red flesh of the blood oranges contrasted with the saturated green of spinach and the bright pink shrimp make for a dramatic presentation!

Serves 4

6 cups baby spinach

2 blood oranges

1¼ pounds shrimp, cleaned, cooked, and chilled

2 tablespoons fresh lemon juice

¼ cup extra-virgin olive oil

¼ teaspoon dry mustard

¼ cup stemmed, loosely packed parsley

1. Divide the spinach among four serving plates.

2. Peel the oranges. Slice them crosswise, about ¼" thick, picking out any seeds. Arrange on top of the spinach. Arrange the shrimp around the oranges.

3. Place the rest of the ingredients in a blender and purée until the dressing is a bright green. Pour over the salads. Serve chilled.

Fresh Spinach—Not Lettuce

When you can, substitute fresh baby spinach for less nutritious iceberg lettuce. White or pale green lettuce can be used as an accent but has less nutritional substance than such greens as spinach, escarole, and watercress.

FIVE-SPICE CRAB MEAT SALAD

This seafood salad makes a wonderful main course for lunch or supper. Mild and delicious, napa or Chinese cabbage keeps well in the refrigerator and adds an excellent crunch to salads.

Serves 4

2 cups shredded napa cabbage

1 pound fresh lump crab meat (any kind)

1 cup Wilma's Mayonnaise (see Chapter 2)

2 tablespoons champagne vinegar or white wine vinegar

2 tablespoons lemon juice

1 tablespoon sesame seed oil

¼ teaspoon Chinese five-spice powder

Salt and pepper, to taste

1. In a large serving bowl, toss the cabbage and crab meat.

2. In a separate bowl, whisk together the rest of the ingredients, add to the cabbage-crab mixture, and toss to coat. Serve chilled.

Exploring Vinegar

Champagne vinegar is made from the same champagne used for drinking. It is aged in oak barrels, and because it is made from light, sparkling wine, it has a bright, crisp taste that is delicious in vinaigrettes.

TURKEY CLUB SALAD WITH BACON, LETTUCE, AND TOMATO

This is a satisfying lunch salad, delicious and easy to make.

Serves 4

1 pound cooked turkey breast

4 strips nitrate/nitrite-free bacon

1 pint cherry tomatoes, halved

1 ripe avocado, peeled and diced

½ cup Wilma's Mayonnaise (see Chapter 2)

½ cup French Dressing (see recipe in this chapter)

2 cups shredded lettuce

1. Thickly dice turkey breast. Fry bacon until crisp, then crumble into a large serving bowl.

2. Mix all ingredients except the lettuce in the bowl. Serve over lettuce.

Salad Dressings

Did you ever study the labels of commercial salad dressings? There are chemicals and preservatives in these dressings that you may not want to ingest. Instead, make your own dressing and store it in an empty, clean olive jar. You'll know everything in it is healthy!

GRILLED TUNA SALAD WITH ASIAN VEGETABLES AND SPICY DRESSING

The fish is hot, the vegetables are spicy, and the greens are chilled! This is an exotic salad that is deceptively easy to make.

Serves 4

3 tablespoons sesame oil

½ cup olive oil

2 cloves garlic, minced

1 teaspoon minced fresh ginger

2 teaspoons sherry vinegar

1 tablespoon coconut aminos

2–3 cups shredded napa cabbage

1 red onion, cut in wedges

2 Japanese eggplants, cut in half lengthwise

4 (¼-pound) tuna steaks

1. In a bowl, whisk together the sesame oil, olive oil, garlic, ginger, sherry vinegar, and coconut aminos. Divide evenly in two bowls and set aside.

2. Place the cabbage on serving plates. Brush the onion, eggplants, and tuna with the dressing from one bowl, being careful not to contaminate the dressing with a brush that has touched the fish.

3. Grill the vegetables and tuna for 3–4 minutes per side over medium-high heat. Arrange the vegetables and fish over the cabbage. Drizzle with the reserved dressing from the second bowl.

A Quick Meal

Tuna is a large fish that is part of the mackerel family. It has a unique circulatory system that allows it to retain a higher body temperature than the cool water it inhabits. This provides tuna with an extra burst of energy that allows it to reach short-distance swimming speeds of over 40 miles per hour!

FILET MIGNON AND RED ONION SALAD

There are few things that taste better cold than filet mignon!

Serves 4

1¼ pounds well-trimmed whole filet mignon

Salt and pepper, to taste

½ cup French Dressing (see recipe in this chapter)

1 red onion, thinly sliced

2 tablespoons capers

16 black olives, pitted and sliced

Bed of chopped romaine lettuce

1. Preheat oven to 400°F. Place the filet mignon on a baking pan. Sprinkle it with salt and pepper. Roast for 15–20 minutes or until temperature reaches 140°F. Rest the meat for 10 minutes before slicing.

2. Slice the filet mignon and place in a bowl with the French Dressing, onion, capers, and olives. Toss gently to coat.

3. Spread the lettuce on a serving platter. Arrange the filet mignon mixture over the top. Serve at room temperature or chilled.

Know Your Beef

Filet mignon is the small part of a beef tenderloin and is considered the most delectable cut of beef because of its melt-in-your-mouth texture. Save yourself some money by preparing this at home instead of dining out!

FRESH TUNA SALAD À LA NIÇOISE

The niçoise salad originates from Nice, a French city on the Mediterranean Sea. This salad is popular in France as the Cobb salad is enjoyed in the United States.

Serves 2

¼ pound asparagus, trimmed and cut into 1" lengths

2 (4-ounce) tuna steaks

2 tablespoons avocado oil

Salt and pepper, to taste

1 head butter lettuce

1½ tablespoons capers

¼ cup niçoise olives

½ cup cherry tomatoes

2 tablespoons Italian Dressing (see recipe in this chapter)

2 hard-boiled eggs, peeled and quartered

1. Cook asparagus in a pot of boiling water, uncovered, until crisp-tender, about 4 minutes, then transfer immediately to a bowl of ice water to stop cooking. Drain asparagus and pat dry.

2. Brush tuna with oil and season with salt and pepper as desired. Grill on lightly oiled rack or grill pan, uncovered, turning over once, until browned on the outside and pink in the center, 6–8 minutes total. Slice tuna into ¼"-thick pieces.

3. Wash lettuce and tear into bite-sized pieces; place in large bowl. Add asparagus, capers, olives, and tomatoes to bowl; coat with Italian Dressing.

4. Divide salad onto two plates. Top with tuna and egg quarters.

Timesaving Tip

If you are tight on time and money, try substituting the tuna steaks with a large can of wild-caught tuna. Canned albacore usually contains more omega-3 fatty acids than chunk light tuna. The salad will still taste authentic without spending extra cash and time grilling the fish.

ARUGULA AND FENNEL SALAD WITH POMEGRANATE

Pomegranates pack a high dose of health-promoting antioxidants. They are in peak season October through January and may not be easy to find at other times of the year. Cranberries can be substituted in this recipe if pomegranates are not available.

Serves 4

2 large navel oranges

1 pomegranate

4 cups arugula

1 cup thinly sliced fennel

4 tablespoons olive oil

Salt and pepper, to taste

1. Cut the tops and bottoms off of the oranges and then cut the remaining peel away. Slice each orange into 10–12 small pieces.

2. Remove seeds from the pomegranate.

3. Place arugula, orange pieces, pomegranate seeds, and fennel slices into a large bowl.

4. Coat the salad with olive oil and season with salt and pepper as desired.

Fennel Facts

Fennel, a crunchy and slightly sweet vegetable, is a popular Mediterranean ingredient. Fennel has a white or greenish-white bulb and long stalks with feathery green leaves stemming from the top. Fennel is closely related to cilantro, dill, carrots, and parsley.

SHAVED FENNEL SALAD WITH ORANGE SECTIONS AND TOASTED HAZELNUTS

Tangelos, mandarin oranges, or any easily sectioned citrus will work wonderfully in this recipe.

Serves 6

3 bulbs fennel, cleaned and trimmed

6 large oranges

6 tablespoons finely chopped hazelnuts

⅓ cup fresh orange juice

2 tablespoons almond oil

1 tablespoon fresh orange zest

1. Finely slice the fennel bulbs. Remove the peel and pith from the oranges. With a small paring knife, remove each section of the oranges and slice away membrane.

2. Form a mound of shaved fennel on each serving plate and arrange the oranges on top. Sprinkle with nuts, then drizzle with the orange juice and oil. Finish with a sprinkle of zest.

FIRE-KISSED CANTALOUPE SALAD

Garnish this light and spicy salad with fresh cilantro or a slice of mango. Serve it as a side to any filling meat dish.

Serves 4

½ medium mango, peeled, diced, and puréed in a blender

1 tablespoon walnut oil

⅛ teaspoon chili powder

⅛ teaspoon sweet paprika

⅛ teaspoon ground red pepper

3 cups cubed cantaloupe

½ cup diced red onion

1. Combine mango purée, oil, chili powder, paprika, and red pepper in a small bowl. Whisk until mixture is emulsified.

2. Add cantaloupe and red onion to a large mixing bowl. Pour dressing over salad. Toss well to mix and coat. Cover salad and let chill in refrigerator for 15 minutes. Remove bowl from refrigerator, toss salad gently, and serve.

CURRIED CHICKEN SALAD

The recipe makes two servings, but you can double or triple the amounts. You can also change the spices around for more variety.

Serves 2

2 tablespoons almond oil

8 ounces chicken breast, cubed

1 stalk celery, sliced

1 small onion, diced

½ English cucumber, diced

½ cup chopped almonds

2 apples, cored, peeled, and chopped

½ teaspoon curry powder

4 cups baby romaine lettuce

1. In skillet, heat oil over medium-high heat and cook chicken, celery, and onion until the chicken is completely cooked, 5–10 minutes. Set aside to cool.

2. In mixing bowl, combine cucumber, almonds, apples, and curry powder with the cooled chicken mixture.

3. Serve over bed of baby romaine lettuce.

BROCCOLI, PINE NUT, AND APPLE SALAD

This quick little salad will tide you over until your next meal. The broccoli and apple taste great together, and the toasted pine nuts add a little bit of crunch.

Serves 2

3 tablespoons almond oil

¾ cup pine nuts

2 cups broccoli florets

2 cups diced green apples

Juice of 1 lemon

1. Heat oil in a small skillet over medium-high heat and sauté the pine nuts until golden brown.

2. Mix broccoli and apples in a medium-sized bowl. Add the pine nuts and oil and and toss.

3. Squeeze lemon juice over salad and serve.

RED PEPPER AND FENNEL SALAD

Fennel has a fantastic licorice flavor that blends nicely with nuts. The red pepper adds a flash of color and a bit of sweetness to the mix.

Serves 2

⅓ cup pine nuts, toasted

3 tablespoons sesame seeds, toasted

2 tablespoons avocado oil

1 medium red bell pepper, seeded and halved

6 leaves romaine lettuce, shredded

½ bulb fennel, diced

1 tablespoon walnut oil

Juice from 1 lime

Black pepper, to taste

1. Preheat broiler.

2. In a medium-sized skillet, sauté pine nuts and sesame seeds in avocado oil over medium heat for 5 minutes.

3. Grill pepper under the broiler about 3 minutes per side, until the skin is blackened and the flesh has softened slightly.

4. Place pepper halves in a paper bag to cool slightly. When cool enough to handle, remove skin and slice peppers into strips.

5. Combine red pepper slices, lettuce, and fennel in a salad bowl.

6. Add walnut oil, lime juice, and black pepper to taste and mix well. Add nut mixture and serve.

Walnut Oil

Walnut oil cannot withstand high heat, so it's best to add it to food that has already been cooked or is served raw, such as a salad. If you choose to cook with it, use a lower flame to avoid burning the oil.

FLORET SALAD

Broccoli is one of the most nutrient-dense green vegetables. Try this floret salad to maximize on taste while simultaneously boosting your health.

Serves 2

⅔ cup fresh cauliflower florets

⅔ cup fresh broccoli florets

2 tablespoons chopped red onion

8 ounces uncured, nitrate/nitrite-free bacon, crisply cooked and chopped

5 teaspoons raw honey

¼ cup walnut oil

2 tablespoons sliced almonds

1. In a medium-sized bowl, combine cauliflower, broccoli, red onion, and bacon.

2. In a small bowl, whisk honey and walnut oil.

3. Combine honey mixture with florets and toss.

4. Top with almonds just before serving.

Broccoli: Superfood

Broccoli is one of the healthiest vegetables you can eat. Ounce for ounce, broccoli has more vitamin C than an orange and as much calcium as a glass of milk. Broccoli is packed with fiber to promote digestive health and it is quite rich in vitamin A.

CRUNCHY FRUIT SALAD

When you're in the mood for a sweet treat, this crunchy salad will fulfill that sugar craving; it's also good for replenishing glycogen storage after workouts.

Serves 2

½ fresh pineapple, peeled, cored, and cubed

1 medium fresh papaya, cubed

1 medium ripe banana, sliced

½ cup halved seedless grapes

1 tablespoon raw honey

¼ cup chopped pecans

¼ cup unsweetened coconut flakes

Combine all ingredients, toss, and serve.

Seasonal Fruits

It is always best to eat foods that are native to your area and in season. If you eat fruits that are imported, they have traveled long distances and their freshness factor cannot be guaranteed. Your hunter-gatherer ancestors only had foods that were in season at the time of the hunt. They did not have the luxury of importing fruits from a neighboring area. Your body is made to change with the seasons.

CHAPTER 4

STOCKS, SOUPS, AND STEWS

CHICKEN STOCK

Homemade stocks can give your soups an incredible depth of flavor you just can't get with canned or boxed products or bouillon cubes. While these recipes take time, remember that you don't have to do any work while they are simmering away. Make a large amount at one time, then freeze in 2-cup containers. Use in any recipe.

Yields 4 quarts

3 tablespoons olive oil

2 roasting chickens

2 onions, cut into eighths, unpeeled

8 cloves garlic, unpeeled

4 carrots, cut into chunks

4 stalks celery, cut into chunks

2 sprigs fresh thyme

1 bay leaf

2 teaspoons salt

12 whole peppercorns

20 cups filtered water

1. In large stockpot, heat olive oil over medium heat. Add chickens, one at a time, breast-side down, and brown well, about 10 minutes. Remove chickens to a plate as they finish browning.

2. Add onions to pot and stir well to loosen pan drippings. Return chickens to pot along with all remaining ingredients.

3. Bring to a boil. Reduce heat to low and simmer, uncovered, for 3 hours, skimming foam off the top from time to time, until the stock is a rich golden color.

4. Strain the stock into a colander. Chill stock overnight.

5. Next morning, remove the fat and reserve to use in recipes. Pour stock into 2-cup freezer containers, label, and freeze up to 3 months.

BEEF STOCK

Beef stock is a delicious soup all on its own. You could just reheat it and add some leftover cooked beef and vegetables for a wonderful soup. This rich and gorgeous stock adds such wonderful flavor to any beef or pork recipe. You could reduce part of this recipe even further to get a more concentrated version of stock, called glace de viande, used to add a rich finishing touch to sauces and gravies.

Yields 5 quarts

2 pounds beef bones

1 oxtail, cut up

1 pound beef stew meat, cut up

2 onions, cut into eighths, unpeeled

1 head garlic, cut in half crosswise

2 carrots, cut into chunks

2 sprigs fresh marjoram leaves

1 bay leaf

1 tablespoon salt

1 teaspoon peppercorns

24 cups filtered water

1. Preheat oven to 375°F. Place the bones and oxtail on a rimmed sheet pan and bake for 40–50 minutes or until well browned.

2. Place the bones, oxtail, and stew meat in a large stockpot or Dutch oven.

3. Carefully pour 1 cup of water into the rimmed sheet pan that held the bones and scrape with a spoon to remove the pan drippings. Add to stockpot along with all remaining ingredients.

4. Bring to a boil. Reduce heat to low and simmer, uncovered, for 6–8 hours or until the stock is rich golden brown.

5. Strain the stock through a colander and refrigerate overnight.

6. Next morning, remove the solidified fat and reserve in the freezer for cooking. Strain the stock through cheesecloth. Freeze in 1-cup containers up to 3 months.

VEGETABLE BROTH

Vegetable broth is crucial in vegetarian recipes. Most commercial brands have lots of additives, colorings, and artificial flavorings you just don't want to eat. And the homemade version is easy to make. For best flavor and color, brown the vegetables well before you add the water and simmer the broth.

Yields 4 quarts

2 tablespoons olive oil

2 onions, peeled and chopped

3 large carrots, chopped

2 cups sliced mushrooms

3 stalks celery, chopped

2 large tomatoes, chopped, if desired

7 cloves garlic, peeled and cut in half

1 teaspoon salt

1 teaspoon peppercorns

1 bay leaf

3 sprigs fresh thyme leaves

20 cups filtered water

1. Heat olive oil in stockpot. Add onions, carrots, mushrooms, and celery and cook over medium heat for 10–15 minutes or until the vegetables brown, stirring frequently.

2. Add tomatoes and garlic and cook for another 5 minutes.

3. Add salt, peppercorns, bay leaf, thyme, and water and stir well to remove pan drippings from bottom of pot.

4. Bring to a boil, then reduce heat to low and simmer, uncovered, for 40 minutes.

5. Strain stock, discarding vegetables. Cool for 30 minutes, then freeze in 2-cup containers up to months.

FISH STOCK

Fish stock adds great flavor to any recipe calling for seafood. It's delicious in sauces and gravies too. Fish stock is difficult to find in the grocery store. If you cook a lot with seafood, this is worth your while to make. Go to a fishmonger and ask for bones and trimmings to make this recipe. If you can find a fish head to add, all the better!

Yields 4 quarts

3 pounds fish bones and trimmings

2 fish heads, if desired

1 leek, chopped

3 stalks celery, chopped

2 carrots, chopped

1 bay leaf

2 sprigs fresh thyme

2 teaspoons salt

1 teaspoon black peppercorns

20 cups filtered water

1. Place all ingredients in a large stockpot.

2. Bring just to a boil, then immediately reduce heat and simmer for about 40 minutes. Skim off and discard foam that forms on the surface.

3. Strain through a colander and discard solids. Then strain the stock through cheesecloth. Cool for 30 minutes, then freeze in 2-cup containers up to 2 months.

BROWN STOCK

When you add ¼ cup of this concentrated stock to a slow-cooked beef dish, you'll get the same succulent flavor as if you first seared the meat in a hot skillet before adding it to the slow cooker. The stock also gives a delicious flavor boost to slow-cooked tomato sauce or tomato gravy.

Yields 4 cups

2 large carrots, scrubbed

2 stalks celery

1½ pounds bone-in chuck roast

1½ pounds cracked beef bones

1 large onion, quartered

Freshly ground black pepper, to taste

4½ cups water

1. Preheat the oven to 450°F. Cut the carrots and celery into large pieces. Put them along with the meat, bones, and onion into a roasting pan. Season with pepper. Put the pan on the middle rack in the oven and roast, turning the meat and vegetables occasionally, for 45 minutes or until evenly browned.

2. Transfer the roasted meat, bones, and vegetables to a 4- or 6-quart slow cooker. Add the water to the roasting pan; scrape any browned bits clinging to the pan and then pour the water into the slow cooker. Cover and cook on low for 8 hours. (It may be necessary to skim accumulated fat and scum from the top of the pan juices; check the broth after 4 hours and again after 6 hours to see if that's needed.)

3. Use a slotted spoon to remove the roast and beef bones. Reserve the roast and the meat removed from the bones for another use; discard the bones.

4. Once the broth has cooled enough to handle, strain it; discard the cooked vegetables. Refrigerate the broth overnight. Remove and discard the hardened fat. The resulting concentrated broth can be kept for 1 or 2 days in the refrigerator, or frozen for up to 3 months.

PORK BROTH

Pork broth is seldom called for in recipes, but it can add layers of flavor when mixed with chicken broth in vegetable soups.

Yields 4 cups

1 (3-pound) bone-in pork butt roast

1 large onion, quartered

12 baby carrots

2 stalks celery, cut in half

4½ cups water

1. Add all the ingredients to a 4-quart slow cooker. Cover and cook on low for 6 hours or until the pork is tender and pulls away from the bone.

2. Strain; discard the celery and onion. Reserve the pork roast and carrots for another use. Once cooled, cover and refrigerate the broth overnight. Remove and discard the hardened fat. The broth can be kept for 1 or 2 days in the refrigerator, or frozen up to 3 months.

Pork Roast Dinner

To make concentrated broth and a pork roast dinner at the same time, increase the amount of carrots, decrease the water to 2½ cups, and add 4 peeled, medium-sized sweet potatoes (cut in half) on top. Cook on low for 6 hours.

TURKEY STOCK

Making turkey stock is the perfect way to put your leftover holiday turkey to good use. This stock can also be used as a substitute in recipes calling for chicken stock.

Yields 16 cups

10 black peppercorns

6 sprigs parsley

4 medium carrots, thickly sliced

4 stalks celery, thickly sliced

4 quarts water

2 medium onions, thickly sliced

2 leeks (white parts only), thickly sliced

1 turkey carcass, cut up

1 cup water

1½ teaspoons dried thyme

Pepper, to taste

1. Combine all the ingredients except pepper in a 6-quart slow cooker. Cover and cook on low for 6–8 hours.

2. Strain the stock through a double layer of cheesecloth, discarding the solids. Season with pepper to taste.

3. Refrigerate 3–5 hours, until chilled. Remove fat from surface of stock. Refrigerate up to 3 days or freeze up to 3 months.

SEAFOOD STOCK

This recipe calls for the shells only because the amount of time it takes to slow-cook the stock would result in seafood that would be too tough to eat.

Yields 4 cups

2 pounds large or jumbo shrimp, crab, or lobster shells

1 large onion, thinly sliced

1 tablespoon fresh lemon juice

4 cups water

1. Add the seafood shells, onion, lemon juice, and water to a 4-quart slow cooker. Cover and cook on low for 4–8 hours.

2. Strain through a fine sieve or wire-mesh strainer. Discard the shells and onions. Refrigerate in a covered container and use within 2 days or freeze for up to 3 months.

Fish or Seafood Stock in a Hurry

For each cup of seafood or fish stock called for in a recipe, you can substitute ¼ cup of bottled clam juice and ¾ cup of water. Just keep in mind that the clam juice is very salty, so adjust any recipe in which you use it accordingly.

MUSHROOM STOCK

Shiitake mushrooms add a rich, bold flavor to this recipe and also provide a variety of beneficial phytonutrients. Be careful not to overcook this stock.

Yields 2 quarts

1 quart water

12 ounces white mushrooms

6 sprigs parsley (with leaves)

1 large onion, sliced

1 leek (white part only), sliced

1 stalk celery, sliced

2 ounces dried shiitake mushrooms

1 tablespoon minced garlic

1½ teaspoons black peppercorns

¾ teaspoon dried sage

¾ teaspoon dried thyme

Freshly ground black pepper, to taste

1. Combine all the ingredients except ground pepper in a 6-quart slow cooker; cover and cook on low for 6–8 hours.

2. Strain, discarding solids; season to taste with pepper. Serve immediately, refrigerate and use within 1–2 weeks, or freeze up to 3 months.

LOADED CAULIFLOWER SOUP

This wonderful soup is full of flavorful and colorful ingredients. It's delicious served for lunch or dinner paired with a nice white wine. You can make it ahead of time and refrigerate the soup and the bacon separately. Reheat the bacon in the microwave until it's crisp, then mix with the cheese and green onions and add to the warmed soup just before serving.

Serves 6

6 slices bacon

2 tablespoons olive oil

1 leek, rinsed and sliced

3 cloves garlic, minced

1 head fresh cauliflower, broken into florets

3 stalks celery, sliced

6 cups chicken stock

1 teaspoon salt

¼ teaspoon pepper

1 cup heavy cream or coconut milk

1½ cups shredded sharp Cheddar cheese, if desired

⅓ cup chopped green onion

1. In large stockpot, cook bacon until crisp, about 8–10 minutes. Remove bacon from the pot, drain on paper towels, crumble, and set aside in the refrigerator.

2. Drain all but 1 tablespoon bacon fat from the pan. Add olive oil to the pan and add the leek and garlic. Cook and stir until crisp-tender, about 5–6 minutes.

3. Add cauliflower and celery to the pot. Cook and stir for 3–4 minutes. Add chicken stock, salt, and pepper and bring to a boil.

4. Reduce heat to low, cover pot, and simmer for 10–15 minutes or until the vegetables are tender.

5. Remove 1 cup of the vegetables from the pot and place in a food processor or blender. Process or blend until smooth. Stir the puréed vegetables back into the soup along with the cream or coconut milk; bring just to a simmer.

6. In small bowl, combine the reserved bacon, Cheddar cheese if using, and green onion. Serve soup in warmed bowls, topped with the bacon mixture.

TOMATO BEEF SOUP

Do not buy beef that is cubed and sold specifically for stew; it is of lesser quality than beef you cube yourself. Sirloin tip steak sounds expensive, but it is a good value and has excellent flavor. This slow-cooker soup cooks all day while you are at work or doing other things. And it makes the house smell incredible! When you get home, just sit down and eat.

6 servings

2 pounds sirloin tip steak, cut into 1½" cubes

1 teaspoon salt

¼ teaspoon pepper

3 tablespoons butter or olive oil

½ pound beef shank bone

1 onion, chopped

4 stalks celery, sliced

3 cloves garlic, minced

2 pounds Roma tomatoes, chopped

1 teaspoon dried marjoram

1 teaspoon dried oregano

1 teaspoon dried thyme

1 bay leaf

2 cups water

4 cups beef stock

2 cups sliced green beans

1. Sprinkle cubed steak with salt and pepper. Melt butter or olive oil in a large skillet and brown the steak, stirring frequently, for 5–6 minutes. Remove the beef to a plate as it browns.

2. In 5- to 6-quart slow cooker, place the shank bone, onion, celery, and garlic. Top with the browned beef.

3. Add tomatoes, then marjoram, oregano, and thyme. Add bay leaf. Pour water and beef stock over all.

4. Cover and cook on low for 7–8 hours or until beef and vegetables are tender. Remove the beef shank bone and cut off any meat and marrow; return to slow cooker. Remove and discard bay leaf.

5. Taste soup for seasoning and add more dried herbs, if desired. Add green beans and stir. Turn the slow cooker to high and cook for 30–40 minutes longer until beans are crisp-tender. Serve immediately.

CAVEMAN GAZPACHO

Gazpacho, a vegetable soup served cold, is perfect for summer entertaining or a light lunch on the porch. You can use any vegetables you'd like. Add green beans, zucchini, yellow squash, or anything that looks good at the market. Serve with a glass of red wine and some grilled shrimp for company.

Serves 6

2 pounds ripe beefsteak tomatoes, chopped

1 cucumber, peeled, seeded, and chopped

1 yellow or orange bell pepper, chopped

1 clove garlic, minced

1–2 jalapeño peppers, minced

1½ cups chicken stock

¼ cup extra-virgin olive oil

2 tablespoons lemon juice

1 tablespoon red wine vinegar

½ teaspoon salt

⅛ teaspoon pepper

2 tablespoons chopped fresh flat-leaf parsley

2 tablespoons chopped fresh dill weed

4 hard-cooked eggs, chopped

⅓ cup chopped green onions

2 avocados, peeled and chopped

1. In large bowl, place one-quarter of the tomatoes. Using a potato masher, mash the tomatoes until smooth. Stir in remaining tomatoes, cucumber, bell pepper, garlic, and jalapeño pepper.

2. Add chicken stock, olive oil, lemon juice, red wine vinegar, salt, pepper, parsley, and dill. Stir and adjust seasonings, if desired. You can serve the gazpacho immediately, or cover and chill for 1–2 hours to blend flavors.

3. In small bowl, combine hard-cooked egg, green onion, and avocados and mix gently. Use this mixture to garnish the soup.

SLOW-COOKER SHORT RIB STEW

Short ribs are sold with the bone and without. For the Paleo diet, use the bones. You'll get more flavor out of the meat, and the marrow adds great nutrition to the recipe. Your slow cooker is a wonderful way to cook soups. They simmer all day while you're doing something else. Serve with Paleo Crackers (see Chapter 5) and a simple green salad.

Serves 6–8

5 slices bacon

3 pounds bone-in beef short ribs

⅓ cup almond flour

2 onions, chopped

5 cloves garlic, minced

3 carrots, cut into chunks

3 sweet potatoes, peeled and cubed

4 large tomatoes, seeded and chopped

5 cups Bone Broth (see recipe in this chapter) or beef broth

1 teaspoon salt

¼ teaspoon pepper

1 teaspoon dried marjoram leaves

1 teaspoon dried basil leaves

1 bay leaf

½ pound green beans, cut in half

1. In a large saucepan, cook bacon until crisp. Remove bacon from pan, drain on paper towel, crumble, and refrigerate.

2. Coat the ribs in the almond flour. Add the ribs to the fat in the pan and brown well on all sides. This should take about 10 minutes.

3. Remove the ribs to a plate and add the onion and garlic to drippings. Stir well, scraping up drippings from bottom of pan, for about 5 minutes.

4. Place the carrots and sweet potatoes in a 4- to 5-quart slow cooker. Top with the onions, garlic, tomatoes, and ribs.

5. Add 2 cups of the broth to the skillet along with salt, pepper, marjoram, basil, and bay leaf, and bring to a simmer. Make sure you scrape the pan to get all of the drippings. Pour into the slow cooker along with remaining 3 cups of the broth.

6. Cover and cook on low for 8–10 hours or until vegetables and ribs are tender. Remove and discard bay leaf.

7. Add beans and reserved bacon to the slow cooker and stir. Cover and cook on high for 20–30 minutes longer or until beans are tender.

HAM BONE CHOWDER

Chowders are usually thickened with flour, or with split peas or other legumes, which aren't on the Paleo diet. This recipe is thickened with some mashed sweet potatoes, which add great texture and flavor to the dish. If you don't see a ham bone at the butcher counter, ask the butcher for one. He or she will most likely be able to find one for you.

Serves 6

2 tablespoons coconut oil

1 onion, chopped

2 cloves garlic, minced

1 large ham bone

3 stalks celery, sliced

2 sweet potatoes, peeled and cubed

4 cups chicken stock

3 cups water

1 teaspoon salt

¼ teaspoon pepper

1 teaspoon dried oregano leaves

3 cups baby spinach leaves, coarsely chopped

1 cup almond milk

1. In large stockpot, melt coconut oil over medium heat. Add onion and garlic; cook and stir until tender, about 5 minutes.

2. Add all remaining ingredients except for the spinach and almond milk. Bring to a simmer, cover, reduce heat to low, then cook for 3–4 hours or until ham and vegetables are tender.

3. Remove the ham bone from the soup and cut off the meat. Discard bone, cube meat, and return to the soup. Remove about ½ cup of the sweet potatoes, mash, and stir back into the soup.

4. Add the baby spinach leaves and almond milk. Cover and simmer for a few minutes until the leaves wilt and soup is hot. Correct seasonings and serve immediately.

BONE BROTH

Bones add such wonderful flavor and texture to stock. The marrow in the bones melts, which adds essential fatty acids, vitamins, and minerals to the stock. By the way, the technical difference between "broth" and "stock" is that broth usually doesn't contain bones, while stock does. But "Bone Broth" has a nice ring to it. You can use any bones you can find at the supermarket in this easy recipe.

Yields 10 cups

1 pound beef bones

½ pound oxtail

1 pound chicken bones

1 onion, chopped

1 leek, well rinsed and chopped

1 carrot, cut into chunks

2 cloves garlic, minced

1 (2") piece fresh gingerroot

1 bunch parsley

1 bay leaf

9 cups water

1½ teaspoons salt

1. Combine all ingredients in a 5-quart slow cooker. Cover and cook on low for 8–12 hours or until broth is richly colored.

2. Strain the broth, discarding all solids. Correct seasonings and refrigerate in 2-cup quantities up to 3 days, or freeze up to 3 months.

MEATBALL ROOT VEGETABLE STEW

Root vegetables are not prohibited on the Paleo diet, except for white and red potatoes. Most people don't know the delicious taste of turnips and parsnips, those staples of days past. Turnips are a sweet vegetable that is low in fat and high in vitamins A, C, E, and K and the B complex. Parsnips are rich in soluble and insoluble dietary fiber, along with antioxidants and anti-inflammatory compounds.

Serves 4–6

2 tablespoons Ghee (see Chapter 2) or coconut oil

1 onion, chopped

3 cloves garlic, minced

2 carrots, peeled and sliced

1 parsnip, peeled and cubed

1 turnip, peeled and cubed

1 sweet potato, peeled and cubed

4 cups Bone Broth (see recipe in this chapter) or beef broth

1 teaspoon salt

¼ teaspoon pepper

1 teaspoon dried marjoram leaves

1 teaspoon dried oregano leaves

1 recipe Primal Meatballs (see Chapter 1), cooked

1. Melt Ghee or coconut oil in large saucepan over medium heat. Add onion and garlic; cook and stir for 5 minutes.

2. Add carrots, parsnip, turnip, sweet potato, and broth and stir. Add salt, pepper, marjoram, and oregano and bring to a simmer. Cover and simmer for 40–45 minutes or until vegetables are tender. At this point you can mash some of the vegetables for a thicker soup.

3. While the soup is simmering, prepare and bake the meatballs. Add to the soup and simmer for another 10–15 minutes until flavors have blended. Serve immediately.

CHICKEN FLORENTINE SOUP

"Florentine" just means spinach is used in the recipe. This delicate soup is good on a cold winter day for lunch or dinner. You could use turkey or pork tenderloin instead of the chicken if you'd like. Serve with Paleo Crackers (see Chapter 5) and a fruit salad for a nice meal.

Serves 4

2 tablespoons olive oil

2 shallots, chopped

2 cloves garlic, minced

3 boneless, skinless chicken breasts, cut into 1" cubes

1 red bell pepper, chopped

4 cups chicken broth

1 teaspoon dried thyme leaves

½ teaspoon salt

⅛ teaspoon white pepper

Pinch fresh grated nutmeg

4 cups chopped fresh baby spinach

1. In large saucepan, heat olive oil over medium heat. Add shallots and garlic; cook and stir for 4 minutes.

2. Add chicken to saucepan; sauté until white, about 4 minutes, stirring frequently. Add bell pepper, broth, thyme, salt, and white pepper and bring to a simmer.

3. Simmer soup for 15 minutes or until chicken is tender. Stir in nutmeg and spinach and cook for 5 minutes longer until spinach is wilted. Serve immediately.

HOT AND SOUR SOUP

Hot and sour is a classic flavoring in Chinese cooking. The "hot" comes from hot chili oil and white pepper, and the "sour" comes from vinegar. This soup is traditionally made with lots of dried exotic mushrooms, dried lily buds, and tofu, but this version is composed of foods that are easy to find at any grocery store.

Serves 6

4 dried shiitake mushrooms

4 dried porcini mushrooms

2 cups warm water

1 tablespoon olive oil

1 onion, finely chopped

2 teaspoons minced fresh gingerroot

½ pound pork tenderloin, cubed

¼ pound fresh Portabello mushrooms, sliced

4 cups chicken stock

2 eggs, beaten

2 tablespoons rice wine vinegar

1 teaspoon sesame oil

1 tablespoon chili oil

1. Soak the dried mushrooms in warm water for 15–20 minutes or until softened. Drain, reserving the soaking liquid, and cut off the tough stems. Slice the dried mushrooms. Strain the soaking liquid through cheesecloth and set aside.

2. In large soup pot, heat oil over medium heat. Add onion and gingerroot; cook and stir for 5 minutes.

3. Add pork tenderloin; cook and stir until pork is browned, about 5 minutes. Add all of the mushrooms; cook and stir for another 4 minutes.

4. Add the reserved mushroom soaking liquid and chicken stock and bring to a simmer. Simmer for 20 minutes.

5. Add the beaten egg to the soup, beating constantly. Stir in the vinegar, sesame oil, and chili oil and serve immediately.

CAULIFLOWER SOUP

Cauliflower is the Paleo substitute for potatoes. It's healthy and delicious and makes a wonderfully creamy soup. This rich soup reheats beautifully. Let cool for 30 minutes, then spoon into a shallow container and refrigerate. To reheat, just pour the soup into a saucepan and heat over low heat, stirring constantly, until warm.

Serves 6

2 tablespoons butter or coconut oil

2 shallots, finely chopped

5 cups vegetable broth or chicken stock

1 head cauliflower, broken into florets

½ teaspoon salt

⅛ teaspoon white pepper

2 egg yolks

½ cup heavy cream or coconut cream

1 tablespoon arrowroot powder

1 tablespoon chopped fresh dill weed

1. In large pot, melt butter over medium heat. Add shallots; cook until soft, about 3–4 minutes.

2. Add broth or stock, cauliflower, salt, and pepper and bring to a simmer. Simmer for 10 minutes or until cauliflower is soft.

3. Purée the soup using a blender or food processor or a stick blender. Return to pot and place over low heat.

4. In small bowl, combine egg yolks, cream, and arrowroot powder and mix with a whisk. Stir into the soup and heat for a few minutes until the soup thickens slightly. Add the dill weed and serve.

GOULASH SOUP

Goulash is a rich mixture of beef and onions, seasoned with paprika and usually served over mashed potatoes or noodles. This soup is just as rich as the classic entrée version of the recipe, but it uses lots of mushrooms and omits the starch. It's the perfect choice for dinner on a cold fall night.

Serves 6

2 tablespoons Ghee (see Chapter 2)

2 pounds boneless chuck roast, cut into 1" pieces

2 onions, chopped

3 cloves garlic, minced

2 cups sliced portabella mushrooms

2 teaspoons paprika

2 teaspoons smoked paprika

1 (6-ounce) can tomato paste

1 teaspoon caraway seed

1 teaspoon salt

¼ teaspoon pepper

6 cups beef broth

1. Heat Ghee in a large stockpot over medium heat. Add the cubed beef; brown well on all sides for about 10 minutes, removing beef to a plate as it browns.

2. Add onions, garlic, and mushrooms to drippings remaining in skillet; cook for 5–6 minutes, stirring to scrape up pan drippings, until tender.

3. Add paprika and smoked paprika to pot; cook for 1 minute longer.

4. Return beef to pot along with tomato paste, caraway seed, salt, pepper, and broth. Bring to a simmer; cover and simmer soup for 1½ hours until beef is tender. Serve garnished with sour cream or crème fraiche, if desired.

AUTHENTIC TEX-MEX CHILI

Did you know that the original chili was made without beans of any kind? Just lots of meat, onion, and chilies are used in the authentic recipe. You can find all kinds of chilies in the market these days. Just remember—the smaller the chili, the hotter the taste. And most of the heat in a chili is in its seeds and inner membranes.

Serves 6

6 slices bacon

2½ pounds sirloin tip steak, cut into 1" cubes

1 onion, chopped

5 cloves garlic, minced

2 red jalapeño peppers, minced

2 chipotle peppers in adobo sauce, minced

2 tablespoons adobo sauce

¼ cup dried ground chili pods

1 tablespoon chili powder

4 cups beef stock

2 cups water

1 tablespoon honey

1½ teaspoons salt

¼ teaspoon pepper

¼ teaspoon crushed red pepper flakes

1. In large stockpot, cook bacon until crisp. Remove bacon, drain on paper towels, crumble, and refrigerate.

2. Brown beef in three batches in the drippings remaining in pot, about 5 minutes per batch. Remove beef from pot and place on a plate as it browns.

3. Cook onions and garlic in drippings in pot, scraping to remove brown bits from bottom of pan. Add jalapeño peppers, chipotle peppers, and 2 tablespoons adobo sauce.

4. Return beef to pot along with ground chili pods, chili powder, stock, water, honey, salt, pepper, and crushed red pepper flakes. Add bacon and stir.

5. Cover and reduce heat to low. Simmer for 2–3 hours, stirring occasionally, until mixture is thickened and beef is tender.

EGG DROP SOUP

This recipe, which only has a few ingredients, really should be made with homemade Chicken Stock (see recipe in this chapter). A good rule of thumb in cooking is, the fewer the ingredients, the fresher they should be. This soup would be a great starter to a Chinese meal of different kinds of stir-fries.

Serves 4

4 cups homemade Chicken Stock (see recipe in this chapter)

¼ cup sliced green onions

1" piece fresh gingerroot

1 tablespoon lemon juice

1 egg

2 egg yolks

Salt and pepper to taste

1. In a medium saucepan, combine stock, green onions, gingerroot, and lemon juice. Bring to a simmer over medium heat.

2. In small bowl, combine egg and egg yolks and beat well with a wire whisk.

3. Remove the gingerroot from the stock and discard.

4. Slowly pour the egg mixture into the simmering soup, stirring constantly with a fork. Egg will cook and form into small strands. Season with salt and pepper and serve immediately.

SLOW-COOKER BEEF STEW

Beef stew is perfect for cold fall and winter nights. The flavor that drifts through your house while this recipe is cooking is completely heartwarming. You can use any vegetables you like in this easy recipe. Top it with a combination of fresh herbs that are chopped just before serving.

Serves 6

2 tablespoons butter or olive oil

2½ pounds sirloin tip steak, cubed

1 onion, chopped

5 cloves garlic, minced

4 carrots, cut into chunks

1 turnip, peeled and chopped

1 (14-ounce) can diced tomatoes, undrained

4 cups beef stock

1 teaspoon salt

⅛ teaspoon pepper

1 teaspoon dried marjoram leaves

1 teaspoon dried oregano leaves

1 bay leaf

1. In large skillet, melt butter over medium heat. Add steak and brown well, stirring frequently, about 8 minutes. Remove meat from skillet and place in 4-quart slow cooker.

2. Add onion and garlic to skillet; cook, scraping up pan drippings, for 5 minutes. Add to slow cooker.

3. Add all remaining ingredients to the slow cooker and stir.

4. Cover and cook on low for 8–9 hours. Remove and discard bay leaf before serving.

TEX-MEX SOUP

Tex-Mex is a hybrid, a combination of cuisines from Texas and Mexico. It uses less-authentic ingredients than traditional Mexican cuisine, and adds its own twist. You can make this soup as mild or as spicy as you like; just use different peppers or add or subtract chili powder and crushed red pepper flakes.

Serves 6

2 tablespoons olive oil

1 onion, chopped

3 cloves garlic, minced

2 jalapeño peppers, minced

1 red bell pepper, chopped

1 orange bell pepper, chopped

1 recipe Primal Meatballs (see Chapter 1), cooked

1 (14-ounce) can diced tomatoes, undrained, if desired

4 cups beef stock

1 tablespoon chili powder

1 teaspoon ground cumin

1 teaspoon dried oregano

1 teaspoon salt

⅛ teaspoon pepper

⅛ teaspoon crushed red pepper flakes

1 tablespoon honey

1. In large pot, heat olive oil over medium heat. Add onion, garlic, and jalapeño peppers; cook and stir for 5 minutes until tender.

2. Add bell peppers; cook and stir for 4 minutes longer.

3. Add meatballs, tomatoes, beef stock, chili powder, cumin, oregano, salt, pepper, red pepper flakes, and honey and bring to a simmer.

4. Reduce heat, cover, and simmer for 15 minutes. Serve immediately.

BASIC CHICKEN SOUP

A major advantage of this soup is that it will be much lower in sodium than canned chicken soups. The only limit is your imagination. Each time you make it, substitute different vegetables and seasonings to tantalize your taste buds.

Serves 6

1 (5- to 6-pound) whole chicken (including giblets)

12 cups water

2 medium carrots

2 stalks celery

4 large yellow onions

¼ bunch parsley

Kosher salt, to taste

Freshly ground black pepper, to taste

1. Clean, trim, and quarter the chicken. Peel and chop all the vegetables. Chop parsley leaves.

2. Place the chicken and giblets in a stockpot, add the water, and bring to a boil. Reduce heat to a simmer and skim off all foam.

3. Add all the vegetables and parsley, season with salt and pepper, and simmer uncovered for about 3 hours.

4. Remove the chicken and giblets from the stockpot; discard giblets. Remove the meat from the bones, discard the bones, and return the meat to the soup. Serve.

BEEF AND VEGETABLE STEW

Fresh herbs brighten this traditional hearty stew. This recipe could be prepared with a variety of seasonal herbs, so experiment for yourself!

Serves 4

2 teaspoons almond oil

1 large onion, diced

2 parsnips, diced

2 large carrots, peeled and diced

2 stalks celery, diced

3 cloves garlic, minced

1 tablespoon minced fresh tarragon

2 tablespoons minced fresh rosemary

1 pound lean beef top round roast, cut into 1" cubes

1½ cups water

1 bulb fennel, diced

1 tablespoon minced parsley

1. Heat the oil in a large skillet over medium-high heat. Sauté the onion, parsnips, carrots, celery, garlic, tarragon, rosemary, and beef for 5–10 minutes, until the ingredients begin to soften and brown. Drain off any excess fat.

2. Place the mixture in a 4-quart slow cooker. Pour in the water. Stir. Cook on low for 8–9 hours.

3. Add the fennel. Cover and cook on high for an additional ½ hour. Stir in the parsley before serving.

BOUILLABAISSE

With one bite, this slightly simplified version of the Provençal fish stew will convert anyone who is skeptical about cooking seafood in the slow cooker into a believer.

Serves 8

1 bulb fennel, sliced

2 leeks, sliced

2 large carrots, peeled and cut into coins

2 shallots, minced

5 cloves garlic, minced

2 tablespoons minced fresh basil

1 tablespoon orange zest

1 tablespoon lemon zest

1 bay leaf

1 (14.5-ounce) can diced tomatoes

2 quarts water or Fish Stock (see recipe in this chapter)

1 pound cubed hake or catfish

8 ounces medium peeled shrimp

1 pound mussels, scrubbed and rinsed

1. Place the vegetables, garlic, basil, zests, bay leaf, tomatoes, and water or stock in a 6-quart slow cooker. Stir. Cook on low for 8 hours.

2. Add the seafood. Cook on high for 20 minutes. Discard bay leaf. Stir prior to serving. Discard any mussels that do not open.

CURRIED CAULIFLOWER SOUP

Orange cauliflower is an excellent variety to use in this recipe. It has 25 percent more vitamin A than white cauliflower and lends an attractive color to the soup.

Serves 4

1 pound cauliflower florets

2½ cups water

1 medium onion, minced

2 cloves garlic, minced

3 teaspoons curry powder

¼ teaspoon cumin

1. Place all the ingredients in a 4-quart slow cooker. Stir. Cook on low for 8 hours.

2. Using an immersion blender or standard blender (in batches), blend until smooth.

CAVEMAN'S CHILI

This chili is medium on the heat-o-meter. If you are looking for five-alarm chili, add more chipotles or a chopped jalapeño or two for some kick!

Serves 8

2 tablespoons coconut oil

1 medium onion, chopped

1 stalk celery, chopped

1 green bell pepper, seeded and chopped

1 red bell pepper, seeded and chopped

1 parsnip, peeled and diced

4 cloves garlic, minced

1 pound grass-fed ground beef

2 tablespoons chopped chipotles in adobo sauce

1 tablespoon cumin

1 tablespoon dried oregano

1 tablespoon chili powder

1½ teaspoons salt

1 (28-ounce) can diced tomatoes

3 cups Brown Stock (see recipe in this chapter) or organic beef stock

1. Heat coconut oil in a large pot over medium heat.

2. Stir-fry onion, celery, peppers, parsnip, and garlic in oil for 10 minutes. Add ground beef and cook until no longer pink (about 7 minutes).

3. Stir in chipotles, cumin, oregano, chili powder, and salt. Add tomatoes and stock. Reduce heat to low and simmer, uncovered, for 45 minutes.

Sauté the Meat When Making Chili

Even though it is not necessary to brown the meat when making chili, sautéing meat before adding it to the slow cooker allows you to drain off any extra fat. Not only is it healthier to cook with less fat, your chili will be unappetizingly greasy if there is too much fat present in the meat during cooking.

NO-BEAN CHILI

For a variation, try this with lean beef sirloin instead of pork.

Serves 6

1 tablespoon avocado oil

1 pound boneless pork tenderloin, cubed

1 large onion, diced

3 poblano chilies, diced

2 cloves garlic, minced

1 teaspoon cumin

1 teaspoon dried oregano

1 cup chicken broth

1 (15-ounce) can crushed tomatoes

2 teaspoons cayenne pepper

1. In a large nonstick skillet, heat the oil over medium heat. Add the pork, onion, chilies, and garlic. Sauté 7–10 minutes, until the pork is no longer visibly pink on any side. Drain off any fats or oils and discard them.

2. Pour the pork mixture into a 4-quart slow cooker. Add the remaining ingredients. Stir.

3. Cook on low for 8–9 hours.

Using Herbs

As a general rule, 1 tablespoon minced fresh herbs equals 1 teaspoon dried herbs. Fresh herbs can be frozen for future use. Discard dried herbs after one year because they will lose flavor.

PALEO "CREAM" OF MUSHROOM SOUP

This Paleo-approved "cream" of mushroom soup is a simple and light main dish. It's also a perfect Paleo-friendly base to use when a recipe calls for canned cream soup.

Serves 4

2 tablespoons avocado oil

2 tablespoons coconut butter

1 cup finely diced fresh mushrooms

4 tablespoons arrowroot powder

2 cups full-fat coconut milk

½ teaspoon pepper

1. Heat the oil and coconut butter in a deep saucepan until sizzling. Add the diced mushrooms and cook until soft, approximately 4–5 minutes.

2. In a medium-sized bowl, whisk the arrowroot powder into the coconut milk. Slowly add to the mushrooms. Cook on medium heat for 5–10 minutes, whisking constantly, until slightly thickened.

3. Carefully pour cream soup into a greased 2½-quart slow cooker. Add pepper and any additional seasonings you would like. Cook on high for 2 hours or on low for 4 hours.

Cream Soup Variations

You can make any number of homemade cream soups with this recipe. If you would rather have cream of celery soup, use 1 cup of finely diced celery instead of the mushrooms. For a cream of chicken soup, use 1 cup finely diced chicken and 2 teaspoons of poultry seasoning.

PALEO "CREAM" OF BROCCOLI SOUP

This Paleo-approved "cream" soup serves as a light meal on its own or can be poured over a chicken or vegetable dish to enhance flavor and richness.

Serves 4

1 (12-ounce) bag frozen broccoli florets, thawed

1 small onion, diced

4 cups chicken broth

Freshly ground black pepper, to taste

1 cup full-fat coconut milk

1. Add the broccoli, onion, broth, and pepper to a 2- or 4-quart slow cooker; cover and cook on low for 4 hours.

2. Use an immersion blender to purée the soup. Stir in the coconut milk. Cover and cook on low, stirring occasionally, for 30 minutes or until the soup is heated through.

MUSHROOM AND ONION SOUP

This soup serves as an excellent opening course for a rich beef or pork dish.

Serves 6

6½ cups Mushroom Stock (see recipe in this chapter)

3 cups thinly sliced onions

2 cups sliced fresh mushrooms

1½ cups thinly sliced leeks

½ cup chopped shallots or green onions

1 teaspoon raw honey (optional)

Pepper, to taste

1. Combine all the ingredients except pepper in a 6-quart slow cooker. Cover and cook on low 6–8 hours.

2. Season with pepper to taste.

CHICKEN AND MUSHROOM STEW

This is a fragrant blend of sautéed chicken, vegetables, and herbs, best enjoyed on a late-autumn night alongside a rich poultry dish.

Serves 6

16–24 ounces boneless, skinless chicken, cut into 1" cubes, browned (in 1 tablespoon avocado oil)

8 ounces fresh mushrooms, sliced

1 medium onion, diced

3 cups diced zucchini

1 cup diced green pepper

4 garlic cloves, minced

1 tablespoon avocado oil

3 medium tomatoes, diced

1 (6-ounce) can tomato paste

¾ cup water

1 teaspoon each dried thyme, oregano, marjoram, and basil

1. Add browned chicken to a 4- or 6-quart slow cooker.

2. In a skillet over medium heat, sauté the mushrooms, onion, zucchini, green pepper, and garlic in oil for 5–10 minutes, until crisp-tender, and add to slow cooker.

3. Add the tomatoes, tomato paste, water, and seasonings to the slow cooker. Stir.

4. Cover and cook on low for 4 hours or until the vegetables are tender. Serve hot.

MEDITERRANEAN SEAFOOD SOUP

This quick and easy soup will give you a taste of the Mediterranean.

Serves 2

2 tablespoons olive oil

½ cup chopped sweet onion

2 cloves garlic, chopped

½ bulb fennel, chopped

½ cup dry white wine or chicken broth

1 cup clam juice

2 cups chopped tomatoes

6 littleneck clams, scrubbed and rinsed

6 mussels, scrubbed and rinsed

8 raw jumbo shrimp, peeled and deveined

1 teaspoon dried basil, or 5 leaves fresh basil, torn

Salt and red pepper flakes, to taste

1. Heat the oil in a large skillet over medium heat and add onion, garlic, and fennel. After 10 minutes, stir in the wine or broth and clam juice and add the tomatoes. Bring to a boil.

2. Drop clams into the boiling liquid. When clams start to open, add the mussels. When mussels start to open, add the shrimp, basil, salt, and pepper flakes. Serve when shrimp curls and turns pink.

PUMPKIN BISQUE

This simple soup is a perfect first course at a holiday meal or as a light lunch. If you aren't making your own pumpkin purée, be sure to choose canned solid-pack pumpkin, not pumpkin pie filling. The pie filling contains sugars and stabilizers.

Serves 4

2 cups puréed pumpkin

4 cups water

1 cup unsweetened coconut milk

¼ teaspoon ground nutmeg

2 cloves garlic, minced

1 large onion, minced

1. Place all ingredients in a 4-quart slow cooker. Stir. Cook on low for 8 hours.

2. Use an immersion blender (or blend the bisque in batches in a standard blender) and blend until smooth. Serve hot.

Make Your Own Pumpkin Purée

Preheat the oven to 350°F. Slice a pie pumpkin or an "eating" pumpkin into wedges and remove the seeds. Place the wedges on a baking sheet and bake until the flesh is soft, about 40 minutes. Scoop out the flesh and allow it to cool before puréeing it in a blender.

PORK AND APPLE STEW

If you prefer a tart apple taste, you can substitute Granny Smith apples for the Golden Delicious. You can also add more apples if you wish. Apples and pork were made for each other!

Serves 8

1 (3-pound) boneless pork shoulder roast

Freshly ground black pepper, to taste

1 large sweet onion, diced

2 Golden Delicious apples, peeled, cored, and diced

2 pounds carrots, peeled and roughly chopped

2 stalks celery, finely diced

2 cups chicken broth

½ cup unsweetened applesauce

1 tablespoon cooking sherry (optional)

2 tablespoons pure maple syrup (optional)

½ teaspoon dried thyme

¼ teaspoon ground allspice

¼ teaspoon dried sage

2 large sweet potatoes, peeled and quartered

1. Trim the roast of any fat; discard the fat and cut the roast into bite-sized pieces. Add the roast to a 4-quart slow cooker along with the remaining ingredients in the order given. (You want to rest the sweet potato quarters on top of the mixture in the slow cooker.)

2. Cover and cook on low for 6 hours or until the pork is cooked through and tender.

CAVEMAN'S CABBAGE SOUP

Slow-cooking cabbage soup preserves the nutrients in the cabbage and other vegetables, versus higher-temperature methods of preparation that tend to destroy many of the nutrients. Add cooked sausage slices to the pot for a well-rounded meal.

Serves 14

1 small head cabbage

2 green onions

1 red bell pepper, if desired

1 bunch celery

1 cup baby carrots

4 cups chicken broth

4 cups water

3 cloves garlic, minced

¼ teaspoon red pepper flakes

¼ teaspoon dried basil

¼ teaspoon dried oregano

¼ teaspoon dried thyme

¼ teaspoon onion powder

1. Chop all vegetables and place them in a 6-quart slow cooker.

2. Pour in the broth and water.

3. Stir in garlic and spices. Cover and cook on low for 8–10 hours.

SIMPLE TOMATO SOUP

If you eat nightshade vegetables, this simple, healthy, three-step soup is made with canned tomatoes, which are available year-round at affordable prices. You can also make this soup with about 4 pounds of chopped fresh tomatoes if you prefer.

Serves 8

1 small sweet onion, finely diced

¼ cup organic unsalted butter or Ghee (see Chapter 2)

3 (14.5-ounce) cans diced tomatoes

1 tablespoon raw honey

15 ounces chicken broth

½ teaspoon lemon juice

1. In a small glass or microwave-safe bowl, cook onions and butter in the microwave on high for 1 minute, until onions are softened.

2. Add onion mixture, tomatoes, honey, and chicken broth to a greased 4-quart slow cooker. Cook on high for 4 hours or on low for 8 hours.

3. Turn off slow cooker. Add lemon juice to the soup. Allow soup to cool for about 20 minutes and then blend using an immersion blender or in batches using a standard blender.

ACORN SQUASH AUTUMN BISQUE

The yellow-orange color of acorn squash comes from its rich vitamin A content. One cup of acorn squash provides more than 100 percent of the daily recommended amount of vitamin A.

Serves 6

2 cups chicken broth

2 medium-sized acorn squash, peeled and cubed

½ cup chopped onion

½ teaspoon cinnamon

¼ teaspoon ground coriander

¼ teaspoon cumin

½ cup unsweetened coconut milk

1 tablespoon lemon juice

Pepper, to taste

1. Combine the broth, squash, onion, cinnamon, coriander, and cumin in a 4-quart slow cooker. Cover and cook on high for 3–4 hours.

2. Blend the squash mixture, coconut milk, and lemon juice in a food processor until smooth.

3. Season with pepper to taste.

BUTTERNUT SQUASH SOUP

This soup is a scrumptious treat on a cool fall day. Warm family and friends with its delightful blend of aroma and flavor.

Serves 4

1 tablespoon almond oil

1 medium onion, chopped

1 pound butternut squash, peeled, seeded, and chopped

2 parsnips, peeled and diced

3 cloves garlic, minced

½ cup almond meal

32 ounces organic low-sodium chicken broth

½ teaspoon cinnamon

¼ teaspoon ground cloves

¼ teaspoon ground nutmeg

1. In a soup pot or Dutch oven, heat oil over medium-high heat. Sauté onion, squash, parsnips, and garlic in oil for 5 minutes.

2. Add almond meal and chicken broth and increase heat to high.

3. Bring to a boil, then turn to low and simmer for 45 minutes.

4. In batches, purée squash mixture in blender or food processor and return to pot or use an immersion blender.

5. Stir in cinnamon, cloves, and nutmeg.

PUMPKIN TURKEY CHILI

Pumpkin keeps for 6 months whole, or for years canned. Pumpkin is most often enjoyed in the fall, but it can be enjoyed year-round.

Serves 6

2 red bell peppers, chopped

1 medium-sized onion, chopped

3–4 cloves garlic, chopped

1 pound ground turkey, browned

1 (14.5-ounce) can pure pumpkin purée

1 (14.5-ounce) can diced tomatoes

½ cup water

1½ tablespoons chili powder

½ teaspoon black pepper

¼ teaspoon cumin

1. In a skillet over medium heat, sauté the peppers, onion, and garlic with the browned turkey for 5–7 minutes.

2. Transfer the turkey and veggies to a 4-quart slow cooker. Add the remaining ingredients.

3. Cover and cook on low for 5–6 hours.

CINCINNATI CHILI

This unusual regional favorite has a spicy-sweet flavor that is wonderfully addictive! Serve over cooked spaghetti squash with any combination of the following toppings: diced raw onion; chopped green, red, yellow, or orange pepper; and shredded carrots.

Serves 8

1 pound ground beef

1 (15-ounce) can crushed tomatoes, undrained

2 cloves garlic, minced

1 large onion, diced

1 teaspoon cumin

1 teaspoon cacao powder

2 teaspoons chili powder

½ teaspoon ground cloves

1 tablespoon lemon juice

1 teaspoon allspice

½ teaspoon cayenne pepper

½ teaspoon cinnamon

1. In a nonstick skillet, quickly sauté the beef over medium heat until it is no longer pink, about 5–6 minutes. Drain all fat and discard it.

2. Place beef and all the other ingredients in a 4-quart slow cooker and stir. Cook on low for 8–10 hours.

LONE STAR STATE CHILI

Texans prefer their chili without beans, which makes this a perfect Paleo meal. Serve it with a tossed salad.

Serves 8

1 stalk celery, finely chopped

1 large carrot, peeled and finely chopped

1 (3-pound) chuck roast, cubed

2 large yellow onions, diced

6 cloves garlic, minced

6 jalapeño peppers, seeded and diced

½ teaspoon freshly ground black pepper

4 tablespoons chili powder

1 teaspoon oregano

1 teaspoon cumin

1 teaspoon raw honey

1 (28-ounce) can diced tomatoes

1 cup beef broth

1. Add all of the ingredients to a 4- or 6-quart slow cooker, in the order given, and stir to combine. The liquid in your slow cooker should completely cover the meat and vegetables. If additional liquid is needed, add more diced tomatoes or broth, or some water.

2. Cover and cook on low for 8 hours. Taste for seasoning, and add more chili powder if desired.

TEXAS FIREHOUSE CHILI

This no-bean chili is similar to dishes entered into firehouse chili cook-offs all over Texas.

Serves 4

1 pound cubed lean beef

2 tablespoons onion powder

1 tablespoon garlic powder

2 tablespoons chili powder

1 tablespoon paprika

½ teaspoon oregano

½ teaspoon freshly ground black pepper

½ teaspoon white pepper

½ teaspoon cayenne pepper

½ teaspoon minced chipotle pepper

8 ounces tomato sauce

1. Brown the beef for 5–7 minutes in a nonstick skillet over medium heat. Drain off any excess grease.

2. Add the meat and all of the remaining ingredients to a 4-quart slow cooker. Cook on low for up to 10 hours.

CHICKEN CHILI VERDE

Enjoy this spicy chili over a Southwestern-themed vegetable medley. Avocado slices work well as a festive garnish.

Serves 8

½ tablespoon avocado oil

2 pounds boneless, skinless chicken breast, cubed

2 (28-ounce) cans whole peeled tomatoes, undrained

1 (4-ounce) can diced green chili peppers, undrained

1 teaspoon thyme

1 teaspoon oregano

1 teaspoon basil

1 tablespoon chili powder

2 teaspoons cumin

1 tablespoon raw honey

1 large onion, minced

3 cloves garlic, minced

½ cup water

1. Heat oil in a skillet over medium heat. Add the chicken. Cook, stirring frequently, until chicken is browned on all sides, about 1–2 minutes per side. Place browned chicken in a greased 4- or 6-quart slow cooker.

2. Add the remaining ingredients over the chicken in the slow cooker.

3. Cover and cook on high for 3 hours or on low for 6 hours.

PUMPKIN AND GINGER SOUP

Relieve some stress with a hot cup of this comforting, seasonal favorite.

Serves 6

2 pounds pumpkin, peeled, seeded, and cubed

3½ cups chicken broth

1 cup chopped onion

1 tablespoon chopped fresh ginger

1 teaspoon minced garlic

½ teaspoon ground cloves

Pepper, to taste

1. In a 4-quart slow cooker, combine all ingredients except the pepper. Cover and cook on high for 4–5 hours.

2. Place the soup in a food processor and blend until smooth.

3. Season to taste with pepper.

TOMATO VEGETABLE SOUP

The array of garden vegetables in this soup produces a light and fresh flavor with a "fall-ish" feel if you eat tomatoes.

Serves 6

1 (28-ounce) can Italian plum tomatoes, undrained

2¼ cups beef broth

1 medium onion, chopped

1 large stalk celery, sliced

1 medium carrot, sliced

1 red bell pepper, chopped

1 teaspoon lemon juice

¾ teaspoon garlic powder

Pinch red pepper flakes

Pepper, to taste

1. Combine all the ingredients except pepper in a 4- or 6-quart slow cooker. Cover and cook on high for 4–5 hours.

2. Process the soup in a blender until smooth; season to taste with pepper. Serve warm.

ZUCCHINI SOUP

This smooth and soothing blend of fresh herbs and spices is perfect for a cold, late-autumn day.

Serves 8

4 cups sliced zucchini

4 cups chicken broth

4 cloves garlic, minced

2 tablespoons lime juice

2 teaspoons curry powder

1 teaspoon dried marjoram

¼ teaspoon celery seeds

½ cup canned unsweetened coconut milk

Cayenne pepper, to taste

Pinch paprika

1. Combine the zucchini, broth, garlic, lime juice, curry powder, marjoram, and celery seeds in a 4- or 6-quart slow cooker, and cook on high for 3–4 hours.

2. Process the soup in batches with the coconut milk in a blender or food processor until combined.

3. Season to taste with cayenne pepper. Serve warm and sprinkle with paprika.

CREAM OF CAULIFLOWER SOUP

Cauliflower is a fantastic vegetable in Paleolithic diet recipes. Blended cauliflower can be used as a thickener in recipes that normally call for potatoes or root vegetables. Best of all, cauliflower won't spike your insulin levels.

Serves 4

1 large head cauliflower, chopped

3 stalks celery, chopped

1 carrot, chopped

2 cloves garlic, minced

1 onion, chopped

2 teaspoons cumin

½ teaspoon ground black pepper

1 tablespoon chopped fresh parsley

1 teaspoon chopped fresh dill, plus additional for garnish

4 slices nitrate/nitrite-free bacon, crisply cooked and crumbled

1. In a soup pot or Dutch oven, combine cauliflower, celery, carrot, garlic, onion, cumin, and pepper.

2. Add enough water to just cover ingredients in pot. Bring to a boil over high heat.

3. Reduce heat to low. Simmer about 8 minutes or until vegetables are tender.

4. Stir in parsley and dill. Garnish with bacon and additional dill before serving.

SCALLION CHIVE SOUP

Chive is a member of the onion family. Chives add a sweet, mildly oniony taste to recipes.

Serves 2

3 teaspoons almond oil

½ cup shredded zucchini

½ cup chopped shallots

1 clove garlic, minced

1 cup chopped scallions

½ cup chopped chives

2 cups no-salt-added chicken broth

½ cup water

1. Heat oil in a soup pot or Dutch oven over medium-low heat. Cook zucchini, shallots, and garlic in oil for 3–5 minutes.

2. Add scallions and chives and cook for 2 minutes more.

3. Add chicken broth and water. Increase heat to high and bring to a boil.

4. Reduce heat to low and simmer for 5 minutes.

5. In batches, purée soup in blender or food processor, or use immersion blender to blend.

CARROT-LEMON SOUP

This is a great "anytime" soup, and can be served either hot or cold.

Serves 6

3 tablespoons almond oil

2 pounds carrots, peeled and diced

2 large yellow onions, peeled and diced

2 cloves garlic, minced

6 cups Vegetable Broth (see recipe in this chapter) or low-sodium canned vegetable broth

1 teaspoon minced fresh ginger

Zest and juice of 1 lemon

Freshly ground black pepper, to taste

3 tablespoons finely chopped parsley (for garnish)

1. Heat the oil over medium heat in a large stockpot and lightly sauté the carrots, onions, and garlic for 5 minutes.

2. Add the broth and simmer for approximately 1 hour. Add the ginger, lemon zest, and lemon juice. Season with pepper.

3. Chill and serve with parsley as garnish.

Lemon Know-How

The thought of lemons may make your cheeks pucker, but they're well worth the powerful dose of cold-fighting vitamin C. The average lemon contains approximately 3 tablespoons of juice. Allow lemons to come to room temperature before squeezing to maximize the amount of juice extracted.

CHICKEN CHOWDER

A warm, traditional taste of home, this chowder makes a great first course to a hearty poultry dish on a cold winter's night.

Serves 5

1 pound boneless, skinless chicken thighs, cut into chunks

1 (14.5-ounce) can diced tomatoes

1 (8-ounce) package fresh, sliced mushrooms

1 large red onion, minced

2 parsnips, peeled and diced

4–6 cloves garlic, minced

½ cup chicken broth

½ cup dry red wine (or additional chicken broth)

1 teaspoon dried oregano

1 teaspoon dried basil

1 teaspoon ground pepper

1. Place all ingredients in a 4-quart slow cooker.

2. Cover and cook on low for 6 hours, stirring occasionally.

SPICY BISON STEW

Bison contains fewer calories, less fat, and more iron per serving than both beef and chicken!

Serves 4

2 small onions, sliced

6 large carrots, peeled and sliced

1 bell pepper, diced

3 stalks celery, diced

2 jalapeño peppers, diced

2 pounds bison meat, cut into 1" cubes

1 (28-ounce) can fire-roasted tomatoes

½ cup unsalted beef broth

Handful of fresh cilantro, chopped

1 tablespoon oregano

Pepper, to taste

1 tablespoon hot sauce

Place onions, carrots, bell pepper, celery, and jalapeño peppers in a 4- or 6-quart slow cooker. Add bison meat and all remaining ingredients. Cover and cook on low for 6–8 hours. Serve hot.

SOUTHWESTERN SOUP

This is a zesty and hearty creation with a perfect balance of herbs and seasonings.

Serves 4

1 pound pork tenderloin, cut into 1" pieces

1 cup chopped onion

1 green bell pepper, seeded and chopped

1 jalapeño pepper, seeded and minced

2 cloves garlic, minced

1 teaspoon chili powder

1 teaspoon cumin

¼ teaspoon freshly ground black pepper

5 cups chicken broth

1 (14.5-ounce) can diced tomatoes

1 cup diced avocado, for garnish

2 tablespoons chopped cilantro, for garnish

Lime wedges, for garnish

1. In the bottom of a 6-quart slow cooker, combine the pork, onion, bell pepper, jalapeño pepper, garlic, chili powder, cumin, and black pepper. Stir to combine.

2. Add broth and tomatoes. Cover and cook on low for 6–8 hours or on high for 3–4 hours.

3. When ready to serve, ladle soup into bowls and top with avocado and cilantro. Serve with lime wedges.

ROSEMARY-THYME STEW

Lots of rosemary and thyme give this surprisingly light stew a distinctive flavor.

Serves 4

1 teaspoon unsalted organic butter or Ghee (see Chapter 2)

1 large onion, diced

1 large carrot, peeled and diced

2 stalks celery, diced

2 cloves garlic, minced

3½ tablespoons minced fresh thyme

3 tablespoons minced fresh rosemary

1 pound boneless, skinless chicken breast, cut into 1" cubes

½ teaspoon freshly ground black pepper

1½ cups water or chicken broth

1 cup diced green, red, and yellow peppers

1. Heat the butter in a large skillet over medium-high heat. Sauté the onion, carrot, celery, garlic, thyme, rosemary, and chicken for 5–7 minutes, until the chicken is white on all sides. Drain off any excess fat.

2. Put sautéed ingredients into a 4-quart slow cooker. Sprinkle with black pepper. Pour in the water or broth and stir. Cook on low for 8–9 hours.

3. Add the diced peppers. Cover and cook on high for an additional ½ hour. Stir before serving.

CHICKEN BOLOGNESE

This easy-to-make chicken stew is sure to please the entire family. Both kids and adults love this delicious recipe. Serve alone or pour the sauce over spaghetti squash or riced cauliflower.

Serves 4

1 pound ground chicken

2 tablespoons bacon fat

4 boneless, skinless chicken breasts, cubed

1 (6-ounce) can tomato paste

1 (28-ounce) can no-salt-added, diced tomatoes

4 garlic cloves, chopped

4 large carrots, sliced

2 red bell peppers, diced

2 green bell peppers, diced

1 tablespoon dried thyme

1 tablespoon chili powder

1. In a medium-sized skillet, cook ground chicken over medium heat until browned, about 5 minutes. Drain and place in a 4- or 6-quart slow cooker.

2. Wipe out the pan and place it over medium-high heat; add bacon fat. Brown the chicken breasts (1–2 minutes per side). Add to slow cooker.

3. Combine all the remaining ingredients in the slow cooker. Cook on high for 5 hours.

4. Serve over your favorite steamed vegetable, such as spaghetti squash.

SIMPLE GROUND TURKEY AND VEGETABLE SOUP

This soup is easy to throw together with pantry ingredients.

Serves 6

1 tablespoon avocado oil

1 pound ground turkey

1 medium onion, diced

2 cloves garlic, minced

1 (16-ounce) package frozen mixed vegetables

4 cups chicken broth

½ teaspoon pepper

1. In a large skillet over medium heat, add oil and heat until sizzling. Cook ground turkey until browned, about 5–6 minutes, stirring to break up the meat. Add meat to a greased 4-quart slow cooker.

2. In the same skillet, sauté onion and garlic until softened, about 3–5 minutes. Add to the slow cooker.

3. Add remaining ingredients to the slow cooker. Cover and cook on high for 4 hours or on low for 8 hours.

STUFFED PEPPER SOUP

This recipe delivers all the flavor of stuffed peppers in a warm and satisfying soup.

Serves 6

1½ pounds ground beef, browned and drained

3 cups diced green bell pepper

2 cups peeled and diced butternut squash

1 (28-ounce) can diced peeled tomatoes

1 (28-ounce) can tomato sauce

¾ cup raw honey

Seasonings of choice (basil, thyme, oregano, onion flakes, etc.), to taste

1. Mix all the ingredients in a 4-quart slow cooker. Cover and cook on low for 3–4 hours or until the green peppers are cooked.

2. Turn heat to high and cook for 20–30 more minutes. Serve.

LAMB STEW

This high-protein concoction is a guaranteed Paleo palate-pleaser.

Serves 4

1½ pounds boneless lamb shoulder, fat trimmed

1 cup beef broth

6 medium carrots, cut into ¾" pieces

12 ounces turnips, cut into ¾" pieces

¾ cup chopped onion

½ tablespoon crushed garlic

¼ teaspoon thyme

¼ teaspoon rosemary, crumbled

½ teaspoon black pepper

1. Cut lamb into 1½" chunks.

2. Combine all the ingredients in a 4-quart slow cooker and cook on low for 8–10 hours.

3. Before serving, skim off and discard fat.

CHAPTER 5

GRAIN-FREE BAKED GOODS AND PASTA

PALEO CRACKERS

Crackers are a wonderful snack to have on hand; kids especially love them. But almost all types of crackers are made with wheat flour. Using two types of nut flour in this easy recipe adds lots of flavor and makes the dough easy to work with. Season these with any type of herb or spice you'd like.

Yields 36 crackers

1 cup almond flour

¾ cup hazelnut flour

¼ cup coconut oil

1 egg, beaten

½ teaspoon dried thyme leaves

½ teaspoon dried marjoram leaves

¼ teaspoon kosher salt

2 tablespoons water, if needed

½ teaspoon coarse salt

1. Combine both flours in a food processor. Add the oil and pulse until particles are fine.

2. Add the egg, herbs, and salt and pulse until dough forms. If the mixture seems dry, add water, a teaspoon at a time, and pulse until the dough forms.

3. Roll dough into 1" balls and place on baking sheet. Flatten with the bottom of a glass dipped in one of the two flours. Sprinkle with coarse salt.

4. Bake for 11–15 minutes or until crackers are firm and light golden around the edges. Cool on wire rack. Store in airtight container at room temperature.

PUMPKIN WAFFLES

You'll need a waffle iron for this recipe. You can use the basic rectangular waffle iron, or choose one that makes round or even heart-shaped waffles. Make sure you don't overfill the waffle iron, or excess batter will come oozing out the sides. It doesn't affect the waffle, but it's difficult to clean.

Serves 6

1 cup solid-pack pumpkin purée

4 eggs, beaten

3 tablespoons honey

⅓ cup coconut milk

1 teaspoon vanilla

1 cup almond flour

⅔ cup coconut flour

½ teaspoon baking powder

½ teaspoon cinnamon

Pinch salt

1. In large bowl, combine pumpkin, eggs, honey, coconut milk, and vanilla and mix well.

2. In medium bowl, combine almond flour, coconut flour, baking powder, cinnamon, and salt and mix until one color.

3. Add dry ingredients to wet ingredients and mix just until combined.

4. Heat waffle iron according to directions and brush with some coconut oil. Ladle batter onto waffle iron according to appliance directions and cook as directed. Serve warm.

BANANA HAZELNUT PANCAKES

Pancakes are a wonderful treat for breakfast during the winter or for the first day of school. Serve with warmed honey or maple syrup, or with nothing but butter. You could also serve them with hazelnut butter; just process hazelnuts until butter forms, about 5–6 minutes. Leftovers can be frozen; reheat in a toaster oven and serve warm.

Serves 4

1 cup hazelnut flour

½ cup coconut flour

¼ cup coconut sugar, if desired

½ teaspoon baking soda

2 ripe bananas, mashed

½ cup coconut milk

2 eggs

2 teaspoons vanilla

2 egg whites

Pinch salt

1 cup chopped hazelnuts

1. In large bowl, combine hazelnut flour, coconut flour, coconut sugar (if using), and baking soda.

2. In small bowl, combine bananas, coconut milk, eggs, and vanilla.

3. In another small bowl, beat egg whites with salt until stiff peaks form.

4. Stir the banana mixture into the flour mixture. Fold in the beaten egg whites.

5. Heat a griddle or skillet until a drop of water sizzles when dropped onto the surface. Grease lightly with coconut oil.

6. Drop batter by ¼ cup measures onto the hot skillet. Sprinkle each pancake with about 1 tablespoon chopped hazelnuts.

7. Cook until bubbles form on the surface and edges look dry, about 3–4 minutes. Carefully flip pancakes and cook for 2–3 minutes on second side. Serve immediately.

MIXED-SQUASH PASTA

There are several kinds of soft-skinned or summer squash that work in this recipe. Zucchini, crookneck summer squash, yellow zucchini, and eight-ball squash are some common types. They are very tender and cook quickly. Be sure you avoid the seeds in the middle when making this recipe. Either cut the seeds out before you cut the squash, or cut to the seed core and discard it. Use a sharp knife, a mandoline, or a "spiralizer" cutter to make the "pasta" strips.

Serves 4

2 yellow summer squash

1 zucchini

2 tablespoons olive oil or coconut oil

1. You can peel the squash and zucchini, but you don't have to. Cut into long slices, then cut the slices into thin strips.

2. Heat the olive oil or coconut oil in a large saucepan. Add the squash and zucchini strips and cook for 2–3 minutes, stirring frequently, until tender. Serve immediately.

NUTTY PASTA

Yes, you can have "pasta" on the Paleo diet. You just have to make your own! It's fun to make pasta; turn it into a family project. If you plan to make this recipe often, buy a pasta maker. It will roll the dough to smooth and even perfection. Fresh pasta always cooks much more quickly than the regular dried boxed pasta. Keep an eye on it every second and taste often as it cooks.

Serves 4

1 cup almond flour

⅓ cup pecan flour

⅓ cup hazelnut flour

½ cup tapioca flour

1 egg

4 egg yolks

1 teaspoon fine salt

1–2 tablespoons olive oil, if needed

1. Combine the almond flour, pecan flour, hazelnut flour, and tapioca flour in a food processor. Process for 2–3 minutes or until the flours are very finely ground. Pour into large bowl.

2. In small bowl, beat egg, egg yolks, and salt until smooth. Add to the flour mixture and start to mix. When the dough is difficult to stir with a spoon, use your hands to mix it.

3. Flour a kneading surface with more of any of the recipe flours, then knead the dough until it is smooth and satiny, adding more flour or olive oil if necessary. Divide the dough into 3 balls and wrap each tightly in plastic wrap; refrigerate for at least 4 hours. You can freeze the balls of dough; thaw overnight in the fridge. They will be slightly sticky; use a bit of flour on the work surface when rolling them.

4. One at a time, roll out each ball of dough to ⅛" thickness—or use a pasta maker, following the directions. Then slice into strips of desired width.

5. This dough should be cooked immediately after rolling. Bring a large pot of water to a boil and add 3 tablespoons of salt. Cook the pasta in two batches for about 2 minutes each, stirring frequently, or until it tastes done when you try a piece. Serve with sauce.

SWEET POTATO PASTA

Sweet potatoes can be turned into "pasta noodles" just as squash and zucchini can. The only real work with this recipe is getting the hard flesh into thin strips. You can do this by yourself with a knife, or try using a mandoline to help. Slice the potatoes into thin slices with the mandoline, then cut into pasta-like strips with your knife. Also try this with butternut squash and pumpkin.

Serves 4

2 large sweet potatoes

2 tablespoons Ghee (see Chapter 2) or olive oil

½ teaspoon salt

¼ cup chicken or vegetable broth

1. Peel sweet potatoes and slice into thin slices. Then cut into thin strips.

2. Melt Ghee in a large saucepan. Add the sweet potatoes and salt; cook and stir until almost tender, about 4 minutes.

3. Add broth and bring to a simmer; simmer for 2–3 minutes or until the "pasta" is tender. Serve immediately.

KELP NOODLES WITH ALMOND PORK SAUCE

Kelp noodles are available commercially. They are made from kelp, which is seaweed or sea vegetable, and a few other ingredients. They are gluten-free, fat-free, and low in carbs and calories. You just need to rinse them or soak them, according to package directions, then combine with a sauce and eat.

Serves 4

1¼ pounds ground pork

1 onion, chopped

3 cloves garlic, minced

1 tablespoon minced fresh gingerroot

2 tomatoes, seeded and chopped

½ teaspoon salt

⅛ teaspoon crushed red pepper flakes

½ cup chicken stock

½ cup almond milk

2 tablespoons almond butter

½ cup sliced almonds

12 ounces kelp noodles

1. In large saucepan, cook pork with onion, garlic, and gingerroot, stirring to break up meat, until pork is done. Drain.

2. Add tomatoes, salt, pepper flakes, stock, and almond milk and bring to a simmer. Simmer over medium heat until thickened, about 5–10 minutes.

3. Meanwhile, in small pan, melt almond butter over medium heat. Add sliced almonds; cook and stir until toasted.

4. Prepare kelp noodles as directed on package. Place on serving plate. Top with pork sauce and sprinkle with toasted almonds. Serve immediately.

GRAHAM CRACKER MUFFINS

Muffins are the perfect breakfast food. You can eat them as you run out the door, or have them as a side dish with scrambled eggs and bacon. This recipe uses the Graham Crackers recipe (see Chapter 13), which is made with gluten-free, legume-free flours and honey. These little muffins aren't very sweet, but they have lots of flavor.

Yields 12 muffins

1½ cups Graham Cracker (see Chapter 13) crumbs

1½ teaspoons baking powder

½ teaspoon baking soda

½ cup coconut milk

⅓ cup melted coconut oil

¼ cup honey

1 egg, beaten

½ cup chopped walnuts

1. Preheat oven to 375°F. Line 12 muffin cups with paper liners and set aside.

2. In large bowl, combine crumbs, baking powder, baking soda, coconut milk, coconut oil, honey, and egg and beat well. Mixture will be thick. Stir in walnuts.

3. Divide among prepared muffin cups.

4. Bake for 18–23 minutes or until set when touched with a finger. Cool on wire rack.

SHIRATAKI NOODLES WITH MUSHROOMS

Shirataki noodles are a Japanese product made from yams. They have almost no calories and almost no carbs. They are ready to eat right out of the package, but should be rinsed with hot water to remove a fishy odor. Their texture is best if they are dry-fried before serving. This rich mushroom sauce adds lots of flavor.

Serves 4

2 tablespoons sesame oil

1 (8-ounce) package sliced cremini mushrooms

3 cloves garlic, minced

2 tablespoons coconut aminos

1 cup chicken stock

1 tablespoon lemon juice

¼ teaspoon white pepper

4 (7-ounce) packages shirataki noodles

2 tablespoons toasted sesame seeds

1. In large saucepan, heat sesame oil over medium heat. Add mushrooms and garlic; cook and stir until mushrooms give up their liquid and the liquid evaporates, about 7 minutes.

2. Add coconut aminos, chicken stock, lemon juice, and pepper and simmer for 8 minutes.

3. Meanwhile, drain the noodles and rinse with hot water; drain again.

4. Heat another skillet over medium-high heat and add the noodles. Cook and stir until the noodles are dry.

5. Place noodles in a serving bowl and pour mushroom sauce over all. Sprinkle with sesame seeds and serve immediately.

BISCUITS

Paleo biscuits are made with non-grain flours. Because these flours do not contain gluten, we need to combine flours and starches with different characteristics to achieve a texture similar to wheat biscuits. Grain-free flours include almond, chestnut, chia, coconut, hazelnut, and sweet potato. Starches that are acceptable include arrowroot and tapioca. These biscuits are light and fluffy and delicious.

Yields 9 biscuits

1 cup almond flour

½ cup coconut flour

¼ cup hazelnut flour

3 tablespoons sweet potato flour

3 tablespoons arrowroot powder

¼ teaspoon salt

1½ teaspoons baking powder

1½ teaspoons baking soda

3 tablespoons butter, cut into pieces, or coconut oil

2 tablespoons coconut oil

⅓ cup almond milk

2 teaspoons vinegar

2 tablespoons honey

2 eggs

1. Preheat oven to 375°F. Line a baking sheet with parchment paper and set aside.

2. In large bowl, combine almond flour, coconut flour, hazelnut flour, sweet potato flour, arrowroot powder, salt, baking powder, and baking soda and mix until one color.

3. Cut in butter and coconut oil until particles are fine.

4. In small bowl, combine almond milk and vinegar; let stand for 5 minutes. Beat in honey and eggs. Add this to the flours and mix until combined. Let stand for 5 minutes.

5. Coat work surface with almond flour. Place dough on surface and sprinkle with more flour. Pat out the dough into a 9" x 9" rectangle. Cut into 9 squares and place on prepared baking sheet, 2" apart.

6. Bake for 15–19 minutes or until biscuits are light golden brown. Cool on wire rack.

KELP NOODLES PAD THAI

Kelp noodles are made with kelp, sodium alginate (which is made from brown seaweed), and water. They are a good source of iodine. They look like rice noodles: thin and transparent. Pad Thai is a Korean stir-fry dish usually made with peanuts. This version uses almonds and chicken.

Serves 4

2 tablespoons coconut oil

3 boneless, skinless chicken breasts, thinly sliced

2 shallots, minced

1 carrot, shredded

1 package kelp noodles, rinsed and drained

2 tablespoons fish sauce

2 tablespoons coconut aminos

2 tablespoons lemon juice

1 tablespoon honey

2 teaspoons minced fresh gingerroot

2 cloves garlic, minced

¼ cup chicken stock

2 eggs, beaten

1. Have all the ingredients ready before you start to cook.

2. Heat a large skillet or wok over medium heat. Add oil and chicken; cook and stir for 2 minutes.

3. Add shallots and carrot; stir-fry for another 3–4 minutes or until chicken is cooked and vegetables are crisp-tender.

4. Add the noodles, fish sauce, coconut aminos, lemon juice, honey, gingerroot, garlic, and chicken stock; cook and stir for another 3 minutes.

5. Push ingredients to the side of the skillet or wok and add eggs; quickly cook until set. Mix everything together for another 2 minutes and serve immediately.

SPAGHETTI SQUASH WITH PRIMAL MEATBALLS

If you enjoyed eating pasta, spaghetti squash should be in regular rotation on your menus. This unique squash separates into threads when cooked, and the texture does mimic wheat spaghetti. Use a fork to scrape the flesh onto a serving platter. Serve with a rich homemade tomato sauce studded with meatballs for a satisfying dinner.

Serves 6

1 large spaghetti squash

2 tablespoons olive oil

1 recipe Primal Meatballs (see Chapter 1)

3 strips bacon

1 onion, chopped

4 cloves garlic, minced

1 (14-ounce) can diced tomatoes, undrained

1 (8-ounce) can tomato sauce

3 tablespoons tomato paste

1 teaspoon dried oregano

1 teaspoon dried basil

½ teaspoon salt

⅛ teaspoon pepper

1 cup grated Parmesan cheese, if desired

1. Preheat oven to 400°F. Cut the squash in half lengthwise and scoop out the seeds. Place cut-side down on baking dish and drizzle with olive oil. Cover with foil.

2. Bake for 10 minutes, then uncover and bake for another 30–40 minutes until tender.

3. Meanwhile, prepare Primal Meatballs.

4. In large saucepan, cook bacon until crisp. Remove bacon, drain on paper towels, crumble, and set aside.

5. Cook onions and garlic in bacon fat until tender. Add tomatoes, tomato sauce, tomato paste, oregano, basil, salt, and pepper. Bring to a simmer. Simmer for 20 minutes, stirring frequently.

6. Add meatballs and bacon to tomato sauce, remove from heat, cover, and set aside.

7. Shred the spaghetti squash flesh with a fork. Place on serving platter and top with tomato and meatball mixture. Top with Parmesan cheese, if desired.

SHIRATAKI NOODLES WITH PESTO

Pesto is usually made with lots of Parmesan or Romano cheese. But you don't have to use cheese to make a satisfying pesto sauce. Most people won't even miss it, since the pine nuts have a silky quality that is a good substitute for the cheese. This recipe must be served at once while the noodles are still hot and the pesto melts into them.

Serves 4

2 cups fresh basil leaves

2 cloves garlic, minced

½ cup pine nuts, toasted

⅓ cup olive oil

1 tablespoon lemon juice

½ teaspoon salt

⅛ teaspoon pepper

12 ounces shirataki noodles

1. In food processor or with a mortar and pestle, combine basil, garlic, and pine nuts until finely chopped.

2. Add the olive oil slowly with the processor running, or while working the mortar and pestle. Season with lemon juice, salt, and pepper.

3. Drain the noodles and rinse with hot water.

4. Heat a large pan over medium-high heat. Add noodles and fry, stirring frequently, until warm and toasted.

5. Pour noodles in serving bowl and add pesto. Toss to coat and serve immediately.

ROASTED TOMATO ZUCCHINI PASTA

Roasting tomatoes concentrates their flavor and sweetness. Use Roma tomatoes for best results in this recipe. They are meatier and have less water and fewer seeds than beefsteak or other types of tomatoes. This recipe is delicious without cheese, but you can add some if you'd like for a finishing touch.

Serves 4

2 large zucchini

14 Roma tomatoes, sliced

1 onion, chopped

2 cloves garlic, sliced

3 tablespoons olive oil, divided

½ teaspoon salt

⅛ teaspoon white pepper

1 tablespoon honey

1 teaspoon dried oregano

½ teaspoon dried basil

½ teaspoon dried thyme

½ cup grated Parmesan cheese, if desired

1. Cut the zucchini into noodle-shaped strips using a sharp knife or a spiral cutter, avoiding the seed center. Set aside.

2. Preheat oven to 325°F. Place the tomatoes on a rimmed baking sheet. Sprinkle with onions, garlic, 2 tablespoons olive oil, salt, and pepper. Drizzle with honey.

3. Roast tomatoes for 1½ hours or until they start to break down and look brown around the edges.

4. In large saucepan, heat remaining 1 tablespoon olive oil. Sauté the zucchini noodles for 2–3 minutes or until tender. Add the tomatoes and all of the scrapings from the pan used to roast the tomatoes along with oregano, basil, and thyme; cook and stir for 1 minute longer. Serve immediately, topped with cheese if using.

MEATBALLS WITH SHIRATAKI NOODLES

Meatballs in sauce with spaghetti is one of the prime comfort foods in life. You can still have this on the Paleo diet if you use shirataki noodles and meatballs made in the primal style. Once again, cheese is an optional topping for this hearty recipe, which is just as good without.

Serves 4

2 cups Slow-Cooker Marinara (see Chapter 2)

1 recipe Primal Meatballs (see Chapter 1), cooked

1 package shirataki noodles

3 tablespoons chopped fresh basil leaves

½ cup grated Parmesan cheese, if desired

1. Place the marinara sauce in a saucepan. Add the meatballs and bring to a simmer.

2. Meanwhile, rinse the noodles and drain. Heat a dry pan over medium heat and cook the noodles, stirring constantly, until they are hot and dry.

3. Add the noodles to the pan with the sauce and meatballs and toss gently to coat. Sprinkle with chopped fresh basil and serve immediately, with cheese if desired.

PALEO SANDWICH BREAD

Yes, you can make bread that is reminiscent of wheat yeast bread. It's best when toasted or grilled in a sandwich. There is some controversy about whether yeast is Paleo. Nutritional yeast is used in many Paleo recipes, so if you use that, try this recipe. A combination of flours and starches will give you the best results. Because there is no gluten in this dough, it doesn't rise long before you bake it; that helps keep the air in the loaf.

Yields 1 loaf

1½ teaspoons active dry yeast

¼ cup warm water

¼ cup almond milk

1 tablespoon honey

½ cup coconut flour

¾ cup almond flour

2 tablespoons hazelnut flour

2 tablespoons arrowroot powder

1 tablespoon ground flaxseed

½ teaspoon salt

3 eggs

2 egg whites

¼ cup puréed canned pears

1 tablespoon olive oil

1. Preheat oven to 350°F. Line a baking sheet with parchment paper and set aside.

2. In small bowl, combine yeast, warm water, almond milk, and honey and mix. Let stand for 5 minutes until foamy.

3. In large bowl, combine coconut flour, almond flour, hazelnut flour, arrowroot powder, ground flaxseed, and salt and mix until the mixture is one color.

4. Add the yeast mixture, eggs, egg whites, pears, and olive oil and beat well.

5. Form into a long loaf shape on the prepared baking sheet. Let stand for 10 minutes.

6. Bake for 30–40 minutes or until the bread sounds hollow when tapped with fingers. You can briefly broil this bread for a golden brown color. Let cool on wire rack; store in airtight container at room temperature.

SOFT BREAKFAST BREAD

Just as a combination of flours will give you the best results when making a gluten-free bread, using a combination of puréed fruits and vegetables will make a more interesting final product. This bread is delicious served as-is for breakfast, or try it as a substitute for ordinary bread in your favorite French Toast recipe.

Yields 1 loaf

½ cup solid-pack pumpkin

½ cup puréed canned pears

2 eggs

½ cup honey

¼ cup maple syrup

¼ cup coconut milk

1 teaspoon vanilla

1 cup almond flour

¾ cup coconut flour

2 tablespoons arrowroot powder

½ teaspoon salt

½ teaspoon baking powder

½ teaspoon cinnamon

¼ teaspoon nutmeg

¼ teaspoon cardamom

1. Preheat oven to 350°F. Line a 9" x 5" loaf pan with parchment paper and set aside.

2. In large bowl, combine pumpkin, pears, eggs, honey, maple syrup, coconut milk, and vanilla and beat well.

3. In medium bowl, combine almond flour, coconut flour, arrowroot powder, salt, baking powder, cinnamon, nutmeg, and cardamom and mix until one color.

4. Add the dry ingredients to the pumpkin mixture and mix well. Pour into loaf pan.

5. Bake for 40–50 minutes or until a toothpick inserted in the center comes out clean. Cool in pan for 15 minutes, then remove to wire rack to cool completely.

CHAPTER 6

VEGETARIAN

CAULIFLOWER PUMPKIN RISOTTO

Risotto is the ultimate comfort food; it's rice cooked in wine and stock until creamy and velvety. But rice isn't on the Paleo diet. So substitute cauliflower "rice"! You can add some shredded or grated Parmesan cheese to this recipe just before serving if you're eating dairy products. But it's just as delicious without. If you do eat cheese on your vegetarian Paleo diet, look for kosher or vegetarian brands. They are made without rennet, which is the lining of a calf's stomach.

Serves 6

1 small sugar pumpkin

1 large head cauliflower

1 tablespoon lemon juice

2 tablespoons Ghee (see Chapter 2) or olive oil

1 leek, chopped

3 cloves garlic, minced

1¼ cups Vegetable Broth (see Chapter 4)

¼ cup coconut milk

½ cup toasted pumpkin seeds

1 tablespoon chopped fresh thyme leaves

1 teaspoon salt

⅛ teaspoon white pepper

½ cup shredded kosher or vegetarian Parmesan cheese, if desired

1. Preheat oven to 375°F. Cut pumpkin in half and scoop out seeds; save for another recipe (such as Cinnamon Pumpkin Seeds in Chapter 13). Place pumpkin halves cut-side down on baking sheet. Roast for 35–40 minutes or until tender. Scrape out the flesh and purée in food processor or push through a sieve. Set aside.

2. Shred cauliflower in a food processor or on the side of a box grater. Toss with lemon juice and set aside.

3. In large saucepan, melt Ghee or heat olive oil over medium heat. Add leek and garlic; cook and stir until tender, about 5 minutes.

4. Drain cauliflower and squeeze in a dishtowel to remove excess moisture.

5. Add the cauliflower to the saucepan and cook for 3 minutes, stirring constantly. Add ½ cup of the broth and cook until absorbed. Add another ½ cup of broth and cook until absorbed. Finally add last ¼ cup of broth and coconut milk and cook, stirring occasionally, until absorbed. This whole process should take about 8 minutes.

6. Stir in the puréed pumpkin, pumpkin seeds, thyme, salt, and pepper and heat through. Add cheese, if using, and serve.

STIR-FRIED "RICE"

Stir-frying is a great way to make a meal in a hurry. But in Paleo Land, rice is a no-no. So we use "cauliflower rice" and the result is remarkably similar to traditional stir-fried rice recipes. Coconut aminos are the soy-free Paleo substitute for soy sauce; that ingredient adds a salty and rich flavor to any dish. If you are eating eggs, use them in this dish; if not, the recipe will be just as delicious without.

Serves 4

1 head cauliflower

1 tablespoon lemon juice

3 tablespoons coconut oil, divided

2 eggs, beaten

1 onion, chopped

2 cloves garlic, minced

1 carrot, chopped

1 red bell pepper, chopped

1 jalapeño pepper, minced

2 tablespoons coconut aminos

½ cup vegetable broth

1 teaspoon toasted sesame oil

½ teaspoon salt

⅛ teaspoon pepper

1. Grate cauliflower in food processor or on box grater, sprinkle with lemon juice, and set aside.

2. In large skillet or wok, heat 1 tablespoon coconut oil over medium-high heat. Add eggs and cook until eggs are done; remove and set aside.

3. Add remaining coconut oil to skillet, then add onion, garlic, and carrot; stir-fry until crisp-tender, about 5–6 minutes. Add red bell pepper and jalapeño pepper and stir-fry for another 2 minutes.

4. Drain cauliflower and add to the skillet. Stir-fry for 6–8 minutes, until cauliflower is tender.

5. Add coconut aminos, broth, sesame oil, salt, and pepper to skillet along with egg. Stir-fry until hot, then serve immediately.

COTTAGE CHEESE SALAD

Cottage cheese has all the protein you need, in just the right combination. You can serve this crunchy and fresh salad any time of the day or night. Cottage cheese is made in either small-curd or large-curd varieties; use your favorite in this recipe. This salad can be made ahead of time and stored in the fridge. Then when you're hungry, pull it out and dig in.

Serves 4

1 (16-ounce) container small-curd cottage cheese

¼ cup Wilma's Mayonnaise (see Chapter 2)

1 cup grape tomatoes

1 red bell pepper, chopped

1 yellow bell pepper, chopped

2 hard-cooked eggs, peeled and chopped

1 tablespoon fresh thyme leaves

½ teaspoon salt

⅛ teaspoon pepper

½ cup sunflower seeds

1. Briefly drain cottage cheese in a sieve and place in medium bowl. Add mayonnaise and stir well.

2. Fold in tomatoes, red bell pepper, yellow bell pepper, hard-cooked eggs, thyme, salt, and pepper. Cover and refrigerate up to 3 days.

3. When ready to eat, sprinkle with sunflower seeds.

SWEET POTATO HASH

This is a delicious recipe and very satisfying. Sweet potatoes have a wonderful texture and nutty taste. Serve along with a simple soup for a tasty meal.

Serves 4

2 sweet potatoes

2 tablespoons olive oil

1 tablespoon coconut oil

1 onion, chopped

3 cloves garlic, minced

1 teaspoon salt

1 teaspoon dried thyme leaves

⅛ teaspoon crushed red pepper flakes

½ cup sliced toasted almonds

¼ cup toasted sesame seeds

1. Peel and chop the sweet potatoes into bite-sized pieces. Place in a large pot and cover with water. Bring to a boil over high heat. Reduce heat to low and simmer until tender, about 10 to 15 minutes. Drain well and place on paper towels to drain.

2. In large skillet heat olive oil and coconut oil over medium-high heat. Add onion and garlic; cook and stir until tender, about 6 minutes.

3. Add the sweet potatoes to the skillet. Cook, stirring frequently, until the potatoes are crusty, about 5–8 minutes. Sprinkle with salt, thyme, red pepper flakes, almonds, and sesame seeds and serve.

It's pretty difficult to be vegetarian on the Paleo diet, so eggs and kosher or vegetarian cheese are featured heavily in most of these types of recipes. But if you don't eat eggs or dairy, you need some combination of foods to create the protein your body needs. That means eating nuts and seeds along with vegetables. Healthy nuts include pecans, walnuts, pistachios, pine nuts, almonds, hazelnuts, and macadamia nuts. Good seeds include sesame, pumpkin, sunflower, and flax. Peanuts are legumes and are not on the Paleo diet.

VEGGIE FRITTATA

A frittata is just a sturdy omelet. It is easier to make than an omelet and can be served hot, warm, or cold. It's ideal for the Paleo vegetarian diet if you're eating eggs; eggs contain 100 percent of the protein your body needs in a perfect balance. This recipe is filled with lots of veggies to add color and flavor.

Serves 4

2 tablespoons olive oil

1 onion, chopped

3 cloves garlic, minced

1 cup chopped mushrooms

2 cups chopped kale

1 cup chopped tomatoes, if desired

10 eggs, beaten

½ cup almond milk

½ teaspoon salt

¼ teaspoon pepper

1 cup crumbled vegetarian goat cheese, if desired

1. Preheat oven to 375°F. In large ovenproof skillet, heat olive oil over medium heat. Add onion and garlic; cook and stir until crisp-tender, about 4 minutes.

2. Add mushrooms to skillet; cook and stir until mushrooms give up their liquid and the liquid evaporates, about 6 minutes.

3. Add kale and tomatoes to skillet and cook for 3 minutes longer.

4. Beat eggs with almond milk, salt, and pepper in large bowl. Pour over vegetables in skillet and cook without stirring for 5 minutes, shaking pan occasionally.

5. Top with cheese, if using, and then bake frittata for 15–20 minutes or until puffed and golden brown. Serve immediately.

EGG SALAD IN TOMATO CUPS

This retro recipe used to be served at ladies' luncheons in the 1950s. Egg and tomato is a good combination, so if you eat eggs, you will love this recipe. The pesto is a more modern addition and adds nice flavor to this classic recipe. Serve with some sliced fresh fruit for a healthy lunch.

Serves 4

6 large eggs

4 large beefsteak tomatoes

¼ cup Wilma's Mayonnaise (see Chapter 2)

3 tablespoons Pumpkin Seed Pesto (see this chapter)

2 green onions, thinly sliced

½ teaspoon salt

⅛ teaspoon white pepper

1. Place eggs in cold water and bring to a boil over high heat. Let boil for 1 minute, then remove pan from heat, cover, and let stand for 11 minutes. Immediately drain eggs, place pan in sink, and add cold water and ice cubes. Let stand for 5 minutes.

2. Crack eggs under the water and carefully peel. Chop eggs and place in medium bowl.

3. Cut the tops from the tomatoes and carefully hollow out, discarding seeds and membranes. Place tomatoes upside down on paper towel to drain.

4. Add mayonnaise, pesto, and green onions to eggs and mix. Season with salt and pepper. Spoon into tomato cups and serve immediately.

CHEESE FONDUE

Fondue is a communal eating experience. Everyone has his or her own long fork, and dips bite-sized pieces of food into melted cheese. The usual dipper is cubes of French bread, but other great dippers include Primal Meatballs (see Chapter 1), avocado slices, apple slices, and cooked pork sausage.

Serves 4

3 tablespoons butter

1 shallot, finely minced

2 cloves garlic, minced

3 tablespoons almond flour

1 cup almond milk

½ cup vegetable broth

1 tablespoon lemon juice

3½ cups grated vegetarian or kosher Swiss cheese

½ teaspoon salt

⅛ teaspoon pepper

1. Have an electric fondue pot or a fondue pot with Sterno ready.

2. In large saucepan, melt butter over medium heat. Add shallot and garlic; cook and stir for 2 minutes until fragrant.

3. Add almond flour and stir, then stir in almond milk and broth; cook and stir until mixture thickens. Stir in lemon juice.

4. Add the cheese, a handful at a time, stirring until cheese melts and mixture is smooth. Season with salt and pepper and pour into fondue pot. Serve immediately.

CRUSTLESS QUICHE

A quiche doesn't have to have a crust! The egg and cheese mixture is just as delicious without a typical flour crust. Some ground almonds or walnuts are a good substitute for a wheat crust; just grease the pan and coat with the nuts. This quiche recipe can be made with almost any cooked vegetable.

Serves 6

1 tablespoon unsalted butter

½ cup ground almonds or walnuts

2 tablespoons olive oil

1 onion, chopped

2 cloves garlic, minced

1 cup chopped mushrooms

1 red bell pepper, chopped

6 eggs, beaten

½ cup almond milk

½ teaspoon salt

⅛ teaspoon pepper

1 teaspoon dried thyme leaves

2 cups shredded vegetarian or kosher Cheddar cheese

½ cup grated vegetarian or kosher Parmesan cheese

1. Preheat oven to 350°F. Grease a 9" pie plate with unsalted butter and sprinkle evenly with ground almonds or walnuts; set aside.

2. In medium skillet, heat olive oil over medium heat. Add onion and garlic; cook and stir for 2 minutes. Add mushrooms and red bell pepper; cook and stir until mushrooms give up their liquid and the liquid evaporates, about 7 minutes longer.

3. In large bowl, combine eggs and almond milk and beat well. Stir in salt, pepper, and thyme.

4. Layer cheeses and cooked vegetables in prepared pie plate. Slowly pour in egg mixture. Bake for 45–55 minutes or until quiche is puffed and golden brown. Let stand 5 minutes, then slice to serve.

MIXED-SQUASH GNOCCHI

Gnocchi is a type of Italian pasta that is shaped into small rounds. They are made from semolina and wheat flour, along with egg, and sometimes with potato or other starchy vegetables. This recipe is made with pumpkin from a can and sweet potato flour. Be sure to buy solid-pack pumpkin, not pumpkin purée with added sugar. Serve the gnocchi with a drizzle of butter in which you have sautéed some fresh herbs. It can also be served with a heartier Slow-Cooker Marinara (see Chapter 2).

Serves 4

1 cup solid-pack pumpkin

1 cup almond flour

½ cup sweet potato flour

1 tablespoon ground flaxseed

1 egg

½ teaspoon salt

⅛ teaspoon nutmeg

½ cup butter or coconut oil

3 tablespoons chopped fresh herbs

1. Combine pumpkin, almond flour, sweet potato flour, flaxseed, egg, salt, and nutmeg in a large bowl and mix well. You may need to add more pumpkin or one of the flours to form a firm dough.

2. Form into two balls and wrap in plastic wrap. Refrigerate overnight.

3. When ready to eat, roll each ball of dough into a long rope. Cut into 1" lengths. If you like, you can press a fork into each gnocchi to make the classic indentations.

4. Bring a large pot of water to a boil; add 2 tablespoons salt. Add half of the gnocchi and cook until they float; remove with skimmer to bowl. Repeat with second half of dough.

5. Serve with melted butter or coconut oil in which you have sautéed herbs such as thyme, sage, or basil.

YELLOW RICE

This recipe is usually made with long-grain white rice cooked with onions, garlic, bell peppers, and tomatoes. Substitute cauliflower rice for the regular long-grain rice; most people won't even be able to tell the difference. Olives make a nice addition to this simple meal and add another layer of flavor. And saffron turns the dish a beautiful golden yellow color.

Serves 4

1 head cauliflower

2 tablespoons lemon juice, divided

¼ teaspoon saffron threads

2 tablespoons olive or coconut oil

1 red onion, chopped

4 cloves garlic, minced

1 green bell pepper, chopped

3 tablespoons water

1 teaspoon dried oregano

½ teaspoon salt

½ teaspoon ground cumin

¼ teaspoon black pepper

1 cup chopped seeded tomatoes, if desired

½ cup sliced green olives

¼ cup chopped flat-leaf parsley

1. Grate cauliflower on a box grater or in a food processor. Sprinkle with 1 tablespoon lemon juice and set aside.

2. In small bowl, combine remaining 1 tablespoon lemon juice and saffron; set aside.

3. In large skillet, heat olive or coconut oil over medium heat. Add onion and garlic; cook and stir for 5 minutes. Add bell pepper; cook and stir for 2 minutes longer.

4. Add cauliflower and water and cook for 5–6 minutes until cauliflower is almost tender. Add saffron in lemon juice, oregano, salt, cumin, pepper, tomatoes, and olives and simmer for another 3 minutes. Garnish with parsley and serve immediately.

STUFFED ARTICHOKES

Artichokes are a great choice for a vegetarian meal. They are high in vitamin C and potassium, as well as fiber and inulin, which is a prebiotic fiber that helps improve digestive health. Plus they are delicious! Choose large globe artichokes for the recipe. To eat, pull off each leaf and scrape the end between your teeth. When all the leaves are gone, eat the filling, then cut the artichoke heart into pieces and enjoy.

Serves 4

4 large globe artichokes

2 tablespoons lemon juice

2 tablespoons coconut oil

1½ cups chopped mushrooms

2 shallots, minced

2 cloves garlic, minced

1 large tomato, seeded and chopped

½ teaspoon dried marjoram leaves

½ teaspoon salt

⅛ teaspoon pepper

½ cup ground almonds

½ cup water

1. Cut the stems off the artichokes so they will stand upright. Slice off the top third of each artichoke using a sharp knife. Pull off the tough, discolored outer leaves. Cut off the sharp tips of the remaining leaves. Pull the leaves apart and scrape out the thistly choke. Place each artichoke in a bowl with 6 cups water and the lemon juice before starting work on another.

2. Preheat oven to 400°F. For filling, heat coconut oil in large skillet. Add mushrooms, shallots, and garlic and cook and stir until mushrooms give up their liquid, the liquid evaporates, and they start to brown.

3. Stir in tomato, marjoram, salt, and pepper and simmer for 5 minutes. Let cool for 15 minutes.

4. Remove artichokes from lemon water and drain well. Place stem-side down on work surface.

5. Stuff each artichoke with about ½ cup of the stuffing, getting it in the center and in between the leaves. Place artichokes in a glass baking dish. Sprinkle with ground almonds. Pour ½ cup water around artichokes.

6. Bake, covered, for about 50 minutes. Check to see if the artichokes are tender; a sharp knife should easily slide into the base. Uncover and bake for another 5–10 minutes or until the almonds start to brown. Serve immediately.

EGGPLANT STEAKS

Eggplant has a very meaty taste and texture when grilled. This unusual vegetable has to be salted before it is cooked or it will release too much moisture and will steam instead of grilling. Topped with a sauce made from butter and sun-dried tomatoes, this vegetarian meal is very appealing.

Serves 4

2 large eggplants

1 tablespoon salt

1 cup hot water

6 sun-dried tomatoes (not packed in oil)

¼ cup butter or olive oil

⅓ cup ground almonds

1 tablespoon lemon juice

2 teaspoons fresh thyme leaves

Pinch salt

⅛ teaspoon white pepper

3 tablespoons olive oil

1. Slice the ends from the eggplants and peel. Slice into ¾" thick slices. Place on a baking sheet and sprinkle with 1 tablespoon salt. Let stand for 1 hour.

2. Rinse the eggplant thoroughly under cool running water. Place between kitchen towels and press down to remove moisture.

3. Combine hot water and sun-dried tomatoes in small bowl; let stand for 15 minutes to rehydrate. Remove tomatoes from water and coarsely chop.

4. In food processor or blender, combine butter or olive oil, tomatoes, almonds, lemon juice, thyme, pinch salt, and pepper. Blend until combined.

5. Prepare and preheat grill. Brush eggplant with olive oil and place on grill rack over medium coals. Grill for 6–8 minutes, turning once, until eggplant slices are tender with nice grill marks. Top each with a spoonful of the tomato mixture and serve immediately.

MUSHROOMS AND GREENS

There are many types of exotic mushrooms available in the market that we couldn't find even 10 years ago. Take some time to browse through the selection and try some mushrooms you haven't tried before. This hearty recipe can be topped with a fried or poached egg if you'd like for more protein.

Serves 4

1 cup sliced cremini mushrooms

1 cup chanterelle or oyster mushrooms, sliced

1 cup sliced shiitake mushrooms

3 tablespoons olive oil

1 tablespoon Ghee (see Chapter 2) or avocado oil

2 shallots, minced

2 cloves garlic, minced

2 cups chopped kale

1 cup chopped Swiss chard

¼ cup water

1 cup baby spinach leaves

2 tablespoons lemon juice

½ teaspoon salt

⅛ teaspoon pepper

1. Trim stems of cremini and chanterelle mushrooms and slice. Remove the stems of the shiitake mushrooms and discard; slice the caps.

2. In large skillet, heat olive oil and Ghee or avocado oil over medium heat. Add shallots and garlic; cook and stir for 2 minutes.

3. Add all of the mushrooms; cook and stir until mushrooms give up their liquid, the liquid evaporates, and they start to brown, about 8–10 minutes.

4. Add the kale and Swiss chard and water; cover and steam for 2 minutes. Remove cover, add spinach, lemon juice, salt, and pepper. Stir, cover, and steam for another 2–4 minutes or until greens are tender. Stir and serve immediately.

SCRAMBLED EGGS IN AVOCADO

Avocados usually aren't heated because they can turn bitter, but the brief heating time in this easy recipe really melds the fruit and eggs together in a luscious way. This wonderful breakfast or dinner recipe is elegant and indulgent and healthy too. Serve with some orange juice and a Berry Smoothie (see Chapter 13).

Serves 4

2 large avocados, cut in half

1 tablespoon lemon juice

2 tablespoons olive oil

6 eggs

¼ cup almond milk

½ teaspoon salt

⅛ teaspoon white pepper

1. Remove the stone from the avocados. Gently scoop out some of the avocado flesh, leaving about ¼" on all sides, and dice. Sprinkle the diced pieces with half of the lemon juice and brush the avocado halves with remaining lemon juice. Set aside.

2. Heat olive oil in large saucepan. Meanwhile, beat eggs with almond milk, salt, and pepper.

3. Pour eggs into pan and cook, stirring occasionally with a spatula, until the eggs are almost set but still moist. Fold in the diced avocado and heat for another minute.

4. Pile the egg mixture into the avocado shells and serve immediately.

MUSHROOM AND BEAN SALAD

Mushrooms are delicious and so good for you. They are high in vitamin D—which is surprising since they're grown in the dark—and a good source of the B vitamin complex. More unusual types include beautiful fan-shaped chanterelles, brown and meaty cremini, earthy morels, rich Portobello, tender oyster, beautiful hen of the woods, and delicate enoki. Choose a variety for this delicious salad.

Serves 4–6

¼ cup olive oil

3 tablespoons lemon juice

2 tablespoons Dijon mustard

1 tablespoon horseradish

½ teaspoon salt

⅛ teaspoon pepper

1 tablespoon chopped fresh dill

1 cup sliced cremini mushrooms

1 cup sliced chanterelle mushrooms

1 cup sliced button mushrooms

1 cup sliced oyster mushrooms

2 cups green beans

2 cups wax beans

6 cups mixed salad greens, if desired

1. In large salad bowl, combine olive oil, lemon juice, mustard, horseradish, salt, pepper, and dill and beat until combined. Add all of the mushrooms and toss to coat.

2. Trim and top the green beans and wax beans. Steam over simmering water until tender, about 7--8 minutes. Drain well.

3. Add beans to mushroom mixture and toss to coat. Serve on mixed salad greens, if desired.

SWEET POTATO PASTA WITH PUMPKIN SEED PESTO

Tender "pasta" made with sweet potatoes is combined with a nutty and crunchy pesto made with pumpkin seeds, basil, and parsley in this delicious recipe. It's colorful and very good for you. You could combine the pesto with any of the other "pasta" recipes in the Grain-Free Baked Goods and Pasta chapter in this book.

Serves 4

1 recipe Sweet Potato Pasta (see Chapter 5)

1 cup pumpkin seeds

1 cup fresh basil leaves

⅓ cup flat-leaf parsley

¼ cup pine nuts

2 cloves garlic, minced

3 tablespoons lemon juice

½ teaspoon salt

⅛ teaspoon pepper

5 tablespoons extra-virgin olive oil

5 tablespoons water, divided

2 tablespoons olive oil

1. Prepare the Sweet Potato Pasta strips, cover, and set aside.

2. In blender or food processor, combine pumpkin seeds, basil, parsley, pine nuts, and garlic. Blend or process until finely chopped.

3. With motor running, add lemon juice, salt, pepper, and olive oil to the blender or food processor. Process until a paste forms. Add up to 2 tablespoons water if needed to reach desired consistency. Place the pesto in a large serving bowl.

4. Heat olive oil in a large skillet over medium heat. Add sweet potato strips; cook and stir until almost tender, about 4 minutes.

5. Add 3 tablespoons water and bring to a simmer. Simmer for 2–3 minutes or until the "pasta" is tender. Immediately pour over the pesto in the serving bowl and gently toss to coat. Serve immediately.

RATATOUILLE

Ratatouille is simply a rich and hearty vegetable stew. You can use any of your favorite veggies in this easy recipe. The colors, flavors, and textures in this dish really highlight produce, whether you're making it in the summer or winter. This recipe does use the nightshade veggies of bell peppers, tomato, and eggplant. You could substitute yellow squash and more mushrooms if you are avoiding those ingredients. Serve with a glass of white wine and some toasted Paleo Sandwich Bread (see Chapter 5).

Serves 4

3 tablespoons olive oil

1 onion, chopped

4 cloves garlic, minced

1 eggplant, peeled and cubed

1 red bell pepper, chopped

1 cup sliced cremini mushrooms

1 cup chopped zucchini

1 cup chopped and seeded tomatoes

½ teaspoon salt

⅛ teaspoon pepper

⅓ cup chopped fresh basil

2 tablespoons chopped fresh parsley

1. Heat olive oil in large skillet over medium heat. Add onion and garlic; cook and stir for 3 minutes. Add eggplant; cook and stir for 5–6 minutes or until eggplant is almost soft.

2. Add bell pepper, mushrooms, and zucchini. Cook and stir for another 2–3 minutes. Add tomatoes, salt, and pepper and bring to a simmer.

3. Simmer for 7–9 minutes or until everything is blended. Sprinkle with basil and parsley and serve immediately.

LOADED BROCCOLI SALAD

This salad really is a meal in one. The vegetables, nuts, and seeds combine to provide your body with the complete protein you need. And it's delicious, flavorful, and full of color and texture. If you'd like, add some sliced fresh fruit to serve on the side. With a nice glass of wine, dinner is complete.

Serves 4

1 head broccoli

1 pound green beans

1 (8-ounce) package mushrooms, sliced

1 red bell pepper, chopped, if desired

1 cup chopped walnuts

½ cup sunflower seeds

¼ cup sliced green onions

½ cup sliced black olives

⅓ cup olive oil

¼ cup lemon juice

3 tablespoons grainy mustard

½ teaspoon salt

⅛ teaspoon pepper

½ cup chopped fresh parsley

2 tablespoons chopped fresh dill

1. Remove florets from broccoli. Peel broccoli stems and slice into ½" rounds.

2. Top and tail beans and cut in half.

3. Bring a large pot of water to a boil. Add broccoli stems; cook for 2 minutes. Add florets and cook for 2–3 minutes more or until tender. Remove with a large strainer and plunge into ice water.

4. Cook the beans in the boiling water until crisp-tender, about 4–5 minutes. Remove and plunge into ice water.

5. Drain vegetables well and place in large serving bowl. Add mushrooms, bell pepper, walnuts, sunflower seeds, green onions, and olives and toss.

6. In small bowl, combine olive oil, lemon juice, mustard, salt, and pepper and mix. Pour over salad and toss to coat. Top with parsley and dill and serve.

BEET AND CAULIFLOWER SALAD

This beautiful salad has such gorgeous colors, it's like a painting! And it's very good for you. Beets are a great source of antioxidants that help reduce the risk of cancer. They are also a great source of folate, magnesium, and potassium. Just remember to wear gloves when you work with beets, or your hands will be stained red for days!

Serves 4

4 large beets

½ cup water

1 head cauliflower

¼ cup extra-virgin olive oil

1 shallot, minced

2 tablespoons red wine vinegar

2 tablespoons coconut milk

1 tablespoon honey

½ teaspoon salt

⅛ teaspoon pepper

6 cups mixed salad greens

½ cup toasted pumpkin or sunflower seeds

½ cup sliced fresh basil leaves

1. Preheat oven to 375°F. Place beets in a baking dish. Add water, cover tightly, and bake for about 65–75 minutes or until a knife slides easily into a beet. Remove from pan and let cool on wire rack.

2. When beets are cool, peel them and cut into ½" cubes. Set aside.

3. Break the cauliflower into florets and set aside.

4. In salad bowl, combine olive oil, shallot, red wine vinegar, coconut milk, honey, salt, and pepper and mix well. Add greens and toss to coat.

5. Add beets and toss to coat.

6. Top with cauliflower florets, seeds, and basil and serve immediately.

CHAPTER 7

BREAKFAST FOR DINNER

STEAK AND EGG ROLL-UPS

Breakfast is the most important meal of the day, and on the Paleo diet, protein is the most important nutrient at breakfast. But bacon and eggs for every meal, no matter how delicious, gets boring. This recipe is variable and reliable. Fill the egg rounds with cooked chicken, sliced roast beef, or shrimp. Leftover vegetables from dinner the night before are a great choice too. Enjoy every bite.

Serves 6

¼ cup butter or olive oil, divided

⅓ cup finely chopped onion

8 eggs

¼ teaspoon salt

⅛ teaspoon pepper

1 cup sliced mushrooms

3 cloves garlic, minced

½ pound asparagus, cut into 1" pieces

1 leftover grilled steak, diced

½ cup heavy cream or coconut cream

1 cup shredded Cheddar or Gruyère cheese, if desired

1 teaspoon lemon juice

1. In 7" skillet over medium heat, melt 2 tablespoons butter or heat olive oil. Add onion; cook and stir until tender, about 5 minutes. Set aside.

2. In medium bowl, beat eggs with salt and pepper. Stir in the onions. Place same skillet over medium heat. Add ¼ cup of the egg mixture and tilt skillet to coat bottom. Cook, shaking pan occasionally, until egg mixture is set. Remove to a plate. Repeat with remaining egg mixture to make 6 rounds. Cover to keep warm and set aside.

3. In medium saucepan, heat remaining 2 tablespoons butter or olive oil over medium-high heat. Add mushrooms and garlic; cook and stir until mushrooms start to give up their liquid, about 4 minutes. Add asparagus; cook and stir until vegetables are tender and liquid evaporates, about 4–5 minutes longer.

4. Stir steak into mushroom mixture along with cream; bring to a simmer. Add cheese, if using, and lemon juice, remove from heat, and stir until cheese melts.

5. Fill each of the egg rounds with about ⅓ cup of the steak mixture and roll up. Serve immediately, or cover and chill in fridge for 1–2 days. Reheat in oven or microwave if desired before serving.

VEGGIE BACON OMELET

Omelets, those light and ethereal creations, must be served as soon as they are cooked. Once you get the hang of making one, they are very simple. Remember that you can add just about any type of meat or any vegetable to this basic recipe. Use sliced mushrooms and green beans instead of the red pepper and broccoli. Leftover cooked salmon or steak is another great addition. And use your favorite cheese, or none at all.

Serves 4

8 slices bacon

1 onion, finely chopped

2 cloves garlic, minced

1 red bell pepper, chopped

1 cup broccoli florets

9 eggs

¼ cup heavy cream or coconut cream

½ teaspoon salt

⅛ teaspoon pepper

1 teaspoon dried thyme leaves

2 tablespoons butter or olive oil

1½ cups shredded sharp Cheddar cheese, if desired

1. In medium skillet, cook the bacon until crisp, about 8 minutes. Remove bacon, drain on paper towels, crumble, and set aside. Remove all but 2 tablespoons drippings from skillet.

2. Add onion and garlic to drippings in skillet; cook and stir until crisp-tender, about 3–4 minutes. Add red bell pepper and broccoli; cook and stir until crisp-tender, about 3–4 minutes. Remove vegetables from skillet and set aside.

3. In large bowl, beat eggs with cream, salt, pepper, and thyme. Melt butter in same skillet. Add egg mixture and cook without stirring for 2 minutes or until eggs begin to set.

4. Lift the edges of the eggs with a spatula and let the uncooked part of the eggs flow underneath to cook. Cook for 3–4 minutes longer, shaking pan occasionally, until eggs are set but still moist.

5. Sprinkle cheese, if using, over egg and add vegetable mixture. Gently fold one half of the omelet over filling and cover pan. Cook for 1–2 minutes longer until cheese melts and omelet is hot. Cut into wedges to serve.

TEX-MEX OVEN FRITTATA

Making a frittata in the oven is a super-simple way to prepare this delicious recipe. And it's also an easy way to make eggs for a crowd. This spicy omelet will jump-start your day. You can make it spicier by adding more jalapeño and chili powder, or reduce those ingredients for a milder dish. Another way to reduce the heat is to remove the seeds and ribs from the jalapeño; they contain the most capsaicin, the chemical that makes the peppers spicy.

Serves 8

1 pound spicy pork sausage

2 tablespoons butter or olive oil

1 onion, chopped

3 cloves garlic, minced

1 jalapeño pepper, minced

1 red bell pepper, chopped

12 eggs

¾ cup heavy cream or coconut cream

2–3 teaspoons chili powder

½ teaspoon cumin

1 teaspoon salt

⅛ teaspoon pepper

⅛ teaspoon crushed red pepper flakes

1½ cups shredded pepper jack cheese, if desired

¼ cup grated Parmesan cheese, if desired

2 avocados, peeled and sliced

1 cup tomato salsa

1. Preheat oven to 350°F. Grease a 13" x 9" pan with unsalted butter and set aside.

2. In large skillet, cook sausage until browned and thoroughly cooked, about 8 minutes, stirring to break up meat. Remove sausage from skillet. Drain all but 1 tablespoon drippings from skillet.

3. Add butter to skillet. Add onion, garlic, and jalapeño pepper; cook and stir for 4–5 minutes until crisp-tender. Add red bell pepper; cook and stir until tender.

4. In large bowl, beat eggs with cream, chili powder, cumin, salt, pepper, and crushed red pepper flakes.

5. Place pork mixture and vegetables in the prepared pan. Pour egg mixture over all. Sprinkle with pepper jack and Parmesan cheeses, if using.

6. Bake for 35–45 minutes or until frittata is puffed and golden brown. Serve with sliced avocados and salsa.

TURKEY PEAR SAUSAGES

Homemade sausages are fun. You can vary this recipe in so many ways! Use ground salmon, turkey, or chicken. Flavor your sausages with herbs and spices. You can form your homemade sausages into patties, or mix up a batch and cook and use it as you would ground beef. You can store cooked sausages in the fridge or freezer. A quick blast in the microwave oven or a slower warm-up in the toaster oven will heat the sausage so it's juicy and tender.

Serves 16

¼ cup butter or olive oil, divided

1 onion, finely chopped

4 cloves garlic, minced

1 pear, peeled and diced

1 tablespoon lemon juice

1 tablespoon Dijon mustard

1 teaspoon salt

¼ teaspoon white pepper

⅛ teaspoon crushed red pepper flakes

2 tablespoons chopped fresh thyme leaves

2 teaspoons chopped fresh marjoram leaves

2 pounds ground turkey, white and dark meat

1. In small skillet, melt 2 tablespoons butter or heat olive oil over medium heat. Add onion and garlic; cook and stir until crisp-tender, about 4 minutes. Add pear and cook 2–4 minutes longer, until liquid evaporates. Remove to large bowl and cool for 10 minutes.

2. Add lemon juice, mustard, salt, white pepper, red pepper flakes, thyme, and marjoram to the onion mixture and stir. Crumble ground turkey into the bowl and mix gently but thoroughly until combined.

3. Cover mixture and chill in the fridge for 1 hour. Then form the mixture into 16 patties, each about ½" thick.

4. Melt remaining 2 tablespoons butter or olive oil in large skillet. Cook sausage patties in two batches until browned, turning once, until a meat thermometer registers 165°F, about 8–11 minutes.

5. Serve patties immediately, or cover and refrigerate up to 2 days. Reheat in microwave or toaster oven. Patties can be frozen up to 2 months. To use, thaw in the refrigerator overnight and then reheat in microwave or toaster oven.

CRUNCHY APPLE NUT MUFFINS

There are certain flours you can use even on the Paleo diet to make muffins and pancakes. These flours are high in protein and are delicious. A combination of gluten-free flours works best, as each one has a different amount of protein and starch to build the structure. Coconut flour is slightly sweet, but doesn't have a strong coconut taste. Hazelnut flour adds a rich flavor. And almond flour is slightly sweet and nutty tasting. Experiment to find the combination you like best.

Serves 12

1½ cups almond flour

½ cup coconut flour

¼ cup hazelnut flour

½ teaspoon baking soda

½ teaspoon baking powder

⅛ teaspoon salt

1 teaspoon cinnamon

½ cup coconut milk

¼ cup organic unsweetened applesauce

3 eggs, beaten

2 teaspoons vanilla

2 tablespoons coconut oil, melted

1 large apple, peeled and finely chopped

½ cup chopped toasted hazelnuts

½ cup slivered toasted almonds

1. Preheat oven to 350°F. Grease 12 muffin cups with unsalted butter or line with paper liners.

2. In large bowl, combine almond flour, coconut flour, hazelnut flour, baking soda, baking powder, salt, and cinnamon. Mix well until the flours are one color to ensure they are well combined.

3. In medium bowl, combine coconut milk, applesauce, eggs, vanilla, coconut oil, and apple and mix well.

4. Stir egg mixture into the flour mixture all at once and stir until combined. Add chopped hazelnuts and almonds. Spoon into prepared muffin cups.

5. Bake for 18–22 minutes or until muffins spring back when lightly touched and a toothpick inserted into the center comes out clean. Remove from the muffin cups and cool on a wire rack.

BARNEY'S MUESLI

Muesli is typically a mixture of raw oats, seeds, nuts, and dried fruits. But here's a surprise: You don't need the oatmeal! Coconut flakes make an admirable substitute. Plus, they are flavorful and filled with fiber and healthy fat. Store the mixture in an airtight container at room temperature. Then combine with milk or water, let stand for a few minutes, and enjoy. For a crunchier muesli, toast the coconut flakes, nuts, and seeds. Spread on a baking sheet and bake at 350°F for 10–15 minutes until fragrant and light brown. Cool before combining with remaining ingredients.

Serves 8

2 cups unsweetened coconut flakes

2 cups slivered almonds

1 cup chopped macadamia nuts

1 cup broken walnuts

½ cup sesame seeds

½ cup pumpkin seeds

1 cup golden raisins

1 cup dried unsweetened cranberries

1 cup chopped Medjool dates

1 teaspoon cinnamon

1 teaspoon ground ginger

½ teaspoon nutmeg

8 cups almond or hazelnut milk

1. In large bowl, combine all ingredients except the milk and mix well. Store in an airtight container at room temperature.

2. To serve, pour about 1 cup of the muesli into a bowl and add 1 cup of the almond or hazelnut milk. Let stand for 5 minutes before eating.

3. You can also make this muesli the night before. Place muesli in a bowl and cover with the milk or water. Cover and let stand overnight in the fridge. When you're ready to eat breakfast, stir the muesli and dig in.

BETTY'S PALEO PANCAKES

Pancakes can be frozen after they are made. Freeze individually, then pack into freezer bags or containers, seal, and label with the date. You can pop them, still frozen, directly into a toaster or toaster oven and heat until hot. Top with butter and applesauce or any nut butter. Devour with crisp bacon and cold almond or coconut milk.

Serves 6

4 eggs, separated

1 tablespoon honey

2 teaspoons vanilla extract

¼ cup melted butter or coconut oil, divided

2 pinches salt, divided

1 teaspoon lemon juice

¾ cup almond flour

½ cup hazelnut flour

½ teaspoon cinnamon

1. In medium bowl, place egg yolks. Whisk in honey, vanilla, and 2 tablespoons melted butter or coconut oil.

2. In another medium bowl, place egg whites. Beat until foamy, then beat in a pinch of salt and the lemon juice. Beat until stiff peaks form.

3. In small bowl, combine almond flour, hazelnut flour, cinnamon, and another pinch of salt; stir until the mixture is one color. Add flour and beaten egg whites alternately to egg yolk mixture, folding gently until combined.

4. Heat large skillet and brush with remaining 2 tablespoons melted butter or coconut oil. Spoon batter onto skillet, using 3 tablespoons batter for each pancake. Cook pancakes until bubbles form on the surface and edges look done, about 2 minutes. Flip pancakes and cook for 2–3 minutes on the second side, until pancakes are browned. Serve immediately.

EGGS AND SAUSAGE IN TOMATO CUPS

Tomatoes make great little cups for scrambled eggs and sausage. This recipe is similar to the sandwiches you get at fast-food joints, but it is Paleo-friendly and much better for you. Serve with some sliced oranges for a great breakfast. If you aren't eating tomatoes, serve this mixture in hollowed-out small zucchini halves. You can sprinkle these with cheese before baking if you'd like.

Serves 4

4 large tomatoes

1 tablespoon butter or olive oil

¼ pound spicy pork sausage

6 eggs, beaten

¼ cup heavy cream or coconut cream

½ teaspoon salt

⅛ teaspoon pepper

1. Preheat oven to 375°F. Cut off the tops of the tomatoes and, using a serrated spoon, gently scoop out the insides and discard. Place the tomato shells on a baking sheet.

2. In medium saucepan, cook the sausage in butter or olive oil over medium heat, stirring to break up meat, until browned.

3. In a medium bowl, beat eggs with cream, salt, and pepper; pour over the sausage. Cook, stirring occasionally, until eggs are almost set.

4. Spoon mixture into tomato shells. Bake for 15–20 minutes or until eggs are set and tomatoes are tender.

SCOTCH EGGS

Scotch eggs are simply hard-cooked eggs that are wrapped in a spicy pork sausage mixture and baked. The traditional recipe uses bread crumbs too, but we use hazelnut flour and chopped hazelnuts for a crisp and nutty crust. You can cool these and serve them cold, or eat them hot; either way, they're delicious!

Serves 6

6 eggs in shells

1½ pounds spicy ground pork sausage

1 shelled egg, beaten

½ cup hazelnut flour

½ cup finely chopped hazelnuts

2 cups coconut oil for frying

1. Place eggs in large saucepan and cover with cold water. Bring to a boil over high heat. Remove pan from heat, cover, and let stand for 11 minutes.

2. Place pan in sink, drain, and run cold water over eggs. Add a few ice cubes. Let stand for 10 minutes. Then crack the eggshells under water and peel eggs. Dry well and set aside.

3. Form the sausage into six pieces and flatten on waxed paper. Put an egg on top of each sausage patty. Wrap sausage around egg to completely cover.

4. Place beaten egg in shallow dish. Combine hazelnut flour and chopped hazelnuts in another dish.

5. Dip sausage-coated eggs into beaten egg, then into hazelnut mixture to coat. Place in refrigerator while the oil is heating.

6. Place oil in deep heavy saucepan and attach deep fry thermometer. Heat to 375°F. Fry eggs, two at a time, until the sausage is cooked and the coating is brown and crisp, about 5–7 minutes. Drain on paper towels and serve.

SAUSAGE EGG BAKE

Use any type of sausage you like in this easy recipe. You can omit the cheese if you're not eating it. Use a spicy pork sausage to wake you up, or a mild sausage if you want comfort. You could also substitute ground chicken or turkey for the sausage for a change of pace, or use a different cheese.

Serves 4

1 pound pork sausage

2 shallots, chopped

1½ cups shredded Gruyère or Swiss cheese, if desired

10 eggs

½ cup heavy cream or coconut cream

½ teaspoon salt

⅛ teaspoon pepper

1 teaspoon dried dill weed

1. Preheat oven to 350°F. Butter a 2½-quart baking dish and set aside.

2. Cook sausage and shallots in medium pan over medium heat until sausage is cooked, stirring to break up meat. Drain and place in bottom of baking dish. Sprinkle with cheese, if using.

3. In large bowl, combine eggs, cream, salt, pepper, and dill weed and beat until combined. Pour over sausage and cheese in pan.

4. Bake for 18–23 minutes or until eggs are puffed and light golden brown. Cut into squares to serve.

CHEESE SOUFFLÉ

Soufflés are beautiful, and seem intimidating, but they're really easy to make. They are just a cheese sauce that is lightened with beaten egg whites and baked. The egg whites puff up in the oven, so the soufflé becomes light and puffy and ethereal. You can add everything from leftover vegetables to cooked meats or seafood to a soufflé. Just put them in the bottom of the dish before you add the egg mixture. There's only one secret to a soufflé: Eat it the second it comes out of the oven, because it falls quickly.

Serves 4

3 tablespoons Ghee (see Chapter 2) or unsalted butter

1 shallot, finely minced

3 tablespoons almond flour

½ teaspoon salt

1¼ cups almond milk

1 tablespoon Dijon mustard

⅔ cup crumbled goat cheese

1¼ cups grated Colby or Gruyère cheese

7 eggs, separated

1 teaspoon lemon juice

1. Preheat oven to 400°F. Butter a 2-quart soufflé dish. Tie a parchment paper strip around the dish so it extends 2" above the edge of the dish. Set aside.

2. Melt Ghee in large saucepan and cook shallot for 5 minutes until tender. Add almond flour and salt and cook for 2 minutes, stirring constantly with wire whisk.

3. Gradually add almond milk, stirring until thickened. Stir in mustard. Beat in cheeses, then add egg yolks, one at a time, beating until combined. Set aside.

4. In large bowl, beat egg whites until soft peaks form. Add lemon juice and beat until stiff.

5. Stir a spoonful of the egg white mixture into the egg yolk mixture to lighten. Fold remaining egg whites carefully into the egg yolk mixture. Spoon into prepared dish.

6. Bake for 20–25 minutes or until the soufflé is puffed and golden brown. Serve immediately.

CHICKEN AND POTATO HASH

Hash is usually made with white potatoes. So for the Paleo plan, use sweet potatoes instead! The change in flavor and color is wonderful. You can usually find ground chicken in the regular supermarket; ground turkey or even chicken sausage would work just as well in this delicious and easy recipe. Top with a poached egg for more protein if you'd like.

Serves 4

2 large sweet potatoes

2 tablespoons butter or olive oil

1 pound ground chicken

1 onion, chopped

1 red bell pepper, chopped

3 cloves garlic, minced

1 teaspoon salt

⅛ teaspoon pepper

1 teaspoon dried marjoram leaves

3 tablespoons coconut milk

1. Preheat oven to 400°F. Scrub sweet potatoes, prick with fork, and bake for 40–50 minutes or until just tender. Let cool for 30 minutes, then peel and cube the potatoes.

2. In a large skillet, melt butter or olive oil over medium heat. Add chicken, onion, red bell pepper, and garlic; cook and stir to break up meat until chicken is thoroughly cooked.

3. Add cubed sweet potatoes, salt, pepper, marjoram, and coconut milk and cook for 5–8 minutes longer, stirring occasionally, until everything is hot and well mixed. Serve with poached eggs, if desired.

NUTTY GRANOLA

Granola is usually made with oatmeal, which is a no-no on the Paleo plan. But there are enough different types of nuts and seeds, together with coconut, to make an admirable granola with no grains. Using raw, or unroasted, nuts adds to the authenticity of the recipe. But if you can't find them, use roasted nuts; just cut the time in the oven by half.

Yields 10 cups

1 cup raw almonds

1 cup raw pecan pieces

1 cup raw hazelnuts

1 cup raw pumpkin seeds

1 cup shelled raw sunflower seeds

2 cups unsweetened coconut flakes

1 cup unsweetened grated coconut

½ cup raw honey

½ cup coconut oil

2 teaspoons cinnamon

1 teaspoon nutmeg

½ teaspoon salt

1 cup golden raisins or dried blueberries

1 cup dried unsweetened cherries

1. Place ¼ cup each of the almond, pecans, hazelnuts, and pumpkin seeds in a blender or food processor. Blend or process until finely chopped.

2. Combine the finely chopped nuts with the remaining almonds, pecans, hazelnuts, and pumpkin seeds in a large bowl. Stir in sunflower seeds, coconut flakes, and grated coconut.

3. In small saucepan, combine honey and coconut oil and heat just until the oil melts. Stir in cinnamon, nutmeg, and salt.

4. Pour honey mixture on top of nut and seed mixture. Stir well.

5. Preheat oven to 325°F. Spread the granola mixture on a large (15" x 10") rimmed baking sheet. Bake for about 30 minutes, stirring every ten minutes, until mixture is golden brown. Let cool completely, and then stir in raisins and cherries. Store in an airtight container at room temperature for a few weeks.

CHICKEN SAUSAGE FRITTATA

Chicken sausage is often sold in major grocery stores. You can sometimes find it in the frozen food section. Be sure to read the ingredient list carefully to make sure there are no Paleo-unfriendly additions, such as starch, wheat, legumes, or artificial ingredients and flavors. If you can't find it, substitute Turkey Pear Sausages (see recipe in this chapter) in this easy recipe.

Serves 4

1 tablespoon olive oil

1 pound bulk chicken or turkey sausage

1 red onion, chopped

2 cloves garlic, minced

½ cup chopped green beans

1 red bell pepper, chopped

12 eggs

¼ cup heavy cream or coconut cream

½ teaspoon salt

⅛ teaspoon pepper

½ teaspoon dried thyme leaves

1 cup shredded Havarti cheese, if desired

1. Preheat oven to 375°F. In large ovenproof skillet, heat olive oil; cook sausage with onion, garlic, and green beans until meat is cooked, stirring to break up meat. Add red bell pepper; cook and stir for another 2 minutes.

2. Meanwhile, in large bowl beat eggs with cream or coconut cream, salt, pepper, and thyme. Pour over ingredients in skillet.

3. Cook for 5 minutes, shaking pan occasionally, until eggs start to set on the bottom.

4. Transfer to oven and bake for 9–14 minutes or until frittata is set and puffed and golden brown on top. Sprinkle with cheese, if desired, and serve.

BACON AND SQUASH HASH

Hash is usually made with red potatoes. Butternut squash makes an admirable substitute. Add onions and bacon for a hearty recipe everyone will love. Top with a poached egg for more protein. If you like your poached eggs runny, or cooked less than well done, please consider using pasteurized eggs for food safety reasons.

Serves 4–6

1 butternut squash

2 tablespoons olive oil

½ teaspoon salt

⅛ teaspoon pepper

10 slices bacon

1 onion, chopped

3 cloves garlic, minced

2 cups baby spinach leaves

1 tablespoon apple cider vinegar

1 tablespoon maple syrup

1. Preheat oven to 350°F. Peel, seed, and cube the squash. Place on a rimmed baking dish. Drizzle with olive oil and sprinkle with salt and pepper. Bake for 15–20 minutes or until just tender.

2. Meanwhile, cook bacon in heavy skillet until crisp. Drain bacon on paper towels, crumble, and set aside. Drain off all but 2 tablespoons bacon fat from pan.

3. Cook onion and garlic in bacon fat until tender, about 6 minutes.

4. Stir in cooked squash and baby spinach leaves; cover and cook until spinach is wilted, about 3 minutes.

5. Uncover and add bacon, vinegar, and maple syrup; cook and stir for another 2–3 minutes until hot. Serve immediately.

SALMON AND EGG SCRAMBLE

Salmon and asparagus is a delicious combination any time, but it's especially good in this egg scramble. You can use salmon fillets you have left over from a cookout or another recipe, or you can use canned salmon. Try to find Alaskan wild canned salmon and drain it well. Crumble the bones into the dish; they add lots of calcium to your diet and will not be detectable in the finished recipe.

Serves 4

1 pound asparagus

2 tablespoons olive oil

3 tablespoons water

1 shallot, minced

10 eggs, beaten

¼ cup almond milk

1 teaspoon dried dill weed

½ teaspoon salt

⅛ teaspoon pepper

2 cooked salmon fillets, flaked, or 1 (14-ounce) can salmon, drained

2 tablespoons minced chives

1. Snap ends off asparagus; cut into 2" lengths and rinse well.

2. Heat olive oil in large skillet. Add asparagus; cook and stir for 2 minutes.

3. Add water; cover pan and simmer asparagus for another 2 minutes.

4. Add shallot to pan and cook, uncovered, for another 2–4 minutes or until water evaporates.

5. Meanwhile, in large bowl, combine eggs, almond milk, dill weed, salt, and pepper and beat well. Add to pan.

6. Cook over medium heat, stirring frequently, until eggs are almost set. Stir in salmon; cover and cook 2 minutes until hot, shaking pan occasionally.

7. Top with chives and serve immediately.

HASH BROWN TURNIPS WITH GREENS

Turnips are a delicious and Paleo-friendly root vegetable. And their greens are an added bonus; so good for you, and the perfect side dish for this savory recipe. Turnip greens are loaded with calcium, vitamin K, and vitamin A. When you buy the turnips for this recipe, look for the freshest-looking tops. You can finish this recipe off with a poached egg if you'd like.

Serves 4

2 large turnips with tops

4 slices bacon

1 onion, chopped

½ teaspoon salt

½ teaspoon smoked paprika

½ teaspoon dried oregano

½ teaspoon dried thyme leaves

¼ teaspoon pepper

1 tablespoon olive oil

3 cloves garlic, minced

¼ cup chicken stock

1. Cut off the turnip greens and sort, discarding any wilted leaves; remove stems if thick. Wash greens and chop; set aside.

2. Peel the turnips and shred on a box grater or in the food processor. Then wring out the turnips in a dishtowel to remove excess liquid. Set aside.

3. In large skillet, cook bacon until crisp. Drain bacon on paper towels, crumble, and set aside.

4. Add onion to the pan with the bacon fat and cook for 3 minutes. Add shredded turnips and sprinkle with salt, paprika, oregano, thyme, and pepper. Cook, stirring frequently, for 12–14 minutes until crisp.

5. Meanwhile, heat olive oil in another large skillet over medium heat. Add turnip greens and garlic; cook for 3–4 minutes until wilted. Add chicken stock and cook, stirring occasionally, until tender.

6. Pile the turnip hash browns on a plate and surround with the greens. Serve with poached eggs, if desired.

SAUSAGE AND VEGGIE BAKE

Your oven does all the work for you in this delicious one-pot dinner. The vegetables cook first, then they are topped with sausage and roasted until everything is tender and the top is slightly crisp. Squeeze the garlic out of its skins on top of your serving of this bake. All you need for a complete meal is a nice green salad or some sliced fruit.

Serves 4–6

2 sweet potatoes, peeled and chopped

2 carrots, peeled and sliced

1 onion, chopped

8 whole cloves garlic, unpeeled

1 parsnip, peeled and chopped

3 tablespoons olive oil

½ teaspoon salt

¼ teaspoon pepper

½ teaspoon dried marjoram leaves

½ teaspoon dried sage leaves

4 kielbasas (Polish sausages)

1. Preheat oven to 375°F. Combine sweet potatoes, carrots, onion, garlic, and parsnip in a large roasting pan.

2. Drizzle with olive oil and sprinkle with salt, pepper, marjoram, and sage. Toss and spread in an even layer.

3. Roast for 20 minutes, then remove from oven and turn with a spatula. Prick sausages with a fork and place on top of vegetables.

4. Roast for another 20–30 minutes or until sausages register 165°F on a meat thermometer and vegetables are tender.

EGG-STUFFED MUSHROOMS

Scrambled eggs are easy to make, but you have to pay attention while they are cooking. Stir occasionally to get nice, soft, fluffy curds of egg. The eggs are spooned into large mushroom caps, then baked until everything is hot and delicious. Serve with roasted asparagus and some crisp bacon on the side.

Serves 4

4 large Portobello mushrooms

1 tablespoon olive oil

½ teaspoon salt, divided

1 tablespoon butter or hazelnut oil

1 shallot, minced

⅔ cup chopped ham

4 eggs

3 tablespoons almond milk

1 cup shredded Havarti cheese, if desired

1. Preheat oven to 375°F. Remove the stems from the mushrooms. Trim the end of the mushroom stems and chop; set aside.

2. Place mushroom caps, stem-side up, on a rimmed baking sheet. Drizzle with olive oil and sprinkle with ¼ teaspoon salt. Roast for about 18–20 minutes or until tender. Drain well, if necessary, and set aside.

3. In medium skillet, melt butter or hazelnut oil over medium heat. Add shallot; cook and stir for 2 minutes. Add ham; cook for another 2 minutes.

4. Beat eggs with almond milk and remaining salt in medium bowl. Add to skillet. Cook, stirring occasionally with a spatula, until eggs are just set but still moist.

5. Fill the mushroom caps with the egg mixture. Top with cheese, if using. Bake for another 5–6 minutes or until cheese is melted. Serve immediately.

MINI FRITTATAS

Mini frittatas are the perfect choice for a quick breakfast or dinner. Because they are small they cook much more quickly than a large frittata. And kids, who love anything miniature, adore these little pies. You can fill them with anything you'd like, but spicy sausage is good and very popular.

Yields 12 frittatas

1 pound bulk spicy pork sausage

1 small onion, chopped

2 cloves garlic, minced

8 eggs

¼ cup almond milk

½ teaspoon dried thyme leaves

½ teaspoon salt

⅛ teaspoon pepper

1 cup shredded Cheddar cheese, if desired

1. Preheat oven to 375°F. Grease 12 regular-sized muffin cups with unsalted butter and set aside.

2. In large skillet, cook sausage with onion and garlic until meat is browned and cooked through, stirring to break up meat. Drain well and set aside.

3. In large bowl, beat eggs with almond milk, thyme, salt, and pepper.

4. Divide pork mixture among the muffin cups. Slowly pour egg mixture into each cup, making sure not to overfill. Sprinkle with cheese, if using.

5. Bake for 15–20 minutes or until the frittatas are puffed and set and golden brown on top. Let stand for 5 minutes, then remove from muffin tins and serve.

CHAPTER 8

BEEF, PORK, AND LAMB

FRUITED BEEF SANDWICHES

The fruit mixture in this recipe (yes, tomatoes and avocados are fruits, although they are classified as vegetables in the market) can be used as a salsa in any other recipe. Just don't mash the blueberries before you stir in the other ingredients. Use the salsa to top broiled salmon or grilled chicken for a nice summer dinner.

Serves 4

1 cup fresh blueberries

1 tomato, chopped

1 avocado, peeled and chopped

1 tablespoon extra-virgin olive oil

1 tablespoon lemon juice

½ teaspoon salt

⅛ teaspoon crushed red pepper flakes

⅛ teaspoon pepper

½ pound cooked roast beef, thinly sliced

8 slices Paleo-approved bread

1. In medium bowl, place blueberries and mash slightly with a fork. Stir in tomato, avocado, olive oil, lemon juice, salt, red pepper flakes, and pepper; mix well.

2. Make sandwiches with the roast beef, fruit mixture, and the Paleo bread. Serve immediately.

GROUND BEEF PAN QUICHE

A pan quiche is a quiche baked in a jellyroll pan. It's kind of like a pizza, but with no crust. This rich mixture is satisfying and delicious. You can omit the cheese if you aren't eating dairy; just add another 2 eggs. Pair it with a green salad tossed with avocado and green onions and some sautéed green beans for a wonderful dinner.

Serves 6–8

½ cup finely chopped almonds

1½ pounds ground beef

1 onion, chopped

1 red bell pepper, chopped

3 tablespoons almond flour

½ teaspoon salt

⅛ teaspoon pepper

1 teaspoon dried marjoram

2 cups shredded Gruyère cheese, if desired

6 eggs, beaten

¾ cup heavy cream or coconut cream

½ cup coconut milk

½ cup beef broth

1. Preheat oven to 375°F. Grease a 15" x 10" jellyroll pan with unsalted butter and sprinkle with almonds; set aside.

2. In large skillet, cook ground beef with onion until beef is browned, stirring to break up meat. Add red bell pepper; cook and stir for another 2 minutes. Drain off excess fat.

3. Add almond flour, salt, pepper, and marjoram to pan and cook for 1 minute longer. Spoon beef into the jellyroll pan over the almonds. Sprinkle evenly with cheese, if using.

4. In large bowl, beat eggs with cream, coconut milk, and beef broth until thoroughly mixed. Slowly pour over the cheese in the pan.

5. Bake for 30–40 minutes or until the quiche is puffed and beginning to brown. Cut into squares to serve.

BETTY'S "SPAGHETTI"

Spaghetti squash is a very unusual vegetable. When cooked, the flesh separates into strings that have the look and texture of cooked pasta. It's an excellent substitute for wheat pasta, which is not allowed on the Paleo diet. One medium spaghetti squash will make enough "pasta" to serve two people. You can top it with any type of sauce.

Serves 4

2 medium spaghetti squash

3 tablespoons olive oil

1 pound grass-fed ground beef

1 onion, chopped

2 cloves garlic, minced

1 (6-ounce) can tomato paste

3 large tomatoes, chopped

1 cup tomato juice

1 cup dry red wine or beef broth

1 teaspoon dried Italian seasoning

½ teaspoon salt

⅛ teaspoon pepper

1. Preheat oven to 400°F. Cut each squash in half and place, cut-side up, on work surface. Using a spoon, firmly scrape out all the seeds and fibers and discard. Drizzle all four halves of the squash with olive oil, put cut-side down on a rimmed baking sheet, and set aside.

2. In large skillet, cook beef with onion and garlic until meat is browned, stirring to break up meat. Drain out most of the fat, then add tomato paste, tomatoes, juice, wine or broth, Italian seasoning, salt, and pepper. Bring to a simmer, reduce heat, cover, and simmer for 40–45 minutes, stirring occasionally.

3. When the sauce starts to simmer, put the squash in the oven. Bake for 35–40 minutes or until the squash is tender.

4. Using a fork, scrape the tender flesh out of the squash skins and divide among four serving plates. Top with the beef sauce and serve immediately.

SLOW-COOKER SWISS STEAK

Swiss steak is made from less tender cuts of beef, cooked slowly in the slow cooker to melt connective tissue and bring out the flavor of the meat. Round steak, either top or bottom cut, is a good choice for this recipe. Serve it over Mashed Cauliflower (see Chapter 11) for an excellent cold weather meal.

Serves 4

3 tablespoons hazelnut flour

1 teaspoon salt

¼ teaspoon pepper

1 teaspoon paprika

1½ pounds bottom round steak

3 carrots, cut into chunks

1 leek, chopped

4 cloves garlic, sliced

1 cup beef broth

1 (14-ounce) can diced tomatoes, undrained

1 tablespoon honey

1. On plate, combine flour, salt, pepper, and paprika. Cut the round steak into 4 pieces and dredge in the flour mixture.

2. Place carrots, leek, and garlic in bottom of 3-quart slow cooker. Top with beef.

3. Pour beef broth and half of the tomatoes over the beef. Stir the honey into remaining tomatoes and pour that into the slow cooker.

4. Cover and cook on low for 8–10 hours or until steak and vegetables are tender.

SLOW-COOKER POT ROAST

The slow cooker and beef roasts were made for each other! Inexpensive roasts have lots of connective tissue that will not soften unless the beef is cooked for a long time in liquid—a process known as braising. You can braise beef in a pan on the stovetop, but using a slow cooker is much easier. When you get home at night, just remove the beef and cover it. Purée some of the vegetable mixture with a stick blender for the gravy, and dig in.

Serves 6

4-pound bottom round roast

2 teaspoons paprika

1 teaspoon salt

¼ teaspoon pepper

2 tablespoons Ghee (see Chapter 2) or olive oil

1 onion, chopped

3 carrots, chopped

1 leek, chopped

7 cloves garlic, sliced

2 sweet potatoes, peeled and chopped

½ cup dry red wine

1 cup beef stock

2 bay leaves

1 teaspoon dried oregano

1 teaspoon dried marjoram

1. Sprinkle the roast with paprika, salt, and pepper on both sides. Heat Ghee in large skillet and brown beef well on both sides, turning once, about 10 minutes total. Remove beef to plate.

2. Add onion to drippings remaining in skillet. Cook for 4 minutes, stirring to remove pan drippings.

3. Meanwhile, place carrots, leek, garlic, and sweet potatoes in 5-quart slow cooker. Top with beef.

4. Pour wine and beef stock into pan with onions; cook for 4 minutes until blended. Pour over beef. Add bay leaves, oregano, and marjoram.

5. Cover and cook on low for 8–10 hours or until beef is tender.

6. To serve, remove bay leaves and discard. Remove beef and most of the vegetables to a platter; cover to keep warm.

7. Using a stick blender, purée remaining vegetables in the liquid in slow cooker to make a gravy. Serve over beef and vegetables.

STEAK WITH RED-EYE GRAVY

Red-Eye Gravy is simply gravy made with brewed coffee; this sauce is usually served with ham. The recipe is so rich because the coffee is used to deglaze the pan in which the steak was cooked. When you're cooking meat, those little brown bits in the bottom of the pan, called "pan drippings," are where a lot of the flavor is concentrated. Never let them go to waste! Always deglaze the pan and add the drippings to the recipe.

Serves 4

4 slices bacon

4 ribeye steaks

1 teaspoon salt

¼ teaspoon pepper

⅛ teaspoon crushed red pepper flakes

1 onion, finely chopped

1 clove garlic, minced

2 tablespoons almond flour

1 teaspoon smoked paprika

1¼ cups brewed coffee

2 tablespoons honey

1 tablespoon butter, if desired

1. Cook bacon in large skillet until crisp. Remove bacon and drain on paper towel; crumble and set aside.

2. Sprinkle steaks with salt, pepper, and crushed red pepper flakes.

3. Add steaks to bacon fat in skillet. Cook steaks on one side until the meat releases easily from the pan, about 5 minutes. Turn and cook for 4–7 minutes longer until desired doneness.

4. Remove steaks from pan, cover, and keep warm.

5. Add onion and garlic to the pan; cook and stir for 5–6 minutes or until tender, scraping pan to remove drippings.

6. Stir in almond flour and cook for 2 minutes. Then add paprika, coffee, and honey; bring to a boil.

7. Simmer for 4–7 minutes or until slightly reduced and thickened. Stir in butter and bacon, remove from heat, pour over steaks, and serve.

STEAK TIPS OVER SQUASH PASTA

When you think about it, any relatively starchy vegetable such as squash or zucchini can be cut into ribbons and cooked, then served as a wheat pasta substitute. Use this "pasta" base for any sauce, including Slow-Cooker Marinara (see Chapter 2), Creamed Chicken (see Chapter 9), or Shrimp Scampi (see Chapter 10).

Serves 4

4 slices bacon

1½ pounds sirloin tip steak, cubed

¼ cup coconut flour

1 onion, chopped

3 cloves garlic, minced

1 (8-ounce) package cremini mushrooms, sliced

2 cups plus 3 tablespoons beef broth, divided

½ teaspoon salt

1 teaspoon dried marjoram leaves

⅛ teaspoon pepper

4 yellow summer squash, cut into long thin strips, seeds discarded

2 tablespoons butter or olive oil

1. Cook bacon in large skillet until crisp; drain bacon, crumble, and set aside.

2. Coat the steak in coconut flour. Add to the bacon fat in pan; brown on all sides and remove.

3. Add onion and garlic to pan; cook and stir for 5 minutes. Then add mushrooms; cook and stir for 5 minutes longer.

4. Add 2 cups broth, salt, marjoram, and pepper and bring to a simmer. Reduce heat, cover, and simmer for 10 minutes until slightly thickened.

5. Meanwhile, in another large pan, sauté the squash in butter for 2 minutes. Add 3 tablespoons broth and bring to a simmer. Simmer for 5–6 minutes or until tender, then drain and cover; set aside.

6. Return beef and bacon to pan and simmer about 5–8 minutes longer until beef is tender. Serve over squash "noodles."

BEEF-STUFFED ZUCCHINI

This excellent and flavorful filling can be used to stuff just about any vegetable. It would be delicious in hollowed-out tomatoes, bell peppers, or even onions. You could substitute ground pork sausage for the beef in this recipe. Just cook it until browned, drain, and continue with the recipe as written.

Serves 4

2 large zucchini

2 slices bacon

½ pound ground beef

1 medium onion, chopped

3 cloves garlic, minced

1 (14-ounce) can diced tomatoes, undrained

½ teaspoon salt

⅛ teaspoon pepper

½ teaspoon dried oregano

¼ cup ground almonds

⅓ cup grated Parmesan cheese, if desired

1. Preheat oven to 375°F. Cut the zucchini in half. Scoop out seeds and much of the flesh; save for another use or discard. Place zucchini, cut-side up, in large baking dish.

2. Cook bacon until crisp; remove bacon, drain, crumble, and set aside. Cook ground beef, onion, and garlic in bacon fat until meat is browned, stirring to break up meat. Drain.

3. Stir in tomatoes, salt, pepper, and oregano and bring to a simmer. Simmer for 5 minutes.

4. Stir in bacon, almonds, and cheese. Use this mixture to stuff zucchini halves.

5. Bake for 30–35 minutes or until zucchini is tender. Serve immediately.

SLOW-COOKER BEEF STROGANOFF

Beef Stroganoff is a rich and elegant dish that is perfect for company. Serve it over Mashed Cauliflower (see Chapter 11) for a delicious dinner. This recipe cooks slowly in the slow cooker so the beef becomes meltingly tender. The onions will turn a dark brown color; don't be alarmed! That just means they're well cooked and very flavorful.

Serves 4–6

1½ pounds sirloin tip steak, cut into strips

1 teaspoon salt

¼ teaspoon pepper

2 tablespoons butter or olive oil

1 onion, chopped

3 cloves garlic, sliced

1 (8-ounce) package mushrooms, sliced

1½ cups beef broth

2 teaspoons Dijon mustard

1 teaspoon dried marjoram leaves

1 bay leaf

½ cup coconut milk

1. Sprinkle beef with salt and pepper. Brown in butter in a medium saucepan; remove beef from pan and place in 4-quart slow cooker.

2. Add onion, garlic, and mushrooms to fat remaining in pan. Cook and stir for 4–5 minutes, scraping up pan drippings.

3. Add beef broth and mustard to pan and simmer for 1 minute, then pour into slow cooker. Add marjoram and bay leaf and stir.

4. Cover and cook on low for 7–8 hours or until beef is tender. Remove bay leaf and discard.

5. Stir in coconut milk. Cover and cook on high for 20 minutes or until mixture is slightly thickened. Serve immediately.

BEEF AND BROCCOLI STIR-FRY

Stir-fry recipes are very quick to cook, but preparation time can be long. You need to have all of the ingredients ready and waiting for you before you put the pan on the heat. So get organized! Put all of the food on separate plates in the order it goes into the pan. Then turn on the heat, grab your spatula, and start cooking.

Serves 4

1¼ pounds beef sirloin steak

2 tablespoons balsamic vinegar

2 tablespoons Paleo-approved hoisin sauce or coconut aminos

1 tablespoon chili paste

1 teaspoon toasted sesame oil

½ cup beef broth

¼ teaspoon pepper

2 tablespoons olive oil

3 cups broccoli florets

½ cup sliced green onions

1. Cut the beef into thin strips against the grain and set aside.

2. In medium bowl, combine vinegar, hoisin sauce or coconut aminos, chili paste, sesame oil, broth, and pepper and mix to combine. Add beef strips; set aside for 15 minutes.

3. Remove beef from marinade; reserve marinade.

4. Heat oil in large skillet or wok over medium-high heat. Stir-fry beef for 3–4 minutes until browned; remove and cover to keep warm.

5. Add broccoli and green onions to skillet; stir-fry for 5–6 minutes or until crisp-tender.

6. Add reserved marinade to pan and bring to a boil. Stir-fry for 2–3 minutes until slightly thickened.

7. Return beef to pan and stir-fry for 2 minutes longer until blended. Serve immediately over Cauliflower Rice (see Chapter 11).

STEAK DIJON

Dijon mustard is made in the French city of Dijon. It is made with verjuice from unripened grapes instead of vinegar. It is spicier than regular yellow mustard and contains mustard seeds that you can see in the finished product. It makes a wonderful crust on tender and juicy steak.

Serves 4

4 ribeye steaks

3 tablespoons Dijon mustard

1 tablespoon honey

1 tablespoon lemon juice

2 cloves garlic, minced

1 tablespoon olive oil

1 teaspoon salt

¼ teaspoon pepper

1. Place steaks on a large platter. In small bowl, combine remaining ingredients and mix well. Rub into steaks.

2. Cover and refrigerate for 4–8 hours.

3. When ready to eat, prepare and preheat grill. Let steaks stand at room temperature for 20 minutes.

4. Grill steak over medium coals for 7–9 minutes per side, turning once, until desired doneness. Let stand, covered, for 5 minutes, then serve.

LAMB SKEWERS

Skewers are fun to make. Make them the next time you entertain. You could set up a "buffet" of sorts with lots of different ingredients; let your guests choose what goes on their skewers. This recipe can be varied by using chicken, pork, or beef in place of the lamb. Serve with chutney or salsa on the side.

Serves 6

2½ pounds boneless lamb

⅓ cup olive oil

⅓ cup lemon juice

2 tablespoons chopped fresh oregano

2 cloves garlic, minced

1 teaspoon salt

¼ teaspoon white pepper

12 fresh bay leaves

24 medium mushrooms

2 red bell peppers, cut into 1½" pieces

2 red onions, cut into eighths

1. Cut the lamb into 2" pieces. In large bowl, combine olive oil, lemon juice, oregano, garlic, salt, pepper, and bay leaves and mix. Add lamb, cover, and refrigerate for 4–12 hours.

2. When ready to eat, prepare and preheat grill. Drain lamb, reserving marinade, bay leaves, and lamb cubes.

3. Thread lamb, bay leaf, mushrooms, bell peppers, and onions onto 12 metal skewers. Grill over medium coals, 6" from heat, brushing occasionally with reserved marinade, until lamb is medium. Discard remaining marinade. Warn guests not to eat the bay leaves!

LAMB CURRY

Curry powder is a combination of many different spices. You can buy curry powder at the store or make your own using those spices. Buy several different brands and see which one you like best. This rich dish is delicious served over Mashed Cauliflower (see Chapter 11) or Mashed Sweet Potatoes (see Chapter 11).

Serves 6

2½ pounds lean boneless lamb

2 tablespoons curry powder

2 tablespoons olive oil

1 cup coconut milk

3 tablespoons red wine vinegar

1 teaspoon salt

¼ teaspoon pepper

3 tablespoons Ghee (see Chapter 2) or coconut oil

1 tablespoon minced fresh gingerroot

4 cloves garlic, minced

1 onion, chopped

1 cup water

3 tomatoes, seeded and chopped

2 cups green beans, trimmed

1 cup walnut pieces, toasted

½ cup chutney

1. Cut lamb into 1½" pieces. In large bowl, combine curry powder, olive oil, coconut milk, red wine vinegar, salt, and pepper. Add lamb, stir, then cover and refrigerate for 8–24 hours.

2. When ready to eat, remove lamb from marinade; reserve marinade.

3. In large pan, heat Ghee over medium-high heat. Add ginger, garlic, and onion; cook and stir for 5 minutes. Add lamb; cook and stir for 5 minutes.

4. Add reserved marinade, water, and tomatoes to skillet. Bring to a simmer, cover, reduce heat to low, and cook for 65–75 minutes or until lamb is tender.

5. Uncover pan and add green beans. Simmer for 5–8 minutes or until beans are tender. Stir in walnuts and chutney, and serve.

SOUVLAKI GRILLED STEAKS

Souvlaki is actually skewered meat marinated in Greek flavors such as olive oil, lemon juice, mint, and oregano. But you can cook steaks or even chicken with this type of marinade and the meat doesn't have to be skewered. Serve this dish with a spinach salad full of vegetables, Cucumber Raita (see Chapter 11), and a nice glass of red wine.

Serves 4

4 chuck or top round steaks

3 tablespoons olive oil

2 tablespoons red wine

2 tablespoons red wine vinegar

1 tablespoon lemon juice

2 tablespoons chopped fresh mint

1 tablespoon chopped fresh oregano

2 cloves garlic, minced

1 teaspoon salt

¼ teaspoon white pepper

1. Pierce steaks with a fork and place in shallow bowl.

2. Combine remaining ingredients and pour over steaks. Cover and refrigerate 4–12 hours.

3. When ready to eat, remove steaks from marinade and pat dry. Discard marinade. Grill steaks over medium coals, 6" from heat, until desired doneness.

SWEET POTATO–TOPPED MEAT LOAF

Meat loaf is such wonderful comfort food. It's rich and soothing and easy to make. It's usually served with mashed potatoes; in this case, it's topped with mashed sweet potatoes, which help keep the meat loaf moist as it bakes. Serve with a green salad tossed with lots of fresh veggies.

Serves 4–6

2 tablespoons butter or olive oil

1 onion, chopped

3 cloves garlic, minced

⅓ cup almond flour

⅓ cup ground almonds

2 eggs, beaten

1 teaspoon salt

¼ teaspoon pepper

1 teaspoon dried marjoram leaves

1 teaspoon dried oregano leaves

1½ pounds lean ground beef

2 cups Mashed Sweet Potatoes (see Chapter 11)

1 egg

½ cup grated Parmesan cheese, if desired

1. Preheat oven to 350°F. Grease a slotted broiler pan with unsalted butter or coconut oil and set aside.

2. In medium skillet, melt butter over medium heat. Add onion and garlic; cook and stir until tender, about 5 minutes. Remove to large bowl and let cool for 10 minutes.

3. Beat almond flour, ground almonds, egg, salt, pepper, marjoram, and oregano into the onion mixture. Stir in ground beef and mix gently but thoroughly.

4. Form mixture into a loaf on the prepared broiler pan. Bake for 55–65 minutes or until a meat thermometer registers 165°F. Remove from oven.

5. Combine sweet potatoes, egg, and cheese, if using. Spread over meat loaf.

6. Heat oven to broil. Broil meat loaf, 6" from heat, for 5–8 minutes or until sweet potatoes are browned and starting to crisp. Serve immediately.

BEEF SATAY

Beef satay is made of marinated meat cooked on a skewer and served with a peanut sauce. But peanuts aren't technically "nuts"—they are legumes, which aren't allowed on the Paleo diet. So let's serve this spicy recipe with an almond sauce! The sauce helps cool the heat from the marinated meat and adds a wonderful flavor.

Serves 4–6

1 cup almond butter

2 tablespoons minced gingerroot, divided

3 cloves garlic, minced, divided

½ cup coconut milk

1 tablespoon lemon juice

¼ teaspoon pepper

3 tablespoons chopped parsley

2 pounds sirloin tip or flank steak

1 teaspoon salt

¼ teaspoon crushed red pepper flakes

1 teaspoon cumin

1 small onion, minced

2 tablespoons honey

½ cup beef stock

1 jalapeño pepper, minced

2 tablespoons fish sauce

1. For almond sauce: In food processor, combine almond butter, half of the gingerroot, half of the garlic, coconut milk, lemon juice, and pepper and process until smooth. Stir in parsley, cover, and refrigerate.

2. Cut beef into 2" strips and set aside.

3. In large bowl, combine remaining gingerroot, remaining garlic, salt, red pepper flakes, cumin, onion, honey, beef stock, jalapeño pepper, and fish sauce. Add beef, cover, and marinate for 4–24 hours in the refrigerator.

4. When ready to eat, remove almond sauce and beef from fridge. Drain beef, discarding marinade.

5. Prepare and preheat grill. Thread beef on skewers. Grill for 4–6 minutes over medium coals until desired doneness. Serve with the almond sauce.

FRUIT-AND-NUT STUFFED FLANK STEAK

Flank steak is a relatively new cut of meat in the general supermarket. It has been used for years in Tex-Mex cuisine as a favorite meat for fajitas. It must be cut against the grain or it will be tough. When marinated and properly sliced, flank steak is tender and juicy. Since the cut is thin, it is easily stuffed and rolled. This beautiful recipe is perfect for entertaining.

Serves 6

1 (2-pound) flank steak

1 teaspoon salt

⅛ teaspoon pepper

6 thin slices prosciutto

1 cup chopped walnuts

½ cup dried cranberries

½ cup golden raisins

1 cup shredded Havarti cheese, if desired

1. Place the flank steak on a work surface so the grain runs from right to left in front of you. Using a very sharp knife, butterfly the steak: Cut it in half horizontally so you can open it up like a book, leaving a ½" "spine" of uncut meat. Open the steak up and pound the spine if necessary so it is even.

2. Sprinkle steak with salt and pepper, then place prosciutto on the steak so it evenly covers the steak.

3. Sprinkle with walnuts, cranberries, and golden raisins. Sprinkle with cheese, if desired.

4. Starting with the edge of the steak nearest to you, roll up tightly. Using kitchen twine, tie the roll every 2 or 3 inches.

5. Preheat oven to 375°F. In a very large skillet, heat oil over medium-high heat. Add the steak roll and brown, turning carefully with two tongs every few minutes to brown all sides, for about 5–6 minutes. Place steak on large rimmed baking sheet.

6. Roast for 20–30 minutes or until steak registers at least 145°F with a meat thermometer. Make sure the probe of the meat thermometer is in the meat, not in the filling. Remove from oven, cover with foil, and let stand 10 minutes. Slice into pinwheels to serve, discarding twine.

SLOW-COOKER SWEET POTATO LASAGNA

Lasagna is a recipe that many people on the Paleo diet miss. But you can still enjoy this classic Italian recipe; just use thinly sliced sweet potatoes in place of the wheat lasagna noodles. To make this recipe even easier, it's cooked in the slow cooker! If you aren't eating dairy or cheese, just omit the ricotta layer; the lasagna will still be delicious. When you get home after a long day at the office, scoop the lasagna out of the slow cooker, make a crisp green salad, and enjoy.

Serves 6

1 pound ground beef

1 onion, chopped

3 cloves garlic, minced

1 green bell pepper, chopped

1 (6-ounce) can tomato paste

1 (8-ounce) can tomato sauce

1⅓ cups beef stock

1 teaspoon dried oregano

1 teaspoon dried basil

½ teaspoon dried marjoram

1 teaspoon salt

¼ teaspoon pepper

1 cup ricotta cheese, if desired

1½ cups shredded mozzarella cheese, if desired

1 egg, if desired

2 large sweet potatoes, peeled and thinly sliced

½ cup grated Parmesan cheese, if desired

1. In large skillet, cook ground beef with onion and garlic until beef is browned, stirring to break up meat. Drain well.

2. Add green bell pepper to meat mixture; cook and stir for 3 minutes. Add tomato paste, tomato sauce, beef stock, oregano, basil, marjoram, salt, and pepper and stir. Bring to a simmer, reduce heat to low, and simmer for 10 minutes.

3. Meanwhile, in medium bowl, combine ricotta, mozzarella, and egg, if desired; mix well.

4. In 4- to 5-quart slow cooker, spread ¼ of meat mixture. Top with ⅓ of the sweet potato slices, then ⅓ of the ricotta mixture, if using. Repeat layers, ending with meat mixture. Sprinkle with Parmesan cheese, if using.

5. Cover and cook on low for 7–9 hours or until sweet potatoes are tender when pierced with a fork.

BEEF BURGERS WITH CRUNCHY SLAW

Grilled burgers are one of the joys of summer. And you can still enjoy them on the Paleo diet; just omit the bun! A word about food safety: Ground beef is not safe to eat unless it is cooked well done. Even organic beef or beef you grind yourself can contain dangerous bacteria. Well-done ground beef can be tough, so some Paleo crackers are soaked in beef stock, then added to the meat to provide moisture and tenderness. Serve on a plate with a knife and fork.

Serves 4

2 cups shredded cabbage

1 red bell pepper, chopped

3 green onions, sliced

1 jalapeño pepper, minced

3 tablespoons apple cider vinegar

2 tablespoons olive oil

1 teaspoon salt, divided

⅛ teaspoon plus ⅛ teaspoon pepper, divided

½ cup crumbled Paleo Crackers (see Chapter 5)

⅓ cup beef stock

2 cloves garlic, minced

2 tablespoons tomato paste

1½ pounds ground beef

1. In medium bowl, combine cabbage, bell pepper, green onions, and jalapeño pepper. Drizzle with vinegar, olive oil, ½ teaspoon salt, and ⅛ teaspoon pepper; toss to mix and set aside.

2. In large bowl, combine crackers and beef stock; let stand for 10 minutes. Add ½ teaspoon salt, ⅛ teaspoon pepper, garlic, and tomato paste and mix well.

3. Add ground beef and mix gently but thoroughly until combined. Form into 4 patties. Make an indentation in the center of each patty with your thumb so the burgers stay flat once they are cooked.

4. Prepare and preheat grill. Grill burgers, turning once, over medium coals until a meat thermometer registers 165°F. Remove from grill, cover, and let stand for 5 minutes.

5. Drain slaw and serve on top of burgers.

PINEAPPLE LAMB SPARERIBS

You may have to order lamb spareribs from the butcher at your grocery store because they aren't often in stock. You need a surprising amount of ribs to serve four people; the bones are heavy and you want enough meat so the meal is satisfying. Marinate the ribs overnight in the fridge, then grill or roast until tender.

Serves 4

1 (8-ounce) can crushed pineapple in unsweetened juice

1 cup chicken stock

3 tablespoons coconut aminos

3 tablespoons lemon juice

4 tablespoons chopped fresh mint, divided

2 cloves garlic, minced

5 pounds lamb spareribs

¼ cup honey

1. In large bowl, combine crushed pineapple with juice, chicken stock, coconut aminos, lemon juice, 2 tablespoons mint, and garlic. Add lamb spareribs; cover and marinate in the refrigerator overnight.

2. When ready to eat, place lamb, with marinade, in roasting pan.

3. Preheat oven to 325°F. Roast for 1½ hours, turning ribs once during cooking time.

4. Preheat oven to broil. Drain ribs and discard cooking liquid. Place ribs on a broiler rack.

5. Combine honey and 2 tablespoons mint in small bowl. Broil ribs 6" from heat source until dark brown, brushing with honey and mint mixture. Serve immediately.

GERMAN SAUSAGE WRAPS

Any of your favorite sausages can be used to make this flavorful wrap sandwich. Some sausages are precooked and can be used without cooking, such as salami and knackwurst. Fresh sausages, which must be cooked before serving, include boudin blanc, bockwurst, and Polish sausage. Check the label; it will tell you whether the sausage is ready to eat or must be cooked first. And use only fresh, naturally fermented sauerkraut for best nutrition.

6 servings

1 pound bratwurst sausages, sliced

1 onion, chopped

3 cloves garlic, minced

1 cup naturally fermented sauerkraut, drained

2 Granny Smith apples, chopped

⅓ cup grainy mustard

6 large red cabbage leaves, thick core cut out

1. In medium skillet, cook bratwurst with onion and garlic until the sausage is slightly crisp and browned, about 8–10 minutes. Remove from skillet with slotted spoon.

2. In medium bowl, combine sausage mixture with sauerkraut and apples and toss to mix. Stir in mustard.

3. Wrap mixture in cabbage leaves and serve immediately, or cover the sausage mixture and chill a few hours before serving.

HONEY-GLAZED BACON

Bacon is in! This incredibly popular meat is put into almost every recipe—even ice cream and cookies! It's a great addition to the Paleo diet because it has so much flavor. Look for bacon that does not contain sodium nitrate, nitrite, or sugar. It's difficult to find, but it's out there. For breakfast, this recipe can't be beat.

Serves 4–6

12 slices thick-cut bacon

¼ cup honey

1 tablespoon Dijon mustard

¼ teaspoon pepper

1. Preheat oven to 400°F. Place bacon on a rack in a rimmed baking sheet.

2. Combine honey, mustard, and pepper in a small bowl and mix well. Brush bacon with some of this mixture.

3. Bake bacon until crisp, about 12–16 minutes, turning once and brushing with honey mixture two more times. Serve immediately.

SAUERKRAUT-STUFFED PORK

Sauerkraut, a German staple, is very good for you despite being high in sodium. It is a natural probiotic, containing many lactobacillus bacteria that help promote digestive health. It's also a great source of vitamin C. And cabbage is a cruciferous vegetable that helps reduce the risk of cancer. So eat up!

Serves 6

6 double-cut rib pork chops

2 tablespoons butter or olive oil

1 onion, chopped

3 cloves garlic, minced

3½ cups sauerkraut, drained, divided

1 cup dried cranberries

2 tablespoons honey

1 teaspoon caraway seeds

¼ teaspoon pepper

2 tablespoons olive oil

1. Preheat oven to 375°F. Cut a slit in the side of each pork chop, gently moving the knife around to enlarge the area. Set aside.

2. In large saucepan, melt butter or olive oil over medium heat. Add onion and garlic; cook and stir until tender, about 6 minutes. Remove from heat and place in large bowl.

3. Add sauerkraut, cranberries, honey, caraway seeds, and pepper to onion mixture and mix gently. Use about 3–4 tablespoons of this mixture to stuff each pork chop.

4. Heat olive oil in large skillet. Brown stuffed pork chops on each side for about 2–3 minutes until browned.

5. Place remaining sauerkraut mixture in 9" x 13" baking dish and top with the pork chops. Bake for 35–45 minutes or until a meat thermometer in the pork chops registers 145°F. Remove from oven and let stand for 5 minutes, then serve.

SLOW-COOKER PULLED PORK

Pulled pork is simply pork that has been cooked for a long time at low heat, so it can be easily shredded into tender bits. It is typically served on sandwich buns, but it's delicious over Mashed Sweet Potatoes (see Chapter 11) or Cauliflower Rice (see Chapter 11). This sweet and salty dish is very delicious.

Serves 6–8

2 onions, chopped

6 cloves garlic, minced

1 teaspoon salt

2 teaspoons smoked paprika

1 teaspoon dried marjoram leaves

½ teaspoon pepper

1 (4-pound) boneless pork shoulder

1 cup chicken broth

¼ cup honey

2 tablespoons Dijon mustard

1. In 4- to 5-quart slow cooker, place onions and garlic.

2. In small bowl, combine salt, paprika, marjoram, and pepper. Rub all over the pork shoulder and place on top of onions in slow cooker.

3. In small bowl, combine broth, honey, and mustard and mix well. Pour over pork.

4. Cover and cook on low for 7–9 hours or until pork is very tender. Shred meat in slow cooker using two forks and mix well with sauce.

BABY BACK RIBS

Baby back ribs are from the top of the pig's rib cage. They are also called loin ribs and have more meat than spare ribs. This tender cut is delicious when slathered with a homemade barbecue sauce.

Serves 4

3 pounds baby back pork ribs

2½ cups Fruity Balsamic Barbecue Sauce (see Chapter 2), divided

¼ cup orange juice

1. The day before you want to serve this recipe, place ribs in a large roasting pan. Combine 1½ cups of the barbecue sauce and the orange juice in medium bowl and pour over ribs. Cover and marinate overnight in the refrigerator.

2. When you want to eat, heat oven to 325°F. Bake the ribs, covered, for 2 hours or until the meat is tender. Uncover and remove from oven.

3. Turn the oven to broil. Drain ribs and place on a broiler rack, meaty side up. Brush with remaining 1 cup barbecue sauce and broil 6" from heat for 10–15 minutes or until ribs are glazed. Serve immediately.

PORK BURGERS WITH SLAW

Burgers made with pork are a delicious change of pace from beef, chicken, and turkey burgers. Using a combination of ground pork, pork sausage, and bacon elevates this recipe to another level. Top it with a crunchy and sweet slaw made from Napa cabbage and apples for another layer of flavor.

Serves 4

2 cups shredded Napa cabbage

1 Granny Smith apple, chopped

2 green onions, sliced

⅓ cup Wilma's Mayonnaise (see Chapter 2)

1 tablespoon lemon juice

½ teaspoon grated lemon zest

1 tablespoon honey

2 tablespoons chopped fresh basil

4 slices bacon

3 green onions, thinly sliced

3 cloves garlic, minced

½ cup peeled and finely chopped apple

1 pound ground pork

⅓ pound spicy pork sausage

½ teaspoon salt

⅛ teaspoon pepper

1. In medium bowl, combine cabbage, Granny Smith apple, and 2 green onions. In small bowl, combine mayonnaise, lemon juice, zest, honey, and basil and mix well. Pour over cabbage mixture and stir to coat. Cover and refrigerate.

2. In medium skillet, cook bacon until crisp. Drain bacon on paper towels and set aside in refrigerator.

3. Cook 3 green onions, garlic, and finely chopped apple in bacon fat until tender, about 3–4 minutes. Remove to large bowl and let cool 10 minutes.

4. Add ground pork, pork sausage, salt, and pepper to onion mixture in bowl and mix with hands until combined.

5. Form into 4 patties. Press a divot into the center of each patty with your thumb; cover and refrigerate.

6. Prepare and preheat grill. Grill burgers 6" from heat over medium coals for 10–14 minutes, turning once, until a meat thermometer registers 165°F. Remove from grill and let stand for 5 minutes; reheat bacon. Top burgers with bacon and slaw and serve.

SAUSAGE-STUFFED PEPPERS

Bell peppers make great vehicles for any type of savory stuffing. The peppers soften and become very tender while the filling heats. You can make this recipe as mild or as spicy as you'd like, depending on the type of sausage you choose. Serve with a fruit salad and some steamed green beans for a nice dinner.

Serves 6

6 green or red bell peppers

1 pound spicy pork sausage

¼ pound ground pork

1 onion, chopped

2 cloves garlic, minced

½ cup finely chopped cauliflower

2 tablespoons Dijon mustard

1 teaspoon dried thyme leaves

½ teaspoon salt

⅛ teaspoon pepper

2 (8-ounce) cans tomato sauce, divided

1. Preheat oven to 350°F. Cut the tops from the bell peppers and remove seeds and membranes from insides. Make sure the peppers will stand upright; if not, cut a small bit from the bottom without cutting through the peppers. Place in glass baking dish and set aside.

2. In large skillet, cook sausage, ground pork, onion, garlic, and cauliflower until meat is browned, stirring to break up meat. Drain well, then stir in mustard, thyme, salt, pepper, and ⅔ cup tomato sauce.

3. Use this mixture to stuff the peppers. Pour remaining tomato sauce over stuffed peppers and cover.

4. Bake for 25 minutes, then uncover and bake for 10–15 minutes longer or until peppers are tender and filling is hot.

PORK FRIED RICE

The "rice" in this recipe is shredded cauliflower. You could also use shredded jicama or turnips if either is more to your taste. This recipe, like all stir-fry recipes, has to have all the components waiting and ready to go before you turn the heat on under the skillet or wok. Then cook and eat.

Serves 4

1 medium head cauliflower

2 teaspoons lemon juice

¼ cup chicken stock

2 tablespoons coconut aminos

1 tablespoon honey

1 tablespoon apple cider vinegar

1 tablespoon fish sauce

⅛ teaspoon white pepper

½ pound chopped pork tenderloin

2 tablespoons coconut oil

1 onion, chopped

2 cloves garlic, minced

2 eggs, beaten

2 tablespoons chopped chives

1. Shred the cauliflower on a box grater or in a food processor. Sprinkle with lemon juice and set aside.

2. In medium bowl, combine chicken stock, coconut aminos, honey, vinegar, fish sauce, and pepper; add pork and stir to coat. Let stand for 10 minutes.

3. Heat coconut oil in large skillet or wok over medium-high heat. Drain pork, reserving marinade, and add pork to skillet; stir-fry until browned, about 4–5 minutes. Remove pork and set aside.

4. Add onion and garlic to skillet or wok; stir-fry until crisp-tender, about 4–5 minutes.

5. Add cauliflower to skillet; stir-fry until tender, about 4 minutes longer. Return pork to skillet and add marinade.

6. Turn heat to high and add eggs to skillet or wok. Stir-fry until egg is cooked and everything is hot. Garnish with chives and serve immediately.

SCALLOPED SWEET POTATOES WITH PORK CHOPS

Scalloped potatoes with pork is a classic comfort food recipe. For the Paleo diet, just substitute sweet potatoes for regular white potatoes for a satisfying dinner. If you don't eat cheese, just leave it out; you won't miss it. If you do eat cheese, pick one that has a good strong flavor such as Gruyère or Gouda to stand up to the rest of the ingredients.

Serves 6

3 large sweet potatoes, peeled and sliced ⅛" thick

2 cups almond milk

2 tablespoons butter or olive oil

6 (1" thick) loin pork chops

1 onion, chopped

3 cloves garlic, minced

3 tablespoons almond flour

1 teaspoon salt

⅛ teaspoon pepper

1 teaspoon dried thyme leaves

1 teaspoon dried marjoram leaves

1 cup shredded Gruyère or Gouda cheese, if desired

1. In large pot, combine sliced sweet potatoes and almond milk and bring to a simmer. Cover and simmer for 6–9 minutes or until potatoes are almost tender. Drain potatoes, reserving milk.

2. In large skillet, heat butter or olive oil over medium heat. Add pork chops and brown on both sides, about 5 minutes total. Remove chops to plate.

3. Add onion and garlic to skillet; cook and stir until tender, about 5 minutes. Add almond flour, salt, and pepper and cook and stir for 2 minutes.

4. Add reserved almond milk, thyme, and marjoram, and beat with wire whisk until slightly thickened. Add cheese, if using, and whisk until melted. Add sweet potatoes, stirring carefully with a spoon.

5. Preheat oven to 350°F. Pour the sweet potato mixture into a 13" x 9" glass baking dish and top with the browned chops.

6. Bake for 45–55 minutes or until chops are 145°F when tested with a meat thermometer and potatoes are bubbling and tender.

SAUSAGE-STUFFED ONIONS

Stuffed onions is not a dish you often see anymore, but it used to be popular in the 1950s and 1960s. When properly made, this dish is really delicious. The onions become sweet and tender as they bake, and the savory filling is the perfect complement. You need large onions for this recipe; pick them out individually rather than buying a bag.

Serves 6

6 large Spanish or red onions

2 slices bacon

¾ pound spicy pork sausage

3 cloves garlic, minced

1 egg, beaten

½ cup Paleo Crackers (see Chapter 5), crushed

⅓ cup tomato sauce

1 teaspoon dried marjoram

1 teaspoon salt

⅛ teaspoon pepper

1 cup grated white Cheddar cheese, if desired

1 cup water

1. Peel onions and cut off the top of each. Bring a large pot of water to a boil and add onions; simmer for about 20 minutes or until onions are almost tender.

2. Preheat oven to 375°F. Carefully remove the centers of the onions, leaving a shell about ½" thick. Mince enough of the onion centers to make ½ cup.

3. Cook bacon in large skillet until crisp; drain on paper towels, crumble, and set aside.

4. Cook sausage, minced onion centers, and garlic in bacon fat until pork is browned, stirring to break up meat. Drain well.

5. Add egg and cracker crumbs to pork mixture; stir in tomato sauce. Season with marjoram, salt, and pepper. Add bacon and cheese, if using.

6. Stuff onions with the sausage mixture. Place in baking dish. Add water to bottom of dish.

7. Bake for 30–35 minutes or until onions are tender and filling is hot.

PRUNE-BRAISED PORK LOIN

Prune juice may sound strange cooked with pork, but the combination is a winner. The prune juice is mildly sweet and tenderizes the pork as it cooks. Pork loin is a great choice for entertaining. The cut serves 6 to 8 people and it is easy to cook. Marinate the pork overnight, then just roast it and serve.

Serves 6–8

3-pound boneless pork loin

¾ cup prune juice

½ cup chicken broth

3 tablespoons coconut aminos

½ cup tomato sauce

3 tablespoons honey

1 bay leaf

3 cloves garlic, minced

1 teaspoon salt

¼ teaspoon pepper

1½ teaspoons dried thyme leaves

1 teaspoon dried basil leaves

1. Place pork in large baking dish. In medium bowl combine prune juice, chicken broth, coconut aminos, tomato sauce, honey, bay leaf, and garlic and mix well. Pour this mixture over pork.

2. Cover and marinate pork in refrigerator for 12–24 hours, turning the pork once or twice during marinating time.

3. Preheat oven to 350°F. Drain marinade from pork, reserving marinade. Sprinkle the loin with salt and pepper. Rub with thyme and basil. Pour 1 cup of the marinade around pork.

4. Roast pork for about 40–50 minutes, basting with the marinade in the pan every 15 minutes. The pork should register 150°F on a food thermometer. Cover pork and let stand for 10 minutes, then slice and serve.

ORIENTAL RIBS

Country-style ribs are the meatiest cut of this pork product. They are from the sirloin or rib end of the pork loin. They are almost always sold boneless, but if there is some bone, cut it out before preparing this recipe. This spicy and Asian-inspired marinade adds great flavor to this tender cut of meat.

Serves 4–6

2½ pounds country-style pork ribs

¼ cup hazelnut flour

¼ teaspoon pepper

¼ cup olive oil

1 onion, chopped

3 cloves garlic

2 cups chicken stock

¼ cup coconut aminos

2 tablespoons honey

3 tablespoons tomato paste

1 teaspoon five-spice powder

1 teaspoon ground ginger

1. Sprinkle ribs with hazelnut flour and pepper. Heat olive oil in large Dutch oven.

2. Add ribs and brown on all sides, working in batches. Remove ribs as they brown.

3. Add onion and garlic to Dutch oven and cook, stirring frequently, until crisp-tender, about 5 minutes.

4. Add stock, coconut aminos, honey, tomato paste, five-spice powder, and ginger to Dutch oven and bring to a simmer. Return ribs to pan.

5. Bring back to a simmer, then reduce heat to low, cover, and simmer for about 1½ hours or until ribs are tender.

SAUSAGE AND PEPPERS

This classic Italian recipe can be made with chicken broth or red wine, if wine is part of your diet. It is simple to make, but rich and delicious. You can serve it as-is, or pour it over Mashed Cauliflower (see Chapter 11) or Mashed Sweet Potatoes (see Chapter 11) for a hearty and filling dinner in the fall or winter.

Serves 4–6

1½ pounds sweet or hot Italian sausages

⅓ cup water

2 tablespoons olive oil

1 leek, chopped

1 onion, chopped

3 cloves garlic, minced

1 red bell pepper, sliced

1 orange bell pepper, sliced

1 green bell pepper, sliced

½ cup chicken stock or dry red wine

½ teaspoon salt

⅛ teaspoon pepper

1. In large skillet, place sausages. Add water and bring to a simmer. Simmer sausages until the water evaporates; then let the sausages brown, turning frequently, until they register 165°F on a meat thermometer. Remove sausages to plate.

2. Add olive oil to pan and add leek, onion, and garlic. Cook, stirring to scrape up pan drippings, until tender, about 5 minutes.

3. Add red, orange, and green bell peppers and cook for 3 minutes.

4. Add stock or wine, salt, and pepper and bring to a simmer. Return sausages to skillet.

5. Simmer for 3–4 minutes or until sausages register 165°F on meat thermometer. Serve immediately.

PORK CHOPS WITH SQUASH

The tender meatiness of pork chops pairs beautifully with sweet squash. Butternut squash is very good for you; it is full of vitamins A and C and is a good source of fiber. It is one of the "winter squashes," with a hard skin. It absorbs the flavors of the pork as this recipe cooks in the oven.

Serves 4

4 boneless pork loin chops

½ teaspoon salt

⅛ teaspoon pepper

1 butternut squash, peeled and seeded

2 tablespoons olive oil

1 onion, sliced

3 cloves garlic, sliced

½ cup chicken stock

⅓ cup honey

3 tablespoons grainy mustard

1. Preheat oven to 400°F. Sprinkle chops with salt and pepper. Cut squash into 1½" chunks.

2. Heat olive oil in a large skillet. Add the chops and brown on both sides, turning once, about 5 minutes total. Remove from pan and set aside.

3. Add onion and garlic to pan, stirring to loosen and incorporate pan drippings. Add squash and cook for 3 minutes.

4. Add stock and bring to a simmer; simmer for 5 minutes, then remove from heat and add honey and mustard. Mix well.

5. Place squash mixture in a glass baking dish. Top with chops.

6. Bake for 25–30 minutes or until chops are 150°F and squash is tender. Serve immediately.

ITALIAN SAUSAGE AND SWEET POTATOES

Italian sausages come in two flavors: sweet and hot. Sweet Italian sausage is flavored with fennel, paprika, basil, oregano, and thyme. Hot Italian sausage usually has crushed red pepper flakes or other peppers added to increase the spiciness factor. You can use either type in this easy recipe.

Serves 4

2 tablespoons olive oil

1½ pounds sweet or hot Italian sausage links

1 onion, chopped

2 sweet potatoes, peeled and cubed

⅓ cup apple cider vinegar

¼ cup Dijon mustard

2 tablespoons grainy mustard

1 tablespoon chopped fresh thyme leaves

½ teaspoon salt

⅛ teaspoon pepper

1. Preheat oven to 400°F. Place olive oil in a large glass baking dish. Add sausage, onion, and sweet potatoes to dish and toss to coat.

2. Bake for 15 minutes.

3. In small bowl, combine vinegar, mustards, thyme, salt, and pepper. Pour over ingredients in dish and toss to coat.

4. Bake for another 10–15 minutes or until sausages are cooked to 165°F and sweet potatoes are tender. Serve immediately.

SAUSAGE POTPIE

Potpies are usually topped with a flour crust of some sort. But you can also top them with mashed sweet potatoes or with this crumbly mixture. The combination of almond and hazelnut flours creates a wonderfully nutty and crisp topping. This rich and satisfying dish is perfect for winter entertaining.

Serves 6

8 tablespoons butter or coconut oil, divided

2 tablespoons olive oil

1 onion, chopped

1 leek, chopped

2 cloves garlic, minced

1 cup sliced cremini mushrooms

1 cup green beans, sliced

2 carrots, sliced

1¼ cups almond flour, divided

3 cups chicken stock

4 links fully cooked bratwurst sausage, sliced

1 teaspoon dried marjoram leaves

1½ teaspoons salt, divided

⅛ teaspoon pepper

½ cup hazelnut flour

1 teaspoon baking powder

1 egg, beaten

½ cup grated Parmesan cheese, if desired

1. Preheat oven to 375°F. Grease a 3-quart casserole dish with unsalted butter and set aside.

2. In large skillet, heat 2 tablespoons butter or coconut oil and olive oil over medium heat. Add onion, leek, and garlic; cook and stir for 5 minutes.

3. Add mushrooms, green beans, and carrots; cook and stir for 4 minutes longer.

4. Sprinkle with ¼ cup almond flour and cook for 2 minutes. Add chicken stock and bring to a simmer. Stir in sausage, marjoram, 1 teaspoon salt, and pepper and stir. Simmer for 10 minutes over low heat, stirring occasionally.

5. Meanwhile, make the topping. Combine remaining 1 cup almond flour and the hazelnut flour in medium bowl. Add baking powder and remaining ½ teaspoon salt and mix.

6. Cut in remaining 6 tablespoons butter or coconut oil until particles are fine. Add egg and cheese, if using, and mix until crumbly.

7. Pour sausage mixture into prepared dish. Sprinkle topping over the top. Bake for 20–25 minutes or until topping is browned and crisp.

MEATY PIZZA

Who says pizza has to have a wheat crust? Or a crust made of any type of flour? A combination of ground pork and pork sausage makes an admirable base to hold a spicy sauce and different toppings. Use your favorite toppings to top each pizza, or offer your guests a choice of different toppings and let them create their own. You don't have to use cheese on this pizza if you aren't eating it.

Serves 4

1 pound ground pork

½ pound pork sausage

1 tablespoon olive oil

1 onion, chopped

4 cloves garlic, minced

1 (8-ounce) can tomato sauce

2 tablespoons Dijon mustard

1 teaspoon dried oregano

½ teaspoon dried basil

½ teaspoon salt

⅛ teaspoon pepper

1 cup sliced mushrooms, if desired

1 green bell pepper, sliced, if desired

½ cup sliced black or green olives, if desired

½ cup sliced pepperoni, if desired

1½ cups shredded cheese, if desired

1. Preheat oven to 400°F. In medium bowl, combine pork and pork sausage and mix gently but thoroughly. Divide into four balls.

2. On waxed or parchment paper, pat the balls into 5" rounds. Carefully invert onto a broiler pan (a pan with slits to drain the grease) and remove the paper.

3. Bake for 12 minutes. Remove from oven.

4. Meanwhile, heat olive oil in medium saucepan. Add onion and garlic; cook and stir for 4 minutes. Add tomato sauce, mustard, oregano, basil, salt, and pepper and bring to a simmer. Simmer while the meat "bases" are in the oven.

5. Spread the sauce over the meat pizza bases and top with desired toppings. Return to the oven and bake another 5–10 minutes or until toppings are tender. Serve immediately.

SAUSAGE "RISOTTO"

Sausage is a delicious addition to risotto; it adds another layer of flavor to this creamy and comforting dish. Cauliflower stands in for the traditional Arborio rice. And dried mushrooms add to the flavor and texture of this recipe. You can find them in most grocery stores; soak them in hot water until tender. The soaking liquid is used in the recipe so you don't lose a drop of flavor.

Serves 4

1 ounce dried mushrooms

⅔ cup hot water

1 pound ground pork sausage

1 onion, chopped

3 cloves garlic, minced

1 head cauliflower, shredded

2 tablespoons heavy cream or coconut cream

½ cup grated Parmesan cheese, if using

1. Place mushrooms in a medium bowl and cover with the hot water. Let stand until softened. Drain off and reserve liquid, being careful to discard any grit. Remove mushroom stems and discard; chop mushroom tops.

2. Cook sausage in large pan over medium heat with onions and garlic until meat is browned, stirring to break up meat. Drain.

3. Add cauliflower and mushrooms to pan; cook for 2 minutes.

4. Add reserved mushroom liquid to the skillet and cook for 3–4 minutes or until cauliflower is tender. Add cream and cheese, if using, and stir for 1 minute. Serve immediately.

TEX-MEX PORK TENDERLOIN

Pork tenderloin is sold in most large grocery stores. It is a very tender and flavorful cut of pork and requires little preparation. It combines well with the flavors and ingredients from every cuisine. Flavored with peppers and sun-dried tomatoes, this dish is delicious and healthy.

Serves 4–6

2 (1-pound) pork tenderloins

3 cloves garlic, slivered

1 tablespoon chili powder

½ teaspoon salt

¼ teaspoon pepper

2 tablespoons olive oil

1 onion, chopped

1 chipotle pepper in adobo sauce, minced

1 tablespoon adobo sauce

1 (8-ounce) can tomato sauce

1 rutabaga, peeled and cubed

3 carrots, peeled and sliced

1. With a sharp knife, pierce slits in the pork tenderloins. Insert slivers of garlic into the pork. Sprinkle pork with chili powder, salt, and pepper.

2. In large skillet, heat olive oil over medium heat. Add onion and cook for 3 minutes. Add chipotle pepper, adobo sauce, and tomato sauce and simmer for 1 minute.

3. Place the rutabaga and carrots in a 4-quart slow cooker. Top with the pork tenderloins. Pour sauce over all.

4. Cover and cook on low for 7–9 hours or until pork registers at least 150°F and the vegetables are tender.

ROSEMARY RACK OF LAMB IN BERRY SAUCE

This rack of lamb recipe is sure to be a winner at any holiday or dinner party. The flavors are strong and the presentation is a winner.

Serves 4

1 rack grass-fed lamb, on the bone

1 teaspoon freshly ground black pepper

2 cloves garlic, crushed and divided

1½ teaspoons dried thyme

2 sprigs fresh rosemary, divided

2 tablespoons olive oil

1 cup mixed berries

1 cup no-salt-added, organic beef stock

1. Place rack of lamb in a roasting pan with a rack. Sprinkle lamb with black pepper, 1 clove crushed garlic, thyme, and 1 sprig of fresh rosemary.

2. Place lamb in a 400°F oven. Roast for 13 minutes per pound or until internal temperature reaches 135°F. Remove from oven and set aside to rest.

3. Prepare sauce by combining remaining garlic and rosemary, olive oil, berries, and beef stock in a medium saucepan over low heat. Stir and cook for about 5 minutes.

4. Reduce sauce until thick (may take another 5 minutes) and pour over cooked lamb.

RUSTIC LAMB SHANKS

This is a French bistro and comfort meal that most people find delicious on a cool evening.

Serves 4

4 lamb shanks, well trimmed

1 teaspoon salt

½ teaspoon freshly ground black pepper

1 tablespoon olive oil

1 large yellow onion, chopped

4 garlic cloves, minced

2 large parsnips, peeled and cut into chunks

1 carrot, peeled and cut into chunks

2 tablespoons tomato paste

1 cup dry red wine or additional chicken broth

1 cup chicken broth

2 bay leaves

¼ cup fresh parsley, chopped

1. Sprinkle the lamb shanks with salt and pepper. In a Dutch oven over medium-high heat, brown lamb in the olive oil, adding onion, garlic, parsnips, and carrot. Cook for 5 minutes. Stir in tomato paste, red wine, chicken broth, bay leaves, and parsley.

2. Cover the pot and simmer for 2 hours. Remove bay leaves before serving.

Not Crazy about Lamb?

When people say they don't like lamb, it's usually the fat, not the lamb, they dislike. When you prepare roast lamb, stew, or shanks, be sure to remove all of the visible fat. It also helps to serve the lamb with something to cut through the fatty taste, such as mint, lemon, or tomato.

GRASS-FED LAMB MEATBALLS

Meatballs are always a kid favorite. These grass-fed lamb meatballs are high in good fats that contribute to their great taste and high health factor.

Serves 6

¼ cup pine nuts

4 tablespoons olive oil, divided

1½ pounds ground grass-fed lamb

¼ cup minced garlic

2 tablespoons cumin

1. In a skillet over medium-high heat, sauté pine nuts in 2 tablespoons olive oil for 2 minutes until brown. Remove from pan and allow to cool.

2. In a large bowl, combine lamb, garlic, cumin, and pine nuts and form into meatballs.

3. Add remaining olive oil to pan and fry meatballs until cooked through, about 5–10 minutes, depending on size of meatballs.

EASY LEG OF LAMB

Although lamb can be an expensive cut of meat, you can often find it on sale during the holidays. When you find good prices, stock up on several cuts and freeze them.

Serves 6

1 (4-pound) bone-in leg of lamb

5 cloves garlic, cut into spears

2 tablespoons olive oil

1 tablespoon dried rosemary

½ teaspoon ground pepper

4 cups chicken broth

¼ cup dry red wine or additional chicken broth

1. Make small incisions evenly over the lamb. Place garlic spears into the incisions.

2. Rub olive oil, rosemary, and pepper over the lamb. Place lamb into a greased 4- or 6-quart slow cooker.

3. Pour broth and wine around the lamb. Cook on high for 4 hours or on low for 8 hours. Remove leg of lamb from slow cooker. Cut off the tender meat or pull it off the bone with a large fork.

4. Serve the roast lamb in bowls. Ladle the sauce from the slow cooker over each serving.

HERBED LAMB CHOPS

The simple herb rub used in this recipe would make a fun holiday gift to give to friends or family members who enjoy cooking! Include this recipe with a small jar of the rub.

Serves 4

1 medium onion, sliced

1 teaspoon dried oregano

½ teaspoon dried thyme

½ teaspoon garlic powder

⅛ teaspoon ground pepper

2 pounds (about 8) lamb loin chops

1 tablespoon olive oil

1. Place the onion on the bottom of a greased 4-quart slow cooker.

2. In a small bowl mix together oregano, thyme, garlic powder, and pepper. Rub herb mixture over the lamb chops.

3. Place herb-rubbed lamb chops over the sliced onions in the slow cooker. Drizzle olive oil over the lamb chops.

4. Cook on high for 3 hours or on low for 6 hours, until tender.

LAMB WITH GARLIC, LEMON, AND ROSEMARY

You can use the spice rub in this recipe as a marinade by applying it to the leg of lamb and refrigerating for several hours (or up to one full day) before cooking.

Serves 4

4 cloves garlic, crushed

1 tablespoon fresh rosemary, chopped

1 tablespoon avocado oil

1 teaspoon ground pepper

1 (3-pound) leg of lamb

1 large lemon, cut into ¼" slices

½ cup chicken or beef stock

1. In a small bowl mix together garlic, rosemary, oil, and pepper. Rub this mixture onto the leg of lamb.

2. Place a few lemon slices in the bottom of a greased 4-quart slow cooker. Place spice-rubbed lamb on top of lemon slices.

3. Add remaining lemon slices on top of lamb. Pour stock around the lamb.

4. Cook on low heat for 8–10 hours or on high for 4–6 hours.

EASY SLOW-COOKER PORK TENDERLOIN

Slow-cooker meals are a great way to cook for your family. Large quantities can be thrown into the cooker hours in advance. Most leftovers can be easily frozen for future meals.

Serves 4

1 (1-pound) lean pork loin

1 (28-ounce) can no-salt-added diced tomatoes

3 medium zucchinis, diced

4 cups cauliflower florets

Chopped fresh basil, to taste

Garlic, to taste

1. Combine all ingredients in a slow cooker.

2. Cook on low for 6–7 hours.

Low-Fat Meat Choice

Pork is a nice low-fat protein source. It is versatile for cooking and quite flavorful. This often-overlooked meat is a fantastic friend of the Paleo lifestyle.

ROASTED PORK LOIN

When you are preparing for a large family gathering and find yourself with a bit more time than expected, this is the recipe to go for. It serves ten easily and will wow your guests with its flavorful punch.

Serves 10

2½ pounds pork loin

Juice of 1 large orange

3 tablespoons lime juice

2 tablespoons red wine

10 cloves garlic, minced

2 tablespoons dried rosemary

1 tablespoon ground black pepper

1. Combine all ingredients in a shallow dish or large zip-top food storage bag. Refrigerate and marinate pork for at least 2 hours.

2. Remove pork from marinade and let stand at room temperature for 30 minutes. Preheat oven to 400°F.

3. Place pork in roasting pan and roast for 20 minutes per pound, or about 50–60 minutes, until internal temperature reaches 145°F.

PORK TENDERLOIN WITH NECTARINES

Pork combined with the flavor of ripe nectarines makes a lovely sweet and slightly tangy sauce. Serve sliced pork and sauce over steamed zucchini strips.

Serves 4

1¼ pounds pork tenderloin

1 tablespoon olive oil

4 ripe but firm nectarines, each peeled and chopped

2 tablespoons lemon juice

Ground black pepper to taste (optional)

1. Rub pork tenderloin with olive oil. Place in a greased 3-quart slow cooker.

2. Place nectarine wedges on top of and around the pork tenderloin. Drizzle lemon juice over the pork and fruit. Cook on high for 3–4 hours or on low for 6–7 hours, until pork is very tender.

3. Remove pork from slow cooker and slice before serving. Pile on a plate and top with the nectarines, which will have cooked down into a sauce. If desired, add pepper, to taste.

PALEO PULLED PORK

This pulled pork recipe has super flavors. Adjust the spices as needed to kick it up a notch or cool it down. Either way, this recipe is sure to please the entire family.

Serves 8

2½ pounds pork loin

1 large onion, chopped

1 (6-ounce) can organic, no-salt-added tomato paste

3 tablespoons olive oil

½ cup lemon juice

½ cup unsalted beef broth

4 cloves garlic

¼ teaspoon cayenne pepper

½ teaspoon paprika

2 teaspoons chipotle chili powder

1 teaspoon thyme

1 teaspoon cumin

1. Combine all ingredients in a slow cooker.

2. Cook on low for 6–8 hours or until pork is tender and thoroughly cooked.

3. Remove pork from slow cooker and shred. Return to slow cooker and mix thoroughly, then serve.

MUSHROOM PORK MEDALLIONS

You would never guess this meal is Paleo-approved. It tastes so amazing, you will swear it was deep fried with flour.

Serves 2

1 pound pork tenderloin

1 tablespoon olive oil

1 small onion, sliced

¼ cup sliced fresh mushrooms

1 clove garlic, minced

2 teaspoons almond meal

½ cup beef broth

¼ teaspoon crushed dried rosemary

⅛ teaspoon ground black pepper

1. Slice tenderloin into ½"-thick medallions.

2. In a skillet, heat olive oil over medium-high heat. Brown pork in oil for 2 minutes on each side.

3. Remove pork from skillet and set aside.

4. In same skillet, add onion, mushrooms, and garlic and sauté for 1 minute.

5. Stir in almond meal until blended.

6. Gradually stir in the broth, rosemary, and pepper. Bring to a boil; cook and stir for 1 minute or until thickened.

7. Lay pork medallions over mixture. Reduce heat; cover and simmer for 15 minutes or until pork is tender and at least 145°F on a meat thermometer.

APPLES-AND-ONIONS PORK CHOPS

Try Sonya or Honeycrisp apples in this sweet and savory dish; they are crisp and sweet.

Serves 4

4 crisp, sweet apples, peeled and cut into wedges

2 large onions, sliced

4 thick-cut boneless pork chops (1 pound total)

½ teaspoon cayenne pepper

½ teaspoon cinnamon

¼ teaspoon allspice

¼ teaspoon ground fennel

1. Place half of the apple wedges in the bottom of a 4-quart slow cooker along with half of the sliced onions.

2. Top with a single layer of pork chops. Sprinkle with spices, and top with the remaining apples and onions.

3. Cook on low for 8 hours.

Slow Cooking with Boneless Pork

Not only is there less waste associated with boneless pork chops or roasts, there is often less fat attached to the meat. Even without much fat, boneless pork is well suited to slow cooking. All of the moisture stays in the dish, ensuring tender pork.

BEEF WITH BELL PEPPERS

Choose a variety of red, yellow, orange, and green bell peppers to bring vibrant color to this one-pot dinner.

Serves 4

1 pound lean beef

4 bell peppers, seeded and chopped

3 cloves garlic, minced

Juice of 2 lemons

½ cup diced button mushrooms

4 stalks celery, chopped

3 large shallots, sliced

Salt and pepper, to taste

1. Preheat oven to 350°F.

2. Cut beef into cubes. Place all ingredients in a casserole dish and stir to combine. Bake for 30–40 minutes or until the beef registers at least 140°F on a meat thermometer.

FILET MIGNON AND ROASTED RED PEPPER WRAPS

This meal is pure Paleo. Your taste buds will dance with the decadence of the filet and the mix of seasoning flavors and textures of the veggies.

Serves 2

4 large leaves romaine lettuce

1 tablespoon avocado oil

1 sweet onion, such as Vidalia, finely chopped

2 cloves garlic, minced

1 teaspoon salt

1 teaspoon freshly ground black pepper

1 (8-ounce) filet mignon, thinly sliced

1 teaspoon Worcestershire sauce

½ teaspoon hot sauce

2 ounces roasted red peppers, chopped

1. Lay the lettuce out on paper towels. Add the oil to the bottom of a medium-sized skillet set over medium heat. Sauté the onion and garlic for 1–2 minutes.

2. Sprinkle salt and pepper on the filet mignon. Add steak to the skillet and sauté for about 3–4 minutes.

3. Scoop onions, garlic, and sliced filet mignon into each lettuce leaf. Sprinkle with Worcestershire sauce and hot sauce. Top with roasted red peppers. Wrap and serve.

LONDON BROIL WITH ONIONS

This will give you a real energy boost! To get the maximum energy out of this recipe, eat slowly and enjoy a smaller portion.

Serves 2

1 tablespoon avocado oil

½ pound London broil, diced

1 teaspoon salt

½ teaspoon freshly ground black pepper

1 teaspoon steak seasoning

½ cup chopped sweet onion

½ teaspoon red pepper flakes, or to taste

1 teaspoon Worcestershire sauce

2 tablespoons salsa

2 large sweet red bell peppers, cored, seeded, and cut in half lengthwise

1. Heat oil over medium heat in a skillet. Season the steak with salt, pepper, and steak seasoning. Add seasoned steak and onions to the pan and sauté until the steak reaches the desired level of doneness. Use a meat thermometer to test the internal temperature of the meat. At 140°F, the steak will be medium-rare.

2. Sprinkle steak with red pepper flakes and Worcestershire sauce. Mix in salsa and stuff the red peppers with the mixture.

BEEF TENDERLOIN WITH CHIMICHURRI

This is simple to make for an easy weeknight meal or perfect for a sophisticated gourmet dinner party.

Serves 2

1 cup parsley

3 cloves garlic

¼ cup capers, drained

2 tablespoons red wine vinegar

1 teaspoon Dijon mustard

2 tablespoons olive oil

Salt and pepper, to taste

2 (5-ounce) beef tenderloins

1. To make the chimichurri sauce, in a blender, blend together parsley, garlic, capers, vinegar, mustard, and oil. Season with salt and pepper as desired.

2. Grill steaks over medium-high heat until internal temperature reaches 140°F (for medium-rare). Serve with chimichurri.

POT ROAST WITH VEGETABLES AND GRAVY

As a family dinner, this can't be beat. The leftovers can be reheated and served over spaghetti squash or mashed cauliflower for a quick lunch or supper.

Serves 6

3 pounds beef bottom round roast, trimmed of fat

2 tablespoons avocado oil

4 medium-sized sweet onions, chopped

4 cloves garlic, chopped

4 carrots, peeled and chopped

4 stalks celery, chopped

8 small bluenose turnips, peeled and chopped

1 (1") piece fresh ginger, peeled and minced

1 (13-ounce) beef broth

½ cup dry red wine (or additional beef broth)

1 teaspoon sea salt

1 teaspoon freshly ground black pepper

1 tablespoon coconut flour

1 tablespoon arrowroot powder

1. Brown the beef in oil in a large pot over medium-high heat. Remove the beef from the pot and set aside. To the same pot add the onions, garlic, carrots, celery, turnips, and ginger and cook, stirring, until wilted. Return the beef to the pot and add the rest of the ingredients. Cover and cook over very low heat for 3 hours.

2. To serve, slice the beef across, not with, the grain. Serve surrounded by vegetables and place the gravy on the side or over the top.

CORNED BEEF AND CABBAGE

The slow cooker is the secret cooking technique of the busy home cook. It requires little attention, and the meat will come out tender and juicy.

Serves 10

3 pounds corned beef brisket

3 carrots, peeled and cut into 3" pieces

3 onions, quartered

1 cup water

½ small head cabbage, cut into wedges

1. Place beef, carrots, onions, and water in a slow cooker. Cover and cook on low for 8–10 hours.

2. Add cabbage to the slow cooker; be sure to submerge the cabbage in liquid. Turn the heat up to high, cover, and cook for 30–40 minutes. Slice the beef against the grain and serve with the vegetables.

BEEF BRISKET WITH ONIONS AND MUSHROOMS

This recipe makes a roast so packed with flavor and so tender that it will melt in your mouth.

Serves 4

4 cloves garlic

1½ teaspoons salt, divided

4 tablespoons avocado oil, divided

2 teaspoons chopped fresh rosemary

1 pound beef brisket

1 teaspoon freshly ground black pepper

3 large onions, quartered

3 cups sliced white mushrooms

3 celery stalks, cut into large chunks

2 cups beef broth

1 (16-ounce) can whole tomatoes, chopped

2 bay leaves

1. Preheat oven to 325°F.

2. Using a mortar and pestle or the back of a spoon and a bowl, mash together the garlic, ½ teaspoon salt, 2 tablespoons oil, and chopped rosemary leaves to make a paste.

3. Season the brisket with pepper and 1 teaspoon salt. Heat remaining oil in a large skillet, place brisket in the pan, and sear over medium-high heat to make a dark crust on both sides. Place in a large roasting pan and spread the rosemary paste on the brisket. Place the onions, mushrooms, and celery in the pan around the brisket. Pour broth and tomatoes over the brisket and toss in the bay leaves.

4. Tightly cover the pan with foil and place in the oven. Bake for about 4 hours, basting with pan juices every 30 minutes, until the beef is very tender.

5. Let the brisket rest for 15 minutes before slicing it across the grain at a slight diagonal. Remove and discard bay leaves before serving.

GINGER BEEF AND NAPA CABBAGE

This stir-fry delivers the perfect balance of sweet, spicy, and savory.

Serves 4

3 tablespoons coconut aminos

2 cloves garlic, minced

1 tablespoon minced fresh ginger

1 teaspoon raw honey

½ teaspoon red pepper flakes

1 pound beef tenderloin or sirloin steak

1 cup beef broth

2 teaspoons arrowroot powder

2 tablespoons sesame oil, divided

1 large onion, thinly sliced

½ head napa cabbage, shredded

3 green onions, sliced, for garnish

1. Combine coconut aminos, garlic, ginger, honey, and red pepper flakes in a small bowl. Slice beef into ¼"-thick strips. Toss beef in ginger-honey sauce. Cover, and place in refrigerator for at least 30 minutes to marinate.

2. Mix broth and arrowroot and set aside.

3. Heat half the oil in a large skillet over medium heat. Add onion to the pan and cook for 5 minutes until tender and slightly brown. Remove from pan and set aside.

4. Heat remaining oil over medium-high heat. Add marinated beef and cabbage to the pan and stir-fry for 5 minutes or until beef is only slightly pink in the center and cabbage is tender. Add cooked onion and broth to the pan. Cook for about 2 minutes, until sauce boils. Reduce heat to low and allow sauce to thicken for about 2 minutes longer.

5. Garnish with green onion before serving.

STEAK-AND-MUSHROOM KEBABS

These meaty, juicy kebabs are a hit at summer barbecues. They can also be cooked indoors on a well-seasoned grill pan.

Serves 3

1 pound sirloin steak

3 tablespoons avocado oil

¼ cup balsamic vinegar

1 tablespoon Worcestershire sauce

½ teaspoon salt

2 cloves garlic, minced

Freshly ground black pepper, to taste

½ pound large white mushrooms

1. Cut steak into 1½" cubes.

2. Combine oil, vinegar, Worcestershire sauce, salt, garlic, and pepper to make a marinade.

3. Wash mushrooms and cut in half. Place steak and mushrooms in shallow bowl with marinade and place in refrigerator for 1–2 hours.

4. Place marinated mushrooms and steak cubes on separate wooden or metal skewers. Grill 4 minutes per side over medium-high heat for medium-rare steak. You may need additional cooking time for mushrooms. Serve.

BOEUF BOURGUIGNON

Boeuf Bourguignon (beef Burgundy) is a well-known classic French beef stew.

Serves 8

2 pounds stewing beef, cut into ½" cubes

1½ teaspoons salt

1 teaspoon freshly ground black pepper

1 tablespoon avocado oil

3 cloves garlic, minced

3 onions, quartered

2 cups dry red wine or beef broth

¾ pound carrots, peeled and sliced

¾ pound white mushrooms, sliced

1 bunch fresh rosemary, chopped

1 bunch fresh thyme, chopped

1–2 cups water, as needed

1. Season beef with salt and pepper.

2. Add oil to a large skillet over medium heat. Place beef in the pan to brown on the outside, about 5 minutes per side. Add garlic and onions to the pan and cook until tender. Add red wine or broth, bring to a boil, and then simmer.

3. Add carrots, mushrooms, and herbs to the pan. Add a few cups of water, as needed, to increase volume of liquid and keep the stew's sauce from cooking down. Cook for 3 hours over low heat, occasionally stirring.

POT ROAST WITH A TOUCH OF SWEET

Serve this roast alongside a hearty portion of Mashed Cauliflower (see Chapter 11).

Serves 8

1 teaspoon freshly ground black pepper

1 teaspoon smoked paprika

1 teaspoon garlic powder

1 teaspoon onion powder

½ cup lime juice

½ cup tomato sauce

2 pounds beef chuck roast

1 large sweet onion, thickly sliced

1 tablespoon coconut or avocado oil

½ cup water

2 tablespoons dry red wine or beef broth

1. In a small bowl, combine the pepper, paprika, garlic powder, and onion powder.

2. In a separate bowl, combine the lime juice and tomato sauce. Set aside.

3. Season all sides of the roast with the prepared spice mixture.

4. Place onion slices on the bottom of a 4-quart slow cooker.

5. Heat the oil in a large skillet over medium-high heat. Brown the roast on all sides in the skillet, about 8 minutes on each side.

6. Place browned roast on top of the onions in the slow cooker. Turn heat under the skillet to low, and add water and wine or broth, scraping to remove pan drippings.

7. Pour pan liquid over the roast, then the lime juice and sauce mixture on top. Cover and cook on low for 8 hours until roast is tender.

SAUSAGE AND SPICY EGGS

This is a very pretty dish that is not only a delicious breakfast but is also good for lunch or a late supper. Be careful not to overly salt the dish—most sausage has quite a lot of salt in it, so taste first.

Serves 4

1 pound sweet Italian sausage

¼ cup water

1 tablespoon avocado or coconut oil

2 sweet red peppers, roasted and chopped

1 jalapeño pepper, seeded and minced

8 eggs

2 tablespoons chopped fresh parsley

1. Cut the sausage in ¼" coins. Place in a heavy skillet with the water and oil. Bring to a boil, then turn down the heat to low to simmer. Turn sausages after 5 minutes to brown both sides.

2. When the water evaporates and the sausages are brown (after about 10 minutes), remove them and place on a paper towel. Add the roasted red peppers and jalapeño pepper to the pan and sauté over medium heat for 5 minutes.

3. While the peppers sauté, beat the eggs vigorously. Add to the pan and gently cook and fold over until puffed and moist.

4. Mix in the reserved sausage, garnish with parsley, and serve hot.

TOMATO-BRAISED PORK

Here the pork is gently cooked in tomatoes to yield beautifully tender meat. If you'd prefer oregano or thyme in place of the marjoram, consider using a bit less than what the recipe calls for, as these herbs tend to have a stronger flavor.

Serves 4

1 (28-ounce) can crushed tomatoes

3 tablespoons tomato paste

1 cup loosely packed fresh basil

½ teaspoon freshly ground black pepper

½ teaspoon marjoram

1¼ pounds boneless pork roast

1. Place the tomatoes, tomato paste, basil, pepper, and marjoram in a 4-quart slow cooker. Stir to create a uniform sauce. Add the pork.

2. Cook on low for 7–8 hours or until the pork easily falls apart when poked with a fork.

HONEY-MUSTARD PORK LOIN

The mixture of mustard and honey keeps the pork from drying out during the long cooking time.

Serves 2

3 tablespoons Dijon mustard

1 tablespoon raw honey

½ pound pork tenderloin

1. In a small bowl, mix the mustard and honey. Spread the mixture on the pork tenderloin in an even layer.

2. Place pork in a 2-quart slow cooker. Cook on low for 6 hours.

PORK TENDERLOIN WITH SWEET-AND-SAVORY APPLES

The tart apples sweeten over the long cooking time and nearly melt into the pork.

Serves 2

¼ teaspoon freshly ground black pepper

¾–1 pound boneless pork tenderloin

½ cup sliced onions

5 fresh sage leaves

2 cups peeled, diced Granny Smith apples

1. Sprinkle pepper on the tenderloin. Place the onion slices on the bottom of a 2-quart slow cooker. Add the tenderloin. Place the sage on top of the meat. Top with the diced apples.

2. Cover and cook on low for 8–10 hours.

BEEF AND COCONUT CURRY

This Indian-inspired recipe has the perfect blend of beef and vegetables, and the finished product is both sweet and savory.

Serves 4

2 tablespoons coconut oil

2 pounds beef chuck roast, cut into 2" pieces

2 large onions, each cut into 8 wedges

4 cloves garlic, finely chopped

2 tablespoons finely chopped fresh ginger

12 ounces coconut milk

2 tablespoons raw honey

1 tablespoon curry powder

1 teaspoon cayenne pepper

1 pint cherry tomatoes

1. In a large skillet, warm oil over medium-high heat. Brown beef on all sides, about 3 minutes per side. Transfer to a 4-quart slow cooker along with onions, garlic, and ginger.

2. In a large bowl, whisk together the coconut milk, honey, curry powder, and cayenne pepper, and pour into skillet. Cook, stirring to loosen pan drippings, for 5 minutes. Pour over meat in slow cooker. Cover and cook on low for 7–8 hours, or on high for 4–5 hours, until meat is tender.

3. Stir in cherry tomatoes and let them warm and soften in stew for 15–20 minutes.

BEEF AND CABBAGE

The longer cooking time for this recipe helps the flavors develop. But because the meat is already cooked, this meal is done when the cabbage is tender. Serve over mashed turnip, cauliflower, or butternut squash.

Serves 4

1 pound cooked stew beef

1 small head cabbage, chopped

1 medium onion, diced

2 large carrots, peeled and thinly sliced

2 stalks celery, sliced in ½" pieces

1 clove garlic, minced

2 cups beef broth

1 (14.5-ounce) can diced tomatoes

¼ teaspoon raw honey

⅛ teaspoon freshly ground black pepper

1. Cut the cooked beef into bite-sized pieces and add it to a 4-quart slow cooker along with the cabbage, onion, carrots, and celery. Stir to combine.

2. Add the garlic, broth, tomatoes, honey, and pepper to a bowl; mix well and pour over the beef. Cook on high for 1 hour or until the cabbage has begun to wilt.

3. Reduce heat to low and cook for 3–4 hours or until cabbage is very tender. Adjust seasonings if necessary.

BEEF AND GINGER CURRY

This hearty and spicy curry dish, typically served over rice, is just as tasty over a bed of Paleo-approved carrots and cauliflower.

Serves 4

1 pound stewing steak

1 tablespoon sesame oil

Pepper, to taste

2 cloves garlic, minced

1 teaspoon chopped fresh ginger

1 fresh green chili, diced

1 tablespoon curry powder

1 (14.5-ounce) can stewed tomatoes, chopped

1 large onion, quartered

8 ounces beef broth

1. In a large skillet, brown the steak in the oil over medium-high heat for 5–10 minutes. Once browned, remove from pan, leaving juices. Season beef with pepper.

2. In the remaining juice from the steak, cook the garlic, ginger, and chili over medium heat for 2 minutes, stirring frequently.

3. Season with curry powder. Mix in the chopped tomatoes.

4. Place the onion on the bottom of a 3- or 4-quart slow cooker, and layer with browned beef.

5. Add mixture from pan to the slow cooker, and add the broth. Cover and cook on low for 6–8 hours.

CHAPTER 9

POULTRY

CHICKEN BACON WRAPS

This recipe may be a bit fussy, but the result is stupendous. Each bit of chicken is wrapped in smoky and salty bacon, making every bite one of the best you'll ever eat. You can serve the bacon-wrapped chicken by itself as an appetizer, perhaps with some guacamole for dipping. If you don't want to wrap each piece of chicken in the bacon, just cube some leftover cooked chicken and make the wraps with bacon you have cooked separately. That will take about 20 minutes off total preparation time.

Serves 4

8 bacon slices, cut into thirds crosswise

2 boneless, skinless chicken breasts

2 large beefsteak tomatoes, chopped

¼ cup chopped green onion

⅓ cup olive oil mayonnaise

4 large romaine lettuce leaves or egg rounds from Steak and Egg Roll-Ups (see Chapter 7)

1. Preheat oven to 425°F. Place bacon in skillet and cook for 4 minutes, turning a few times, until the bacon has rendered some fat and is partially cooked but still pliable. Drain on paper towels.

2. Cut chicken breasts into 1" pieces. Wrap each piece of chicken with a piece of the partially-cooked bacon and secure with a toothpick.

3. Place bacon-wrapped chicken pieces on a baking pan with sides. Bake for 7 minutes, then turn chicken over and bake for 7–9 minutes longer or until bacon is crisp and chicken is thoroughly cooked.

4. In medium bowl, combine tomatoes, green onions, and mayonnaise and mix.

5. Arrange lettuce on work surface. Remove toothpicks from chicken, divide chicken among leaves and top with tomato mixture. Roll up and serve immediately.

CREAMY SPINACH-STUFFED CHICKEN BREASTS

This wonderful recipe is perfect for company. You can make it ahead of time. Make the chicken rolls and store in the fridge; don't brown them until your guests have arrived. Then brown the rolls and bake until done. If you are avoiding cheese, use 1 cup Yogurt Cheese (see Chapter 2) in the filling in place of the cream cheese. Serve with roasted asparagus and a spinach salad, along with Apple Cranberry Crisp (see Chapter 15) for dessert.

Serves 8

3 slices bacon

2 tablespoons butter or olive oil

1 onion, finely chopped

1 (8-ounce) package cream cheese, softened

¼ cup sour cream

1 cup frozen chopped spinach, thawed and well drained

Pinch nutmeg

8 boneless, skinless chicken breasts

½ teaspoon salt

⅛ teaspoon white pepper

2 eggs, beaten

2 cups ground almonds

1. Cook bacon in medium skillet until crisp. Drain on paper towels, crumble, and set aside. Drain all but 1 tablespoon bacon fat from pan. Add butter or olive oil to pan and melt over medium heat.

2. Cook onion in this mixture until tender, about 5–6 minutes. Remove from heat and let cool for 10 minutes.

3. Meanwhile, beat cream cheese in medium bowl until smooth. Stir in sour cream and mix well. Add onion, crumbled bacon, spinach, and nutmeg and mix.

4. Place chicken breasts on parchment paper and cover with more parchment paper. Pound with meat mallet until about ¼" thick; don't tear the chicken. Season chicken with salt and pepper. Divide spinach mixture among breasts and roll up to enclose filling; secure with toothpick.

5. Dip chicken bundles into egg, then into ground almonds to coat. At this point you can cover chicken and refrigerate.

6. When ready to eat, preheat oven to 375°F. Place chicken in pan and bake for 25–35 minutes or until thoroughly cooked. Remove toothpicks and serve.

CHICKEN TIKKA

"Tikka" means an Indian dish of spicy marinated small pieces of meat or vegetables. The food, usually some type of poultry, is often marinated in yogurt to tenderize the meat before cooking. This spicy and flavorful dish is delicious served with cooked spaghetti squash or Mashed Cauliflower (see Chapter 11). Add some fruit on the side for a cooling contrast.

Serves 6

2½ pounds boneless, skinless chicken breasts

½ cup whole milk yogurt

½ cup heavy cream or coconut cream

2 tablespoons Ghee (see Chapter 2) or melted butter or olive oil

3 cloves garlic, minced

1 tablespoon curry powder

1 teaspoon ground ginger

½ teaspoon smoked paprika

½ teaspoon ground cumin

⅛ teaspoon ground cardamom

2 tablespoons lemon juice

1 teaspoon salt

⅛ teaspoon pepper

¼ teaspoon crushed red pepper flakes

1. Cut chicken into 1½" pieces and set aside.

2. In large bowl, combine yogurt, cream, Ghee, and remaining ingredients; stir to combine. Add chicken and stir to coat.

3. Cover bowl and marinate in refrigerator for at least 6 hours, up to 24 hours.

4. When ready to eat, prepare and preheat grill. Drain chicken and thread onto 12 metal skewers. Discard remaining yogurt mixture.

5. Grill chicken 6" from medium coals until chicken registers 165°F on a meat thermometer and juices run clear, about 10–14 minutes, turning occasionally. Serve immediately.

CHICKEN-STUFFED ACORN SQUASH

Squash is flavorful and so good for you. It is packed with vitamin A, the B complex vitamins, and vitamin C. It is also high in potassium and magnesium, as well as being a great source of fiber. The vegetable is stuffed with cranberries, nuts, chicken, and apple in this appetizing recipe that's perfect for a fall dinner.

Serves 6

3 medium acorn squash

¼ cup water

2 tablespoons coconut oil

1 onion, chopped

1 pound ground chicken or turkey

1 green apple, peeled and chopped

½ cup dried cranberries

½ cup chopped pecans

2 tablespoons honey

½ cup chicken broth

1 teaspoon salt

1 teaspoon dried thyme leaves

⅛ teaspoon pepper

1. Preheat oven to 350°F. Cut acorn squash in half and remove seeds. If necessary, cut off a small piece of squash on the opposite side from the cut so the squash is stable and sits upright. Place, cut-side down, on rimmed baking sheet; add water. Bake for 30 minutes.

2. Meanwhile, heat coconut oil in large pan over medium heat. Add onion and chicken; cook and stir until chicken is cooked. Add apple and cook for 4 minutes longer. Stir in dried cranberries, pecans, honey, broth, salt, thyme, and pepper, and simmer for 5 minutes.

3. Remove squash from oven and turn cut-side up. Fill with chicken mixture. Bake for 20–25 minutes longer or until squash is tender. Serve immediately.

SWEET-AND-SOUR GLAZED CHICKEN

Sweet-and-sour is a classic flavor combination in Chinese cooking. The "sweet" is usually from brown sugar, but honey or even maple syrup is a Paleo-friendly substitute. Serve this recipe over Mashed Sweet Potatoes (see Chapter 11) to soak up the sauce.

Serves 4

½ cup apple cider vinegar

¼ cup tomato sauce

¼ cup honey

1 tablespoon Worcestershire sauce

½ cup chicken broth

3 cloves garlic, minced

⅛ teaspoon pepper

½ teaspoon ground ginger

2 tablespoons Ghee (see Chapter 2) or coconut oil

4 boneless, skinless chicken breasts

1. In small bowl, combine vinegar, tomato sauce, honey, Worcestershire sauce, chicken broth, garlic, pepper, and ginger.

2. Heat Ghee or coconut oil in large skillet over medium-high heat. Add chicken; brown on one side until chicken releases easily from pan.

3. Turn chicken and pour sauce over all. Bring to a simmer, then reduce heat to low and simmer for 15–20 minutes or until sauce is slightly thickened and chicken registers 165°F on a meat thermometer.

CHICKEN IN TUNA SAUCE

This is a takeoff on vitello tonnato, which is veal in tuna sauce. The meat is cooked, then sliced thin and covered with a creamy sauce made from tuna, capers, and mustard. It's ideal for entertaining, and perfect for dinner on a hot summer night. This recipe must be made ahead of time. Serve with some fresh fruit and a spinach salad.

Serves 6

2 tablespoons olive oil

1 shallot, finely chopped

2 cloves garlic, minced

1 carrot, sliced

4 cups chicken broth

1 teaspoon salt

⅛ teaspoon pepper

6 boneless, skinless chicken breasts

1 (6-ounce) can tuna in oil

2 tablespoons Dijon mustard

2 tablespoons lemon juice

¼ cup coconut milk

2 tablespoons drained capers

1. In large skillet, heat olive oil over medium heat. Add shallot and garlic; cook and stir for 2 minutes. Add carrot, broth, salt, and pepper and bring to a boil. Boil for 3 minutes.

2. Add chicken breasts and reduce heat. Simmer, covered, for 8–12 minutes or until the chicken reaches 165°F on a meat thermometer. Remove from heat.

3. Place chicken in baking dish; pour some of the cooking liquid over it. Cover and chill until cold. Discard remaining cooking liquid.

4. While chicken is chilling, drain tuna, reserving 3 tablespoons oil. Place tuna, reserved oil, mustard, lemon juice, and coconut milk in blender or food processor. Blend or process until smooth. Cover and refrigerate.

5. When chicken is cold, remove from marinade and slice each into 6 pieces crosswise. Arrange on a serving plate and spread with the tuna sauce. Sprinkle with capers, then cover and chill for another 4–8 hours before serving.

CREAMED CHICKEN

Creamed Chicken is a wonderful old-fashioned recipe that is pure comfort food. You can serve it over Roasted Tomato Zucchini Pasta (see Chapter 5), Cauliflower Rice (see Chapter 11), or Mashed Sweet Potatoes (see Chapter 11). Add some steamed carrots and a green salad for a delicious dinner.

Serves 4

2 tablespoons Ghee (see Chapter 2) or coconut oil

1 onion, chopped

3 cloves garlic, minced

1½ pounds boneless, skinless chicken breast, cubed

3 tablespoons coconut flour

1 teaspoon salt

⅛ teaspoon pepper

1½ cups chicken stock

½ cup coconut milk

2 tablespoons Dijon mustard

1 teaspoon dried thyme leaves

1. In large saucepan, heat Ghee over medium heat. Add onion and garlic; cook and stir until tender, about 5 minutes.

2. Toss chicken with coconut flour, salt, and pepper. Add to skillet; cook for 4–5 minutes or until browned.

3. Add stock, coconut milk, mustard, and thyme and bring to a simmer. Reduce heat to low and simmer for 6–9 minutes or until chicken is thoroughly cooked and sauce is slightly thickened. Serve immediately.

CHICKEN LETTUCE WRAPS

Lettuce is the wrap of choice to replace bread in Paleo sandwiches. You can choose any type of sturdy lettuce, including romaine, butter lettuce, or Boston. Separate the leaves carefully and wash and dry. Serve this recipe immediately with a cold glass of milk or iced tea and a fruit salad.

Serves 4

2 tablespoons coconut oil

1 pound boneless, skinless chicken thighs, cubed

2 cloves garlic, minced

4 green onions, chopped

1 cup shredded carrot

1 red bell pepper, chopped

1 tablespoon lemon juice

2 tablespoons Paleo-friendly hoisin sauce or coconut aminos

½ teaspoon salt

⅛ teaspoon crushed red pepper flakes

⅓ cup Wilma's Mayonnaise (see Chapter 2)

8 lettuce leaves

1. In large skillet, heat coconut oil over medium heat. Add chicken and brown, stirring frequently, for about 6 minutes.

2. Add garlic, green onions, carrot, and bell pepper and cook for another 4 minutes.

3. Stir in lemon juice, hoisin sauce, salt, and red pepper flakes. Simmer until chicken is thoroughly cooked to 165°F.

4. Remove from heat and stir in mayonnaise. Serve in lettuce leaves.

TANDOORI CHICKEN KEBABS

Tandoori is a special Indian way of cooking meat. A tandoori oven is made of clay or metal and is round. The meat is cooked on the side of the oven, where temperatures can reach 900°F. But "tandoori" can also be used to describe the marinade of a recipe, which usually uses yogurt to tenderize. The cream that is on the top of a can of coconut milk is an admirable substitute, as long as lemon juice is added for acidity. You can also use Almond Yogurt (see Chapter 1) in place of the coconut cream.

Serves 4

⅓ cup coconut cream or Almond Yogurt (Chapter 1)

⅓ cup lemon juice

2 tablespoons minced gingerroot

4 cloves garlic, minced

2 tablespoons curry powder

1 teaspoon ground turmeric

½ teaspoon salt

¼ teaspoon crushed red pepper flakes

6 boneless, skinless chicken breast halves

2 red bell peppers, cut into strips

2 red onions, cut into eighths

1. In glass baking dish, combine cream from coconut milk or Almond Yogurt, lemon juice, gingerroot, garlic, curry powder, turmeric, salt, and red pepper flakes and mix well.

2. Cut chicken into 1½" pieces. Add to marinade and turn to coat. Cover and marinate in the refrigerator for 12–24 hours.

3. When ready to eat, prepare and preheat grill. Remove chicken from marinade; discard marinade. Thread chicken, bell peppers, and onions onto metal skewers.

4. Grill over medium-high coals until chicken is cooked to 165°F and vegetables are tender. Serve immediately.

TURKEY HAWAIIAN

This is a great recipe to make with leftover Thanksgiving turkey. Use the cooked turkey within 4 days; after that time, freeze it. This sweet-and-sour recipe is different from the Thanksgiving staple and a nice change of pace for the holidays. Plus, it's easy to make!

Serves 4

2 tablespoons olive or coconut oil

1 onion, chopped

2 cloves garlic, minced

1 tablespoon minced fresh gingerroot

3 tablespoons coconut flour

1 tablespoon coconut aminos

⅛ teaspoon pepper

1 (14-ounce) can unsweetened pineapple tidbits in juice, drained, reserving juice

1½ cups chicken broth

1 red bell pepper, chopped

3 cups cubed cooked turkey

½ cup toasted coconut

1. In large saucepan, heat olive or coconut oil over medium heat. Add onion, garlic, and gingerroot; cook and stir until crisp-tender, about 4 minutes. Add coconut flour; cook and stir for 2 minutes.

2. Add coconut aminos, pepper, pineapple juice, and chicken broth and bring to a simmer; simmer for 3 minutes.

3. Add bell pepper; simmer for 4 minutes longer.

4. Stir in pineapple tidbits and turkey and simmer for 4–6 minutes or until hot. Serve over Cauliflower Rice (see Chapter 11) or Jicama Rice (see Chapter 11), topped with toasted coconut.

TURKEY KEBABS

You can often find turkey breast tenderloin in the meat section of the supermarket. If you can't find it, ask the butcher for this cut. It is part of the breast, but not the whole breast, which weighs about 4 pounds. The tenderloin is a very tender cut and doesn't need to marinate for a long time; about an hour in the fridge will flavor it nicely.

Serves 4

1 (24-ounce) turkey tenderloin

⅓ cup olive oil

¼ cup lemon juice

¼ cup Dijon mustard

2 cloves garlic, minced

1 teaspoon dried thyme leaves

1 teaspoon salt

⅛ teaspoon pepper

16 whole medium mushrooms, trimmed

1 red bell pepper, cut into 1" chunks

1. Cut the turkey into 1½" cubes and set aside.

2. In large bowl, combine olive oil, lemon juice, mustard, garlic, thyme, salt, and pepper and mix well. Add turkey and stir to coat. Cover and refrigerate for at least 1 hour, up to 8 hours.

3. When ready to eat, prepare and preheat grill. Remove turkey from marinade, reserving marinade.

4. Thread turkey, mushrooms, and bell pepper on 4 metal skewers. Brush with marinade, then discard marinade. Grill 6" from medium coals for about 12–15 minutes or until turkey registers 165°F on a meat thermometer. Serve immediately.

PANCETTA-WRAPPED CHICKEN

Pancetta is a type of Italian bacon that is cured but not smoked. It has a delicate spicy flavor. You can find it in the deli department of most supermarkets. It is sliced very thin and is the perfect thing to wrap around a boneless, skinless chicken breast. This easy recipe is perfect for entertaining.

Serves 6

6 boneless, skinless chicken breasts

2 cloves garlic, minced

1 teaspoon salt

1 tablespoon Dijon mustard

1 tablespoon lemon juice

½ teaspoon dried thyme leaves

⅛ teaspoon pepper

6 thin slices pancetta

2 tablespoons olive oil

⅔ cup chicken broth

2 tablespoons butter, if desired

1. Place chicken breasts on work surface. On a cutting board, mince the garlic with the salt, working the mixture with a side of a knife to form a paste. Transfer to small bowl and add mustard, lemon juice, thyme, and pepper and mix well.

2. Rub this mixture into both sides of the chicken breasts. Wrap the chicken with the pancetta.

3. Heat the olive oil in a large pan. Add the chicken and cook, turning once, until chicken registers 165°F on a meat thermometer and the pancetta is crisp, about 5–7 minutes on each side. Transfer to a platter and cover to keep warm.

4. Add chicken broth to pan and simmer for 3 minutes, scraping pan drippings, until reduced. Swirl in the butter, if using, until just melted, then pour sauce over chicken and serve.

ROAST CHICKEN

Roasting chickens are small, usually about 2½–3 pounds. If you're serving more than 3 or 4 people you'll need to roast two (or three) chickens. A roast chicken will perfume a house like nothing else. And it is easy to complement with just about any side dish or salad. Stuff the chicken with lemon, garlic, and bacon for fabulous flavor. You can add cut-up carrots, onions, and other vegetables to the pan to roast with the chicken for a complete dinner.

Serves 3–4

1 (3-pound) roasting chicken

1 lemon, cut in half

8 whole cloves of garlic

3 slices bacon, cooked and drained

3 tablespoons butter

½ cup chicken stock

1. Preheat oven to 375°F. Pat the chicken dry (do not rinse it, because rinsing can spray bacteria around your kitchen). Place in a roasting pan.

2. Stuff one lemon half inside the chicken. Juice the other lemon half, reserving the juice, and place the juiced half in the pan. Stuff the garlic and bacon into the chicken too. Truss if desired.

3. Rub the chicken with butter and 1 tablespoon of the reserved lemon juice. Pour chicken stock and remaining lemon juice into the pan.

4. Roast for 60–80 minutes, basting every 20 minutes with pan juices, until chicken registers 165°F on a meat thermometer. Cover and let stand for 10 minutes, then carve and serve.

SPICY BACON CHICKEN

Chicken thighs are wrapped in bacon and baked, then topped with a creamy and spicy mixture and broiled until a crust forms. This unusual recipe is a great choice for entertaining. Serve it with some steamed asparagus and Tomato Salad (see Chapter 3), and with Blueberry Coconut Crisp (see Chapter 15) for dessert.

Serves 4

8 slices bacon

8 boneless, skinless chicken thighs

1 tablespoon olive oil

1 tablespoon lemon juice

½ teaspoon salt

¼ teaspoon pepper

⅓ cup Wilma's Mayonnaise (see Chapter 2)

¼ cup prepared horseradish

2 tablespoons grainy mustard

1. Preheat oven to 350°F. Wrap one slice of bacon around the sides of each chicken thigh so the top of the chicken is exposed; secure with toothpick. Place on a baking sheet and drizzle with olive oil and lemon juice. Sprinkle with salt and pepper.

2. Bake for 35–40 minutes or until chicken registers 165°F and bacon is crisp.

3. Meanwhile, in small bowl combine mayonnaise, horseradish, and mustard.

4. Remove chicken from oven and remove toothpicks. Turn oven to broil. Place chicken on broiler pan. Divide mayonnaise mixture among the chicken thighs.

5. Broil for about 1–2 minutes or until the sauce just starts to bubble and brown. Serve immediately.

CHICKEN IN PARCHMENT

You can find parchment paper at any grocery store in the country. It is thick white paper that stands up well to the oven's heat. It can be used to bake chicken or fish; the paper holds the moisture inside so the end result is juicy and tender. Use any tender vegetable you like in this easy recipe; use whatever looks good at the market or what suits your taste at the time.

Serves 4

4 boneless, skinless chicken breasts

½ teaspoon salt

⅛ teaspoon pepper

1 cup sliced mushrooms

1 red bell pepper, chopped

1 yellow summer squash, chopped

1 sprig fresh rosemary

2 teaspoons fresh thyme leaves

¼ cup olive oil

¼ cup lemon juice

1. Preheat oven to 400°F. Cut four 12" x 15" squares of parchment paper and place on work surface.

2. Place each chicken breast in the center of each parchment paper square and sprinkle with salt and pepper.

3. Divide mushrooms, bell pepper, and squash among the parchment paper squares. Divide rosemary leaves on the vegetables and top with thyme. Drizzle with olive oil and lemon juice.

4. Fold ends of the paper together twice, then fold the other ends to make a packet. Make sure to leave some room in the packet for heat expansion.

5. Place parchment paper bundles on a baking sheet and bake for 20–30 minutes or until chicken registers 165°F on a meat thermometer. Open the bundles at the table, being careful of the steam.

GREEK CHICKEN WINGS

The flavors of Greece—lemon, olive, garlic, and oregano—are combined with crisp and tender chicken wings for a wonderful dinner. Yes, you can serve wings for dinner. Each serving should be about one pound of the uncooked wings. Buy wings labeled "drumettes" because they have the most meat per pound. Serve these wings with a spinach salad, and sliced strawberries for dessert.

Serves 4

¼ cup lemon juice

2 tablespoons chopped fresh oregano leaves

3 tablespoons olive oil

3 tablespoons honey

2 tablespoons yogurt or coconut milk

1 teaspoon Tabasco sauce

3 cloves garlic, minced

1 teaspoon salt

¼ teaspoon white pepper

4 pounds chicken drumettes

½ cup crumbled feta cheese, if desired

1. In very large zip-top food storage bag, combine lemon juice, oregano, olive oil, honey, yogurt or coconut milk, Tabasco, garlic, salt, and pepper and mix. Add drumettes and massage to coat. Seal bag, place in large baking dish, and refrigerate for 8–24 hours.

2. When ready to eat, preheat oven to 400°F. Remove drumettes from marinade; discard marinade. Place wings on 15" x 10" jellyroll pan.

3. Bake drumettes for 40–45 minutes, turning once, until meat thermometer registers 165°F. Sprinkle chicken with feta cheese, if using, and serve immediately.

SLOW-COOKER SPICY CHICKEN THIGHS

Chicken thighs cook beautifully in the slow cooker. The higher fat content of the thighs means that the meat will not overcook; instead, it becomes tender and juicy. This simple recipe is a delicious choice when you're just too busy to cook. Just throw the ingredients together in the morning and let it cook all day while you work or run errands.

Serves 4

10 boneless, skinless chicken thighs

½ teaspoon salt

⅛ teaspoon crushed red pepper flakes

1 onion, chopped

3 cloves garlic, minced

1 jalapeño pepper, minced

1 cup Roasted Veggie Salsa (see Chapter 2)

1 tablespoon arrowroot powder, if desired

¼ cup water, if desired

1. Combine all ingredients except arrowroot powder and water in a 4-quart slow cooker and stir to combine. Cover and cook on low for 7–9 hours or until chicken registers 165°F on an instant-read meat thermometer.

2. You can thicken the liquid if you like by dissolving arrowroot powder in water. Add to the slow cooker. Cover and cook on high for 20 minutes until thickened.

SPATCHCOCKED CHICKEN

Chicken that is "spatchcocked" is just chicken that is flattened out so it cooks evenly and quickly on the grill. The backbone is cut out of the whole chicken, then it is flattened, marinated, and grilled. The end result is tender and juicy with nicely crisped skin. If you're serving more than 3 or 4 people, grill more chickens!

Serves 3–4

1 (3½-pound) whole chicken

2 tablespoons olive oil

2 tablespoons lemon juice

2 cloves garlic, minced

1 teaspoon paprika

1 teaspoon smoked paprika

1 teaspoon dried thyme leaves

1 teaspoon dried basil leaves

½ teaspoon salt

¼ teaspoon white pepper

1. Place the chicken on a work surface, breast-side down. Using kitchen shears, cut along the backbone on both sides. Remove the backbone and save for Chicken Stock (see Chapter 4).

2. Turn the chicken skin-side up and press down on the breast to flatten until you hear a cracking noise. Place the chicken in a 9" x 13" glass baking dish.

3. In small bowl, combine remaining ingredients and mix well. Rub this mixture on the chicken. Cover and marinate for 2–8 hours.

4. When ready to eat, prepare and preheat grill, creating a two-level fire. That means one side should have fewer coals than the other so it is at a lower temperature. For a gas grill, heat one side to medium-high and the other to medium-low by turning off one of the burners on the cooler side. Place chicken over the cooler side of the grill, skin-side up, and cover. Grill for 10 minutes.

5. Turn the chicken skin-side down over the hotter side of the grill and press on the bird using a large spatula. Grill, covered for another 10 minutes.

6. Move the chicken again to the cooler side of the grill. Cover and grill for another 5–10 minutes until the chicken registers 165°F. Remove from grill and let stand for 5 minutes, covered, then cut apart to serve.

PHEASANTLY PLEASANT

Wild game like pheasants move more frequently than the average chicken and therefore contain less saturated fat and calories per ounce. They are also less tender so are best cooked slowly for a long period of time.

Serves 6

Boneless meat from 2 pheasants, cut into small, 1–2" chunks

¼ cup almond flour, seasoned with a pinch of pepper

4 tablespoons avocado or coconut oil

4 tablespoons coconut butter

1 clove garlic

1 large onion, diced

1 cup dry white wine or additional chicken broth

1 tablespoon raw honey

1 (10.75-ounce) can chopped mushrooms

10 ounces chicken broth

1. Coat pheasant pieces in seasoned almond flour.

2. In a skillet over medium heat, sauté the pheasant for 5–7 minutes in oil and butter. Transfer pheasant to a 4-quart slow cooker.

3. Mash garlic clove in skillet juices, add onion, wine, honey, mushrooms, and broth. Heat to bubbling and simmer 5 minutes, then pour over pheasant in the slow cooker.

4. Cover and cook on low for 6–8 hours.

GROUND TURKEY JOES

This easy, sweet-and-sour turkey dish comes together quickly and serves well over puréed cauliflower, mashed sweet potatoes, or turnips. If you prefer, you can use ground chicken or ground beef as a substitute for the ground turkey.

Serves 4

2 teaspoons organic butter or Ghee (see Chapter 2) or olive oil

1 pound lean ground turkey

½ cup finely chopped onion

½ cup finely chopped green pepper

1 teaspoon garlic powder

1 tablespoon prepared yellow mustard

¾ cup Homemade Ketchup (see Chapter 2)

3 tablespoons raw honey

¼ teaspoon lemon juice

½ teaspoon ground pepper

1. In a large skillet, heat butter over medium-high heat. Brown ground turkey, onion, and green pepper for approximately 5–6 minutes. Drain off any grease.

2. Add turkey mixture to a greased 2½- or 4-quart slow cooker. Add garlic powder, mustard, ketchup, honey, lemon juice, and pepper.

3. Mix ingredients together and cook on low for 4 hours or on high for 2 hours.

TURKEY MEATBALLS

This is a fairly generic meatball recipe with some basic additions. You can substitute any type of ground meat you prefer: bison, beef, chicken, or pork. Flaxseed meal can replace the almond meal as well.

Yields 24 meatballs

2 pounds (93% lean) ground turkey

1 cup almond meal

2 large eggs

5 scallions, chopped

1 red bell pepper, seeded and diced

2 cloves garlic, minced

1 tablespoon dried basil

1 tablespoon dried oregano

2 tablespoons avocado oil

1. Preheat oven to 400°F.

2. Combine all ingredients except oil in a large bowl. Mix well with clean hands. Add oil to turkey mixture and mix well.

3. Form turkey mixture into 24 meatballs and place on 2 rimmed baking pans.

4. Bake for 20–25 minutes or until meat thermometer inserted into a meatball registers 165°F.

Fat Content in Ground Meats

Although most people make sure to buy ground meat with the lowest fat content, it is more beneficial to buy fattier ground meat when it is from grass-fed or barn-roaming animals. This meat is lower in saturated fat than most commercial ground meat, and the fat profiles favor the omega-3 fatty acids to fight inflammation and heart disease in your body.

MANGO DUCK BREAST

Slow-cooked mangoes soften and create their own sauce in this easy duck dish.

Serves 4

2 boneless, skinless duck breasts

1 large mango, peeled and cubed

¼ cup duck or chicken stock

1 tablespoon ginger juice

1 tablespoon minced hot pepper

1 tablespoon minced shallot

1. Place all ingredients in a 4-quart slow cooker. Cover and cook on high for 4–5 hours or on low for 6–8 hours or until duck is tender.

2. Remove duck from slow cooker and cover to keep warm. Skim fat from top of sauce remaining in slow cooker. Serve duck with the sauce.

THYME-ROASTED TURKEY BREAST

Slow-cooked turkey is so moist there's no basting required!

Serves 10

2 large onions, thinly sliced

1 (6–7-pound) turkey breast, skin on

½ cup minced thyme

½ tablespoon freshly ground black pepper

½ tablespoon dried parsley

½ tablespoon celery flakes

½ tablespoon mustard seed

1. Arrange the onion slices in a thin layer on the bottom of a 6- or 7-quart slow cooker.

2. Make a small slit in the skin of the turkey and spread the thyme between the skin and meat. Smooth the skin back onto the turkey.

3. In a small bowl, stir the pepper, parsley, celery flakes, and mustard seed. Rub the spice mixture onto the skin of the turkey.

4. Place the turkey in the slow cooker on top of the onion layer. Cook for 8 hours. Remove the skin and discard before serving. Serve the turkey with cooked onions.

POACHED CHICKEN

Use this moist, tender poached chicken in any recipe that calls for cooked chicken. It is especially good in salads and sandwiches.

Serves 8

4–5 pounds whole chicken or chicken parts

1 large carrot, peeled

1 stalk celery

1 medium onion, quartered

1 cup water

1. Place the chicken into an oval 6-quart slow cooker. Arrange the vegetables around the chicken. Add the water. Cook on low for 7–8 hours until chicken registers 165°F on a meat thermometer.

2. Remove the skin before eating.

FOOLPROOF CHICKEN

This is just about the simplest chicken recipe there is, and it's perfect for any occasion.

Serves 6

3 pounds boneless, skinless chicken breasts or thighs

24 ounces tomato sauce

Place chicken in a 4-quart slow cooker and add sauce. Cover and cook on low for 8 hours or on high for 4–5 hours. Once cooked, shred the chicken with a fork and enjoy.

HOT BUFFALO CHICKEN BITES

Love buffalo wings? Then you will love these chicken bites even more; they are made with juicy chicken breasts so you won't have to worry about bones. They are super easy and much less messy! Serve with celery and carrot sticks.

Serves 6

3 large boneless, skinless chicken breasts, cut into 2" strips

2 tablespoons almond flour

¼ cup melted coconut oil

3 cloves garlic, minced

⅓ cup hot sauce

1. Place chicken strips in a greased 2½-quart slow cooker.

2. In a saucepan, whisk together the almond flour and melted coconut oil for 2–3 minutes to toast the flour.

3. Slowly whisk in the garlic and hot sauce. Pour sauce over chicken in the slow cooker.

4. Cover and cook on high for 3 hours or on low for 6 hours. Serve with celery and carrot sticks.

Fresh Garlic versus Garlic Powder

In a pinch you can use 1½ teaspoons garlic powder in this recipe. The garlic flavor won't be quite as pungent and rich as it is when you use fresh garlic, but it will still be easy and enjoyable.

CHICKEN PICCATA

Chicken is a staple for the Paleolithic eater. This lunchtime treat is a pleasant departure from the ordinary.

Serves 4

1 cup unsalted chicken broth

½ cup lemon juice

4 boneless, skinless chicken breasts

3 tablespoons almond oil

1 cup chopped onion

1 clove garlic, minced

2 cups chopped fresh artichoke hearts

3 tablespoons capers

1 teaspoon pepper

1. Combine chicken broth, lemon juice, and chicken in shallow dish. Cover and marinate overnight in the refrigerator.

2. Heat oil in a medium-sized skillet over medium heat and cook onion and garlic until softened, about 2 minutes.

3. Remove chicken from marinade, reserving marinade. Add chicken to pan and brown each side, 5–10 minutes.

4. Add artichoke hearts, capers, pepper, and reserved marinade. Reduce heat and simmer until chicken is thoroughly cooked, approximately another 10 minutes.

SHREDDED CHICKEN WRAPS

These are a great way to get the feel of a wrap without the forbidden carbohydrates of a tortilla. You can easily substitute your favorite meat or fish for the chicken to vary your lunchtime menu.

Serves 8

2 cooked boneless, skinless chicken breasts (baked, poached, or broiled)

2 stalks celery, chopped

¼ cup chopped basil

2 tablespoons almond oil

2 tablespoons lemon juice

1 teaspoon minced garlic

Ground black pepper, to taste

1 teaspoon hot sauce

1 head radicchio or romaine lettuce

1. Shred chicken and place in a medium-sized bowl.

2. Mix chicken with celery, basil, oil, lemon juice, garlic, pepper, and hot sauce.

3. Separate radicchio or lettuce leaves and place on 8 plates.

4. Spoon chicken mixture onto lettuce leaves and roll up.

CHICKEN ENCHILADAS

If you have been craving a Mexican feast, try this spicy Paleolithic alternative. This recipe has most of the taste of traditional enchiladas without the carbohydrates.

Serves 8

2 tablespoons avocado oil

2 pounds boneless, skinless chicken breast, cut in 1" cubes

4 cloves garlic, minced

½ cup finely chopped onion

2 cups chopped tomatoes

1 teaspoon cumin

1 teaspoon chili powder

½ cup fresh cilantro

Juice from 2 limes

1 (10-ounce) package frozen chopped spinach, thawed and drained

¼ cup sliced green olives

8 collard green leaves

1. Heat oil in a medium-sized skillet. Sauté chicken, garlic, and onion in the hot oil until thoroughly cooked, about 10 minutes.

2. Add tomatoes, cumin, chili powder, cilantro, and lime juice and simmer for 5 minutes.

3. Add spinach and simmer for 5 more minutes. Remove from heat. Stir in olives.

4. In a separate pan, quickly steam collard greens to soften, about 3 minutes.

5. Wrap chicken mixture in collard greens and serve.

CHICKEN WITH SAUTÉED TOMATOES AND PINE NUTS

Sautéed tomatoes and pine nuts add a nice nutty flavor to an ordinary dish. This topping can be added to fish or beef just as easily.

Serves 2

¼ cup avocado oil

1 cup halved cherry tomatoes

¼ cup chopped green chilies

¼ cup cilantro

½ cup pine nuts

2 boneless, skinless chicken breasts

1. Heat oil in a medium-sized skillet over medium-high heat. Sauté tomatoes, chilies, cilantro, and pine nuts until golden brown, about 5 minutes. Remove from pan and set aside.

2. In the same pan, cook chicken 5 minutes on each side.

3. Return tomato mixture to pan and cover. Simmer on low for 5 minutes until chicken is fully cooked.

PECAN-CRUSTED CHICKEN

This pecan crust recipe is quite versatile. It works for fish as well as chicken, and other nuts can be substituted for different flavors.

Serves 4

1 cup ground pecans

2 large eggs, beaten

4 boneless, skinless chicken breasts

1. Preheat oven to 350°F.

2. Place ground nuts in a shallow bowl and eggs in a separate shallow bowl.

3. Dip each chicken breast in egg and then in nuts. Place coated chicken breasts in a shallow baking dish.

4. Bake for 25 minutes or until a meat thermometer registers 165°F. Let chicken stand for 5 minutes, then serve.

SPICY CHICKEN SLIDERS

You can substitute ground turkey or pork for the chicken. Adjust the quantity of pepper flakes to control the spiciness.

Serves 4

1 pound ground chicken breast

¼ cup finely chopped yellow onion

¼ cup finely chopped red bell pepper

1 teaspoon minced garlic

¼ cup thinly sliced scallions

½ teaspoon red pepper flakes

½ teaspoon chili powder

½ teaspoon sea salt

Freshly ground black pepper, to taste

1. Clean and oil broiler rack. Preheat broiler to medium.

2. Combine all the ingredients in a medium-sized bowl, mixing lightly. Form mixture into 8 small patties.

3. Broil the burgers for 3–4 minutes per side until firm through the center, the juices run clear, and a food thermometer registers 165°F. Transfer to a plate and tent with tinfoil to keep warm. Allow to rest 1–2 minutes before serving.

NO-CRUST CHICKEN POTPIE

This is a traditional comfort food converted to satisfy even the hardest-to-please Paleo palate.

Serves 4

2 teaspoons organic butter or Ghee (see Chapter 2)

10 ounces coconut milk

1 teaspoon dried parsley

1 teaspoon dried onion flakes

1 (16-ounce) package frozen cauliflower, broccoli, and carrot blend

1 pound boneless, skinless chicken breasts, cut into ½" cubes

1. Melt butter and pour into a 4-quart slow cooker.

2. Add coconut milk, parsley, and onion flakes to the slow cooker.

3. Stir in the frozen vegetables and chicken pieces. Cover and cook on low for 8 hours until chicken is cooked. Mix well before serving.

CHICKEN WITH EGGPLANT

Adding chicken to a typical Asian-inspired eggplant dish makes for a well-balanced dinner.

Serves 4

4 boneless, skinless chicken breasts

1 pound eggplant

2 tablespoons avocado oil

2 cloves garlic, minced

1 medium red bell pepper, finely chopped

½ cup water

¼ cup coconut aminos

¼ cup red wine vinegar

2 tablespoons raw honey

2 tablespoons sesame oil

¼ teaspoon red pepper flakes

1. Cut chicken breasts lengthwise into ½"-wide strips. Cut eggplant lengthwise into 1"-wide strips.

2. Heat avocado oil in a large skillet over medium-high heat and cook chicken until well done. Transfer to a bowl and set aside.

3. Return pan to high heat and add eggplant, garlic, bell pepper, and water. Bring to a boil, then reduce heat to medium-low, cover pan, and cook until eggplant is very soft and liquid has evaporated, stirring occasionally.

4. In a small bowl, mix coconut aminos, vinegar, honey, and sesame oil. Add cooked chicken, coconut aminos mixture, and red pepper flakes to pan with cooked eggplant and bring to a boil. Reduce heat to medium and cook, occasionally stirring, for about 5 minutes. Serve.

CHICKEN AND VEGETABLE FRITTATA

Eggs and chicken make this satisfying meal both high in protein and a complete one-pot dish.

Serves 4

1 teaspoon organic butter or Ghee (see Chapter 2)

3 shallots, sliced

2 cloves garlic, minced

½ teaspoon salt

½ teaspoon freshly ground black pepper

8 ounces boneless, skinless chicken breast, diced

1 cup broccoli florets

1 cup sliced zucchini

1 cup sliced yellow squash

12 asparagus spears, chopped into 1" pieces

8 eggs

1. Preheat oven to 350°F. Melt butter in a small skillet over medium heat and sauté shallots and garlic until soft, about 3 minutes. Be careful not to burn garlic.

2. Sprinkle salt and pepper over diced chicken breast as desired. Add chicken to pan with shallots and garlic and sauté until chicken is cooked, about 7 minutes.

3. Grease a round casserole dish. Place all vegetables and chicken with shallots into the greased dish.

4. Whisk eggs and pour over contents in the dish.

5. Bake at 350°F for 20–25 minutes, until eggs are set but not brown.

POACHED CHICKEN WITH PEARS AND HERBS

Any seasonal fresh fruit will make this dish very special. Pears go very well with all poultry. Try this for a quick treat and double the recipe for company.

Serves 2

1 ripe pear, peeled, cored, and cut into chunks

2 shallots, minced

½ cup dry white wine or chicken broth

1 teaspoon dried rosemary or 1 tablespoon fresh

1 teaspoon dried thyme or 1 tablespoon fresh

1 teaspoon salt

½ teaspoon freshly ground black pepper

2½ pounds boneless, skinless chicken breasts

1. Prepare the poaching liquid by mixing pear, shallots, wine or broth, rosemary, and thyme and bringing to a boil in a medium saucepan.

2. Salt and pepper the chicken and add to the pan. Simmer over low heat for 10–12 minutes or until chicken registers 165°F on a food thermometer.

3. Serve with pears on top of each piece of chicken.

GRILLED SAN FRANCISCO–STYLE CHICKEN

This is a quick chef's delight. It's excellent, and everyone at your table will ask "What is in this?" (in a good way)!

Serves 4

1 tablespoon almond oil, plus more for grilling

1 tablespoon Dijon mustard

2 tablespoons raspberry white wine vinegar

1 small chicken (about 2½–3 pounds), cut in quarters

1 teaspoon celery salt

½ teaspoon freshly ground black pepper

1. Heat grill to 400°F or build a two-level fire, with one side hot and the other medium. In a small bowl, mix 1 tablespoon oil, mustard, and vinegar.

2. Sprinkle the chicken with celery salt and pepper. Paint the skin side of the chicken with the mustard mixture.

3. Grill the chicken, skin side up, for 15 minutes. Reduce heat to 325°F or move chicken to cooler side of grill, skin side down; Cover and cook for 15–20 minutes or until chicken registers 165°F on a food thermometer.

BRAISED CHICKEN WITH CITRUS

Chicken is wonderfully flavored by lemons, oranges, and grapefruits. Try using the sauce in this recipe over riced cauliflower or chilled in a salad.

Serves 2

¼ cup freshly squeezed orange juice

¼ cup freshly squeezed grapefruit juice

1 tablespoon raw honey

1 teaspoon dried summer savory

½ teaspoon lemon zest

1 teaspoon almond oil

½ pound boneless, skinless chicken breasts, cut in chunks

1 teaspoon salt

½ teaspoon freshly ground black pepper

1. In shallow pan, combine orange juice, grapefruit juice, honey, savory, lemon zest, and almond oil. Bring to a simmer over low heat.

2. Sprinkle the chicken with salt and pepper and add to the pan. Poach chicken for 8–10 minutes or until chicken registers 165°F on a meat thermometer. Serve warm or chilled.

LEMON CHICKEN

This is a classic citrus chicken with fresh herbs that isn't too sour—it calls for the perfect amount of lemon!

Serves 6

⅓ cup lemon juice

2 tablespoons lemon zest

3 cloves garlic, minced

2 tablespoons chopped fresh thyme

2 tablespoons chopped fresh rosemary

2 tablespoons almond oil

1 teaspoon salt

1 teaspoon fresh ground black pepper

3 pounds bone-in chicken thighs

1. To make the marinade, combine lemon juice, lemon zest, garlic, thyme, rosemary, oil, salt, and pepper in a small bowl. Place chicken in a large bowl and pour marinade on top. Let marinate in the refrigerator for 2 hours.

2. Heat oven to 425°F. Place marinated chicken in one layer in a large baking dish. Spoon leftover marinade over top of chicken.

3. Bake until chicken is completely cooked through, about 50 minutes. The internal temperature will be 165°F.

BRAISED CHICKEN WITH KALE

This dish is inspired by a traditional Tuscan kale and white bean soup.

Serves 4

1 pound boneless, skinless chicken breasts

1 teaspoon salt, divided

1 teaspoon freshly ground black pepper, divided

2 tablespoons almond oil

½ onion, chopped

2 cloves garlic, minced

1 large bunch kale, chopped

1 teaspoon red pepper flakes

1 tablespoon fresh rosemary, chopped

1 (15-ounce) can diced tomatoes

1 (14.5-ounce) can chicken broth

1. Slice chicken breasts into small pieces. Season chicken with ½ teaspoon salt and ½ teaspoon pepper.

2. Heat oil in a large skillet over medium-high heat and sauté onion and garlic for 3–4 minutes. Add chicken and cook an additional 4 minutes.

3. Add kale in batches to the pan with the chicken and cook until wilted, about 2 minutes. Season with red pepper flakes and rosemary.

4. Add tomatoes, broth, ½ teaspoon salt, and ½ teaspoon pepper to the pan; stir and simmer for 10–15 minutes.

STEWED CHICKEN WITH VEGETABLES

This is a good old-fashioned way to prepare chicken for the family.

Serves 4

1 frying chicken, cut up

1 cup chicken stock

16 pearl onions

2 large carrots, peeled and cut into 1"
pieces

2 stalks celery, cut in chunks

2 cloves garlic, smashed with the side of a
knife

1 bulb fennel, trimmed and cut into chunks

4 small bluenose turnips, peeled and cut
into chunks

1 teaspoon dried thyme, or 3 teaspoons
fresh

1 teaspoon dried rosemary

2 bay leaves

3 cups chicken broth

Salt and pepper, to taste

1. In a large stew pot, mix all ingredients. Bring to a boil. Reduce heat to a simmer; cover and cook over very low heat for 50 minutes.

2. Remove and discard bay leaves before serving. You may also want to remove and discard the chicken skin before serving.

BAKED CHICKEN LEGS

This is so simple—an everyday baked chicken that requires no fuss or hassle.

Serves 6

6 bone-in chicken legs and thighs

2 tablespoons avocado oil, divided

2 tablespoons paprika

1½ tablespoons onion powder

1 teaspoon salt

1. Preheat oven to 400°F. Pat chicken dry. Coat the bottom of a large roasting pan with 1 tablespoon oil.

2. Coat chicken pieces lightly with remaining oil. Cover chicken evenly with paprika, onion powder, and salt. Place chicken pieces skin-side up in the pan.

3. Bake chicken at 400°F for 30 minutes, then lower the temperature to 350°F and cook for 10–15 minutes. The internal temperature of the chicken thighs should be 165°F.

CHICKEN CACCIATORE

This classic Italian dish, also called hunter's stew, is cooked slowly until the chicken is falling off the bone.

Serves 6

3 tablespoons avocado oil

1 whole chicken, cut up

1 cup chopped onion

1 cup chopped red bell pepper

3 cloves garlic, minced

2 (15-ounce) cans stewed tomatoes

¾ cup chicken broth

1 tablespoon Italian seasoning

1 teaspoon salt

½ teaspoon freshly ground black pepper

1 bay leaf

3 tablespoons capers

1. Heat oil in a medium-sized skillet over medium-high heat. Brown chicken thoroughly, turning frequently with tongs, about 10 minutes. Remove chicken from pan. Add onion, bell pepper, and garlic to the hot pan; sauté until onion is tender, about 10 minutes.

2. Stir in tomatoes, broth, Italian seasoning, salt, pepper, and bay leaf. Add chicken back into the pan with sauce and bring to a boil.

3. Reduce heat to low, cover, and simmer for 40–45 minutes. Stir in capers. Remove and discard bay leaf from the sauce before serving.

THAI CHICKEN STEW WITH VEGETABLES IN COCONUT CREAM

Asian flavorings can provide so many minimal yet wonderful additions to rather ordinary foods. This vegetable-loaded chicken stew is spicy and tastes very rich.

Serves 4

2 cloves garlic, minced

1 (1" piece) fresh ginger, peeled and minced

2 tablespoons almond oil

2 carrots, shredded

1 cup canned unsweetened coconut cream

1 cup chicken broth

2 cups shredded napa cabbage

4 boneless, skinless chicken breasts (about 5 ounces each), cut into bite-sized pieces

¼ cup coconut aminos

2 tablespoons Asian fish sauce

1 teaspoon Thai chili paste (red or green) or hot sauce

1 tablespoon sesame oil

½ cup chopped scallions (green parts only)

¼ cup chopped cilantro

1. In a medium-sized skillet over medium-high heat, sauté the garlic and ginger in the almond oil for 1–2 minutes. Add the carrots, coconut cream, and chicken broth and simmer for 10 minutes. Add the cabbage, chicken, coconut aminos, and fish sauce.

2. Whisk in the chili paste. Stir in the sesame oil, scallions, and cilantro. Simmer for 20 minutes, stir, and serve.

JERK CHICKEN

This is a milder take on this typically ultra-spicy Caribbean favorite.

Serves 8

2 pounds chicken pieces

1 small onion, chopped

2 green onions, chopped into large pieces

1 jalapeño pepper, seeded

3 cloves garlic

1 teaspoon black pepper

¾ teaspoon salt

½ teaspoon dried thyme

¼ teaspoon cayenne pepper

1 tablespoon coconut aminos

¼ cup lime juice

3 tablespoons avocado oil

1. Place chicken in a large glass baking dish.

2. In a food processor or blender, combine onion, green onion, jalapeño, and garlic. Pulse to chop, then add black pepper, salt, thyme, cayenne pepper, coconut aminos, lime juice, and oil. Process until smooth.

3. Pour mixture over chicken and stir well to coat evenly. Cover with plastic wrap and refrigerate for 12 hours or overnight.

4. Preheat oven to 425°F. Arrange chicken in single layer in pan. Bake for approximately 50–55 minutes or until meat thermometer registers 165°F.

TUSCAN CHICKEN

This simple dish is perfect served over grilled or oven-roasted asparagus.

Serves 4

1 pound boneless, skinless chicken breast tenderloins

1 cup chicken broth

4 cloves garlic, minced

1 shallot, minced

2 tablespoons lime juice

1 tablespoon lemon juice

1 tablespoon minced fresh rosemary

1. Place all the ingredients in a 2½–3-quart slow cooker. Stir.

2. Cook on low for 4 hours or until the chicken is fully cooked. Stir well and serve.

COCONUT MANGO SPICED CHICKEN

This simple sweet and spicy dish requires just four ingredients and is easily prepared in just a few minutes.

Serves 4

1 can unsweetened coconut milk

1 large, firm mango, peeled and cubed (save mango pit)

1 pound boneless, skinless chicken breasts or thighs, cubed

1 tablespoon dried paprika flakes

1. Pour coconut milk into a 2½–3-quart slow cooker.

2. Place the cubes of mango in the slow cooker, along with the pit of the mango. Add the chicken and paprika flakes. Stir well.

3. Cook on high for 3 hours or on low for 5–6 hours or until chicken registers 165°F on a meat thermometer.

GINGER-ORANGE CHICKEN BREAST

This recipe is great chilled, sliced, and served on a crispy green salad.

Serves 4

2 tablespoons avocado oil

4 (5-ounce) boneless, skinless chicken breasts

½ teaspoon seasoned salt

Freshly ground black pepper, to taste

2 cloves garlic, minced

2 tablespoons grated fresh ginger

2 teaspoons orange zest

½ cup freshly squeezed orange juice

1. Heat the oil in a small nonstick skillet over medium-high heat. Season the chicken with salt and pepper. Brown the chicken in the oil, turning it once, about 8 minutes per side. Transfer the chicken to a plate and cover to keep warm.

2. Add the garlic to the pan and cook for about 1 minute, stirring frequently to prevent burning. Add the ginger, orange zest, and orange juice and bring to a simmer.

3. Add the chicken and any chicken juices and heat through, about 4–5 minutes. Test chicken to make sure it registers 165°F on a meat thermometer. Adjust seasoning to taste. Serve hot with the sauce.

CHAPTER 10

FISH AND SEAFOOD

SALMON AND VEGGIE FRITTATA

Frittatas are a type of omelet, but they are sturdier and easier to make. A frittata can be chilled and served later either cold or at room temperature. And salmon is the perfect addition to a frittata. You can use other vegetables in this easy recipe; green beans or sliced bell peppers would be delicious.

Serves 6

4 tablespoons olive oil, divided

2 (6-ounce) salmon fillets

1 teaspoon salt, divided

¼ teaspoon pepper, divided

1 onion, chopped

2 cloves garlic, minced

8 ounces asparagus, cut into 1" pieces

10 eggs, beaten

⅓ cup heavy cream or coconut cream

1 teaspoon five-spice powder

1 cup shredded Havarti cheese, if desired

1. In 10-inch ovenproof skillet, heat 2 tablespoons olive oil over medium heat.

2. Sprinkle salmon with ½ teaspoon salt and ⅛ teaspoon pepper and add to skillet. Cook, turning once, until the fish flakes when tested with a fork, about 10 minutes.

3. Remove salmon from skillet and place on a plate. Remove skin and flake salmon into large pieces.

4. Return skillet to medium heat. Add remaining 2 tablespoons olive oil. Cook onion and garlic for 5–6 minutes until tender. Add asparagus and cook 4–5 minutes longer, until crisp-tender.

5. Meanwhile, in large bowl beat eggs with cream, five-spice powder, ½ teaspoon salt, and ⅛ teaspoon pepper. Stir in salmon and pour into skillet over vegetables.

6. Cook frittata over medium heat, shaking pan and moving egg mixture around occasionally, for 4–5 minutes or until it starts to set. Then cook, undisturbed, for 4–5 minutes or until bottom is golden.

7. While frittata is cooking, preheat broiler. Place frittata under broiler. Broil, rotating skillet occasionally, for 5 minutes until puffed. Sprinkle with cheese, if using, and return to broiler. Broil until frittata is puffed, set, and golden, about 5–10 minutes longer. Cut into wedges to serve.

BACON-WRAPPED GRILLED SCALLOPS

There are two sizes of scallops in the market: bay and sea. It's easy to remember the difference! Bay scallops are smaller than sea scallops, since a "bay" is smaller than the "sea." They should smell sweet and not at all fishy when you buy them. If a small muscle is attached to a scallop, pull it off and discard; it gets tough when cooked.

Serves 4

6 slices bacon

12 sea scallops, small muscles removed if needed

2 tablespoons tomato sauce

1 tablespoon Dijon mustard

1 tablespoon apricot preserves

1 tablespoon red wine vinegar

½ teaspoon salt

⅛ teaspoon pepper

1. Cut bacon slices in half crosswise. In large skillet, cook bacon until much of the fat is rendered but the bacon is still pliable. Wrap around the sea scallops and hold with a toothpick.

2. Prepare and preheat grill. Meanwhile, combine tomato sauce, mustard, apricot preserves, vinegar, and 1 tablespoon bacon fat in small bowl.

3. Sprinkle scallops with salt and pepper. Grill over medium coals for 3 minutes, then turn. Brush with the tomato mixture as they grill for another 3–4 minutes or until scallops are opaque and bacon is crisp. Serve immediately.

CURRIED SALMON STEAKS

Salmon is a wonderful choice for a Paleo dinner. The flesh of this fish is tender and nutty and is full of healthy fats. Choose wild salmon if you can find it because it is more flavorful and has more nutrients. Combined with curry, an antioxidant powerhouse, this recipe is as healthy as it is delicious.

Serves 4

4 salmon steaks

2 teaspoons curry powder

2 tablespoons butter or olive oil

½ teaspoon salt

⅛ teaspoon white pepper

3 tablespoons mango chutney

1. To prepare salmon, place on a board. You will notice the round body of the steak, with two thin flaps that extend from the body. Trim the skin from the outside of one of the thin flaps of the fish up to the body of the steak. Hold the skin away from the thin flap and curl the flap into the steak. Curl the other thin flap around the first flap, flesh side together, and then fold the skin back to make a compact bundle. Tie with kitchen string.

2. Prepare broiler. Place salmon steaks on a broiler pan. Broil for 5 minutes about 6" from the heat source.

3. Meanwhile, combine curry powder, butter or olive oil, salt, pepper, and chutney. Remove salmon from broiler.

4. Turn salmon, return to broiler, and broil for 2 minutes. Remove from broiler and spoon curry powder mixture evenly over steaks. Return to broiler and broil for 3–5 minutes longer until salmon is desired doneness and fish is glazed.

BAVARIAN FISH

Bavaria is a part of Germany that serves hearty food. Traditional dishes include red cabbage, sauerkraut, pickles, horseradish, and lots of smoked sausages. Adding sausage to a seafood dish adds a lot of flavor and interest to the dish. This delicious recipe will convert people who think they don't like fish!

Serves 4

2 tablespoons butter or olive oil

1 cup chopped fully cooked bratwurst

1 onion, chopped

3 cloves garlic, minced

¼ cup chopped dill pickle

2 tablespoons dill pickle juice

½ cup Fish Stock (see Chapter 4)

4 fish fillets (walleye or cod)

½ cup sour cream or Almond Yogurt (see Chapter 1)

1 tablespoon arrowroot powder

1. In large skillet, melt butter or olive oil over medium heat. Add bratwurst; cook and stir until sausage releases some juices.

2. Add onion and garlic to skillet; cook and stir for 5 minutes. Then add dill pickle, the pickle juice, and the Fish Stock. Bring to a simmer.

3. Add the fish fillets to the skillet and reduce heat to low. Simmer for 5–8 minutes or until fish flakes when tested with fork.

4. Remove fish from pan and cover to keep warm. Add sour cream or yogurt and arrowroot powder to sauce in skillet and stir to combine; cook for 1–2 minutes until slightly thickened. Pour over fish and serve.

SHRIMP SCAMPI

Shrimp scampi is an elegant recipe that is perfect for company. It's just shrimp sautéed in butter, with garlic and lemon juice added for flavor. Be sure that when you buy shrimp you give it a good sniff. Shrimp should smell fresh and of the sea. If it has any off odor at all, don't buy it. Remove the shell and rinse out the dark vein or remove it with the tip of a knife before cooking.

Serves 4

1½ pounds medium raw shrimp

2 tablespoons butter

3 tablespoons extra-virgin olive oil

1 onion, chopped

4 cloves garlic, minced

¼ cup lemon juice

½ teaspoon lemon zest

¾ cup Fish Stock (see Chapter 4)

½ teaspoon salt

¼ teaspoon pepper

1 tablespoon chopped fresh basil

1. Remove shells from shrimp and make a cut along the back. Rinse out the dark vein or remove it with the tip of a knife. Pat shrimp dry and set aside.

2. In large skillet melt butter with olive oil over medium heat. Add onion and garlic; cook and stir until softened, about 5 minutes.

3. Add shrimp; cook until shrimp just begin to curl. Remove shrimp from skillet.

4. Add lemon juice, zest, stock, salt, and pepper to skillet and bring to a boil. Reduce heat and simmer for 4 minutes.

5. Return shrimp to sauce and simmer for 1 minute. Sprinkle with basil and serve immediately.

CRAB CAKES

Any fresh crab meat you buy is already cooked, so in this recipe you're really just reheating it. Don't overcook these cakes or the seafood will be tough. Serve with Flintstone Guacamole (see Chapter 1) or any type of salsa. This recipe makes a wonderful appetizer, or it can be a whole meal served with a green salad and some white wine.

Serves 4

1 pound jumbo lump crab meat

½ cup ground almonds

½ cup finely chopped celery

3 green onions, finely chopped

2 tablespoons lemon juice

1 teaspoon lemon zest

2 tablespoons Dijon mustard

½ cup Wilma's Mayonnaise (see Chapter 2)

3 eggs, beaten

½ teaspoon salt

¼ teaspoon white pepper

1. In large bowl, combine crab meat with almonds, celery, and green onions and toss, taking care not to break up crab meat too much.

2. In small bowl, combine lemon juice, zest, mustard, mayonnaise, eggs, salt, and pepper and beat. Add to crab meat mixture and stir to coat. Cover and chill for 1 hour.

3. When ready to eat, preheat oven to 375°F. Form crab mixture into patties using a ⅓ cup measure and shape with your hands. Place on parchment paper–lined baking sheet and bake for 12–17 minutes or until light golden brown.

ALMOND SHRIMP

Shrimp is graded and sold in varying sizes according to how many shrimp are in a pound. Really tiny shrimp are about 60 per pound, and medium shrimp are around 45 per pound. Large shrimp are around 30 per pound, and jumbo shrimp are around 20 per pound. For this recipe, choose medium cooked shrimp. All you do is thaw them under running water and they're ready to use.

Serves 6

¼ cup butter or olive oil

1 onion, chopped

2 cloves garlic, minced

2 pounds medium cooked shrimp

3 cups Cauliflower Rice (see Chapter 11)

1 teaspoon salt

⅛ teaspoon pepper

⅓ cup sliced black olives

1 (14-ounce) can diced tomatoes, undrained

½ cup almond milk

1 cup ground almonds

1. In medium saucepan, heat butter or olive oil over medium heat. Add onion and garlic; cook and stir until tender, about 6 minutes.

2. In large bowl, combine onion mixture, shrimp, Cauliflower Rice, salt, pepper, and olives and toss.

3. Add tomatoes with their liquid and almond milk. Turn into 2-quart baking dish. Sprinkle with the ground almonds.

4. Bake for 25–30 minutes or until top starts to brown. Serve immediately.

SHRIMP DIJON

Shrimp Dijon is a very simple recipe that is full of flavor. You can serve it on its own or over cooked spaghetti squash or Cauliflower Rice (see Chapter 11). Be sure to get a good quality Dijon mustard for this recipe, because the flavor is crucial. Serve with steamed asparagus and a fruit salad.

Serves 4

2 tablespoons butter or olive oil

1 onion, chopped

2 cloves garlic, minced

1 (8-ounce) package mushrooms, sliced

1 cup almond milk

½ cup Fish Stock (see Chapter 4)

1 tablespoon almond flour

1½ pounds raw medium shrimp, shelled and deveined

3 tablespoons Dijon mustard

2 teaspoons chopped fresh thyme leaves

1 tablespoon lemon juice

½ teaspoon salt

⅛ teaspoon white pepper

1. In large saucepan, heat butter or olive oil over medium heat. Add onion and garlic; cook and stir until tender, about 5 minutes.

2. Add mushrooms; cook and stir until mushrooms give up their liquid and the liquid evaporates, about 5 minutes longer.

3. Add almond milk and bring to a simmer. Combine Fish Stock and almond flour in a small bowl and add to saucepan; simmer until thickened.

4. Add shrimp and simmer until shrimp curl and turn pink, about 3 minutes.

5. Add mustard, thyme, lemon juice, salt, and pepper and stir until combined. Serve immediately.

PROSCIUTTO-WRAPPED SHRIMP

Prosciutto is an Italian product that is made in a similar process as ham, but it is dry-cured. It is sold very thinly sliced at the deli counter of most supermarkets. When wrapped around shrimp and cooked, the prosciutto's flavor intensifies. It protects the shrimp from the heat and keeps it moist and tender. Serve this recipe over mixed greens with pan juices drizzled on top.

Serves 4

¼ cup extra-virgin olive oil

3 tablespoons lemon juice

1 tablespoon Dijon mustard

¼ teaspoon salt

⅛ teaspoon pepper

4 cups arugula

4 cups torn endive

1½ pounds large raw shrimp, shelled and deveined

4 ounces thinly sliced prosciutto

1 tablespoon butter or olive oil

¼ cup Fish Stock (see Chapter 4)

1. In large bowl, combine extra-virgin olive oil, lemon juice, mustard, salt, and pepper and whisk to combine. Add arugula and endive and toss to coat; set aside.

2. Wrap each shrimp with a piece of prosciutto.

3. Heat butter or olive oil in large skillet. Add half the shrimp and cook, turning, until the shrimp curl and turn pink and prosciutto is slightly crisp. Remove and set aside as the shrimp cook. Repeat with remaining shrimp.

4. Place cooked shrimp on the greens in the bowl. Add the Fish Stock to the pan that you used to cook the shrimp and bring to a boil. Drizzle over shrimp and greens and serve immediately.

SHRIMP CREOLE

Creole cooking is a blend of French, Spanish, Southern, and Italian cuisines. It originated in Louisiana along with Cajun cuisine. The foods most often used in Creole cooking are tomatoes, seafood, red peppers, mustard, allspice, and garlic. This easy recipe takes just a few minutes to prepare. Make it as mild or spicy as you'd like.

Serves 4

2 tablespoons olive oil

1 onion, chopped

3 cloves garlic, minced

½ cup chopped celery

1 green bell pepper, chopped

1 (14-ounce) can diced tomatoes, undrained

1 (8-ounce) can tomato sauce

2 tablespoons coconut aminos

½ teaspoon salt

¼ teaspoon white pepper

⅛ teaspoon crushed red pepper flakes

1 tablespoon chili powder

⅛ teaspoon Tabasco sauce

Pinch allspice

1 pound raw medium shrimp, shelled and deveined

1. In large saucepan, heat oil over medium heat. Add onion and garlic; cook and stir for 3 minutes. Add celery and bell pepper; cook and stir for 3 minutes longer.

2. Add diced tomatoes, tomato sauce, coconut aminos, salt, white pepper, crushed red pepper flakes, chili powder, Tabasco sauce, and allspice and bring to a simmer. Simmer, uncovered, for 20 minutes.

3. Stir in raw shrimp and bring back to a simmer. Cook for 4–5 minutes or until shrimp just curl and turn pink. Serve immediately.

FISH WITH MUSHROOMS

There are many different species of fish fillets. The white fish used in this recipe can be pollock, grouper, haddock, cod, halibut, or sole. Choose what looks best at the market. Fish should never smell "fishy," but clean and slightly of the sea. The fillets should be firm and not slimy. This delicate mushroom sauce complements the tender fish perfectly.

Serves 4

1½ pounds fish fillets

2 tablespoons lemon juice

2 tablespoons butter, melted, or olive oil

1 shallot, finely chopped

2 tablespoons olive oil

1 (8-ounce) package mushrooms, sliced

1 tablespoon almond flour

1 cup almond milk

½ teaspoon salt

⅛ teaspoon pepper

1 teaspoon dried thyme leaves

1. Preheat oven to 350°F. Place fish in a 9" x 13" glass baking dish. In small bowl, combine lemon juice, butter or olive oil, and shallot and mix. Pour over fish.

2. Bake fish for 15–20 minutes or until it flakes when tested with a fork.

3. Meanwhile, heat 2 tablespoons olive oil in medium pan. Add mushrooms; cook and stir until mushrooms give up their liquid and the liquid evaporates, about 8 minutes.

4. Sprinkle with almond flour and cook for 1 minute longer.

5. Add almond milk, salt, pepper, and thyme and cook, stirring with a wire whisk, until mixture thickens.

6. When fish is done, remove from oven and place on serving platter. Top with mushroom sauce and serve immediately.

MAPLE BACON SALMON

The suave smoothness of salmon pairs beautifully with the sweetness of maple syrup and the salty crispness of bacon. This combination is a knockout. Serve it when you are entertaining with Green-on-Green Salad (see Chapter 3) and Cauliflower Rice (see Chapter 11), with Dark Chocolate Brownies (see Chapter 15) for dessert.

Serves 6

6 slices thick-cut bacon

6 salmon fillets

1 teaspoon salt

¼ teaspoon white pepper

2 shallots, minced

2 cloves garlic, minced

⅓ cup maple syrup

2 tablespoons lemon juice

1. In large skillet, cook bacon until crisp; drain on paper towels, crumble, and set aside. Remove all but 2 tablespoons bacon fat from pan.

2. Sprinkle salmon with salt and pepper and add to fat in pan, skin-side up. Cook for 4–5 minutes or until golden brown. Carefully turn salmon and cook until skin is crisp and salmon feels firm to the touch, about 3–5 minutes longer. Remove salmon from pan and cover to keep warm.

3. Add shallot and garlic to fat in pan; cook and stir for 2 minutes until crisp-tender. Add maple syrup and lemon juice and simmer for 2 minutes. Return salmon to pan, turn in the glaze, and sprinkle with bacon.

4. Cook for another 1–2 minutes or until salmon is hot. Serve immediately.

GRILLED FISH WITH PICO DE GALLO

Pico de gallo is a type of Mexican salsa that is uncooked. Its name means "rooster's beak," which may refer to roosters pecking at their food, or the small sizes of the pieces of food in the salsa. Any fish can be grilled, but tender white fillets are best placed on a grill rack or a piece of foil before being added to the grill. The delicate flesh can tear and stick easily when on the grill itself.

Serves 4

2 tomatoes, diced

1 red onion, finely chopped

1 jalapeño pepper, minced

2 tablespoons lime juice

1 clove garlic, minced

¼ cup chopped fresh cilantro

¼ teaspoon salt

⅛ teaspoon crushed red pepper flakes

4 white fish fillets

1 tablespoon unsalted butter or olive oil

1. In medium bowl, combine tomatoes, red onion, jalapeño, lime juice, garlic, cilantro, ¼ teaspoon salt, and crushed red pepper flakes and blend well.

2. Prepare and preheat grill. Grease a fine-mesh grill rack or foil with unsalted butter or olive oil. Add fish.

3. Grill fish for 5–8 minutes, without turning, until fish flakes when tested with a fork. Serve with the salsa.

NUT-CRUSTED SHRIMP

You can use your favorite nuts to coat the shrimp in this recipe. Almonds are more delicate, while walnuts and pecans have a stronger flavor. Just be sure to cook the shrimp only until they curl and turn pink so they aren't tough. Serve this with Kale and Fruit Salad (see Chapter 3), Maple-Roasted Carrots (see Chapter 13), and Plum Blueberry Coconut Crumble (see Chapter 15) for dessert.

Serves 4

¼ cup honey

3 tablespoons Dijon mustard

1 tablespoon butter, melted or olive oil

1¼ pounds large shrimp, shelled and deveined

1½ cups ground almonds

1. Preheat oven to 400°F. Line a baking pan with sides with parchment paper and set aside.

2. On shallow plate, combine honey, mustard, and butter or olive oil. On another plate, put the ground almonds.

3. Dip shrimp into the honey mixture, then into the ground almonds. Place on prepared baking pan.

4. Bake for 12–17 minutes or until shrimp are curled and turn pink and are firm to the touch. Serve immediately.

POACHED SALMON

Poaching salmon is a wonderful way to cook this tender fish. The important thing to note about poaching is that the poaching liquid should never boil; it shouldn't even come to a simmer. The French say that the liquid is "smiling"; bubbles rise to the surface but don't really break. The poaching liquid can be cooled and frozen and used again if you'd like.

Serves 4

3 cups Fish Stock (see Chapter 4)

1 cup dry white wine or water

1 lemon, thinly sliced

2 tablespoons lemon juice

1 tablespoon peppercorns

2 teaspoons fennel seeds

1 teaspoon mustard seeds

½ teaspoon salt

4–6 salmon fillets

1. In large saucepan, combine Fish Stock, wine, lemon, lemon juice, peppercorns, fennel seeds, mustard seeds, and salt and bring to a simmer. Simmer for 5 minutes.

2. Reduce heat to low so the liquid in the pan is barely moving and add the fillets to the poaching liquid. Spoon liquid over the salmon if the fillets are not covered.

3. Cover and cook for about 8–10 minutes, making sure the liquid never comes to a complete simmer, until salmon just flakes when tested with a fork and a meat thermometer registers at least 145°F. Remove salmon from liquid with a slotted spatula and serve.

SALMON CAESAR SALAD

Caesar salad is traditionally served with garlic bread croutons. But toasted mixed nuts make an admirable substitute and add flavor and texture to this salad. And don't be afraid of the anchovy fillet; it blends beautifully into the dressing and adds a salty and slightly spicy note.

Serves 4

4 salmon fillets

2 tablespoons olive oil

½ teaspoon salt, divided

⅛ teaspoon pepper

1 tablespoon Ghee (see Chapter 2)

½ cup walnut pieces

½ cup pine nuts

2 cloves garlic, minced

1 anchovy fillet, drained and chopped

2 teaspoons coconut aminos

2 tablespoons Dijon mustard

⅓ cup Wilma's Mayonnaise (see Chapter 2)

2 tablespoons lemon juice

2 tablespoons coconut milk

6 cups torn romaine lettuce

½ cup shredded Parmesan cheese, if desired

1. Preheat oven to 350°F. Place salmon in a baking dish; drizzle with oil and sprinkle with ¼ teaspoon salt and pepper. Bake for 20–25 minutes or until salmon just flakes with a fork. Set aside.

2. Meanwhile, heat Ghee in small skillet. Add walnuts and pine nuts and toast until fragrant. Set aside.

3. In large serving bowl, combine garlic and anchovy with remaining ¼ teaspoon salt; mash into a paste. Add coconut aminos and mustard and mix well. Stir in mayonnaise, lemon juice, and coconut milk.

4. Add lettuce to serving bowl and toss to coat with dressing.

5. Flake salmon and add to lettuce mixture and toss. Top with toasted nuts and cheese, if using, and serve immediately.

BACON-WRAPPED FISH

Bacon adds wonderful flavor to fish. But the two meats cook at different times. So for this recipe to work, you must partially cook the bacon, then wrap it around the fish and finish in the oven. Choose a sturdy white fish for this recipe, such as cod or halibut. Serve with roasted or steamed green beans or asparagus and a nice mixed green salad.

Serves 4

8 slices bacon

4 cod or halibut fillets

½ teaspoon salt

⅛ teaspoon pepper

2 tablespoons lemon juice

1 tablespoon chopped fresh dill

1. Preheat oven to 375°F. In a large skillet, partially cook the bacon until it is transparent and much of the fat is rendered out. Do not cook the bacon until it is crisp; it should still be pliable. Drain bacon on paper towels. Reserve 1 tablespoon bacon fat.

2. Sprinkle fish with salt and pepper.

3. In small bowl, combine lemon juice and 1 tablespoon bacon fat. Brush this over the fillets. Sprinkle with dill.

4. Wrap two pieces of bacon around each piece of fish, covering it as much as possible. Place seam-side down in a baking dish.

5. Bake for 13–18 minutes or until bacon is crisp and the fish just flakes when tested with a fork. Serve immediately.

SEAFOOD AND SALMON SALAD

You can use any combination of seafood you'd like in this luscious salad. Even cooked mussels and oysters would be a nice addition! This chunky salad is good served as-is, or can be served in avocado halves or on lettuce leaves. Put it into stemmed mushrooms for a quick appetizer, or spread it on Paleo Crackers (see Chapter 5) for an appetizer. It's versatile and easy to make and keeps in the fridge for 3 days.

Serves 4

2 tablespoons olive oil

2 salmon fillets

½ teaspoon salt

⅛ teaspoon pepper

½ pound medium raw shrimp, shelled and deveined

½ pound jumbo lump crab meat, pre-cooked and picked over

4 stalks celery, chopped

1 red bell pepper, chopped

4 green onions, sliced

1 cup Wilma's Mayonnaise (see Chapter 2)

3 tablespoons Dijon mustard

1 tablespoon grainy mustard

2 tablespoons honey

1 tablespoon chopped fresh dill

2 teaspoons chopped fresh thyme leaves

1. Heat olive oil in large skillet over medium heat. Season salmon with salt and pepper and place, skin-side down, in skillet. Cook for 5 minutes, then carefully turn and cook for another 3–5 minutes or until salmon just flakes when tested with a fork. Remove from skillet and set aside.

2. Add shrimp to the skillet and cook, stirring frequently, just until shrimp curl and turn pink, about 4–5 minutes. Remove from skillet.

3. Remove skin from salmon and break flesh into large chunks. Place in bowl with shrimp, crab meat, celery, red bell pepper, and green onions.

4. In small bowl, combine mayonnaise, Dijon mustard, grainy mustard, honey, dill, and thyme and mix well. Pour over seafood mixture and stir to coat.

5. Cover and chill for 2–8 hours before serving.

SALMON GUMBO

Gumbo is a classic Louisiana dish that is made of seafood; the "holy trinity" of celery, bell peppers, and onions; and thickened stock. It is traditionally served over rice; you can serve it over Cauliflower Rice (see Chapter 11) or Jicama Rice (see Chapter 11). It is spicy, so add a cooling fruit salad as the perfect partner to this Southern specialty.

Serves 6

¾ pound Andouille sausage, sliced

3 (6-ounce) salmon fillets

1 tablespoon coconut oil

2 tablespoons bacon drippings or butter

1 tablespoon olive oil

2 tablespoons almond flour

2 tablespoons coconut flour

1 onion, chopped

5 cloves garlic, minced

4 stalks celery, sliced

1 green bell pepper, chopped

1 (14-ounce) can diced tomatoes, undrained

2 cups Fish Stock (see Chapter 4)

3 tablespoons tomato paste

2 tablespoons lemon juice

1 teaspoon Tabasco sauce

1 teaspoon salt

¼ teaspoon pepper

¼ teaspoon crushed red pepper flakes

1. In large heavy saucepan, cook the sausage until some of the fat renders out. Remove sausage from pan and set aside. Cook the salmon fillets in the fat in the pan, turning once, until the salmon just flakes, about 8–9 minutes. Remove salmon from pan and set aside.

2. Add coconut oil, bacon fat or butter, and olive oil to the pan and place it over medium heat. Add almond flour and coconut flour and mix. Cook this mixture (which will become a roux), stirring constantly with a wire whisk, until it turns brown. This can take about 15 minutes. Don't let the mixture burn.

3. Add onion, garlic, celery, and bell pepper to the roux and cook, stirring constantly, until tender, about 8 minutes. Add the sausage to the pan.

4. Add tomatoes, Fish Stock, tomato paste, lemon juice, Tabasco, salt, pepper, and red pepper flakes to pan. Bring to a simmer; simmer for 30 minutes.

5. Remove skin from salmon and break into large chunks. Stir into the pan and heat for another 5–10 minutes or until everything is hot. Serve immediately.

CRAB BURGERS IN JUMBO MUSHROOMS

Many grocery stores regularly carry very large mushrooms that can be up to 4" in diameter. These are usually Portobello mushrooms. They are meaty tasting and quite substantial and are a great substitute for wheat burger buns. This excellent dish is a great combination of textures and flavors; the mix of tender mushrooms, savory crab burgers, and crisp and fresh slaw is wonderful.

Serves 4

1½ cups shredded green cabbage

1 red bell pepper, chopped

2 stalks celery, sliced

4 tablespoons olive oil, divided

3 tablespoons lemon juice, divided

4 large Portobello mushrooms

1 pound jumbo lump crab meat, picked over

¼ cup Wilma's Mayonnaise (see Chapter 2)

½ cup crushed Paleo Crackers (see Chapter 5)

2 green onions, sliced

1 tablespoon Dijon mustard

1 tablespoon grainy mustard

1 egg, beaten

1. In medium bowl, combine cabbage, bell pepper, and celery. Drizzle with 2 tablespoons olive oil and 2 tablespoons lemon juice and toss; set aside.

2. Trim mushroom stems, remove the stems, and chop finely; set aside.

3. Heat remaining 2 tablespoons olive oil in large skillet over medium heat. Add the mushroom caps, stem-side down, and cook for 2 minutes. Turn and cook for another 3–4 minutes until just tender. Remove caps and set aside.

4. Add mushroom stems to the skillet and cook until they give up their liquid and the liquid evaporates, about 5 minutes. Remove to bowl and let cool for 10 minutes.

5. Add crab meat, mayonnaise, crushed crackers, green onions, both mustards, and egg to mushroom stems in bowl. Mix gently but thoroughly.

6. Form crab mixture into patties. Cook in the oil and drippings remaining in skillet over medium heat, turning once, about 5–7 minutes or until the patties are crisp and golden.

7. Place mushroom caps, stem-side up, on serving plate. Top each with a crab patty and divide cabbage mixture among them. Serve immediately.

SHRIMP WITH SQUASH PURÉE

Squash makes a lovely purée, somewhat like mashed potatoes but with a sweeter taste and lighter texture. The squash is steamed to hold in all the flavor and nutrients, then puréed with butter or coconut oil and fresh herbs. Choose large shrimp for this recipe; they should be about 30 shrimp per pound.

Serves 4

1 butternut squash

3 tablespoons butter or coconut oil, divided

1 shallot, minced

2 tablespoons chopped fresh basil

2 teaspoons chopped fresh thyme leaves

½ teaspoon salt

⅛ teaspoon pepper

1¼ pounds large raw shrimp, peeled and deveined

1. Peel and seed squash and cut into 1" pieces. Prepare a steamer, or place a large colander over a pot of boiling water. Steam the squash, covered, for about 7–9 minutes or until tender.

2. Meanwhile, melt 2 tablespoons butter or coconut oil in a small saucepan. Sauté shallot just until tender.

3. When squash is done, transfer to a food processor. Process the squash, then add butter with shallot, basil, thyme, salt, and pepper. Cover to keep warm.

4. Melt remaining 1 tablespoon butter or coconut oil in large skillet. Add the shrimp; cook just until shrimp curl and turn pink, about 3–4 minutes.

5. Place squash purée on a serving dish and top with shrimp. Serve immediately.

STEAMED KING CRAB LEGS

Shellfish is a healthy and flavorful protein source. It is naturally low in fat and has a nice, sweet taste—a great alternative to the usual poultry or beef dish.

Serves 4

2 tablespoons coconut oil

3 cloves garlic, crushed

1 (1") piece fresh ginger, crushed

1 stalk lemongrass, crushed

2 pounds Alaskan king crab legs

1 teaspoon ground black pepper

1. Heat the oil in a large pot over medium-high heat.

2. Add the garlic, ginger, and lemongrass; cook and stir until brown, about 5 minutes.

3. Add crab legs and pepper. Cover and cook, tossing occasionally, for 15 minutes or until the crab legs turn a bright orange or red color and are thoroughly cooked.

SALMON CAKES

These salmon cakes are a great party appetizer. Even non-Paleo dieters will rave about them.

Serves 10

3 pounds salmon, finely diced

5 egg whites

1 teaspoon dried dill

¼ teaspoon ground ginger

¼ teaspoon cayenne pepper

¼ cup black pepper

¼ cup freshly squeezed lemon juice

¼ cup sesame oil

2 tablespoons arrowroot powder

1 cup almond meal

1. Preheat broiler.

2. Mix salmon, egg whites, dill, ginger, cayenne, black pepper, lemon juice, oil, and arrowroot powder together in a large bowl. Form about 20 small patties from the mixture.

3. Pour almond meal into a shallow dish. Dredge patties in almond meal and place on an ungreased baking sheet. Broil each side for 4 minutes.

Super Omega

The more omega-3 fatty acid you ingest, the better chance you will have at fighting silent inflammation. This compound is also proven to significantly reduce your recovery time from workouts or endurance races. The more omega-3 you consume, the better for optimum health all around.

SALMON IN PARCHMENT WITH BABY BRUSSELS SPROUTS

Cooking the salmon in parchment paper works to keep the fish from drying out, a common problem when cooking fish in the oven. The paper also helps to contain flavors so they are not cooked off.

Serves 2

2 (4- to 5-ounce) salmon fillets or steaks

2 tablespoons finely chopped petite Brussels sprouts

2 cloves garlic, crushed

2 dashes lemon juice

1 tablespoon avocado oil

1. Preheat oven to 425°F.

2. Place each piece of salmon on a large (12") circle of parchment paper.

3. Cover each salmon piece with a spoonful of Brussels sprouts, a clove of crushed garlic, a dash of lemon juice, and a drizzle of oil.

4. Fold the paper over into a packet and seal the edges by crimping and folding like a pastry. Place on a baking sheet.

5. Bake for 15 minutes, or until fish flakes easily with a fork.

CITRUS-BAKED SNAPPER

Snapper is a tasty fish that absorbs the flavors in this recipe quite nicely. If cleaning and scaling a fish is overwhelming for you, ask your grocer or fishmonger to do it for you.

Serves 4

1 (3-pound) whole red snapper, cleaned and scaled

3½ tablespoons grated fresh ginger

3 green onions, chopped

1 tomato, seeded and diced

¼ cup freshly squeezed orange juice

¼ cup freshly squeezed lime juice

¼ cup freshly squeezed lemon juice

3 thin slices lime

3 thin slices lemon

1. Preheat the oven to 350°F.

2. Make three slashes across each side of the fish using a sharp knife. This will keep the fish from curling as it cooks.

3. Combine ginger, green onions, and tomato. Place half in a shallow baking dish or roasting pan. Top with the fish and cover with remaining tomato mixture.

4. Combine juices and drizzle over snapper, then place lime and lemon slices on top.

5. Cover with aluminum foil and bake until the flesh is opaque and can be flaked with a fork, about 20 minutes.

Snapper and Omega-3

Snapper is not the fish that comes to mind when you're thinking about omega-3, but this cold-water fish does have some beneficial DHA fatty acid packed inside. Those with elevated blood triglycerides will benefit greatly from even small amounts of EPA and DHA.

FRIED SARDINES

There are not many fried items in a Paleolithic diet, because most fried dishes are made with flour. This is a healthier alternative to traditional frying. The alcohol in the wine is mostly cooked off, so you will not have to worry about the alcohol either.

Serves 6

1 cup almond flour

2 pounds boneless, skinless, no-salt-added sardines

¾ cup plus 1 tablespoon almond oil, divided

2 cloves garlic, chopped

1 cup dry white wine

1 cup apple cider vinegar

½ cup chopped mint leaves

1. Pour almond flour into a shallow dish. Roll sardines in flour.

2. Heat ¾ cup oil in a large skillet over medium-high heat.

3. When the oil is hot, fry the sardines until brown and crispy, approximately 5 minutes. Drain on paper towels and keep warm.

4. In another skillet over medium heat, warm garlic in remaining 1 tablespoon oil. Cook for 1 minute.

5. Add the wine and vinegar. Simmer mixture, stirring occasionally, until the liquid has reduced by half, about 15 minutes.

6. Pour the sauce over the sardines, and sprinkle with fresh mint.

HADDOCK FISH CAKES

This version of a familiar fish cake has the fresh flavor of haddock. Serve this with a spicy sauce or a fresh spritz of lemon.

Serves 6

1 pound haddock

2 leeks

1 red bell pepper

2 egg whites

2 teaspoons Old Bay Seasoning

1 teaspoon sea salt

½ teaspoon freshly ground black pepper

1 tablespoon almond oil

1. Finely shred the raw fish with a fork. Dice the leeks and red pepper.

2. Combine all the ingredients except oil in a medium-sized bowl; mix well. Form the mixture into small oval patties.

3. Heat the oil in a medium-sized skillet over medium heat. Place the cakes in the pan and loosely cover with the lid; sauté the cakes for 4–6 minutes on each side until firm. Drain on a rack covered with paper towels; serve immediately.

FRESH TUNA WITH SWEET LEMON LEEK SALSA

The tuna can be prepared the night before, refrigerated, then either reheated or served at room temperature.

Serves 6

Tuna

1½ pounds fresh tuna steaks (cut into 4-ounce portions)

¼–½ teaspoon almond oil

Freshly ground black pepper, to taste

Salsa

1 teaspoon almond oil

3 fresh leeks (light green and white parts only), thinly sliced

1 tablespoon fresh lemon juice

1 tablespoon raw honey

1. Preheat grill to medium-high.

2. Brush each portion of the tuna with the oil and drain on a rack. Season the tuna with pepper, then place the tuna on the grill; cook for 3 minutes. Shift the tuna steaks on the grill to form an X grill pattern on the fish; cook 3 more minutes.

3. Turn the steaks over and grill 3 more minutes, then change position again to create an X grill pattern. Cook to desired doneness.

4. For the salsa: Heat the oil in a medium-sized skillet on medium heat, then add the leeks and sauté for about 3 minutes, just until leeks are wilted. Add the lemon juice and honey. Plate each tuna portion with a spoonful of salsa.

LIME-POACHED FLOUNDER

Lime brings out the delicate flavor of the fish and complements the zip of the cilantro.

Serves 6

¾ cup sliced leeks

¼ cup cilantro leaves (reserve the stems)

1½ pounds flounder fillets

1¾ cups fish stock

2 tablespoons fresh lime juice

½ teaspoon fresh lime zest

¼ teaspoon ground black pepper

1 cup shredded yellow onion

⅔ cup shredded carrots

⅔ cup shredded celery

2 tablespoons extra-virgin olive oil

1. Place the leek slices and cilantro stems (reserve the leaves) in a large skillet over medium-high heat, then lay the flounder on top.

2. Add the stock, lime juice, lime zest, and pepper. Bring just to a boil, reduce heat, and cover. Simmer for 7–10 minutes, until the flounder is thoroughly cooked. Remove from heat. Discard the liquid.

3. To serve, lay the shredded onions, carrots, and celery in separate strips on serving plates. Top with flounder, drizzle with the olive oil, and sprinkle with the reserved cilantro leaves.

PECAN-CRUSTED CATFISH

Catfish and tilapia rank among the most popular fish in the United States today. They are relatively inexpensive and have a nice flavor. You can use either fish in this recipe.

Serves 4

½ cup almond meal

½ cup finely chopped pecans

¼ teaspoon ground black pepper

1½ pounds catfish

2 tablespoons coconut oil

1. In a shallow dish, mix almond meal, pecans, and pepper. Dredge the catfish in the mixture, coating well.

2. Add coconut oil to medium-sized skillet over medium-high heat. Place catfish in pan and fry 3–5 minutes on each side or until fish registers at least 140°F on a meat thermometer. Serve.

COCONUT SHRIMP

This is an irresistibly sweet way to enjoy a commonly served first-course dish.

Serves 6

3½ cups chicken broth

1 cup water

1 teaspoon ground coriander

1 teaspoon cumin

Cayenne pepper, to taste

Zest of 1 lime

⅓ cup lime juice

7 cloves garlic, minced

1 tablespoon minced fresh ginger

1 large onion, chopped

1 red bell pepper, diced

1 large carrot, peeled and shredded

½ cup unsweetened coconut flakes

1½ pounds large or jumbo shrimp, peeled and thawed if frozen

Toasted coconut, for garnish

1. Mix the chicken broth, water, coriander, cumin, cayenne pepper, lime zest, lime juice, garlic, and ginger in a 4- or 6-quart slow cooker.

2. Stir in the onion, bell pepper, carrot, and coconut. Cover and cook on low for 3 hours.

3. Stir in the shrimp. Cover and cook another 30 minutes or until shrimp curl and turn pink. Serve garnished with toasted coconut.

SALMON WITH LEEKS

Salmon and leeks complement each other well. This recipe is a nice combination of the two.

Serves 4

4 leeks

2 tablespoons coconut oil

1 tablespoon raw honey

3 carrots, cut into matchsticks

2 pounds salmon fillets

2 teaspoons avocado oil

1 teaspoon ground black pepper

1. Preheat oven to 425°F.

2. Trim leeks and discard root end and outer leaves. Cut lengthwise.

3. Melt coconut oil in a large skillet over medium-high heat. Add leeks and cook until soft, about 5 minutes.

4. Drizzle the leeks with honey and cook until they turn brown, 15–20 minutes.

5. Stir in carrots and cook until tender, about 10 minutes.

6. Line a baking sheet with parchment paper. Place salmon on baking sheet. Brush salmon with oil and sprinkle with black pepper.

7. Roast the salmon in the oven until flesh is pink and flaky, about 6–8 minutes. Serve salmon topped with leek-and-carrot mixture.

GRILLED HALIBUT HERB SALAD

If you don't care for oranges or don't have any fresh ones handy, use drained capers to garnish this entrée salad instead.

Serves 2

2 (6-ounce) halibut fillets

4 teaspoons orange juice

3 tablespoons avocado oil

¼ teaspoon lemon pepper

¼ teaspoon garlic powder

¼ teaspoon sweet paprika

2 cups torn romaine lettuce

¼ cup chopped flat-leaf parsley

1 tablespoon chopped fresh basil

1 tablespoon sliced fresh chives

2 orange slices

1. Place a large grill pan over medium-high heat. Sprinkle each fillet side with 1 teaspoon of orange juice and lightly rub it in. Brush both sides of each fillet with oil. Sprinkle each side with a little lemon pepper, garlic powder, and paprika.

2. Add fillets to hot grill pan and cook for 5 minutes on each side until the fish is firm and flakes when gently tested with a fork. Remove fillets from pan as soon as they are cooked and place on a plate. Let fillets rest for 3 minutes, then slice each one widthwise into 2" slices.

3. Combine romaine, parsley, basil, and chives in a large salad bowl. Toss to mix. Split salad between two plates. Top each salad with a sliced fillet. Squeeze an orange slice over each salad, garnish with slice, and serve.

SHRIMP FRA DIAVOLO

Serve this spicy sauce over hot "Paleo pasta"—that is, spaghetti squash. Spaghetti squash is an excellent substitute for pasta. When cooked in the oven for 40–50 minutes, the squash becomes soft enough to lightly separate with a fork, forming an angel hair–like "pasta."

Serves 4

1 teaspoon avocado oil

1 medium onion, diced

3 cloves garlic, minced

1 teaspoon red pepper flakes

1 (15-ounce) can diced fire-roasted tomatoes

1 tablespoon minced Italian parsley

½ teaspoon freshly ground black pepper

¾ pound medium-sized shrimp, shelled

1. Heat the oil in a nonstick skillet over medium-high heat. Sauté the onion, garlic, and red pepper flakes for 8–10 minutes, until the onion is soft and translucent.

2. Add the onion mixture, tomatoes, parsley, and black pepper to a 4-quart slow cooker. Stir. Cook on low for 2–3 hours.

3. Add the shrimp. Stir, cover, and cook on high for 15 minutes or until the shrimp is fully cooked.

GINGER-LIME SALMON

The slow cooker does all the work in this recipe, creating a healthy yet impressive dish that requires virtually no hands-on time.

Serves 12

1 (3-pound) salmon fillet, bones removed

¼ cup minced fresh ginger

¼ cup lime juice

1 lime, thinly sliced

1 large onion, thinly sliced

1. Place the salmon skin-side down in an oval 6- or 7-quart slow cooker. Pour the ginger and lime juice over the fish. Arrange the lime slices and then the onion slices in single layers over the fish.

2. Cook on low for 3–4 hours or until the fish is fully cooked and flaky. Remove the skin before serving.

Cracked!

Before each use, check your slow cooker for cracks. Even small cracks in the glaze can allow bacteria to grow in the ceramic insert. If there are cracks, replace the insert or the whole slow cooker.

SALMON WITH LEMON, CAPERS, AND ROSEMARY

Salmon is amazingly moist and tender when cooked in the slow cooker.

Serves 2

8 ounces salmon

⅓ cup water

2 tablespoons lemon juice

3 thin slices fresh lemon

1 tablespoon nonpareil capers

½ teaspoon minced fresh rosemary

1. Place the salmon on the bottom of a 1-quart slow cooker. Pour the water and lemon juice over the fish.

2. Arrange the lemon slices in a single layer on top of the fish. Sprinkle with capers and rosemary.

3. Cook on low for 2 hours. Discard lemon slices prior to serving.

ROMAINE-WRAPPED HALIBUT STEAKS

Enjoy this very healthy, lean seafood dish that is so tender it'll flake with just a light touch of a fork.

Serves 4

1 cup chicken broth

10–14 large romaine leaves

4 (4-ounce) halibut steaks

1 teaspoon bouquet garni or dried tarragon

Pepper, to taste

½ cup thinly sliced fresh spinach

1. Pour broth into a 4-quart slow cooker. Cover and cook on high for 20 minutes. Immerse leaves of romaine (removing center stem) in boiling water for about 30 seconds, until wilted. Drain leaves.

2. Sprinkle halibut with herbs, pepper, and spinach. Wrap each steak in 2–4 romaine leaves. Place the wrapped halibut, seam side down, in slow cooker.

3. Cover and cook on high for 1 hour or until the fish is tender and can be flaked with a fork.

Bouquet Garni

Bouquet garni is a classic herb mixture frequently used for flavoring in meat and vegetable dishes. The herbs are typically contained within a cheesecloth pouch, which is removed before the dish is served. The herbs traditionally used include dried parsley, thyme, bay leaf, and sage.

FOILED FISH FILLETS

This recipe makes a simple, low-calorie, high-protein dish that is ready in just 2 hours.

Serves 2

2 firm white fish fillets (e.g., tilapia)

1 small bulb fennel, thinly sliced

1 tomato, thinly sliced

1 red onion, sliced into rings

1 teaspoon dried dill

Juice of 1 lime

Pepper, to taste

1. Place fish fillets on aluminum foil and top with fennel, tomato, and onion.

2. Sprinkle on dill and lime juice. Fold the foil over and connect the edges, making a packet.

3. Place the packets in a 3-quart slow cooker. Cover and cook on high for 2 hours. Season to taste with pepper.

CAVEMAN'S CATFISH

First time trying catfish? This recipe is easily spruced up with any combination of flavorful veggies (e.g., tomatoes, onions, peppers, spinach . . .).

Serves 4

4 catfish fillets

½ teaspoon dried dill

½ teaspoon dried basil

½ teaspoon dried thyme

2 lemons (1 juiced, 1 sliced into rounds)

1. Place fish fillets on aluminum foil, sprinkle with spices, and squeeze the juice of 1 lemon over fish.

2. Place the lemon slices on the fish, and fold the foil over and connect the edges, making a packet.

3. Place the packets in a 4-quart slow cooker. Cover and cook on high for 2 hours or until fish flakes when tested with a fork.

ORANGE TILAPIA

This dish provides a sweet taste of the sea. Serve it with a medley of colorful summer vegetables.

Serves 4

4 tilapia fillets

2 tablespoons lime juice

1 tablespoon raw honey

1 (10-ounce) can mandarin oranges, drained

Pepper, to taste

1. Place fish fillets on aluminum foil, drizzle with lime juice and honey, and top with oranges.

2. Fold the foil over the fish and connect the edges, making a packet. Place the packets in a 4-quart slow cooker.

3. Cover and cook on high for 2 hours. Add pepper to taste.

MAHI MAHI AND GREEN VEGETABLE MEDLEY

This is a super-healthy (and easily prepared) meal, packed with fiber, protein, iron, omega-3s, B vitamins, and phytonutrients.

Serves 2

8 stalks asparagus

2 cups broccoli florets

2 cups fresh spinach

1 tablespoon walnut oil

¼ teaspoon black pepper

½ teaspoon red pepper flakes

¼ cup lemon juice, divided

1 pound mahi mahi

1. Place the vegetables in a 3-quart slow cooker.

2. In a separate bowl, combine the oil, black pepper, red pepper flakes, and 1 tablespoon of lemon juice. Brush mixture on both sides of the mahi mahi, and place fish on top of vegetables in the slow cooker.

3. Add remaining lemon juice. Cover and cook on low for 2–3 hours. The fish should flake easily with a fork when it is done.

HERBED TILAPIA STEW

Any type of white fish fillets (such as haddock or cod) will also work in this recipe. Fish cooks very, very quickly even on the low setting in a slow cooker, so this is one recipe you will need to set a timer for.

Serves 6

2 pounds frozen boneless tilapia fillets

4 tablespoons organic butter or Ghee (see Chapter 2), melted

1 (14.5-ounce) can diced tomatoes, undrained

4 cloves garlic, minced

½ cup sliced green onions

2 teaspoons Asian fish sauce

2 tablespoons chopped fresh thyme or 1 teaspoon dried

1. Place all the ingredients in a 4-quart slow cooker.

2. Cover and cook on high for 1½–2 hours or on low for 2½–3 hours. Watch the cooking time. If your fish fillets are very thin you may need to reduce the cooking time.

3. When fish is cooked through, fillets will easily separate and flake with a fork. Break up the fish in the tomatoes and cooking liquids and serve.

SCALLOP AND SHRIMP JAMBALAYA

This version of a "red" jambalaya originated in the French Quarter of New Orleans when saffron wasn't readily available. This Creole-type jambalaya contains tomatoes, whereas a rural Cajun jambalaya (also known as "brown jambalaya") does not.

Serves 8

2 tablespoons organic butter or Ghee (see Chapter 2)

1 large onion, chopped

2 medium celery stalks, chopped

1 medium green bell pepper, chopped

3 garlic cloves, minced

1 (28-ounce) can diced tomatoes, undrained

1 tablespoon dried parsley

½ teaspoon dried thyme

½ teaspoon salt

¼ teaspoon pepper

¼ teaspoon hot sauce

2 teaspoons Creole seasoning

¾ pound uncooked, frozen scallops, thawed

¾ pound uncooked, peeled, deveined medium shrimp, thawed if frozen

¼ cup fresh parsley, chopped

1. In a large skillet, melt the butter over medium heat. Sauté the onions, celery, and bell pepper until softened, about 3–5 minutes. Add garlic and cook for 1 minute more.

2. Place sautéed vegetables and all remaining ingredients except the scallops, shrimp, and fresh parsley in a 4-quart slow cooker.

3. Cover and cook on low for 6 hours or on high for 3 hours.

4. Add scallops and shrimp and continue to cook on low for 45–60 minutes, or until scallops are opaque and shrimp curls and is bright pink. Serve jambalaya over a root-vegetable medley and garnish with fresh parsley.

FISH "BAKE"

The stewed tomatoes help prevent the fish from overcooking and make the perfect sauce for serving the fish over steamed cabbage or alongside a vegetable dish of your choice.

Serves 4

2 tablespoons organic butter or Ghee (see Chapter 2), melted

4 flounder or cod fillets

1 clove garlic, minced

1 small onion, thinly sliced

1 green bell pepper, seeded and diced

1 (14.5-ounce) can stewed tomatoes

½ teaspoon dried basil

½ teaspoon dried oregano

1 teaspoon dried parsley

Freshly ground black pepper, to taste

1. Add the butter to a 3- or 4-quart slow cooker. Use the melted butter to coat the bottom and the sides of the insert.

2. Add fish to the slow cooker in a single layer over the butter.

3. Evenly distribute the garlic, onion, and bell pepper over the fish. Pour the stewed tomatoes over the fish. Evenly sprinkle the basil, oregano, parsley, and black pepper over the tomatoes.

4. Cover and cook on low for 4–6 hours or until the fish is opaque and flakes apart.

CIOPPINO

Cioppino is a versatile summer dish. You can replace the cod with haddock and add lobster, crab, crayfish, and clams. Enjoy this beautiful and healthy bounty from the sea!

Serves 6

2 tablespoons organic butter or Ghee (see Chapter 2)

1 large sweet onion, diced

2 stalks celery, finely diced

2 cloves garlic, minced

3 cups bottled clam juice or fish stock

2 cups water

1 (28-ounce) can diced or whole peeled tomatoes

1 cup dry red wine or chicken broth

2 teaspoons dried parsley

1 teaspoon dried basil

1 teaspoon dried thyme

Red pepper flakes, to taste

1 teaspoon raw honey

1 bay leaf

1 pound cod, cut into 1" pieces

½ pound medium or large raw shrimp, peeled and deveined

½ pound scallops

1. Add the butter, onion, celery, and garlic to a 4-quart slow cooker. Stir to mix the vegetables together with the butter. Cover and cook on high for 30 minutes or until the onions are transparent.

2. Add the clam juice or fish stock, water, tomatoes, wine or broth, parsley, basil, thyme, red pepper flakes, honey, and bay leaf. Stir to combine. Cover, reduce the slow cooker setting to low, and cook for 5 hours.

3. If you used whole peeled tomatoes, use a spoon to break them apart. Gently stir in the cod, shrimp, and scallops. Increase the slow cooker setting to high. Cover and cook for 30 minutes or until the seafood is cooked through. Remove and discard bay leaf, then ladle stew into soup bowls and serve immediately.

ALMOND-STUFFED FLOUNDER

Making this dish in the slow cooker lets you layer the fish and stuffing rather than stuffing and rolling the fillets. You can substitute sole for the flounder. Serve with a tossed salad and a seasoned vegetable medley of your choice.

Serves 4

2 teaspoons coconut oil

4 (4-ounce) fresh or frozen flounder fillets

½ cup slivered almonds

1 tablespoon freeze-dried chives (optional)

Sweet paprika, to taste

¼ cup dry white wine or chicken broth (optional)

1 tablespoon coconut oil

½ cup grated carrots

1 tablespoon almond flour

¼ teaspoon dried tarragon

White pepper, to taste

1 cup (full-fat) coconut milk

1. Lightly grease the insert of a 3- or 4-quart slow cooker with coconut oil.

2. Lay 2 fillets flat in the slow cooker. Sprinkle the almonds and chives (if using) over the fillets. Place the remaining fillets on top. Sprinkle paprika over the top fillets. Pour the wine or broth around the fish.

3. Add the oil and carrots to a microwave-safe bowl. Cover and microwave on high for 1 minute; stir and microwave on high for 1 more minute. Stir in the flour, tarragon, and pepper. Whisk in half the coconut milk. Cover and microwave on high for 1 minute. Stir in the remaining coconut milk. Pour the sauce over the fish.

4. Cover and cook on low for 2 hours or until the fish is cooked through and the sauce is thickened.

5. Turn off the slow cooker and let rest for 15 minutes. To serve, use a knife to cut into four wedges. Spoon each wedge onto a plate (so that there is fish and filling in each serving). Sprinkle with additional paprika before serving if desired.

POACHED SWORDFISH WITH LEMON-PARSLEY SAUCE

Swordfish steaks are usually cut thicker than most fish fillets, plus swordfish is a firmer fish so it takes longer to poach. You can speed up the poaching process a little if you remove the steaks from the refrigerator and put them in room-temperature water during the 30 minutes that the onions and water are cooking.

Serves 4

1 tablespoon coconut oil

4 thin slices sweet onion

2 cups water

4 (6-ounce) swordfish steaks

1 lemon

2 tablespoons extra-virgin olive oil

2 teaspoons fresh lemon juice

¼ teaspoon Dijon mustard

Freshly ground white or black pepper, to taste (optional)

1 tablespoon fresh flat-leaf parsley, minced

1. Use the coconut oil to grease the bottom and halfway up the sides of a 4-quart slow cooker.

2. Arrange the onion slices in the bottom of the slow cooker, pressing them into the butter so that they stay in place. Pour in the water. Cover and cook on high for 30 minutes.

3. Place a swordfish steak over each onion slice.

4. Thinly slice the lemon; discard the seeds, and place the slices over the fish. Cover and cook on high for 45 minutes or until the fish is opaque. Transfer the (well-drained) fish to individual serving plates or to a serving platter.

5. In a small bowl add the olive oil, lemon juice, mustard, and white or black pepper, if using, and whisk to combine.

6. Immediately before serving the swordfish, fold the parsley into the sauce. Evenly divide the sauce between the swordfish steaks.

MANHATTAN SCALLOP CHOWDER

Serve this chowder with a tossed salad. Unlike the popular New England clam version, this scallop chowder is red!

Serves 6

2 tablespoons butter, melted

2 stalks celery, finely diced

1 medium green bell pepper, seeded and diced

1 large carrot, peeled and finely diced

1 medium onion, diced

2 medium butternut squash or turnips, scrubbed, peeled, and diced

1 (15-ounce) can diced tomatoes

1 (15-ounce) can tomato purée

2 cups bottled clam juice or Fish Stock (Chapter 4)

1 cup dry white wine or chicken broth

¾ cup water

1 teaspoon dried thyme

1 teaspoon dried parsley

1 bay leaf

¼ teaspoon freshly ground black pepper

1½ pounds bay scallops

Fresh parsley, minced (optional)

Fresh basil (optional)

1. Add the butter, celery, bell pepper, and carrot to a 4- or 6-quart slow cooker; stir to coat the vegetables in the butter. Cover and cook on high for 15 minutes. Stir in the onion. Cover and cook on high for 30 minutes or until the vegetables are soft.

2. Stir in the squash or turnips, tomatoes, tomato purée, clam juice, wine or broth, water, thyme, parsley, bay leaf, and pepper. Cover, reduce the temperature to low, and cook for 7 hours or until the squash is cooked through.

3. Add scallops to the slow cooker.

4. Increase the temperature to high, cover, and cook for 15 minutes or until the scallops are firm.

5. Remove and discard the bay leaf. Taste and adjust seasonings if necessary. Ladle into soup bowls. If desired, sprinkle minced fresh parsley over each serving and garnish with fresh basil.

HATTERAS CLAM CHOWDER

This cozy, Paleo-creamy chowder is thickened by turnips in place of potatoes. Serve it with a fresh green salad or hearty main dish of your choice.

Serves 4

1 small onion, diced and sautéed in 1 tablespoon olive oil

2 medium turnips, peeled and diced

1 (8-ounce) bottle clam juice

2–3 cups water

½ teaspoon freshly ground black pepper

2 (6.5-ounce) cans minced clams, undrained

1. Add cooked onions to a greased 2½-quart slow cooker.

2. Add turnips, clam juice, and enough water to cover. Add pepper.

3. Cover and cook on high for 3 hours until turnips are very tender.

4. One hour prior to serving, add in the clams along with broth from the cans and cook on high for 20–30 minutes or until heated through.

MAHI MAHI WRAPS WITH AVOCADO AND FRESH CABBAGE

These California-style "tacos" can be prepared with any meaty, mild fish or shrimp.

Serves 4

1 pound mahi mahi fillets

1 teaspoon salt

½ teaspoon freshly ground black pepper

1 teaspoon avocado oil

1 avocado

4 Bibb lettuce cups

2 cups shredded cabbage

2 limes, quartered

1. Season fish with salt and pepper. Heat oil in a large pan over medium heat. Once the oil is hot, sauté fish for about 3–4 minutes on each side. Slice or flake fish into 1" pieces.

2. Slice avocado in half. Remove seed and, using a spoon, remove the flesh from the skin. Slice the avocado halves into ½"-thick slices.

3. Place one-fourth of the mahi mahi on each lettuce leaf; top with avocado and cabbage. Serve with lime wedges.

CHAPTER 11

SIDE DISHES

CAVEMAN VEGETABLE ROAST

Roasted vegetables are easy and a satisfying side dish. They can even be dinner, served with a green salad and some fruit. Roasting concentrates the flavors of the veggies and brings out their sweetness, and makes the vegetables very tender. Season them with just about any herb or spice. For a change of pace, curried roasted vegetables are delicious, as are veggies roasted with Asian spices.

Serves 6

1 onion, cut into eighths

12 whole cloves garlic, peeled

1 sweet potato, peeled and cubed

1 parsnip, peeled and cubed

1 red bell pepper, cut into strips

1 yellow bell pepper, cut into strips

¼ cup olive oil

1 tablespoon red wine vinegar

1 teaspoon dried thyme leaves

1 teaspoon salt

⅛ teaspoon pepper

1. Preheat oven to 400°F. In a large rimmed baking sheet, combine all the vegetables. Drizzle with oil and vinegar and sprinkle with thyme, salt, and pepper; toss to coat.

2. Roast for 40–50 minutes or until the vegetables are tender and browned on the edges, stirring every 15 minutes. Serve warm or cool.

ROASTED CRUCIFEROUS VEGETABLES

Cauliflower, Brussels sprouts, and broccoli are all cruciferous vegetables. That means they belong to the cabbage family of vegetables. These nutrition powerhouses contain fiber, phytochemicals, antioxidants, and vitamins so they help fight the risk of many diseases, including cancer and heart disease. When roasted, the bitterness of broccoli and Brussels sprouts is reduced, so even broccoli and/or Brussels sprouts haters will love this dish.

Serves 6–8

1 head cauliflower

1 head broccoli

2 cups Brussels sprouts

5 cloves garlic, sliced

2 tablespoons coconut oil

2 tablespoons olive oil

½ teaspoon salt

⅛ teaspoon pepper

1. Preheat oven to 400°F. Line a 9" x 13" baking dish with parchment paper and set aside.

2. Break the cauliflower into florets, discarding the leaves and tough core. Place in pan.

3. Cut the broccoli into florets. You can use the stem; just peel it and cut into 2" sections. Place in pan with the cauliflower.

4. Remove discolored or torn leaves from the Brussels sprouts. Trim off the stem end and place in pan. Top with garlic slices.

5. Melt coconut oil and olive oil and drizzle over the vegetables. Toss to coat, then sprinkle with salt and pepper.

6. Roast the vegetables for 50–60 minutes or until browned and tender, stirring occasionally. Serve warm.

MASHED CAULIFLOWER

This is a classic substitute for mashed potatoes, which are not on the Paleo diet. This substitution is surprisingly similar to potatoes, especially when served as a base for a stew or a pot roast such as Pot Roast with Vegetables and Gravy (see Chapter 8). Just make sure the cauliflower is steamed until very tender. Add whatever you'd usually add to mashed potatoes: bacon, butter, shredded cheese, chives, green onions, etc. You may even fool people into thinking they're eating mashed potatoes!

Serves 8

1 large head cauliflower, cut into florets

3 cloves garlic, peeled

3 ounces softened cream cheese or 6 tablespoons Yogurt Cheese (see Chapter 2)

3 tablespoons butter, softened, or olive oil

2 tablespoons buttermilk or Almond Yogurt (see Chapter 1)

3 tablespoons heavy cream or coconut cream

1 teaspoon salt

Pinch freshly grated nutmeg

⅛ teaspoon white pepper

1. Place the cauliflower and garlic in a steamer, or in a colander that fits over a heavy pot. Put water in the pot, or in the steamer. Cover and steam until very tender, about 8–9 minutes.

2. Place the cauliflower and garlic in a food processor. Cover and let stand 2 minutes. Then add cream cheese or Yogurt Cheese and butter or olive oil and process until smooth. Add buttermilk or Almond Yogurt, cream, salt, nutmeg, and pepper and blend again. You may need to add more liquid for desired consistency. Serve immediately.

CAULIFLOWER RICE

Cauliflower makes a surprisingly delicious substitute for rice. The creamy flesh of this cruciferous vegetable shreds nicely to mimic the texture of the grain. Just be sure you don't overcook it. You want each little piece of cauliflower to be tender, but slightly firm to stand up to the sauces and foods you'll serve with it.

Serves 4

1 head cauliflower

1 tablespoon lemon juice

2 tablespoons Ghee (see Chapter 2) or coconut oil

3 shallots, minced

2 cloves garlic, minced

1 teaspoon salt

⅛ teaspoon white pepper

1. Rinse the cauliflower and pat dry. Break into florets. You can grate this on a box grater or use a food processor. Grate or process until the cauliflower is in tiny pieces. Toss with lemon juice so the cauliflower stays nice and white, and set aside.

2. In large skillet, melt Ghee or coconut oil over medium-high heat. Add shallots and garlic; cook and stir until tender, about 5 minutes.

3. Add the cauliflower and sprinkle with salt and pepper. Cook for 4–5 minutes, stirring frequently, until cauliflower is tender but with some firmness in the center. Serve immediately.

MASHED SWEET POTATOES

Sweet potatoes are an excellent substitute for white potatoes when you want something creamy, comforting, and delicious. These tubers are full of vitamin A and fiber and pair well with everything from beef to pork to chicken. Sweet potatoes are often called yams, but the two are not the same. Yams are a large pale starchy root with a crumbly texture.

Serves 6

4 large sweet potatoes, peeled and cubed

2 tablespoons coconut oil

3 cloves garlic, minced

½ cup coconut milk

½ cup applesauce

½ teaspoon ground ginger

1 teaspoon salt

⅛ teaspoon white pepper

1. Place sweet potatoes in a large pot and cover with cold water. Bring to a boil over high heat. Reduce heat to medium, cover, and simmer for about 15 minutes until tender.

2. Drain sweet potatoes and return to hot pot. Cover and set aside.

3. Melt coconut oil in small saucepan; cook garlic until just fragrant.

4. Pour oil and garlic into sweet potatoes and mash. Add coconut milk, applesauce, ginger, salt, and pepper and mash until smooth. Serve immediately.

RIBBON SALAD

Your vegetable peeler can turn ordinary root vegetables and squash into a gorgeous side salad. This recipe takes a bit of time, but the end result is just beautiful and very delicious. Choose your favorite hard veggies for this recipe. It's delicious served with grilled chicken or steak.

Serves 6

2 medium zucchini

2 large carrots

2 yellow summer squash

2 tablespoons olive oil

3 tablespoons lemon juice

1 tablespoon Dijon mustard

1 tablespoon chopped fresh dill weed

½ teaspoon salt

⅛ teaspoon pepper

1. Rinse the vegetables and pat dry; cut off ends. Using a vegetable peeler or a mandoline, shave all of the vegetables into thin, wide ribbons. Don't shave the seedy core of the zucchini and squash; discard that when you get to it.

2. In large bowl, combine olive oil, lemon juice, mustard, dill weed, salt, and pepper and mix well. Add the vegetable ribbons and toss to coat. Serve immediately, or cover and refrigerate up to 24 hours before serving.

SWEET POTATOES ANNIE

Sweet potato fries are a real treat, especially if you miss the classic French-fried potato. But this recipe takes the average fry to another level. The potatoes are coated with hazelnut flour for some sweet nuttiness, and lots of herbs, then baked in a combination of ghee and coconut oil. They get crisp and brown and are packed with flavor. Serve with a grilled steak for a wonderful meal.

Serves 4

3 sweet potatoes

1 egg white

¼ cup hazelnut flour

⅓ cup shredded toasted coconut, ground

1 teaspoon dried oregano leaves

1 teaspoon dried marjoram leaves

1 teaspoon salt

⅛ teaspoon crushed red pepper flakes

¼ cup Ghee (see Chapter 2) or olive oil

¼ cup coconut oil

1. Preheat oven to 400°F. Peel the sweet potatoes and cut into strips.

2. In small bowl, beat egg white until foamy. Pour over potatoes and toss to coat.

3. In small bowl, combine flour, coconut, oregano, marjoram, salt, and crushed red pepper flakes and mix well. Sprinkle over potatoes and toss to coat.

4. Place Ghee or olive oil and coconut oil in a heavy-duty half sheet pan (15" x 10") and place in oven until fats melt. Carefully remove from oven.

5. Add coated potatoes in a single layer. Return to oven and bake for 30–45 minutes, turning with a spatula every 15 minutes, until fat is absorbed and potatoes are golden brown and tender. Serve immediately.

JICAMA RICE

You can make "rice" out of jicama just as you can out of cauliflower! Jicama are slightly sweeter and a bit more starchy tasting than cauliflower. The knobby white root is low in calories and high in fiber and antioxidants. It's also a good source of vitamins C and B, in addition to magnesium, copper, and iron.

Serves 4

1 large jicama

1 tablespoon lemon juice

2 tablespoons butter or coconut oil

2 shallots, minced

½ teaspoon salt

⅛ teaspoon white pepper

1. Peel the jicama and grate on a box grater or in the food processor. Sprinkle with lemon juice and mix.

2. In large skillet, melt butter or coconut oil over medium heat. Add shallots; cook and stir until tender, about 4 minutes.

3. Add the jicama rice to the skillet; cook and stir until the jicama releases some of its water and the water evaporates, about 5–6 minutes. Taste the jicama to see if it's tender. If not, cook another minute or two. Then sprinkle with salt and pepper and serve.

VEGGIE KEBABS WITH CHIMICHURRI SAUCE

When you're grilling steak, pork, or chicken, it's always nice to serve some grilled vegetables too. Just remember to use vegetables that have about the same cooking time, or precook the harder produce so it all cooks to tender perfection at once. You can serve extra chimichurri sauce on the side; it's also good on any grilled meat or chicken.

Serves 4

1 red bell pepper

1 yellow bell pepper

1 red onion, cut into eighths

16 large button mushrooms

1 yellow squash, cut into chunks

2 tablespoons olive oil

⅓ cup Chimichurri Sauce (see Chapter 2)

1. If using bamboo skewers, soak in cool water for 30 minutes to prevent burning.

2. Thread vegetables onto bamboo or metal skewers, alternating the produce. Brush with olive oil.

3. Grill 6" from medium coals, turning frequently, until vegetables are slightly charred on the edges and tender. Brush with chimichurri sauce, grill for 1 more minute, then serve.

GRILLED SWEET POTATO SLICES

Grilled sweet potatoes are like a brand new vegetable. The grill adds a wonderful smoky flavor and brings out the sweetness of this root veggie. Because sweet potatoes take a long time to cook, they must be precooked before they are finished on the grill. You can do this ahead of time, then grill the potatoes just before serving.

Serves 6

2 sweet potatoes, well scrubbed

2 tablespoons coconut oil

1 tablespoon honey

2 teaspoons curry powder

1 teaspoon paprika

1 teaspoon salt

⅛ teaspoon pepper

1. Preheat oven to 350°F. Pierce sweet potatoes with a fork and bake for 30 minutes or until almost tender but still firm. Cool 30 minutes.

2. Slice the sweet potatoes into ½" thick slices.

3. In small saucepan, combine coconut oil, honey, curry powder, paprika, salt, and pepper and heat until blended. Brush on the sweet potatoes.

4. Grill the sweet potatoes for 2–4 minutes or until nice grill marks appear, turning once and brushing frequently with the honey sauce.

CELERY ORIENTAL

Cooked celery is a vegetable that not many have tried, but it is very delicate and delicious. It is a good accompaniment to any grilled meat or chicken recipe. Celery leaves, which are not often used in recipes, are a good source of beta-carotene and other antioxidants that help lower the risk of cancer. And celery is a good source of fiber, vitamin K, and folic acid.

Serves 6

2 tablespoons olive oil

2 cloves garlic, minced

3 cups sliced celery

¼ cup water

1 tablespoon coconut aminos

½ teaspoon five-spice powder

½ cup chopped celery leaves

⅛ teaspoon crushed red pepper flakes

⅓ cup sliced almonds, toasted if desired

1. In large saucepan, heat olive oil over medium heat. Add garlic; cook for 1 minute.

2. Add celery; cook for 2–3 minutes or until crisp-tender. Add water and coconut aminos; bring to a simmer. Cover pan, reduce heat, and simmer for 4 minutes.

3. Uncover pan and add five-spice powder, celery leaves, and crushed red pepper flakes; cook for 2 minutes longer. Sprinkle with almonds and serve immediately.

SCALLOPED ONIONS

Onions are an assertive root vegetable that change character completely when cooked. Any strong onion will become sweet and tender when slowly cooked for a long time. This excellent recipe uses three kinds of onions for a beautiful presentation. It's delicious served with grilled steak or chicken.

Serves 6

¼ cup butter or olive oil

4 large yellow onions, chopped

2 leeks, chopped

1 (16-ounce) package frozen pearl onions, thawed

4 cloves garlic, minced

2 tablespoons almond flour

1 teaspoon salt

¼ teaspoon white pepper

1½ cups full-fat coconut milk

2 tablespoons mustard

2 tablespoons lemon juice

1½ cups grated Gruyère cheese, if desired

1 cup ground almonds

1. Preheat oven to 375°F. In large pan, melt butter or heat olive oil over medium heat. Add yellow onions and leeks; cook and stir for 10 minutes until crisp-tender. Add pearl onions and garlic; cook, stirring occasionally, for another 5–7 minutes until tender.

2. Sprinkle flour, salt, and pepper over mixture; cook and stir for 2 minutes longer. Then add coconut milk and cook, stirring occasionally, until thickened. Add mustard and lemon juice and 1 cup of cheese, if using.

3. Pour into 3-quart casserole and top with ground almonds and remaining cheese, if using. Bake for 25–35 minutes or until mixture is bubbly and almonds and cheese are browned.

ONIONS AND APPLES

This is an old-fashioned recipe that has fallen out of style, but it's delicious and easy to make. It is a great accompaniment to roasted chicken or pork for a fall or winter dinner. Choose tart apples that aren't too sweet and are firm, such as Granny Smith or Braeburn.

Serves 4

1 tablespoon butter or coconut oil

1 tablespoon olive oil

2 onions, chopped

2 cloves garlic, minced

3 apples, sliced

3 tablespoons honey

1 tablespoon lemon juice

½ teaspoon salt

½ teaspoon dried thyme leaves

1. In large pan, melt butter or coconut oil and olive oil over medium heat. Add onions and garlic and cook until crisp-tender, about 4 minutes.

2. Add apples and stir. Drizzle with honey and lemon juice and sprinkle with salt and thyme leaves.

3. Cover and cook on low for about 7–9 minutes or until apples are tender. Serve immediately.

ROASTED FRUIT

Roasting fruit brings out its sweetness and tenderness. Although this is a sweet recipe it's an excellent side dish for grilled and roasted meats. Stone fruits roast the best; they retain their shape and texture even after cooking. Serve warm from the oven, or cool the fruit, cover, and chill it in the fridge for a few hours before serving.

Serves 6

4 peaches, pitted and cut into quarters

4 nectarines, pitted and cut into quarters

6 apricots, pitted and cut in half

1 tablespoon olive oil

2 tablespoons lemon juice

½ teaspoon salt

½ teaspoon dried thyme leaves

⅛ teaspoon ground white pepper

1½ cups red grapes

1. Preheat oven to 400°F. Place the peaches, nectarines, and apricots, cut-side up, in a roasting dish. Drizzle with olive oil and lemon juice. Sprinkle with salt, thyme, and pepper.

2. Roast, uncovered, for 15 minutes. Add grapes to the pan and stir gently. Roast for another 5–10 minutes or until fruit is tender.

CUCUMBER RAITA

Raita is an Indian side dish that serves as a cooling complement to spicy dishes. It's usually made of cucumber, sour cream, and some herbs. You can certainly use sour cream, but coconut milk is a more Paleo alternative. Because cucumbers contain a lot of water, they are salted and left to drain for about an hour before they are mixed with the coconut milk.

Serves 4–6

1 (5-ounce) can full-fat coconut milk

1 cucumber, peeled and seeded

½ teaspoon salt

⅓ cup minced red onion

1 clove garlic, minced

2 tablespoons lemon juice

1 tablespoon chopped fresh mint

½ teaspoon ground cumin

⅛ teaspoon white pepper

1. Place the can of coconut milk in the fridge for at least 8 hours. Spoon off the solids from the top; reserve the thin liquid for another use.

2. Slice the cucumber thinly and sprinkle with salt. Place in colander and place in the sink; let stand for 30 minutes. Rinse the cucumber, drain, and pat dry with paper towels.

3. In medium bowl, combine coconut milk solids, cucumber, red onion, garlic, and lemon juice and mix well. Stir in mint, cumin, and pepper. Cover and chill for 1 hour before serving.

SAUTÉED CABBAGE

If you eat a lot of bacon, and enjoy cooking with bacon fat, it's a good idea to save the fat every time you make a batch of this smoky meat. When the bacon is cooked, let the pan sit off the heat for about 10 minutes. Then carefully pour the fat into a container. You can strain it if you'd like. Store it in the freezer in 1- or 2-tablespoon quantities and use in cooking.

Serves 6

3 tablespoons bacon fat or coconut oil

1 onion, chopped

3 cloves garlic, minced

4 cups chopped green cabbage

3 cups chopped red cabbage

¼ cup water

1 tablespoon coconut aminos

1 teaspoon salt

⅛ teaspoon pepper

1. In large skillet, heat bacon fat or coconut oil over medium heat. Add onion and garlic; cook and stir until crisp-tender, about 4 minutes.

2. Add cabbages to the pan and cook and stir for 4 minutes.

3. Add water, coconut aminos, salt, and pepper and bring to a simmer. Cover and cook for 5–8 minutes longer until cabbage is tender.

BROCCOLI AND BELL PEPPERS

This colorful side dish is delicious and easy and very good for you. Broccoli is a cruciferous vegetable with cancer-fighting properties, and bell peppers are a great source of vitamin C and fiber. There are many colors of bell peppers on the market, from red to green to orange and even white and purple. Use what you like best.

Serves 4

1 head broccoli

2 tablespoons Ghee (see Chapter 2) or coconut oil

1 onion, chopped

1 red bell pepper

1 orange bell pepper

3 cloves garlic, sliced

3 tablespoons water or vegetable stock

½ teaspoon salt

⅛ teaspoon pepper

1. Cut the florets off the broccoli stems. Peel the stems and cut into 1" slices. Steam the broccoli until crisp-tender, about 3–4 minutes. Drain and set aside.

2. In large skillet, melt Ghee or coconut oil over medium heat. Add onion and cook for 3 minutes.

3. Add all of the bell peppers and cook for another 3 minutes, stirring occasionally.

4. Add broccoli, garlic, water, salt, and pepper to pan. Bring to a simmer, then cover and simmer for 3–4 minutes until everything is hot.

ROASTED BRUSSELS SPROUTS

Brussels sprouts are very healthy, but not many people like them because they are so bitter. One way to get rid of the bitter taste is to cook them very well. In this recipe they are roasted until very tender, with crisp and brown exteriors. The bacon fat aids in the browning and adds great flavor. Serve with your fall and winter meals.

Serves 4–6

4 slices bacon

1½ pounds fresh Brussels sprouts, trimmed

1 head garlic, cut in half crosswise

1 teaspoon salt

⅛ teaspoon pepper

2 tablespoons lemon juice

1. Preheat oven to 400°F. In ovenproof skillet, cook bacon until crisp. Drain bacon on paper towels, crumble, and set aside.

2. Add Brussels sprouts to bacon fat in pan along with garlic, cut-side down; cook for 3 minutes. Turn garlic cut-side up.

3. Sprinkle with salt and pepper and place in oven. Roast for 30–40 minutes or until the vegetables are deep golden brown.

4. Remove garlic from pan and, holding in an oven mitt, squeeze the cloves over the Brussels sprouts. Sprinkle with bacon and lemon juice, stir, and serve.

SAUTÉED KALE AND BROCCOLI RABE

Kale is a magnificent cruciferous vegetable, as is broccoli rabe. They are both leafy green vegetables with fabulous nutritional profiles. Both vegetables are bitter, so cook them until tender to reduce that flavor profile. Adding sweet vegetables, such as onion, can help add another layer of flavor. In this recipe, the greens are first steamed, then sautéed with the onion and garlic.

Serves 4–6

1 bunch broccoli rabe

1 bunch kale

2 tablespoons butter or olive oil

1 onion, chopped

3 cloves garlic, minced

2 tablespoons lemon juice

1 teaspoon salt

⅛ teaspoon white pepper

1. Trim the base of the broccoli rabe stems and cut into 2" pieces. Trim the thick ribs and stems off the kale and cut into 4" pieces.

2. Steam the broccoli rabe and kale for about 3 minutes. Drain and set aside.

3. In large skillet, melt butter or olive oil over medium heat. Add onion and garlic; cook and stir until tender, about 5 minutes.

4. Add broccoli rabe and kale to skillet; cook and stir for 3 minutes. Add lemon juice, salt, and pepper and cook for another 2–3 minutes until tender. Serve immediately.

CARAMELIZED ONIONS

Caramelized onions are a wonderful accompaniment to any grilled or roasted meat, and just about any cooked vegetable. The only trick to this recipe is to cook over low heat so the onions do not burn before they are done. When done, the onions will be a deep golden brown color and be very sweet and tender.

Serves 4–6

2 tablespoons butter or coconut oil

1 tablespoon olive oil

4 large onions, peeled and sliced

½ teaspoon salt

2 tablespoons water

1 tablespoon honey

1 tablespoon red wine vinegar

1. In a large, heavy skillet, melt butter or coconut oil and olive oil over medium-high heat. Add onions; cook and stir for about 5 minutes until tender.

2. Reduce heat to low and cook for about 10 minutes longer. Sprinkle with salt and add water.

3. Cook onions for another 40–50 minutes, stirring frequently, until deep golden brown. Drizzle with honey and red wine vinegar and stir well. Serve immediately, or refrigerate up to 3 days. Freeze for longer storage.

ASPARAGUS WITH BACON

Asparagus is a wonderful Paleo-friendly vegetable that used to be a real extravagance. Now you can find fresh asparagus in the market almost year-round. Whether the spears are thin or thick doesn't matter; just cook it until tender but still with a bit of firmness in the center.

Serves 4

1 pound asparagus

4 slices bacon

1 shallot, minced

2 tablespoons water

½ teaspoon salt

⅛ teaspoon pepper

1. Break off the ends of the asparagus spears; they will naturally snap where the stalk starts to become tough. Rinse well and set aside.

2. In large skillet, cook bacon until crisp. Drain bacon on paper towels, crumble, and set aside.

3. Drain off all but 2 tablespoons bacon fat from pan. Add shallot; cook for 2 minutes.

4. Add asparagus to pan and cook for 2 minutes. Add water, cover, and steam for another 2 minutes or until asparagus is tender.

5. Remove cover, add bacon, salt, and pepper, and heat until hot. Serve immediately.

SAUTÉED ASPARAGUS

Asparagus makes a healthy and filling side complement to any main course. Try this dish with any meat, poultry, or fish recipe.

Serves 4

1 bunch asparagus

2 tablespoons walnut oil

2 cloves garlic, chopped

1. Cut bottoms off asparagus, then cut remainder of stalks into 2" pieces.

2. Add walnut oil to a skillet set on medium heat.

3. Add garlic and cook for about 30 seconds, then add asparagus.

4. Stir-fry until asparagus is tender when pierced with fork, approximately 5–8 minutes.

ROASTED ASPARAGUS

Use thicker asparagus to withstand the heat of the grill. Be sure to remove the woody ends of the stalks first.

Serves 6

2 bunches asparagus

1 tablespoon walnut oil

1 tablespoon lemon juice

Freshly ground black pepper, to taste

Preheat grill to medium. Toss the asparagus in the oil, then drain on a rack and season with lemon juice and pepper. Grill the asparagus for 1–2 minutes on each side (cook to desired doneness). Serve immediately.

CITRUS-STEAMED CARROTS

This recipe includes figs, which are said to be the fruit of gods and goddesses. Enjoy the pleasure yourself!

Serves 6

1 pound carrots

1 cup orange juice

2 tablespoons lemon juice

2 tablespoons lime juice

3 fresh figs

1 tablespoon extra-virgin olive oil

1 tablespoon capers

1. Peel and julienne the carrots. In a pot, combine the citrus juices and heat over medium-high heat. Add the carrots, cover, and cook until al dente, about 5 minutes. Remove from heat, strain, and let cool.

2. Cut the figs into wedges. Mound the carrots on a serving plate and arrange the figs around the carrots. Sprinkle the olive oil and capers on top and serve.

BAKED SWEET POTATO STICKS

These fries are good for you and make a delicious and energizing side dish that substitutes for traditional French fries. Great for kids!

Serves 2

1 large sweet potato, peeled and cut like French fries

1 tablespoon almond oil

1 teaspoon salt

½ teaspoon freshly ground black pepper

1 teaspoon dried thyme

1 teaspoon dried sage

1. Cook the potato slices in boiling water for 4–5 minutes. Drain potatoes and dry on paper towels.

2. Sprinkle with oil, salt, pepper, and herbs. Bake on an aluminum pan at 350°F until crisp, about 10 minutes.

CELERIAC SLAW

Celeriac is a vegetable in the celery family. You can put this slaw next to most meat, fish, or poultry for a tasty counterpoint.

Serves 6

1 bulb celeriac, peeled and coarsely grated

1 tablespoon Wilma's Mayonnaise (see Chapter 2)

1 tablespoon white wine vinegar

Pinch dried thyme

½ teaspoon salt

½ teaspoon freshly ground black pepper

1 teaspoon ground mustard

Place the celeriac in a bowl. In a separate bowl, mix mayonnaise, vinegar, thyme, salt, pepper, and mustard. Pour over the celeriac and serve as a garnish or as part of an appetizer tray.

NAPA CABBAGE WITH ASIAN SAUCE

You can use napa cabbage (cooked or raw) instead of pasta as a bed for sauces and meats or as a salad green. Try it steamed with various sauces. It's an easy way to add fiber and antioxidants to your meals. This sauce can be adapted to your taste, from fruity to hot.

Serves 2

4 tablespoons sesame oil

6 scallions, sliced

1 (1") piece fresh ginger, peeled and minced

1 clove garlic, minced

3 tablespoons coconut aminos

½ head napa cabbage, cut crosswise in thin slices and separated into ribbons

Heat the oil in a medium skillet over medium-high heat. Sauté the scallions, fresh ginger, and garlic. Add the coconut aminos. Rinse the cabbage and drain on paper towels; toss with sauce.

Asian-Style Garnishes

To add flair to the presentation of this dish, try topping it with 1 tablespoon of toasted sesame seeds and the juice of half a lime. Serve with lime wedges and chopsticks.

CHIPOTLE-LIME MASHED SWEET POTATOES

Sweet potatoes are a great post-workout food. These chipotle-lime mashed potatoes will be a favorite at any family table.

Serves 10

3 pounds sweet potatoes

1½ tablespoons coconut oil

1¼ teaspoons chipotle powder

Juice from ½ large lime

1. Peel the sweet potatoes and cut into cubes.

2. Steam the cubes until soft, approximately 5–8 minutes. Transfer to a large bowl.

3. In a small saucepan, heat coconut oil and whisk in the chipotle powder and lime juice.

4. Pour the mixture into the bowl with the sweet potato cubes and mash with fork or potato masher.

OKRA STUFFED WITH GREEN PEPPERCORNS

This is a delightful Indian dish. You can make it in advance and warm it up before serving. It's a great side dish for curry, and okra is a nice vegetable alternative if you get sick of the usual broccoli, asparagus, and zucchini.

Serves 2

6 okra, stemmed

½ cup vegetable broth

3 teaspoons green peppercorns, packed in brine and drained

1 teaspoon organic butter or Ghee (see Chapter 2)

1 teaspoon cumin

½ teaspoon salt

½ teaspoon freshly ground black pepper

1. In a large saucepan, poach the okra in the vegetable broth until slightly softened, about 4 minutes. Remove from the broth and place on a work surface, reserving broth in the saucepan.

2. Rinse peppercorns and poke them down into the center of the okra. Return to broth; add butter, cumin, salt, and pepper.

EGGPLANT SOUFFLÉ

Smooth and creamy in texture, this is an Indian favorite. Often the eggplant is simply puréed and spiced—this is more of a fusion dish.

Serves 4

2 medium eggplants

1 teaspoon water

1 tablespoon avocado oil

2 cloves garlic, minced

1 small white onion, minced

4 eggs, separated

1 teaspoon salt

½ teaspoon freshly ground black pepper

1 teaspoon curry powder, or to taste

1. Wrap the eggplant in aluminum foil with water. Roast the eggplant at 400°F in a roasting pan for 1 hour, or until very soft when pricked with a fork. Cool, cut in half, scoop out flesh, and discard skin. Keep oven on.

2. In a medium-sized skillet, heat oil and sauté garlic and onion over medium heat until softened, about 8–10 minutes. Mix with eggplant and purée in a food processor or blender until very smooth. Mix in egg yolks and pulse, adding salt, pepper, and curry powder. Place in a greased 1-quart soufflé dish.

3. Beat the egg whites until stiff. Fold into the eggplant mixture. Bake until puffed and golden, about 45 minutes.

BRUSSELS SPROUTS HASH WITH CARAMELIZED SHALLOTS

Even people who say they dislike Brussels sprouts will love this dish.

Serves 6

1 pound Brussels sprouts

2 shallots, thinly sliced

¼ cup avocado oil

1 teaspoon salt

½ teaspoon freshly ground black pepper

3 tablespoons balsamic vinegar

1. Preheat oven to 400°F.

2. Trim stems off Brussels sprouts and slice in half lengthwise. Place Brussels sprouts and shallots in a shallow baking dish. Coat Brussels sprouts with oil; season with salt and pepper.

3. Bake for 20 minutes. Remove dish from the oven, and drizzle vinegar evenly over Brussels sprouts. Return dish to the oven and bake for 3–4 more minutes.

MARINATED BABY ARTICHOKE HEARTS

Here's where frozen artichoke hearts work perfectly! They save you the time and energy of cutting out the choke and removing the leaves of fresh artichokes, and they taste delicious when marinated.

Serves 4

2 (10-ounce) boxes frozen artichoke hearts

½ cup white wine vinegar

¼ cup olive oil

1 teaspoon Dijon mustard

½ teaspoon ground coriander

Salt and freshly ground black pepper

1. Thaw and cook the artichokes according to package directions. Drain and set aside.

2. Whisk the rest of the ingredients together in a bowl large enough to hold the artichokes. Add the warm artichokes and cover with dressing. Cover and marinate for 2–4 hours. Serve as antipasto.

BAKED STUFFED ARTICHOKES

These are worth a bit of effort. You can make them in advance, then finish cooking just before serving.

Serves 4

2 large artichokes

¼ cup lemon juice

2 tablespoons avocado oil

2 cloves garlic, chopped

½ sweet onion, chopped

1 cup almond meal

1 tablespoon minced lemon peel

8 medium shrimp, peeled and deveined

4 tablespoons fresh parsley

½ teaspoon freshly ground black pepper

4 quarts plus ½ cup water

Juice and rind of ½ lemon

½ teaspoon ground coriander

1. Remove any tough or brown outside leaves from the artichokes. Using a sharp knife, cut off artichoke tops, about ½" down. Slam the artichokes against a countertop to loosen leaves. Cut in half, from top to stem, and remove the thistly choke with a spoon. Trim the stem end. Place in a bowl of cold water mixed with ¼ cup lemon juice; set aside.

2. Heat the oil in a large skillet over medium heat. Add the garlic and onion and sauté for 5 minutes, stirring. Add the almond meal, lemon peel, shrimp, parsley, and pepper. Cook until shrimp turns pink. Pulse in the food processor or blender.

3. Boil the artichokes in 4 quarts water with lemon juice, lemon rind, and coriander for 18 minutes. Remove the artichokes but reserve the cooking water. Place the artichokes in a baking dish with ½ cup water on the bottom. Pile with shrimp filling.

4. Preheat oven to 375°F. Drizzle the stuffed artichokes with a bit of the cooking water and bake for 25 minutes until the filling is browned on top. Serve.

PINEAPPLE-ONION SALAD

This sweet and tangy recipe does not keep well, so make sure to throw it together right before eating. If you prefer a little more zing, add another tablespoon of lime juice and a sprinkle of cayenne pepper.

Serves 4

1 cup cubed fresh pineapple

½ cup chopped red onion

3 cups mixed baby greens

1 tablespoon lime juice

1 tablespoon extra-virgin olive oil

1. Place pineapple cubes in a large salad bowl. Mix onion and baby greens into the pineapple.

2. Sprinkle lightly with lime juice and olive oil. Toss to coat and serve immediately.

ROASTED PEPPERS

Many people don't know that peppers become very sweet when roasted.

Serves 6

2 tablespoons avocado oil

2 green bell peppers

2 yellow bell peppers

2 red bell peppers

6 cloves garlic, minced

Freshly ground black pepper, to taste

1. Pour the oil in a stainless-steel bowl. Dip the peppers in the oil, then roast or grill them over an open flame (reserve the bowl with the oil in it). Put the peppers into a paper bag and close; let stand 5 minutes to steam. Then remove the peppers from the bag and remove the skins.

2. Julienne the peppers and add them to the bowl with the oil, along with the garlic and black pepper.

3. Let sit at room temperature in serving bowl up to an hour, until ready to serve.

PALEO STUFFED PEPPERS

Peppers are chock-full of great vitamins and minerals that everyone needs. These peppers are so fun to eat, you won't even guess how healthy they are.

Serves 4

4 red bell peppers

2 tablespoons avocado oil

3 cloves garlic, chopped

1 large onion, chopped

1 pound ground chicken

2 green bell peppers, chopped

1 cup diced celery

1 cup sliced mushrooms

2 tablespoons chili powder

1 tablespoon cumin

1 (28-ounce) can organic, no-salt-added diced tomatoes

1 (6-ounce) can organic, no-salt-added tomato paste

1. Cut off the tops of red peppers and remove seeds and ribs. Set aside.

2. Heat the oil in a large skillet over medium-high heat and sauté garlic and onion for 2 minutes.

3. Add ground chicken and cook until browned, about 5 minutes.

4. Add green peppers, celery, mushrooms, chili powder, and cumin and continue cooking for 5 minutes.

5. Stuff mixture into red peppers and place in a 4-quart slow cooker.

6. In medium bowl, stir together diced tomatoes and tomato paste. Pour around and over peppers, then cover slow cooker and cook on high for 5 hours.

CANDIED BUTTERNUT SQUASH

Butternut squash has a delicious natural sweetness and is an excellent replacement for sweet potatoes. Also, you can now buy cut-and-peeled butternut squash in many grocery stores (in the produce section), making this recipe incredibly easy to assemble.

Serves 4

4–5 cups peeled, seeded, and cubed butternut squash

⅓ cup raw honey

1 tablespoon orange zest

½ teaspoon cinnamon

½ teaspoon ground cloves

Add all the ingredients to a greased 2-quart slow cooker. Cook on high for 3–4 hours or on low for 6–8 hours, until squash is fork-tender. You can serve this as-is, or mash the squash as you would potatoes.

BISON-STUFFED ZUCCHINI

Bison meat is both low in fat and high in protein. It has a great taste that resembles beef but with a little more flavor. This is sure to be a big hit at any party or holiday gathering.

Serves 6

3 large zucchini, halved

2 tablespoons coconut oil

1 cup diced onion

1 cup chopped cauliflower

1½ pounds bison meat, cubed

¼ teaspoon cayenne pepper

1 teaspoon oregano

1 (14.5-ounce) can no-salt-added diced tomatoes

1 (6-ounce) can, no-salt-added tomato paste

1 large egg

1. Preheat oven to 400°F.

2. Scrape out seeds of zucchini and save in a mixing bowl.

3. Heat coconut oil in a large skillet over medium-high heat and sauté onion, cauliflower, and zucchini seeds until caramelized, about 12 minutes.

4. Add bison, cayenne pepper, and oregano to skillet and brown meat, approximately 8–10 minutes. Drain.

5. Add tomatoes and tomato paste and stir to combine.

6. Add egg and mix. Stuff each zucchini half, forming a large mound on top.

7. Place in large baking dish with a little water on the bottom and bake 40 minutes until zucchini are tender and the filling starts to brown.

STUFFED TOMATOES

This is a great side dish or light vegetarian lunch that is packed with flavor.

Serves 3

3 large beefsteak tomatoes

6 small white mushrooms, sliced

4 cloves garlic, minced

6 sun-dried tomatoes, chopped

1 teaspoon ground black pepper

½ teaspoon paprika

1 teaspoon thyme

8 leaves fresh basil, torn

1. Preheat oven to 350°F.

2. Cut tomatoes in half and hollow them out, reserving tomato pulp. Place tomatoes in a small baking dish.

3. Mix tomato pulp with mushrooms, garlic, sun-dried tomatoes, pepper, paprika, thyme, and basil.

4. Fill tomatoes with tomato pulp mixture and bake for 25 minutes or until tops start to brown.

VEGETABLE KEBABS ON ROSEMARY SKEWERS

Serve these kebabs as an appetizer at parties so your guests can easily handle the food without using cutlery. Using rosemary for the skewers adds an extra dimension of flavor to the grilled vegetables.

Serves 4–6

12 large rosemary sprigs with strong woody stems

1 large red bell pepper

1 large yellow bell pepper

1 large green bell pepper

1 medium red onion, peeled and cut into wedges

1 medium zucchini, sliced into 1" rounds

1 tablespoon avocado oil

Freshly ground black pepper, to taste

1. Strip the leaves from the bottom two-thirds of the rosemary sprigs (reserve the leaves for another use).

2. Trim and seed the bell peppers and cut them into 2" squares.

3. Thread the bell peppers, onions, and zucchini onto the rosemary sprigs and brush all sides of the vegetables with oil. Season with black pepper.

4. Place the skewers on the grill or under the broiler, paying close attention as they cook, as they can easily burn. Cook for 8–10 minutes, turning occasionally, until the vegetables are fork-tender.

An Alternative to Rosemary Skewers

If you can't find sturdy rosemary sprigs, you can use wooden skewers. Make sure you soak them in water for an hour before spearing the vegetables. Soaking the skewers prevents them from burning on the grill.

SPICED "BAKED" EGGPLANT

Serve this as a main dish over a garden salad, or as a side dish.

Serves 4

1 pound cubed eggplant

⅓ cup sliced onion

½ teaspoon red pepper flakes

½ teaspoon crushed rosemary

¼ cup lemon juice

Place all the ingredients in a 2-quart slow cooker. Cook on low for 3 hours or until the eggplant is tender. Stir and serve.

SLOW-COOKED BROCCOLI

This is a great way to cook a large amount of broccoli while preserving all its nutrients.

Serves 5

1 pound broccoli

½ cup water or chicken broth

2 tablespoons organic butter or Ghee (see Chapter 2)

½ teaspoon lemon juice

¼ teaspoon black pepper

1. Cut the main stalk off of broccoli with a sharp kitchen knife, and then rinse the broccoli under cool running water. Place the broccoli in a 3-quart slow cooker.

2. Add water or broth, butter, lemon juice, and pepper to the slow cooker with the broccoli. Cover and cook on low for 3 hours or until the broccoli is tender.

3. Serve immediately, or allow to stay warm in the slow cooker for up to another hour.

"ROASTED" ROOTS

This is a perfect substitute for a starchy side dish such as potatoes.

Serves 6

1 pound baby carrots

12 ounces turnips, peeled and cubed

1 medium onion, chopped

2 cloves garlic, minced

2 tablespoons water

3 tablespoons organic butter or Ghee (see Chapter 2)

¼ teaspoon lemon juice

⅛ teaspoon pepper

1. Combine all the ingredients in a 3- or 4-quart slow cooker and stir to mix.

2. Cover and cook on low for 7–9 hours or until vegetables are tender when pierced with a fork.

ZUCCHINI CASSEROLE

This highly nutritious and delicious vegetable compilation is great for a side dish or a light lunch.

Serves 4

4 medium zucchini, sliced and unpeeled

1 red onion, sliced

1 green pepper, cut in thin strips

1 (16-ounce) can diced tomatoes, undrained

1 teaspoon lemon juice

½ teaspoon pepper

½ teaspoon dried basil

1 tablespoon avocado oil

1. Combine all ingredients except oil in a 4-quart slow cooker. Cook on low for 3 hours.

2. Drizzle casserole with oil. Cook on low for 1½ hours more or until vegetables are tender.

SLOW-COOKED FENNEL WITH ORANGE

Fennel is crunchy and a bit sweet and is most often associated with Italian cuisine.

Serves 4

3 small bulbs fennel, halved

1 (13.5-ounce) can chopped tomatoes

Juice and zest of 1 small orange

2 tablespoons raw honey

Pepper, to taste

1. Place the halved fennel in a 3- or 4-quart slow cooker.

2. In a large mixing bowl, combine the remaining ingredients. Pour mixture over the fennel in the slow cooker.

3. Cover and cook on high for 4–5 hours.

SLOW-COOKED SWEET POTATOES

This is the simplest way to prepare this primal-approved carbohydrate-rich side dish, perfect for the Paleo-athlete.

Serves 2

2 large sweet potatoes

1. Wash off the sweet potatoes, but don't dry them. You'll want the moisture in the slow cooker.

2. Stab each sweet potato with a fork 5–6 times. Place the sweet potatoes in a 3-quart slow cooker.

3. Cover the slow cooker and cook on low for 5–6 hours or until potatoes are tender.

DILL CARROTS

The carrots in this side dish keep a firm texture even when fully cooked.

Serves 6

1 pound carrots, cut into coins

1 tablespoon minced fresh dill

⅓ teaspoon almond oil

3 tablespoons water

Place all the ingredients in a 2- to 3-quart slow cooker. Stir. Cook on low 1½–2 hours or until the carrots are fork-tender. Stir before serving.

Dill Details

Dill is a delicate plant that has many culinary uses. The seeds are used as a spice, and the fresh and dried dill plant is used as an herb. Dill is an essential ingredient in dill pickles and gravlax, a type of cured salmon.

STEWED TOMATOES

For an Italian variation on these tomatoes, add basil and Italian parsley.

Serves 6

1 (28-ounce) can whole tomatoes in purée, cut up and undrained

1 tablespoon minced onion

1 stalk celery, diced

½ teaspoon oregano

½ teaspoon thyme

Place all the ingredients in a 2-quart slow cooker. Stir. Cook on low for up to 8 hours.

CHAPTER 12

GLUTEN- AND DAIRY-FREE MEALS

BACON SALMON BITES

Bacon and salmon really go together well. The salty crispness of the bacon complements the smooth rich taste of the salmon. Use wild Pacific salmon if you can find it. Make these ahead of time; just refrigerate the bacon-wrapped salmon and the sauce separately. Then bake the salmon and reheat the sauce right before serving.

Serves 6

1 tablespoon olive oil

1 small onion, chopped

3 cloves garlic, minced

1 (8-ounce) can tomato sauce

1 tablespoon honey

2 tablespoons Dijon mustard

1 tablespoon lemon juice

½ teaspoon smoked paprika

½ teaspoon salt

⅛ teaspoon crushed red pepper flakes

2 (6-ounce) salmon fillets, skin removed

12 slices bacon, cut into thirds

1. In small saucepan, heat olive oil over medium heat. Add onion and garlic; cook and stir until tender, about 5 minutes. Add tomato sauce, honey, mustard, lemon juice, paprika, salt, and red pepper flakes and bring to a simmer. Simmer for 15 minutes, stirring occasionally.

2. When ready to eat, preheat oven to 375°F. Cut the salmon fillets into 1" pieces. Wrap each piece of salmon in the bacon; you may need more bacon slices. Secure with a toothpick.

3. Place the wrapped salmon pieces on a rimmed baking sheet lined with parchment paper or foil.

4. Bake for 15–20 minutes or until bacon is crisp. While the salmon is baking, reheat the sauce. Brush each piece of salmon with the sauce and serve remaining sauce on the side.

CELERY MUSHROOM SOUP

Soups can be thick and hearty, or they can be delicate and beautiful. This is the delicate type of soup. It's good for when you're feeling a bit under the weather. And it's also great for packing into a thermos for lunch, either for school or for work. Make your own Chicken Stock (see Chapter 4) for this recipe for best results. Canned and boxed stocks just can't compare to homemade.

Serves 6

2 tablespoons olive oil

1 shallot, finely minced

1 (8-ounce) package cremini mushrooms, sliced

1 bunch celery, sliced

6 cups Chicken Stock (see Chapter 4)

1 teaspoon dried thyme leaves

1 teaspoon salt

⅛ teaspoon white pepper

1 tablespoon lemon juice

1. In large pot, heat olive oil over medium heat. Add shallot; cook until softened, about 3 minutes.

2. Add mushrooms; cook and stir until mushrooms give up their liquid.

3. Add celery and cook for 4 minutes longer. Add stock, thyme, salt, and pepper, and bring to a simmer.

4. Cover pot, reduce heat to low, and simmer for 15–20 minutes or until soup is blended. Stir in lemon juice and serve immediately.

ANTIPASTO

Antipasto is simply a platter filled with marinated vegetables and spiced meats. You can choose any vegetables or meats you'd like; just arrange them beautifully and serve with a glass of red wine. Antipasto can be mild or hot. If you like your appetizer spicy, add a minced jalapeño pepper or sprinkle the vegetables with crushed red pepper flakes.

Serves 8

1 cup water

½ cup white wine vinegar

⅓ cup olive oil

2 tablespoons honey

2 cloves garlic, minced

1 teaspoon salt

1 teaspoon dried Italian seasoning

¼ teaspoon pepper

1 head cauliflower, broken into florets

3 carrots, cut into thin strips

3 stalks celery, cut into strips

1 cup ripe black olives

1 (10-ounce) jar artichoke hearts, drained

½ pound pancetta, rolled

½ pound gluten-free salami, sliced

1. In large pot, combine water, vinegar, olive oil, honey, garlic, salt, Italian seasoning, and pepper and bring to a simmer.

2. Add cauliflower and carrots; simmer for 4–6 minutes until tender.

3. Remove pot from heat and add celery; let cool for 30 minutes, then refrigerate.

4. When ready to serve, drain vegetables and arrange on a platter with olives, artichoke hearts, pancetta, and salami.

COFFEE-CRUSTED STEAK

Coffee makes a fabulous crust on grilled steak. If you aren't consuming coffee, try using 2 tablespoons cacao nibs instead. Combined with some honey and spices, coffee or cacao add a wonderful flavor to the moist and tender meat. Choose a good quality steak for this recipe, such as ribeye or tenderloin. The marinade won't really tenderize the steak; it is just for adding flavor.

Serves 4

3 tablespoons ground coffee beans

2 tablespoons honey

2 tablespoons gluten-free tomato sauce

1 tablespoon gluten-free Dijon mustard

2 teaspoons chili powder

1 teaspoon paprika

1 teaspoon salt

¼ teaspoon pepper

4 bone-in ribeye steaks or 4 filet mignon steaks

1. In small bowl, combine coffee, honey, tomato sauce, mustard, chili powder, paprika, salt, and pepper and mix well.

2. Rub this mixture into both sides of the steak. Let stand at room temperature for 20 minutes, or cover and marinate up to 4 hours.

3. When ready to eat, prepare and preheat grill. Grill steaks 6" from medium coals, turning once, about 5–6 minutes per side until desired doneness. Let stand 5 minutes, then serve.

ORANGE BEEF STIR-FRY

Orange and beef is a good combination. The acid in the orange tenderizes the beef and adds wonderful flavor. A bit of ginger and garlic add some kick to this simple stir-fry recipe. Serve over Cauliflower Rice (see Chapter 11) or just alone in a bowl with some chopsticks.

Serves 4

½ cup orange juice

¼ cup beef stock

1 tablespoon red wine vinegar

3 cloves garlic, minced

2 teaspoons grated orange zest

1 tablespoon finely minced fresh gingerroot

1 pound beef sirloin steak, cut into strips

2 tablespoons olive oil or coconut oil

1 onion, chopped

1 red bell pepper, cut into strips

½ pound asparagus, cut into 2" lengths

1 tablespoon arrowroot powder

1. In medium bowl, combine orange juice, beef stock, vinegar, garlic, orange zest, and gingerroot. Add steak; set aside for 20 minutes.

2. Heat oil in large skillet or wok. When hot, drain steak, reserving marinade, and stir-fry steak for 2 minutes. Remove beef from skillet.

3. Add onion to skillet; stir-fry for 4 minutes. Then add bell pepper and asparagus; stir-fry for 3–4 minutes longer.

4. Whisk arrowroot powder into reserved marinade. Add marinade and steak to skillet with vegetables. Stir-fry for 2–3 minutes or until steak is done and sauce is slightly thickened. Serve immediately.

STEAK ITALIANO

Round steak or chuck steak tastes best and has the best texture when it is simmered for a long time in liquid. The connective tissue in the meat dissolves with long cooking times and the meat stays juicy. The flavoring in this simple recipe is Italian: onions, garlic, oregano, and basil.

Serves 6

2 pounds round steak, cut into 1½" cubes

1 teaspoon salt

¼ teaspoon pepper

2 tablespoons olive oil

1 onion, chopped

5 cloves garlic, sliced

1½ cups beef broth

1 cup water or red wine

1 (6-ounce) can gluten-free tomato paste

1 teaspoon dried oregano

1 teaspoon dried basil

1. Sprinkle steak with salt and pepper. Heat olive oil in large saucepan over medium heat.

2. Add beef cubes and brown, turning frequently, for about 5 minutes; remove to plate as they finish cooking. Drain fat, leaving 1 tablespoon in pan.

3. Add onion and garlic to pan; cook, stirring to remove pan drippings, until tender, about 6 minutes. Return beef to pan and add broth, water or wine, tomato paste, oregano, and basil.

4. Bring mixture to a simmer. Reduce heat, cover, and simmer for about 1½ hours or until meat is very tender.

BLUEBERRY SOUP

Fruit soups are delicious and refreshing. They can be served as an appetizer, as part of a meal, or as dessert. Blueberries make a wonderful soup, thick and rich and vibrantly colored. If you can find wild blueberries, use them. They are smaller and more intensely flavored than cultivated blueberries.

Serves 4

3 cups fresh blueberries, divided

2 cups water, divided

½ cup freshly squeezed orange juice

2 tablespoons lemon juice

1 cinnamon stick

2 tablespoons honey

Pinch salt

2 tablespoons quick cooking tapioca, ground

1 teaspoon vanilla

1. In large saucepan, combine 2½ cups blueberries, 1 cup water, orange juice, lemon juice, cinnamon stick, honey, and salt. Bring to a simmer over medium heat.

2. Reduce heat to low and simmer for 10 minutes or until blueberries pop.

3. Purée soup in batches in blender or food processor and return to pan.

4. Dissolve tapioca in remaining 1 cup water and add to the soup. Simmer for another 5 minutes until thickened.

5. Cool soup for 30 minutes, then stir in vanilla. Cover and refrigerate until cold. Stir in remaining ½ cup blueberries before serving.

LAMB AND MINT MEATBALLS

Mint is a natural partner with lamb. Since lamb fat is quite cloying, the fresh sharp taste of mint cuts right through it. If you've never had ground lamb before, you are in for a treat. It's rich and tender with a wonderful flavor. Serve this recipe with Fruit and Nut Salad (see Chapter 3) and Mashed Cauliflower (see Chapter 11).

Serves 4

1 tablespoon olive oil

½ cup minced onion

2 cloves garlic, minced

1 egg, beaten

2 tablespoons chopped fresh mint

½ teaspoon salt

⅛ teaspoon white pepper

1¼ pounds ground lamb

2 small zucchini, cut into 1½" pieces

1. In small skillet, heat olive oil over medium heat and cook onion and garlic until tender, about 5 minutes. Remove to large bowl to cool for 10 minutes.

2. Add egg, mint, salt, and pepper to onion mixture and stir. Then add lamb and work with your hands gently but thoroughly until combined.

3. Form into 1" meatballs and chill in refrigerator for 1 hour.

4. When ready to eat, prepare and preheat grill. Thread the meatballs onto metal skewers alternately with the zucchini.

5. Grill meatballs, turning occasionally, over medium coals for 8–12 minutes or until meat registers 165°F on a meat thermometer. Let stand for 5 minutes, then serve with Mint Pesto (see Chapter 2), if desired.

CURRIED APPLE SOUP

Curry powder is made of many different spices and herbs. You can make your own, using turmeric, cumin, ginger, cinnamon, mustard seed, red pepper flakes, pepper, and coriander, or buy a premade blend. This spice blend is a wonderful complement to sweet and tart apples in this delicious soup.

Serves 6

3 tablespoons butter

1 leek, chopped

2 cloves garlic, minced

4 apples, peeled and chopped

1–2 tablespoons gluten-free curry powder

4 cups gluten-free chicken stock

2 tablespoons lemon juice

1 teaspoon salt

⅛ teaspoon white pepper

1 cup coconut milk

1. Melt butter in large saucepan. Add leek and garlic; cook and stir for 3 minutes. Then add apples; cook and stir for 4 minutes longer.

2. Add curry powder; cook and stir for 2 minutes.

3. Add stock and lemon juice; simmer until apples and leeks are very soft, about 20–25 minutes.

4. Purée using a stick blender, keeping some of the vegetables and fruit whole if you'd like.

5. Season to taste with salt and pepper. Stir in coconut milk and heat for 1–2 minutes until steaming. Serve immediately.

ROOT VEGETABLE SOUP

Red, white, and russet potatoes may be verboten on the Paleo diet, but that doesn't mean all root vegetables are taboo. Parsnips, turnips, carrots, onions, and rutabagas are all fine, as are sweet potatoes in moderation. Those veggies do not contain saponins such as solanine that are in the white-fleshed potatoes that are objectionable to the Paleo plan. Enjoy this hearty soup with a spinach salad.

Serves 6

¼ cup olive oil

2 onions, chopped

6 cloves garlic, minced

1 small butternut squash, peeled, seeded, and cubed

3 carrots, sliced

1 rutabaga, peeled and chopped

5 cups Chicken Stock (see Chapter 4)

1 teaspoon dried marjoram leaves

1 teaspoon dried thyme leaves

1 teaspoon salt

¼ teaspoons pepper

1. In large soup pot or Dutch oven, heat olive oil over medium heat. Add onion and garlic; cook and stir for 4 minutes.

2. Add squash, carrots, and rutabaga; cook and stir for about 10 minutes or until vegetables start to brown.

3. Add stock, marjoram, thyme, salt, and pepper and bring to a simmer. Reduce heat to low, cover, and simmer for 45–55 minutes or until vegetables are tender. Correct seasoning, if needed, and serve.

CHICKEN AND SAUSAGE

Spicy and well-seasoned sausage complements tender and juicy chicken perfectly. You can make this recipe as spicy or as mild as you like depending on which sausage you choose. Polish sausage and bockwurst are mild, while hot Italian sausage or Andouille packs a kick. Serve this recipe over Mashed Cauliflower (see Chapter 11) or Mashed Sweet Potatoes (see Chapter 11) for a hearty dinner.

Serves 6

1 pound uncooked gluten-free sausage

3 tablespoons olive oil

6 bone-in, skin-on chicken breasts

1 teaspoon salt

¼ teaspoon pepper

1 onion, chopped

1 red bell pepper, sliced

4 cloves garlic, sliced

½ cup gluten-free chicken broth

1 tablespoon fresh thyme leaves

1. Prick sausages with a fork and place in large skillet over medium heat. Brown sausages on all sides, but do not cook through. Remove from pan; drain pan but do not wipe.

2. Add olive oil to pan. Sprinkle chicken with salt and pepper and add to pan, skin-side down. Brown well, then turn chicken. Cook for 3 minutes longer, then remove from pan.

3. Add onion, bell pepper, and garlic to pan and cook, stirring frequently, for another 4 minutes.

4. Meanwhile, cut sausages in thirds crosswise. Add to pan with chicken, broth, and thyme.

5. Bring to a boil, then reduce heat to low, cover, and simmer 20 minutes or until chicken and sausages are thoroughly cooked to 165°F. Serve immediately.

PORK CHOPS AND SAUERKRAUT SKILLET

One-dish meals are a wonderful way to get dinner on the table in a hurry. This flavorful recipe combines pork chops, sauerkraut, apples, onions, and rutabaga. All you need for a complete meal is some sliced fresh fruit. This is a good recipe for a cold fall or winter day.

Serves 6

6 bone-in loin pork chops

½ teaspoon salt

⅛ teaspoon pepper

¼ cup almond flour

3 tablespoons olive oil

1 onion, chopped

4 cloves garlic, minced

1 rutabaga, peeled and cubed

2½ cups naturally fermented sauerkraut, drained

⅓ cup apple cider vinegar

2 tablespoons honey

1 cup chicken stock

1 teaspoon fennel seeds

2 Granny Smith apples, sliced

⅓ cup almond milk

1. Sprinkle chops with salt, pepper, and almond flour. Heat olive oil in large skillet. Brown chops, turning once, for about 5 minutes. Remove chops from skillet.

2. Add onion, garlic, and rutabaga to pan; cook and stir for 5 minutes. Add sauerkraut, vinegar, honey, chicken stock, and fennel seeds and bring to a simmer.

3. Return pork chops to pan along with apples. Cover and simmer for 10–15 minutes or until pork reaches 150°F on a meat thermometer. Stir in almond milk, heat through, and serve.

SOUTHWEST ALMOND SOUP

This type of recipe is usually made with peanuts, which are not allowed on the Paleo diet because they are actually legumes. This soup is spicy, thick, and rich, with a wonderful texture and flavor combination. Serve with a glass of white wine and Kale and Fruit Salad (see Chapter 3) for an elegant dinner.

Serves 6

3 tablespoons olive oil

1 onion, chopped

2 cloves garlic, minced

1 jalapeño pepper, minced

3 tablespoons almond flour

1 teaspoon ground cumin

5 cups gluten-free chicken broth

⅔ cup almond butter

⅓ cup almond milk

½ teaspoon salt

⅛ teaspoon pepper

⅔ cup sliced almonds, toasted

½ cup Kale Pesto (see Chapter 2)

1. In large soup pot, heat olive oil over medium heat. Add onion, garlic, and jalapeño; cook and stir for 5 minutes.

2. Add almond flour and cumin; cook for 1 minutes. Then beat in chicken broth and simmer for 2 minutes until thickened.

3. Add almond butter, almond milk, salt, and pepper. Simmer for 10 minutes until flavors are blended. Season with additional salt and pepper if desired.

4. In small bowl combine almonds with Kale Pesto and mix. Serve soup with this mixture for topping.

SHELLFISH CASINO

Clams and oysters are two varieties of shellfish that are often cooked with bacon and vegetables. Serving a combination of the two adds interest to your meal and satisfies those who love clams and those who love oysters. You can find clams and oysters fresh on the half shell, but if you can't, shuck them yourself. Be sure that clams and oysters are tightly closed before you start to open them. If any are open and don't close when you tap on the shells, discard.

Serves 4

2 pounds raw oysters on the half shell

2 pounds raw clams on the half shell

6 slices bacon

1 onion, chopped

1 red bell pepper, chopped

1 cup chopped mushrooms

3 cloves garlic, minced

3 tablespoons lemon juice

1 teaspoon salt

½ teaspoon Tabasco sauce

1. Arrange the oysters and clams on two rimmed baking sheets in a single layer, with clams on one and oysters on the other.

2. Cook bacon in a large skillet over medium heat until crisp. Drain on paper towels, crumble, and set aside.

3. Add onion to bacon fat in pan; cook for 3 minutes. Add red bell pepper, mushrooms, and garlic; cook until mushrooms give up their liquid and liquid evaporates.

4. Add lemon juice, salt, Tabasco, and bacon to the pan.

5. Preheat broiler. Top oysters and clams with a spoonful of the bacon mixture.

6. Broil clams for 8–10 minutes or until edges curl. Broil oysters for 4–6 minutes or until edges curl. Serve with more lemon wedges, if desired.

MUSTARD-ROASTED PORK TENDERLOIN

There are so many different types of mustards on the market. You can find Dijon, grainy mustard, yellow mustard, mustard made with fruit or honey, Irish mustard, brown mustard, and English mustard. Use a combination of your favorites in this easy and flavorful recipe.

Serves 4–6

2 (1-pound) pork tenderloins

2 shallots, minced

1 tablespoon caraway seeds

3 tablespoons gluten-free Dijon mustard

2 tablespoons gluten-free grainy mustard

2 tablespoons prepared gluten-free horseradish

1 teaspoon salt

¼ teaspoon pepper

1. Remove silver skin from tenderloins, if necessary. Place on a rimmed baking sheet and prick all over with a fork.

2. In small bowl, combine remaining ingredients. Spread the mixture over the tenderloins, coating on all sides. Let stand at room temperature while oven preheats.

3. Preheat oven to 400°F. Roast the tenderloins for 20–30 minutes or until meat thermometer registers 145–150°F. Cover and let stand for 5 minutes, then slice to serve.

CHAPTER 13

CHILDREN'S FAVORITES

MINI CAVEMAN'S SQUASH (BABY FOOD)

Babies seem to love this nutrient-rich and creamy sweet squash. It's full of vitamins A and C, along with the anti-inflammatory pigment beta-carotene.

Serves 6

2 butternut squash, peeled and cubed

¼ cup water

1. Place the squash in a 4- or 6-quart slow cooker, add water, cover, and cook on high for 3 hours.

2. Use a blender or food processor to purée into baby food. Cool and refrigerate up to 3 days. You can freeze this for longer storage; freeze up to 3 months. To use, thaw overnight in the refrigerator.

MINI CAVEMAN'S SWEET POTATOES (BABY FOOD)

Turnips could also be used here in place of the sweet potatoes.

Serves 6

2 medium-sized sweet potatoes, peeled

¾ cup water

1. Place the sweet potatoes in a 4- or 6-quart slow cooker, add water, cover, and cook on high for 3 hours.

2. Use a blender or food processor to purée into baby food. Chill, then refrigerate up to 3 days. Freeze up to 3 months for longer storage. To use, thaw overnight in the refrigerator.

MINI CAVEMAN'S CARROTS (BABY FOOD)

These puréed carrots can be incorporated into another recipe—to thicken a soup, for example.

Serves 6

12 ounces carrots, peeled and chopped

¼ cup water

1. Place the carrots in a 4- or 6-quart slow cooker, add water, cover, and cook on high for 3 hours.

2. Use a blender or food processor to purée into baby food. Chill and refrigerate up to 3 days. Freeze up to 3 months for longer storage. To use, thaw overnight in the refrigerator.

NUTTY BAKED CHICKEN CHUNKS

Chicken fingers and chicken nuggets are beloved by children. But fast food and packaged products are full of wheat, preservatives, and sugar. Make your own—they're easy and fun. Let the kids help too. But make sure they wash their hands carefully after handling raw chicken. And wash your hands too!

Serves 4

1 pound boneless, skinless chicken breasts

1 tablespoon lemon juice

1 tablespoon Worcestershire sauce

1 tablespoon maple syrup

½ teaspoon salt

1 cup ground almonds

1. Preheat oven to 400°F. Cut chicken into 1½" pieces.

2. Toss chicken with lemon juice, Worcestershire sauce, maple syrup, and salt and let stand for 20 minutes. Then toss with almonds and place in single layer on parchment paper–lined baking sheet.

3. Bake for 18–23 minutes or until chicken is thoroughly cooked. Serve with any salad dressing or guacamole for dipping.

GRAHAM CRACKERS

It's hard to believe that you can make graham crackers that are Paleo acceptable. But the explosion in gluten-free products and flours means you can make this childhood treat without any type of wheat or grain. Coconut and hazelnut flours are naturally sweet and this cracker has a mild nutty taste. The kids will love it; serve with almond or coconut milk for dunking.

Makes 30–36 crackers

1 cup hazelnut flour

¾ cup coconut flour

¼ cup tapioca starch

1 teaspoon baking powder

2 teaspoons cinnamon

¼ teaspoon salt

⅓ cup honey

3 tablespoons coconut oil

¼ cup coconut milk

1 tablespoon water

2 teaspoons vanilla

1. Preheat oven to 350°F. In large bowl, combine hazelnut flour, coconut flour, tapioca starch, baking powder, cinnamon, and salt, and mix until one color.

2. In small saucepan, combine honey, coconut oil, coconut milk, and water and heat until oil melts.

3. Add coconut milk mixture to dry ingredients along with vanilla and mix until dough forms. You may need to add more of either of the flours or more water for the right consistency. Wrap in plastic wrap and refrigerate for 1 hour.

4. Roll dough into 2" balls and place on parchment paper–lined baking sheet about 3" apart. Top with another sheet of parchment paper and flatten the balls using a rolling pin to ⅛" thickness. Carefully peel off the top piece of paper. Prick the dough with a fork.

5. Bake for 12–15 minutes or until the crackers are set and golden brown. Cool on wire racks. Store in airtight container at room temperature.

MINI POTATO-TOPPED MEAT LOAVES

Kids love anything that's been miniaturized. These little meat loaves are easier for them to eat, and they're so cute! You can use ground lamb, pork, chicken, or ground beef for the filling. This is a good way to get them to eat veggies, since they're not apparent in the loaf. Make sure the meat is cooked to 165°F before you take the little loaves out of the oven.

Serves 6–8

1 tablespoon olive oil

1 onion, finely chopped

1 clove garlic, minced

⅓ cup shredded carrot

⅓ cup tomato sauce

2 tablespoons hazelnut flour

1 tablespoon honey

1 egg, beaten

1 tablespoon yellow mustard

½ teaspoon salt

⅛ teaspoon pepper

1 pound extra lean ground beef

2 cups Mashed Sweet Potatoes (see Chapter 11)

1. Preheat oven to 350°F. Grease 12 regular muffin cups with unsalted butter or Ghee (see Chapter 2) and set aside.

2. In medium saucepan, heat olive oil over medium heat. Add onion and garlic; cook for 3 minutes. Add carrot; cook for 3–5 minutes longer or until vegetables are tender.

3. Place vegetables in large bowl. Add tomato sauce, hazelnut flour, honey, egg, mustard, salt, and pepper and mix well.

4. Stir in ground beef and mix gently but thoroughly until combined. Divide among the prepared muffin cups and press down gently. Top each meat loaf with a spoonful of the Mashed Sweet Potatoes.

5. Bake for 25–30 minutes or until the meat is thoroughly cooked and sweet potato topping starts to brown. Let stand for 5 minutes, then gently remove from cups and serve.

TOASTED NUT "CEREAL"

Kids love any type of sweetened cereal with a cartoon character on the box. But these products are loaded with artificial colors, sweeteners, and preservatives. Make your own "cereal" and your kids will gobble it up. You can serve it in a bowl with milk and they won't miss that packaged stuff one bit.

Yields 10 cups

1½ cups pumpkin seeds

1 cup sunflower seeds

1½ cups sliced almonds

1½ cups chopped pecans

1½ cups shredded coconut

⅓ cup honey

⅓ cup coconut oil, melted

1 teaspoon cinnamon

2 teaspoons vanilla

1 cup dried cranberries

1 cup chopped dried apricots

1 cup golden raisins

1. Preheat oven to 375°F. Line a rimmed baking sheet with parchment paper.

2. In large bowl, combine pumpkin seeds, sunflower seeds, almonds, pecans, and coconut and mix.

3. In small saucepan, combine honey and coconut oil and heat gently. Remove from heat and stir in cinnamon and vanilla.

4. Drizzle honey mixture over the mixture on baking sheet and toss to coat. Spread evenly.

5. Bake for 20–30 minutes, stirring every 10 minutes, until light golden brown and fragrant. Remove from oven and stir in cranberries, dried apricots, and raisins. Let stand until cool, stirring occasionally. Store in airtight container at room temperature.

CAULI-MAC

Macaroni and cheese is a classic favorite beloved by all children. But even gluten-free pastas contain grains; they are usually made from rice. Substitute chopped cauliflower for the macaroni and the kids will likely not be able to tell the difference! This creamy and rich dish is perfect served with some fresh fruit.

Serves 4

1 large head cauliflower, finely chopped

1 tablespoon lemon juice

2 tablespoons butter

2 shallots, minced

2 tablespoons almond flour

1½ cups almond milk

1 cup chicken broth

1 tablespoon mustard

1 cup shredded Cheddar cheese

1 cup shredded Havarti or Swiss cheese

½ teaspoon salt

⅛ teaspoon white pepper

1. Sprinkle cauliflower with lemon juice. Bring a large pot of water to a boil and cook the cauliflower until just tender, about 3–5 minutes. Drain well.

2. Preheat oven to 375°F. Grease a 3-quart baking dish with unsalted butter and set aside.

3. In large saucepan, melt butter over medium heat. Add shallots and cook and stir until tender, about 4 minutes. Add almond flour and cook for 2 minutes.

4. Add almond milk and chicken broth to pan and stir with a wire whisk until thickened. Stir in mustard, cheeses, salt, and pepper and remove from heat.

5. Add cauliflower to sauce and stir gently. Pour into prepared dish.

6. Bake for 25–30 minutes or until top is browned and casserole is bubbling. Serve immediately.

NUTS AND SEEDS GRANOLA BARS

Granola bars are a go-to snack for school, backpacking, and after-school treats. But most commercial varieties are loaded with sugar and artificial ingredients. Make your own granola bars for a satisfying snack. You can vary the nuts and fruits in these bars as you'd like.

Yields 24 bars

1½ cups slivered almonds

1½ cups sunflower seeds

1 cup chopped pecans

1½ cups shredded coconut

1 cup dried unsweetened cherries

¼ cup honey

¼ cup maple syrup

⅔ cup almond butter

2 teaspoons vanilla

1 teaspoon cinnamon

¼ teaspoon nutmeg

½ teaspoon salt

1. Preheat oven to 350°F. Line a 9" x 13" pan with parchment paper and set aside.

2. Place half of the nuts and seeds in a food processor and process until finely chopped. Combine with remaining nuts, coconut, and cherries in a large bowl.

3. In saucepan, combine honey and maple syrup and bring to a simmer. Simmer for 1 minute. Pour over ingredients in bowl.

4. Add almond butter, vanilla, cinnamon, nutmeg, and salt and mix until well combined.

5. Place into prepared pan and press down firmly with buttered hands or more parchment paper until even.

6. Bake for 20–30 minutes or until the bars are light golden brown. Cool completely, then refrigerate overnight. Cut into bars to serve.

MAPLE-ROASTED CARROTS

Carrots are naturally sweet, and their sweetness intensifies when they are cooked. Kids almost always like carrots, and they will especially love them when paired with the sweetness of maple syrup. To pique their interest, you can cut carrots into unusual shapes—sticks or circles or on an angle.

Serves 6

1 tablespoon butter or coconut oil

2 tablespoons maple syrup

1 teaspoon coconut aminos

1 pound carrots, peeled and cut

1. Preheat oven to 400°F. In large ovenproof saucepan, combine butter or coconut oil and maple syrup and heat until melted. Add the coconut aminos and the carrots; cook and stir for 2 minutes.

2. Place the pan in the oven and roast for 15–20 minutes, turning once, or until carrots are tender and glazed. Serve immediately.

CINNAMON PUMPKIN SEEDS

When you carve pumpkins for Halloween, always save the seeds for this recipe. It's a great snack for after-school treats or to include in your child's lunchbox. The only trick is to separate the seeds from the fibers. Put the seeds and fibers in a large bowl, cover with water, and let stand for about 10 minutes. The seeds will start to float. Then work with your hands to remove the seeds from the stringy part. Discard the stringy part, pat the seeds dry, and begin.

Yields 2 cups

2 cups pumpkin seeds

1 tablespoon coconut oil, melted

2 tablespoons coconut sugar, if desired

2 teaspoons cinnamon

½ teaspoon salt

¼ teaspoon nutmeg

1. Preheat oven to 325°F. Place pumpkin seeds on a rimmed baking sheet. Drizzle with coconut oil and stir to coat. Spread into a single layer.

2. Sprinkle with coconut sugar, if using.

3. Roast for 18–23 minutes, stirring once during cooking, until seeds are light golden brown. Sprinkle with cinnamon, salt, and nutmeg and toss to coat. Cool completely before storing in an airtight container for up to 1 week.

PALEO PIZZA

Yes, you can buy Paleo pizza crust mixes. There are several different brands; experiment and find the one you like best. Get your kids to help with this recipe. Teaching them how to cook is part of teaching them how to take care of themselves. And getting them interested in cooking also teaches math, science, chemistry—and patience! Use your child's favorite pizza toppings in this easy recipe.

Serves 4

1 prepared Paleo pizza crust or pizza crust mix

1 (8-ounce) can tomato sauce

2 tablespoons mustard

½ teaspoon dried Italian seasoning

2 Roma tomatoes, seeded and chopped

½ cup pepperoni or ½ cup cooked, drained ground beef, if desired

⅓ cup sliced black or green olives, if desired

1½ cups shredded mozzarella cheese, if desired

1. Preheat oven to 400°F. Prepare the pizza crust as directed on mix, or place the prepared crust on a baking sheet.

2. Combine tomato sauce, mustard, Italian seasoning, and chopped tomatoes in a small bowl. Spread over crust.

3. Top with desired toppings. Bake for 15–20 minutes or until crust is browned and toppings are hot. Cheese will start to brown and bubble when the pizza is ready.

BERRY SMOOTHIES

Smoothies are easy to make as long as you have a good blender. Look for one with reverse action or one that is marketed as good for making crushed ice. You can vary this recipe any way you'd like, using the berries and fruits your child likes best. This recipe even sneaks in a tomato to add more nutrition, but it can be omitted.

Serves 3

1 cup sliced strawberries

1 cup raspberries

1 Roma tomato, seeded and chopped

1 cup coconut milk

2 tablespoons honey

½ teaspoon vanilla

3 ice cubes

Combine all ingredients in a blender and blend until smooth. Pour immediately into three glasses and serve.

PRIMAL FISH STICKS

Every child loves fish sticks. They are mild and easy to eat and fun to make too. All children love things that are sized for their smaller hands and mouths. But commercial fish sticks are coated in wheat bread crumbs and contain lots of junk you don't want your child to eat. Make your own fish sticks and serve with Homemade Ketchup (see Chapter 2) and some fruit for a great quick lunch.

Serves 4

1 pound white fish fillets such as cod or haddock

1 egg

2 egg whites

¾ cup almond flour, divided

½ cup ground almonds

½ teaspoon salt

½ teaspoon paprika

⅛ teaspoon white pepper

1. Preheat oven to 400°F. Line a baking sheet with a wire rack and set aside.

2. Pat fish dry and cut into desired size sticks.

3. Beat egg and egg white in shallow bowl. Combine ½ cup almond flour, ground almonds, salt, paprika, and pepper in another shallow bowl.

4. Sprinkle the fish with the ¼ cup plain almond flour to coat. Dip into egg mixture, then dip into the ground almond mixture. Place on wire rack as you work.

5. Bake for 12–17 minutes or until the fish flakes when tested with a fork and the topping is light golden brown.

MINI QUICHES

Little quiches are perfect for an easy breakfast or for a snack anytime. Mini muffin tins are smaller than regular muffin tins and they make a perfect child-sized quiche. You can use cheese or leave it out; it's up to you. It all depends on what you want your child to eat and what she likes and can tolerate.

Yields 24 mini quiches

6 slices bacon

1 red bell pepper, finely chopped

1 cup chopped broccoli

5 eggs

⅓ cup almond milk

½ teaspoon salt

1 cup shredded cheese, if desired

1. Preheat oven to 400°F. Grease a 24-cup mini muffin pan with unsalted butter or coconut oil and set aside.

2. In medium skillet, cook bacon until crisp. Remove bacon from pan, drain on paper towels, crumble, and set aside. Drain off all but 1 tablespoon bacon fat from pan.

3. Add red pepper and broccoli to fat in pan; cook and stir until tender. Remove pan from heat and set aside to cool.

4. In large bowl, beat eggs, almond milk, and salt until smooth. Stir in the crumbled bacon and the vegetables.

5. Divide among the mini muffin cups. Top with cheese, if using. Bake for about 15–20 minutes or until quiches are set and tops are light golden brown. Let cool for 5 minutes, then remove from pan and serve.

ALMOND COOKIES

Almond butter is a good substitute for peanut butter in Paleo recipes. It's rich and delicious and is full of fiber, iron, and calcium. These cookies are flavorful and not too sweet. You can add some chopped dark chocolate to the cookies if you'd like, but they're also delicious served as-is.

Yields 36 cookies

1 cup almond butter

⅓ cup honey

1 egg

2 egg whites

2 teaspoons vanilla

⅓ cup almond flour

3 tablespoons coconut flour

1 teaspoon baking powder

¼ teaspoon salt

½ cup chopped sliced almonds

1. Preheat oven to 350°F. Line baking sheets with parchment paper and set aside.

2. In large bowl, combine almond butter with honey and beat well. Beat in egg and egg whites along with vanilla.

3. In small bowl, combine almond flour, coconut flour, baking powder, and salt and mix until one color. Add to almond butter mixture and stir until blended. Stir in almonds.

4. Drop by tablespoons onto baking sheets. Bake for 9–11 minutes or until just set. Cool on pans for 5 minutes, then remove to wire racks to cool completely.

LEMON CHICKEN

Lemon and chicken go together like peanut butter and jelly. This recipe has a mild lemon flavor to make it suitable for kids. If your child likes lemon, by all means add more lemon juice. The acid in the lemon makes this chicken meltingly tender.

Serves 4

3 boneless, skinless chicken breasts

⅓ cup lemon juice

2 tablespoons olive oil

2 tablespoons coconut milk

1 tablespoon honey

½ teaspoon salt

½ teaspoon lemon zest

2 teaspoons chopped fresh thyme leaves

1. Cut each chicken breast into four strips crosswise.

2. In medium bowl, combine remaining ingredients and mix well. Add chicken and stir to coat. Cover and refrigerate for 1–3 hours.

3. Preheat oven to 350°F. Arrange chicken strips on a parchment paper–lined rimmed baking sheet. Bake for 15–20 minutes or until chicken is light golden brown and 165°F on a meat thermometer. Let cool 5 minutes and serve.

CHICKEN IN A BISCUIT

Biscuits make great sandwiches for kids. Make the Biscuits as directed (see Chapter 5), cutting the dough into 16 squares instead of 9 and baking for a shorter time. The tender biscuits are a great foil for the chicken, avocado, and lettuce. Or let your kids make their own sandwiches using their favorite ingredients!

Serves 8

1 recipe Biscuits (see Chapter 5)

1½ cups chopped cooked chicken

1 avocado, peeled and diced

2 teaspoons lemon juice

⅓ cup Wilma's Mayonnaise (see Chapter 2)

1 tablespoon yellow mustard

Butter lettuce

1. Make the Biscuits as directed, except cut the dough square into 16 squares. Bake for 8–12 minutes or until light golden brown. Cool on wire rack.

2. Meanwhile, in medium bowl combine chicken, avocado, lemon juice, mayonnaise, and mustard.

3. Split biscuits and make sandwiches with the biscuits, lettuce, and filling. Serve immediately.

SEEDED CHICKEN DRUMMIES

Chicken drummies are sold in most major grocery stores. They are just the meaty part of the chicken wing. The tips and the less meaty side are cut off. They really do look like miniature drumsticks, which makes them perfect for kids. The crunchy sesame and sunflower seed coating adds great texture.

Serves 4

1½ pounds chicken drummies

2 tablespoons olive oil

2 tablespoons honey

1 tablespoon coconut aminos

1 tablespoon apple cider vinegar

½ teaspoon salt

⅛ teaspoon pepper

½ cup sesame seeds

⅓ cup chopped sunflower seeds

1. Place chicken drummies in a zip-top food storage bag. Add olive oil, honey, coconut aminos, vinegar, salt, and pepper. Close bag and massage to mix.

2. Place bag on a rimmed baking sheet and refrigerate for 1–3 hours.

3. When ready to eat, remove chicken wings from bag. Preheat oven to 375°F.

4. Combine sesame and sunflower seeds on a shallow plate. Dip the chicken drummies into this mixture, then place on a wire rack in a baking pan.

5. Bake for 25 minutes, then turn wings and bake 10–15 minutes longer or until meat thermometer registers 165°F and the wings are golden brown. Cool for 5 minutes and serve.

PORK AND MUSHROOM SLIDERS

Sliders are little burgers that are very popular. They are usually served in mini wheat hamburger buns. But they are also good served with small Portobello mushrooms as the "bun." Wrap the whole sandwich in some parchment paper to make it easier to eat. This flavorful pork burger recipe can be varied to suit your child's tastes. And use her favorite toppings too—cheese if you are eating it, and avocado and lettuce.

Serves 4–5

5 slices bacon

20 (2") Portobello mushrooms

1 clove garlic, minced

1 pound ground pork

½ teaspoon salt

⅛ teaspoon pepper

½ teaspoon dried thyme leaves

10 small slices Cheddar or Monterey jack cheese, if desired

1 avocado, peeled and thinly sliced

Butter lettuce

1. Cook bacon in large skillet until crisp. Drain bacon on paper towels, cut each piece in half, and set aside.

2. Remove stems from mushrooms. Trim stem ends and finely chop stems; set aside.

3. Cook the mushroom caps in the bacon fat in skillet, turning once and pressing down gently with a spatula, until tender, about 5–8 minutes. Drain on paper towels.

4. Cook mushroom stems and garlic in remaining fat in pan until tender, about 3–5 minutes. Remove to medium bowl. Add pork, salt, pepper, and thyme and mix.

5. Form pork mixture into 10 small patties about ½" thick. Cook the patties in skillet for 4–6 minutes on each side, turning once, until meat thermometer registers 165°F.

6. Make sandwiches with the cooked mushroom caps, patties, cheese, avocado, bacon, and lettuce.

GRILLED CHEESE AND CHICKEN SANDWICH

Grilled cheese sandwiches are one of the joys of childhood. But it's nice to branch out and serve your child something a little more sophisticated. This sandwich, with chicken and avocado, is delicious and easy. Use Paleo Sandwich Bread (see Chapter 5) for this recipe, or look for special Paleo-friendly breads at the grocery stores. And remember, if you aren't eating cheese, you can just omit it. Mash an avocado and use that instead.

Serves 4

8 slices Paleo Sandwich Bread (see Chapter 5)

8 slices Monterey jack or Swiss cheese

¼ cup Fruity Balsamic Barbecue Sauce (see Chapter 2)

4 slices cooked chicken breast

1 avocado, sliced

2 tablespoons softened butter or coconut oil

1. Place bread slices on work surface. Top each with a piece of cheese.

2. Spread barbecue sauce over cheese, then top half of the slices with a piece of chicken. Top with avocado slices. Put together to make four sandwiches.

3. In large skillet, melt butter or coconut oil over medium heat.

4. Add sandwiches; cover and cook for 4–5 minutes or until bottom is golden brown. Flip sandwiches, then cover and cook for another 3–5 minutes or until bread is golden brown and cheese is melted. Serve immediately.

SLOW-COOKER CHICKEN TENDERS

Here's a Paleo-approved version of a traditional kid-friendly favorite. These flavorful chicken tenders partner perfectly with a side of Turnip Tots (see next recipe).

Serves 4

2 tablespoons avocado oil

1 clove garlic, minced

6 sprigs fresh thyme, stripped and chopped

1 tablespoon lemon zest

¼ cup lemon juice

1 pound chicken breast tenders

Pepper, to taste

1. In a large mixing bowl, combine the oil, garlic, chopped thyme, lemon zest, and lemon juice.

2. Season the chicken tenders with pepper.

3. Place chicken in a 2- to 3-quart slow cooker, and pour avocado oil mixture over chicken, stirring until coated.

4. Cover and cook on low for 4–6 hours until chicken is thoroughly cooked, registering 165°F on a meat thermometer.

TURNIP TOTS

This is a healthier, Paleo-approved substitute for frozen Tater Tots, and the perfect accompaniment to Slow-Cooker Chicken Tenders (see previous recipe). Serve with Homemade Ketchup (see Chapter 2).

Serves 4

4 medium turnips, peeled and cubed

2 tablespoons avocado oil

2 tablespoons raw honey

1 tablespoon brown mustard

¼ teaspoon pepper

1. Place the turnips in a 2- or 4-quart slow cooker, drizzle with oil, and toss.

2. In a small bowl, mix together the honey, brown mustard, and pepper. Drizzle over turnips, and toss.

3. Cover and cook on low for 5 hours. Serve alongside Slow-Cooker Chicken Tenders.

SLOW-COOKED SLOPPY JOEYS

Serve over mashed cauliflower, turnips, or winter squash.

Serves 4

1 pound lean ground beef or turkey

1 (6-ounce) can tomato paste

2 tablespoons raw honey

1 tablespoon onion flakes

1 tablespoon paprika

1 teaspoon cumin

1 teaspoon lemon juice

½ teaspoon garlic powder

¼ teaspoon dry mustard

¼ teaspoon celery seed

¼ teaspoon black pepper

1 cup warm water

1 teaspoon almond meal

1. Cook beef or turkey in medium skillet over medium heat until browned, stirring to break up meat; drain well. Place meat, tomato paste, honey, and seasonings into a 4-quart slow cooker. Add water and almond meal and stir.

2. Cover and cook on low for 6–7 hours or on high for 3–5 hours. Serve warm.

"ROASTED" FALL VEGETABLES

You won't have to beg the kids to eat their veggies with this yummy recipe. You won't even have to ask them twice!

Serves 10

1½ pounds sweet potatoes

1 pound parsnips

1 pound carrots

2 large red onions, coarsely chopped

¾ cup chopped cranberries

1 tablespoon raw honey

3 tablespoons avocado oil

2 tablespoons lemon juice

½ teaspoon freshly ground black pepper

⅓ cup chopped fresh flat-leaf parsley

1. Peel the sweet potatoes, parsnips, and carrots and cut into 1½" pieces.

2. Combine the parsnips, carrots, onions, and cranberries in a lightly greased 5- to 6-quart slow cooker; layer sweet potatoes over the top.

3. In a small bowl, mix together the honey, oil, lemon juice, and pepper; pour over vegetable mixture. (Do not stir.)

4. Cover and cook on high for 4–5 hours or until vegetables are tender. Toss with parsley just before serving.

SOFT "SHELL" BEEF TACOS

The romaine leaves could also be placed under the broiler until crispy, for use as a "hard" taco shell.

Serves 12

2 (16-ounce) jars mild or medium tomato-based salsa, divided

2 tablespoons lime juice

5 teaspoons chili powder

1½ pounds beef chuck pot roast, fat trimmed

12 large leaves romaine lettuce

3 cups shredded lettuce

1 avocado, diced

1. Spoon 1 cup salsa into a small bowl; set aside.

2. In a 4-quart slow cooker, combine remaining salsa with lime juice and chili powder.

3. Stir in beef, cover, and turn heat to low. Cook for 10–12 hours. Shred the meat, using 2 forks, and spoon into a serving bowl.

4. Lay out the romaine leaves for use as taco "shells," and place a small portion of slow-cooked beef on each.

5. Place shredded lettuce, diced avocado, and reserved salsa in small separate bowls for serving. Add toppings to tacos, wrap lettuce leaves tightly, and enjoy.

TURKEY LETTUCE WRAPS

Turkey is a low-fat protein source that kids are sure to love. Although these wraps are a bit complex to make, you can make a larger batch of the filling and serve it over salad at a later meal. If your kids aren't used to spicy food, use a jalapeño pepper that is milder than a Serrano pepper, or omit it.

Serves 4

3 tablespoons walnut oil

3 shallots, chopped

1 piece lemongrass, thinly sliced

1 serrano chili pepper, thinly sliced, if desired

½ teaspoon fresh ground black pepper

1½ pounds ground turkey

⅓ cup fresh lime juice

2 tablespoons sesame oil

4 tablespoons coconut oil

½ cup thinly sliced basil leaves

8 large butter lettuce leaves

1. In a large skillet, heat walnut oil over medium heat.

2. Add shallots, lemongrass, serrano pepper, and black pepper. Cook until the shallots soften, about 4 minutes.

3. Add ground turkey and stir frequently until cooked through, approximately 8–10 minutes.

4. Add lime juice, sesame oil, and coconut oil and cook for 1 minute.

5. Turn the heat off and mix in basil leaves.

6. Wrap mixture in lettuce leaves and serve.

BAKED APPLES

You will feel as if you're eating apple pie when you eat these, and your house will smell like Thanksgiving dinner.

Serves 6

6 Pink Lady apples

1 cup unsweetened coconut flakes

Cinnamon, to taste

1. Preheat oven to 350°F.

2. Remove cores to ½" above the bottom of the apples.

3. Place apples in a medium baking dish.

4. Fill apple hollows with coconut flakes and sprinkle with cinnamon.

5. Bake for 10–15 minutes. Apples are done when they are completely soft and brown on top.

PALEO CHOCOLATE BARS

Your kids will be thrilled when they see these chocolate bars in their lunch boxes. These bars are quick to whip up and quick to eat. The amount of honey can be varied depending on your desired sweetness level.

Serves 8

1 tablespoon raw honey

4 tablespoons coconut oil

¼ cup ground almonds

¼ cup ground hazelnuts

¼ cup sunflower seeds

¼ cup cacao powder

¾ cup shredded unsweetened coconut flakes

1. Melt honey and coconut oil in saucepan over medium heat.

2. In a mixing bowl, combine almonds, hazelnuts, sunflower seeds, cacao powder, and coconut. Mix thoroughly.

3. Add honey mixture to bowl and mix well.

4. Pour dough into an 8" × 8" baking pan and store in refrigerator until firm, about 10 minutes in the freezer or 1 hour in the refrigerator.

5. Cut into squares and enjoy.

KIDS' FAVORITE TRAIL MIX

For kids who love potato chips, this recipe will be a nice alternative. It has a sweet and salty taste that will satisfy all their cravings.

Serves 8

½ cup raw sunflower seeds

½ cup almonds

½ cup macadamia nuts

½ cup pistachios, shelled

4 tablespoons raw honey

1 teaspoon sea salt

½ teaspoon ground black pepper

¼ teaspoon cumin

1 teaspoon curry powder

Pinch ground cloves

1 teaspoon cinnamon

1. Preheat oven to 300°F.

2. Place sunflower seeds and nuts on a large baking sheet and bake for 10–12 minutes, taking care they do not burn. Remove from oven and let cool approximately 5 minutes.

3. In a small bowl, mix honey, salt, pepper, cumin, curry powder, cloves, and cinnamon.

4. In a large saucepan over medium heat, place the honey mixture. When the mixture begins to melt, mix in the toasted nut mixture.

5. Shake the pan until all the nuts are coated and glazed, about 5–8 minutes.

6. Cool on wax paper. Use a spoon to separate nuts that stick together.

OLD-FASHIONED SWEET POTATO HASH BROWNS

These sweet potato hash browns are likely to become a family favorite. They are easy to make and packed with flavor your entire family will love.

Serves 6

3 tablespoons coconut oil

3 medium sweet potatoes, peeled and grated

1 tablespoon cinnamon

1. Heat the coconut oil in large skillet over medium-high heat.

2. Cook grated sweet potatoes in hot oil for 7 minutes, stirring often.

3. Once brown, sprinkle with cinnamon and serve.

CARROT PUDDING

Serve this pudding chilled in the summer and enjoy warm in the winter.

Serves 4

4 large carrots, cooked and mashed

1 small onion, grated

¼ teaspoon nutmeg

1 tablespoon raw honey

1 cup canned unsweetened coconut milk

3 eggs, beaten

½ teaspoon lemon juice

1. Mix together all ingredients.

2. Pour into a 2- or 3-quart slow cooker and cook on high for 3–4 hours until the mixture is set. Serve immediately or remove from slow cooker, cover, and refrigerate for at least two hours to serve cold.

AWESOME APPLESAUCE

Serve warm or chilled, or as a complement to a main pork, chicken, or beef dish. Or freeze for an icy, sweet summer treat!

Serves 6

3 pounds Jonathan apples, peeled, cored, and coarsely chopped

½ cup water

½ cup pure maple syrup

Cinnamon, to taste

1. Combine all ingredients except cinnamon in a 6-quart slow cooker and cover.

2. Cook on high until apples are very soft and form applesauce when stirred, about 2–2½ hours. You can leave the mixture chunky, or mash the apples for a smoother texture. Sprinkle with cinnamon just before serving.

CHAPTER 14

GRILLING TIME

GRILLED LEMON AND DILL SWORDFISH STEAKS

This recipe calls for preparation on the grill but could easily be cooked in the oven using the broiler.

Serves 4

4 (4-ounce) swordfish steaks

1 tablespoon almond oil

1 lemon

4 sprigs dill

1. Lightly coat swordfish steaks with oil.

2. Slice lemon into circles and place on top of swordfish steaks.

3. Place 1 fresh dill sprig on each swordfish steak.

4. Grill over medium-high heat, about 5 minutes per side, depending on thickness of steaks, until a meat thermometer registers 145°F for medium. Cover and let stand for 5 minutes before serving.

SALMON SKEWERS

Salmon has a wonderful omega profile—it is one of the highest sources of omega-3 fatty acids.

Serves 4

8 ounces salmon fillets

1 red onion, cut into wedges

2 red bell peppers, seeded and cut into 2" pieces

12 mushrooms

12 cherry tomatoes

12 (2") cubes fresh pineapple

1. Cut salmon into cubes.

2. Thread all ingredients on metal skewers, alternating vegetables, pineapple, and meat.

3. Grill over medium-high heat until salmon is light pink, about 10 minutes, depending on thickness of salmon cubes.

TILAPIA WITH TOMATO AND BASIL

Tilapia is a very low-fat fish choice with a light flavor. It cooks quickly and absorbs flavors from spices quite nicely.

Serves 6

6 tilapia fillets

½ teaspoon salt

⅛ teaspoon pepper

2 large beefsteak tomatoes, sliced

12 whole basil leaves

1. Place each tilapia fillet on a square of aluminum foil. Sprinkle with salt and pepper.

2. Cover each fillet with 2–3 slices of tomato and 2 basil leaves.

3. Fold and seal foil over each fillet and grill over medium heat for 6–8 minutes, or until fish flakes easily when tested with a fork.

SPICY GRILLED FLANK STEAK

Flank steak is one of the leanest steak cuts. It pairs well with many different spices and ingredients. It must be sliced against the grain for the most tender texture.

Serves 4

2 tablespoons raw honey

1 teaspoon cinnamon

1 teaspoon chili powder

½ teaspoon salt-free lemon-pepper seasoning

1½ pounds lean flank steak

½ cup sliced green onions

1. Combine honey, cinnamon, chili powder, and lemon-pepper seasoning in a small bowl.

2. Grill flank steak over medium-high heat for 6 minutes on each side. Baste often with honey mixture. Remove steak from grill.

3. Thinly slice the steak against the grain.

4. Serve sprinkled with green onions as garnish.

LIME THYME GRILLED SWORDFISH

Thyme is a useful spice that adds flavor without overpowering a dish, and it blends well with other spices.

Serves 4

4 (5-ounce) swordfish steaks

½ cup water

4 tablespoons fresh lime juice

4 bay leaves

1 teaspoon crushed dried thyme

½ teaspoon salt

⅛ teaspoon pepper

1. Preheat grill to 350°F.

2. Place each swordfish steak on a large sheet of heavy-duty aluminum foil. Pour the water and lime juice over fish. Top each steak with a bay leaf. Sprinkle the thyme, salt, and pepper over the fish and wrap the foil closed.

3. Cook for 10–15 minutes or until the fish flakes easily when tested with a fork and is opaque all the way through. Tell your guests not to eat the bay leaf.

SHRIMP SKEWERS

These skewers are easy to make and can be served as a main dish or an appetizer. They are fantastic at parties or holiday celebrations.

Serves 4

1½ pounds large shrimp, peeled and deveined

Juice of ½ lime

1 teaspoon ground black pepper

12 white mushrooms

1 medium summer squash, sliced in 1" pieces

1 large red bell pepper, sliced in 2" pieces

1 large green bell pepper, sliced in 2" pieces

4 cloves garlic, finely minced

2 tablespoons coconut oil, melted

1. Soak 8 wooden skewers in water for at least 30 minutes.

2. In a large bowl, drizzle shrimp with lime juice and season with pepper. Set aside for 5 minutes.

3. Add vegetables, garlic, and oil to the shrimp and toss to coat.

4. Alternate vegetables and shrimp on skewers.

5. Grill over medium heat for 5 minutes or until shrimp turns pink, then turn skewers to cook other side an additional 5 minutes until vegetables are tender and shrimp curls.

ASIAN GRILLED SALMON

Salmon is a traditional barbecue item and a staple in the Paleolithic diet.

Serves 4

2 pounds salmon fillets, skin on

¼ cup sesame oil

¼ cup coconut aminos

¼ cup lemon juice

4 green onions, thinly sliced

3 tablespoons minced fresh parsley

2 teaspoons minced fresh rosemary

¼ teaspoon sea salt

⅛ teaspoon pepper

1. Place salmon in a shallow dish.

2. Combine remaining ingredients in a medium-sized bowl and mix well. Set aside ¼ cup for basting and pour the rest over the salmon.

3. Cover and refrigerate salmon for 30 minutes.

4. Grill salmon over medium heat, skin-side down, for 15–20 minutes. Baste with marinade often. Discard any remaining marinade before serving.

JALAPEÑO STEAK

When you want a little kick of flavor instead of the more traditional steak meals, give this recipe a shot. Jalapeños and lime juice give this meal a multicultural feel.

Serves 6

4 jalapeño peppers, stemmed, seeded, and roughly chopped

4 cloves garlic

¼ cup fresh cilantro leaves

1½ teaspoons fresh cracked black pepper

1 tablespoon sea salt

¼ cup lime juice

1½ pounds top sirloin steak

1. Combine jalapeños, garlic, cilantro, pepper, sea salt, and lime juice in a blender. Blend until smooth.

2. Place steak in a shallow pan and pour marinade over it. Cover and marinate for 8 hours in the refrigerator.

3. Drain and discard marinade. Grill steak over high heat for 5 minutes per side, or to desired doneness.

BBQ CHICKEN

This mouthwatering chicken will become a staple in your home regardless of the season.

Serves 4

3 tablespoons avocado oil

¼ cup tomato paste

1½ cups apple cider vinegar

½ cup raw honey

Juice of 1 lemon

¼ teaspoon ground black pepper

2 sprigs fresh sage, chopped

2 pounds bone-in chicken breasts

1. In a small bowl combine oil, tomato paste, vinegar, honey, lemon juice, pepper, and sage.

2. Place chicken breasts on hot grill and baste with sauce.

3. Cook for 45–60 minutes, turning every 10–15 minutes, until the chicken registers 165°F on a meat thermometer. Baste with sauce after each turning. Discard any remaining sauce when the chicken is done.

GRILLED TROUT

Cooking the fish inside the foil packets keeps it tender and moist.

Serves 2

2 whole trout, heads removed, cleaned and butterflied

1 teaspoon ground black pepper

2 cloves garlic, minced

½ teaspoon chopped fresh rosemary

1 teaspoon chopped fresh parsley

6 sprigs fresh rosemary

1 lemon, halved; one half thinly sliced

1. Place each trout on a square piece of aluminum foil. Season both sides of trout with pepper, garlic, rosemary, and parsley.

2. Fold fish closed and top with rosemary sprigs and a few slices of lemon. Squeeze the lemon half over each fish. Wrap each fish securely inside the sheet of aluminum foil, leaving some room for heat expansion.

3. Grill packets over medium-high heat for 6–7 minutes on each side or until fish flakes when tested with a fork.

GRILLED PINEAPPLE

Pineapple has such a profound flavor, and grilling just intensifies it. The addition of some raw honey will make this a really special treat at any barbecue or party.

Serves 6

1 tablespoon avocado oil

1 fresh pineapple, cored, peeled, and cut into 1" rings

¼ cup raw honey

2 tablespoons chopped macadamia nuts

1. Coat grill rack with oil before starting the grill.

2. Grill pineapple over medium heat for 5 minutes. Turn pineapple over and grill 5 more minutes. Brush with honey and sprinkle with macadamia nuts.

GRILLED WATERMELON

If you haven't tried grilled fruit, you are missing out. Not only does the heat enhance the flavor, but the little bit of sea salt really brings out the natural sweetness of the fruit.

Serves 6

1 tablespoon avocado oil

1 small (4-pound) watermelon, sliced

1 teaspoon sea salt

1. Coat grill rack with oil before starting the grill. Season both sides of watermelon slices with salt.

2. Grill watermelon over medium heat for 5 minutes. Turn watermelon over and grill 3–5 minutes longer or until tender with nice grill marks.

GRILLED SALMON

Grilling salmon is a nice way to get maximum flavor while cooking. The marinade in this recipe doubles as a basting sauce to really seal in the flavor.

Serves 4

2 pounds skin-on salmon fillets

½ cup avocado oil

½ cup lemon juice

4 green onions, thinly sliced

3 tablespoons minced fresh parsley

1½ teaspoons minced fresh rosemary

⅛ teaspoon pepper

1. Place salmon in a shallow dish.

2. In a medium-sized bowl, combine remaining ingredients and mix well. Set aside ¼ cup for basting; pour the rest over the salmon.

3. Cover and refrigerate for 30 minutes. Drain, discarding marinade.

4. Grill salmon over medium heat, skin-side down, for 15–20 minutes or until fish flakes easily with a fork. Baste occasionally with reserved marinade. Discard any remaining marinade before serving.

CHAPTER 15

DESSERTS

CHOCOLATE NUT BARS

Luckily, dark chocolate is on the Paleo-approved list! Just make sure it's good quality chocolate with as few ingredients as possible. You don't want to eat polyglycerol polyricinoleate (PGPR), which is a new cheap additive that corporations are adding to chocolate in place of cocoa butter. Good dark chocolate should have just a few ingredients: all natural dark chocolate, and sugar. And it should be at least 70 percent cacao.

Serves 12

1 cup hazelnuts

1 cup walnuts

1½ cups pecans

1 pound dark chocolate, cut into small pieces

1. Preheat oven to 350°F. Place hazelnuts, walnuts, and pecans on a baking sheet. Bake for 10–15 minutes or just until nuts are fragrant and start to brown. Remove from oven and cool completely.

2. Coarsely chop the nuts and place on a parchment paper–lined baking sheet.

3. Reserve ⅓ cup of the chocolate; place the remaining chocolate in a heavy saucepan over low heat. Melt, stirring occasionally, until mixture is smooth. Remove from heat and stir in reserved chocolate until melted; this tempers the chocolate so it will stay solid at room temperature.

4. Pour chocolate over nuts to coat. Let stand until set, then break into bars. Store in airtight container at room temperature.

SLOW-COOKER STUFFED APPLES

This is a classic recipe for fall. The fragrance that drifts through your house as these apples slowly cook is incredible. Choose apples that don't brown quickly and that stay firm while cooking for best results. Granny Smith, Cortland, and Rome Beauty are good choices. For a real treat, pour some cold heavy cream over each apple as you serve it.

Serves 4

4 large apples

2 tablespoons lemon juice

2 tablespoons unsweetened dried cherries

2 tablespoons chopped hazelnuts

2 tablespoons unsweetened coconut flakes

½ teaspoon cinnamon

⅛ teaspoon cardamom

½ cup unsweetened apple juice

½ cup water

1. Peel a strip around the top of the apples. Using an apple corer, remove the core. If you want to fit more filling inside, carefully use a knife to cut away the hole in the center to make it bigger. Brush apples with lemon juice.

2. In small bowl, combine cherries, hazelnuts, coconut, cinnamon, and cardamom.

3. Place apples in a 3- to 4-quart slow cooker. Fill each with the cherry mixture, mounding it up tall as it will sink as the apples cook. Pour apple juice and water around the apples.

4. Cover and cook on low for 2–4 hours or until apples are tender. Serve warm.

APPLE CRANBERRY CRISP

Apple crisp is usually made with a topping of sweetened oatmeal and butter. Since oatmeal is a no-no on the Paleo diet, substituting nuts and coconut works very well. Choose an apple that keeps its shape after baking for this recipe: Granny Smith, Honeycrisp, and Mutsu are good choices.

Serves 6

1 cup chopped walnuts

½ cup unsweetened shredded coconut

½ cup coconut flour

1 teaspoon cinnamon

⅛ teaspoon cardamom

Pinch salt

⅓ cup butter or coconut oil, melted

2 pounds apples, peeled and sliced

½ cup dried unsweetened cranberries

2 tablespoons honey or maple syrup

2 tablespoons orange juice

1. Preheat oven to 375°F. In medium bowl, combine walnuts, coconut, coconut flour, cinnamon, cardamom, and salt and mix. Add melted butter or coconut oil and mix until crumbly; set aside.

2. In a glass baking dish, arrange the apples and cranberries. In small bowl, combine honey or maple syrup and orange juice and mix well. Drizzle over the apple mixture. Top with the walnut mixture.

3. Bake for 25–35 minutes or until the apples are tender and juices are bubbling. Serve warm with heavy cream, if desired.

BERRY NUT CRISP

Berries are full of vitamins and fiber. They're all good for you, but raspberries have a lot of vitamin C, blueberries are packed with antioxidants, and blackberries contain anthocyanin, a powerful phytonutrient that may help prevent cancer. Plus they taste wonderful, especially in this warm and comforting dessert. Pour some cold heavy cream over each portion before serving.

Serves 6

3 cups blueberries

2 cups blackberries

2 tablespoons orange juice

1 cup raspberries

1 cup chopped pecans

½ cup shredded coconut

½ cup coconut flour

3 tablespoons coconut oil, melted

2 tablespoons honey or agave nectar

1. Preheat oven to 350°F. In 2-quart baking dish, combine blueberries and blackberries and toss gently. Sprinkle with orange juice, then top with raspberries; set aside.

2. In medium bowl, combine pecans, coconut, and coconut flour and mix. Add melted coconut oil and honey or agave nectar; stir until mixture is crumbly. Spoon over fruit in baking dish.

3. Bake for 20–30 minutes or until fruit is bubbling and topping is browned. Serve warm.

FROZEN YOGURT BARS

Frozen yogurt bars are a cool and sweet summertime treat. You can purchase specially made popsicle forms to make these bars, or freeze in small custard cups or in a baking dish. Use your favorite whole milk yogurt and kefir (fermented yogurt drink) in this easy recipe, and your favorite fruits.

Serves 4

1 cup whole milk Greek yogurt

1 cup kefir

1 cup raspberries

1½ cups sliced strawberries

1 teaspoon vanilla extract

2 teaspoons agave nectar, if desired

1. Combine all ingredients in a blender or food processor and blend or process until puréed.

2. Pour into small cups or popsicle molds. Cover and freeze until firm; unmold to serve. You can also pour this mixture into a 2-quart baking dish and freeze, then slice and serve.

MIXED-FRUIT MINI PIES

Mixing fruit is a great way to give pies more flavor and interest. But you must choose fruit that cooks at about the same time so they are all tender and sweet. Delicate fruits such as peaches, raspberries, and blueberries will become tender at the same time. When topped with a sweet and crunchy mixture, these individual pies are irresistible.

Serves 6

½ cup coconut flour

¼ cup hazelnut or almond flour

½ cup chopped toasted hazelnuts or almonds

¼ cup coconut

⅓ cup melted coconut oil

1 tablespoon honey

Pinch salt

3 ripe peaches, peeled and chopped

1 cup blueberries

1 cup raspberries

1 teaspoon vanilla

1 tablespoon orange juice

1 tablespoon honey

1. Preheat oven to 400°F. Grease 6 1-cup ovenproof custard cups with unsalted butter or Ghee (see Chapter 2) and set aside.

2. In medium bowl, combine coconut flour, hazelnut flour, hazelnuts, and coconut and toss. Add the melted coconut oil, 1 tablespoon honey, and salt and mix until crumbly; set aside.

3. In medium bowl, combine peaches, blueberries, and raspberries. Sprinkle with vanilla, orange juice, and 1 tablespoon honey and toss gently. Divide among prepared custard cups. Top with crumble mixture.

4. Place on a rimmed baking sheet and bake for 20–30 minutes or until the fruit is bubbly and tender and topping is browned. Serve warm or cool.

BLUEBERRY COCONUT CRISP

Among their many virtues, blueberries are low on the glycemic index, in spite of their inherent sweetness. Taste the berries before you make this recipe. You may find you don't need any honey at all to sweeten them.

Serves 6–8

4 cups fresh blueberries

¼ cup honey, if needed

1½ teaspoons vanilla

1 tablespoon lemon juice

1 cup chopped pecans

1 cup shredded coconut

⅓ cup coconut flour

6 tablespoons butter, softened, or coconut oil

⅛ teaspoon salt

1. Preheat oven to 400°F. Butter an 8" square glass pan with unsalted butter.

2. Combine blueberries, honey, vanilla, and lemon juice in the pan and toss gently; set aside.

3. In medium bowl, combine pecans, coconut, and coconut flour. Add butter or coconut oil and salt and mix until crumbly. Sprinkle over blueberries.

4. Bake for 35–40 minutes or until blueberry mixture is bubbly. Serve warm or cool.

GRILLED STONE FRUITS

Stone fruits are fruits that have a stone, or pit, in the center. They include peaches, nectarines, plums, apricots, and pluots, which are a cross between a plum and an apricot. When quickly grilled, these fruits become even more juicy and succulent and their flavor is intensified. Serve with cold heavy cream for a decadent treat.

Serves 4

2 peaches, cut in half, stone removed

3 plums, cut in half, stone removed

4 nectarines, cut in half, stone removed

3 tablespoons butter, melted

½ teaspoon cinnamon

⅛ teaspoon cardamom

1. Prepare and preheat grill. Place fruits, cut-side up, on plate.

2. In small bowl, combine butter, cinnamon, and cardamom and mix well. Brush this mixture over the fruits.

3. Add the fruits to the grill, peaches first, cut-side up. Grill for 2 minutes, then add the plums and nectarines and grill, covered, 1 minute longer.

4. Carefully turn all of the fruits. Grill for another minute or two until the flesh is scored with grill marks and fruit is easily pierced with a fork. Remove fruits as they are done. Serve warm.

CHOCOLATE GRAHAM CRACKER BARS

It's nice to have a sweet treat every once in a while, even on a diet. Just make sure that the sweets you eat are high quality and very delicious. For the Paleo diet, dark chocolate is a must. Look for chocolate with a high percentage of cacao since it has much less sugar than milk chocolate varieties. Try to find chocolate with less than 10 grams of sugar added. Then enjoy every bite.

Serves 8

1 cup finely chopped walnuts

1 cup grated unsweetened coconut

3 cups crushed Graham Crackers (see Chapter 13)

⅔ cup coconut milk

14 ounces chopped dark chocolate

2 teaspoons vanilla

1. Grease a 9" square pan with coconut oil and set aside. Combine walnuts, coconut, and Graham Cracker crumbs in large bowl and set aside.

2. In saucepan, combine coconut milk and dark chocolate. Melt over low heat, stirring frequently, until smooth. Stir in vanilla. Reserve ⅓ cup of this mixture.

3. Pour remaining chocolate mixture over Graham Cracker crumb mixture and stir to coat.

4. Press into prepared pan and spread reserved chocolate over top. Place in refrigerator until set; cut into small squares to serve.

PLUM BLUEBERRY COCONUT CRUMBLE

Plums are in season in summer and early fall. These sweet stone fruits are low in carbs with a low glycemic index rating and rich in vitamins A and C. And their natural sweetness is a boon to those on the Paleo diet with a sweet tooth. Serve this crumble warm from the oven, topped with heavy cream if you're eating dairy.

Serves 4

8 plums, stones removed, sliced

2 cups blueberries

2 tablespoons honey

2 tablespoons lemon juice

1 tablespoon arrowroot powder

2 cups coconut flakes

1 cup chopped pecans

⅔ cup coconut flour

1 teaspoon baking powder

Pinch salt

⅓ cup coconut oil, melted

1. Preheat oven to 350°F. Grease a 9" square baking dish with coconut oil.

2. Combine plums and blueberries in prepared dish. Drizzle with honey, lemon juice, and arrowroot powder and toss to coat.

3. In medium bowl, combine coconut flakes, pecans, coconut flour, baking powder, and salt and mix. Add coconut oil and mix until crumbly. Pat on top of fruit in dish.

4. Bake for 40–45 minutes or until fruit is bubbly and topping is golden. Serve warm.

RASPBERRY PIE

Using the Graham Crackers recipe from this book (see Chapter 13), an excellent pie crust can be made using melted butter or coconut oil and chopped walnuts. Fill it with fresh fruit mixed with heavy cream that is flavored with crushed fruit. This dazzling recipe is wonderful for parties.

Serves 6–8

2 cups crushed Graham Crackers (see Chapter 13)

½ cup finely chopped walnuts

½ cup butter or coconut oil, melted

3 cups fresh raspberries, divided

1½ cups heavy whipping cream

2 tablespoons honey

1 teaspoon vanilla

1. Preheat oven to 400°F. In medium bowl, combine Graham Cracker crumbs, walnuts, and melted butter or coconut oil and mix. Press into bottom and up sides of a 9" pie plate. Bake for 8–10 minutes or until set. Cool completely.

2. Set aside 2½ cups raspberries. Crush remaining ½ cup raspberries in small bowl.

3. In large bowl, beat heavy cream until stiff peaks form. Beat in honey, crushed raspberries, and vanilla. Fold in remaining whole raspberries.

4. Pile into pie crust. Refrigerate for 3–4 hours until firm. Slice to serve. This pie can also be frozen until firm. Let stand at room temperature 10 minutes before slicing to serve.

STRAWBERRY APPLE SOUP

Cold soups actually make wonderful desserts, especially on hot summer nights. Use beautiful organic berries and apple juice for the best flavor in this refreshing recipe. Garnish with sliced berries and a sprig of fresh mint and serve in large flat soup bowls with silver spoons.

Serves 4

1½ cups water

¼ cup honey

1 stick cinnamon

1½ cups unsweetened apple juice

2 cups sliced strawberries

1 tablespoon lemon juice

1 tablespoon arrowroot powder

½ cup water

1 teaspoon vanilla

Pinch salt

1. In large saucepan, combine 1½ cups water, honey, stick cinnamon, and apple juice and simmer for 10 minutes. Remove and discard cinnamon.

2. Pour 1 cup of this mixture into blender or food processor. Add strawberries and purée. Return to saucepan along with lemon juice.

3. Dissolve arrowroot powder in ½ cup water and add to pan. Simmer for 4–5 minutes or until thickened. Add vanilla and salt.

4. Cover and chill for 3–4 hours before serving.

WATERMELON RASPBERRY GRANITA

Watermelon is a wonderful fruit to serve on the Paleo diet. It is a great source of lycopene, an antioxidant that helps protect against cell damage. It's also an excellent source of vitamin C and potassium. Plus it's delicious and naturally sweet. A granita is a bit different from sherbets or sorbets. The fruit mixture is scraped with a fork several times while freezing so it has a beautiful crystalline structure.

Serves 4

4 cups chopped watermelon

1 cup raspberries

¼ cup honey

2 tablespoons lemon juice

Pinch salt

1. In two batches, combine watermelon, raspberries, honey, lemon juice, and salt in a blender or food processor. Blend or process until smooth.

2. Pour mixture into a 9" x 9" baking dish. Freeze for 3 hours, then remove from freezer and use a fork to scrape the mixture into small pieces, paying special attention to the sides of the pan. Return to freezer and freeze for another hour.

3. Scrape mixture again with a fork. Serve immediately, or spoon lightly into a bowl and freeze, covered, up to 2 days. Scrape with a fork into serving dish and eat immediately.

WATERMELON POPS

Frozen pops, or Popsicles, are the quintessential frozen summer treats. For this recipe you can freeze servings of the sweet puréed mixture in muffin cups, paper cups, or molds you buy at specialty stores. You will need flat Popsicle sticks to serve as handles for your homemade creations. Vary the fruit used in this recipe to suit your own tastes and enjoy this refreshing and easy treat.

Yields 8 pops

2 cups cubed seeded watermelon

½ cup coconut milk

1 tablespoon lime juice

1 tablespoon honey

1. Combine all ingredients in blender or food processor and blend or process until smooth.

2. Pour into frozen-pop molds and insert sticks. If using paper cups or muffin tins, freeze for about an hour, then insert sticks. Cover and freeze until firm, about 5–7 hours. Unmold to serve.

COCONUT DROPS

This recipe couldn't be simpler or more delicious. With just two ingredients, you do need to buy the best chocolate and best and freshest coconut you can find. When melting chocolate, if you hold some back and add that after the chocolate is removed from the heat, the chocolate will be "tempered" and will stay solid at room temperature.

Yields 2 pounds

1½ pounds dark chocolate, chopped

2½ cups shredded unsweetened coconut

1. In heavy saucepan, melt all but ½ cup of the chocolate over low heat, stirring frequently, until melted and smooth.

2. Remove pan from heat and stir in the reserved chocolate. Stir constantly until mixture is smooth again.

3. Add the coconut and mix well.

4. Drop mounds of this mixture onto parchment paper. Let stand until set. Store in airtight container at room temperature.

DARK CHOCOLATE BROWNIES

With good quality dark chocolate and cocoa powder, along with some honey and various gluten-free and Paleo-friendly flours, you can actually make a brownie that is very dense, fudgy, and flavorful. Cut these into small squares because they are very rich. Store in an airtight container to keep them moist.

Yields 25 brownies

⅓ cup unsalted butter

⅓ cup coconut oil

⅓ cup honey

¼ cup coconut sugar

1 square unsweetened chocolate, chopped

3 eggs

1½ teaspoons vanilla

⅓ cup cocoa powder

¼ cup coconut flour

¼ cup almond flour

Pinch salt

1. Preheat oven to 325°F. Grease a 9" square pan with unsalted butter and set aside.

2. In large saucepan, combine butter and coconut oil and melt over low heat. Add honey, coconut sugar, and chopped chocolate and stir over low heat until mixture is smooth.

3. Remove from heat and beat in eggs, one at a time, until well mixed. Stir in vanilla.

4. Add cocoa powder, coconut flour, almond flour, and salt and mix just until combined. Pour into prepared pan.

5. Bake for 20–25 minutes or just until a toothpick inserted near the center comes out clean. Do not overbake. Cool completely, then cut into squares to serve.

MINI CHERRY GRANOLA PIES

Fresh cherries are in season in July and August. The rest of the year, you can make this recipe with frozen cherries. The topping is made using the Nutty Granola (see Chapter 7) recipe in this book, but you can use any Paleo-friendly granola. The little tart pans can be found at specialty stores.

Serves 4

4 cups pitted Bing cherries

1 tablespoon lemon juice

⅓ cup honey

5 tablespoons coconut flour, divided

1 teaspoon vanilla

2 cups Nutty Granola (see Chapter 7)

¼ cup butter, melted

1. Preheat oven to 375°F. In large bowl, combine cherries, lemon juice, honey, 2 tablespoons coconut flour, and vanilla and toss to coat. Divide among four 4" mini pie tins.

2. In medium bowl, combine Nutty Granola, remaining 3 tablespoons coconut flour, and butter and mix until crumbly. Pat on top of the cherry mixture.

3. Place pies on a baking sheet and bake for 25–30 minutes or until cherries are bubbling and topping is browned. Cool completely before serving.

AMBROSIA CRUMBLE

Ambrosia is an old-fashioned recipe that used to be served as a salad. It contained orange segments, maraschino cherries, coconut and mini marshmallows and was usually enveloped in sweetened whipped topping. This version omits the marshmallows and uses real cherries. And it becomes a dessert with a crumbly, nutty topping.

Serves 8

2 large oranges, peeled and chopped

2 cups Bing cherries, pitted

1 cup unsweetened coconut, divided

1 tablespoon lemon juice

1 cup coconut flour

1 cup chopped pecans

¼ cup honey

¼ cup coconut oil, melted

2 tablespoons butter, melted, or more coconut oil

2 eggs, beaten

¼ teaspoon salt

1 teaspoon cinnamon

1. Preheat oven to 350°F. Combine oranges, cherries, ½ cup coconut, and lemon juice in a 2-quart baking dish and set aside.

2. In large bowl, combine coconut flour, remaining ½ cup coconut, and pecans. Add honey, coconut oil, and butter and mix. Add eggs, salt, and cinnamon and mix until crumbly.

3. Top fruit with the crumble mixture. Bake for 30–35 minutes or until topping is golden brown. Serve warm.

RICH ICE CREAM

Coconut milk is naturally sweet and it freezes beautifully. Combine that with some mashed banana and egg yolks for a super-simple ice cream that is Paleo-friendly. Taste this mixture before you freeze it. If you think that it's not quite sweet enough, you could add some honey or maple syrup. But if the bananas are nice and ripe, it should be perfect.

Yields 1 quart

2 cups full-fat coconut milk

4 egg yolks

4 ripe bananas, mashed

2 teaspoons vanilla

1. In heavy saucepan, combine coconut milk and egg yolks. Cook over medium-low heat, stirring constantly, until mixture reaches 160°F and thickens slightly.

2. Cool for 30 minutes, stirring occasionally.

3. Place coconut milk mixture in blender or food processor and add bananas and vanilla. Blend or process until smooth.

4. Chill mixture until very cold. Freeze in ice cream maker according to manufacturer's instructions. Keep in freezer, tightly covered, up to 2 weeks.

INDIVIDUAL YOGURT FRUIT TRIFLES

Yogurt may not be sweet enough to qualify as a dessert in and of itself, but when paired with sweet in-season fruits, it makes an admirable trifle filling. Use your favorite fruits in this simple recipe, and use a purchased Paleo-approved granola, or the Nutty Granola recipe from this book (see Chapter 7).

Serves 6

1 cup chopped cherries

2 cups blueberries

2 cups sliced strawberries

2 bananas, sliced

1 cup raspberries

4 cups yogurt

2 teaspoons vanilla

4 cups granola

1. In large bowl, combine cherries, blueberries, strawberries, bananas, and raspberries and mix. In medium bowl, combine yogurt and vanilla and mix well.

2. In six jelly jars or parfait glasses, layer the fruit mixture, yogurt mixture, and granola. Serve immediately, or chill for 3 hours before serving.

STANDARD U.S./METRIC MEASUREMENT CONVERSIONS

VOLUME CONVERSIONS

U.S. Volume Measure	Metric Equivalent
⅛ teaspoon	0.5 milliliter
¼ teaspoon	1 milliliter
½ teaspoon	2 milliliters
1 teaspoon	5 milliliters
½ tablespoon	7 milliliters
1 tablespoon (3 teaspoons)	15 milliliters
2 tablespoons (1 fluid ounce)	30 milliliters
¼ cup (4 tablespoons)	60 milliliters
⅓ cup	90 milliliters
½ cup (4 fluid ounces)	125 milliliters
⅔ cup	160 milliliters
¾ cup (6 fluid ounces)	180 milliliters
1 cup (16 tablespoons)	250 milliliters
1 pint (2 cups)	500 milliliters
1 quart (4 cups)	1 liter (about)

WEIGHT CONVERSIONS

U.S. Weight Measure	Metric Equivalent
½ ounce	15 grams
1 ounce	30 grams
2 ounces	60 grams
3 ounces	85 grams
¼ pound (4 ounces)	115 grams
½ pound (8 ounces)	225 grams
¾ pound (12 ounces)	340 grams
1 pound (16 ounces)	454 grams

OVEN TEMPERATURE CONVERSIONS

Degrees Fahrenheit	Degrees Celsius
200 degrees F	95 degrees C
250 degrees F	120 degrees C
275 degrees F	135 degrees C
300 degrees F	150 degrees C
325 degrees F	160 degrees C
350 degrees F	180 degrees C
375 degrees F	190 degrees C
400 degrees F	205 degrees C
425 degrees F	220 degrees C
450 degrees F	230 degrees C

BAKING PAN SIZES

U.S.	Metric
8 × 1½ inch round baking pan	20 × 4 cm cake tin
9 × 1½ inch round baking pan	23 × 3.5 cm cake tin
11 × 7 × 1½ inch baking pan	28 × 18 × 4 cm baking tin
13 × 9 × 2 inch baking pan	30 × 20 × 5 cm baking tin
2 quart rectangular baking dish	30 × 20 × 3 cm baking tin
15 × 10 × 2 inch baking pan	30 × 25 × 2 cm baking tin (Swiss roll tin)
9 inch pie plate	22 × 4 or 23 × 4 cm pie plate
7 or 8 inch springform pan	18 or 20 cm springform or loose bottom cake tin
9 × 5 × 3 inch loaf pan	23 × 13 × 7 cm or 2 lb narrow loaf or pâté tin
1½ quart casserole	1.5 liter casserole
2 quart casserole	2 liter casserole

INDEX